D0389690

THE MERGER

THE
MERGER

THE CONGLOMERATION OF
INTERNATIONAL ORGANIZED CRIME

JEFFREY ROBINSON

THE OVERLOOK PRESS

First published in the United States in 2000 by
The Overlook Press, Peter Mayer Publishers, Inc.
Lewis Hollow Road
Woodstock, New York 12498

Library of Congress Cataloging-in-Publication Data

Robinson, Jeffrey.
The merger : the conglomeration of international
organized crime / Jeffrey Robinson.
p. cm.
Includes bibliographical references (p.) and index.
1. Transnational crime. 2. Organized crime. I. Title.
HV6252.R6   2000   364.1'06—dc21   00-026068

Book design and type formatting by Bernard Schleifer
Manufactured in the United States of America
FIRST EDITION
1 3 5 7 9 8 6 4 2
ISBN 1-58567-030-8

For Estelle and Carl
With love from your biggest fans

CONTENTS

THE MERGER

PROLOGUE

O N THE OUTSKIRTS OF VIENNA, ABOUT SIX MILES from the center of town, past the Ferris wheel where Harry Lime plied his trade in *The Third Man*, the City Club is a massive hotel and leisure complex, the heart of which is the huge climate-controlled glass-pyramid hothouse where a swimming pool sits in a tropical jungle. It is artificial global warming at its most luxurious. It is also where, over Easter 1990, some twenty men with disparate backgrounds met for the first time, to get to know another and to explore the feasibility of strategic alliances.

There were Italians, including Sicilian mafiosi, members of the Camorra from Naples, members of the 'Ndrangheta from Calabria and representatives of the Christian Democrats political party. There were Russians, mostly from Moscow but also a few living in Hungary and the Czech Republic. There were some Poles. And there were some Colombians.

They knew one another on a one-to-one basis, but there'd never been a meeting of all these men together. Their cover was a forum sponsored by "The Italian Association." The City Club management was told, somewhat ironically, that the topic of the meeting was how European countries could help South American countries develop their economy in Europe. For security reasons, the group insisted on renting the entire complex for that weekend.

They'd originally tried to book a Club Med, but the management there wanted them to pay in advance, and when the money wasn't paid,

Club Med refused to hold their reservations. So they wound up at the City Club, sitting around long tables in conference rooms, exactly like the life-insurance salesmen and bankers and heart surgeons who have met there since. Except that, every now and then—according to staff working there at the time—the men who appeared to be the leaders of each faction would get up and walk out into the hallway, where they could speak quietly among themselves, where there was no possibility of conversations being overheard.

Any worries they might have had about their meeting being bugged were misplaced. The only person who realized the significance of this secret meeting—the first time that this many diverse criminal groups sat down together—was a French Foreign Intelligence Service agent assigned to the nearby United Nations. Having spotted some faces that looked vaguely familiar, he did what little he could to find out who was there and what they were talking about. He even dispatched a report to Paris, suggesting that these men were meeting specifically to form joint ventures and strategic alliances.

Italians. Russians. Colombians. Politicians.

The report was filed away, never to be seen again.

Except for that lone French intelligence agent, there were no other witnesses to the birth of modern transnational crime.

1

SPREADING THE VIRUS

As legitimate business understood and adjusted to the complexities
of this new global marketplace, so did international criminal organizations.

—Arnaud de Borchgrave
Center for Strategic International Studies

T HE ANUS OF THE EARTH IS CUT INTO THE JUNGLE ON
the Paraguay side of the Paraná River—a home-away-from-home for the
South American drug cartels, Chinese Triads, Japanese Yakuza, Italian gangsters, Russian gangsters, Nigerian gangsters and Hezbollah terrorists—and
is called Ciudad del Este.

A city of two hundred thousand hustlers, whores, hoodlums, revolu-
tionaries, thugs, drug traffickers, drug addicts, murderers, racketeers, pirates,
mobsters, extortionists, smugglers, hit men, pimps and wannabes, it was
the creation of Paraguay's former dictator, Alfredo Stroessner. The same
man who welcomed fugitive Nazis like Josef Mengele, he originally named
it after himself and it remained Ciudad de Stroessner until he was deposed
in 1989.

Its very remoteness is the major factor in its appeal. Despite a recent
influx of tourists to the nearby Iguacu Falls, few people ever stumble into
Ciudad. It's one of those places where, in order to get there, you have to
want to get there. Which is why Ciudad has always been an ideal spot for
secret meetings. High government officials mingled there with agents of

Taiwanese and South Korean counterfeiters, filling their own coffers with kickbacks as the counterfeiters filled the town with phony goods. Military dictators gathered there to cement friendships while they ruled the Southern Cone of South America.

The world's organized criminals still break bread there, in harmony, with one another.

Hezbollah guerrillas based themselves in Ciudad while planning and carrying out the 1992 bombing of the Israeli embassy in Argentina, which killed twenty-nine people, and the 1994 bombing of a Buenos Aires Jewish community center, which killed eighty-six people. In January 1999, the Uruguayans arrested Egyptian terrorist El Said Hassan Ali Mohamed Mukhlis when he crawled out of his hiding place—he'd been living in Ciudad like a Cold War mole for five years—on his way to plant a bomb in Britain. A suspect in the 1997 killings of fifty-eight foreign tourists and four Egyptian nationals at Luxor, he is also believed to have knowledge of the bombings of the U.S. embassies in Kenya and Tanzania.

More than one hundred landing strips are scattered around the Tri-Border, as the region is known, none of them regulated by any authority, all of them in constant use by small planes. Convoys of trucks and vans and private cars leave Rio de Janeiro nightly—and other cities in Brazil and Argentina—arriving in Ciudad del Este early the next morning, creating a massive, noisy and fume-riddled daily traffic jam. The two-lane bridge from the Brazilian border town of Foz do Iguaçu brings in thirty thousand people a day. Beneath the bridge, young boys shift boxes and crates from the Paraguay side to the Brazil side, often in plain sight of the police. They come to Ciudad because it's a market town where they can buy absolutely anything, *caveat emptor* being the only law of the land, as just about every-thing on sale in the five thousand shops that fill the twenty-block center of this cesspool is fake.

Except the drugs. Three tons of cocaine move through Ciudad every month on its way to the U.S., Canada, Europe and South Africa. Colom-bian heroin comes through as well. Marijuana, grown in Paraguay, gets smuggled from there into Brazil and Argentina, while chemicals needed to refine cocaine are smuggled from Argentina into Ciudad—although "smuggled" might not be the right word, because fifteen hundred to two thousand TIR-sized trucks drive across the bridge in each direction every month, and rarely are any of them ever stopped. Much of the money that the Colombians earn there is washed through an illegal betting racket in Rio de Janeiro, set up as a money-laundering sink-for-hire, under the ultimate direction of the American Cosa Nostra.

The weapons that are bought, sold and negotiated there are also real. It was in Ciudad that the Italian P-2 Lodge facilitated the sale of Exocet missiles and spare parts to the Argentines for use against the British during the Falklands War.

The lives that are trafficked there are real as well. There is an abundance of cheap sex, cheap slaves, wholesale body parts for medical transplants and murder for hire. Killing someone in Ciudad costs as little as $1,000 for a nonwhite, only slightly higher for a Caucasian.

You can even buy a new identity. A Chinese Triad gang has cornered the market on counterfeit Argentine identity papers. Most are sold in batch lots to other organized crime groups with interests in alien smuggling. But anybody looking for a set of papers can find one, the benefit being that Argentina is currently the only Latin American nation whose citizens do not need to apply in advance for visas to enter the United States.

Today, Ciudad is not only the continent's most important black market, it is the city with the third largest volume of cash transactions, behind Hong Kong and Miami.

Counterfeit designer goods, counterfeit currency, counterfeit passports, pirated CDs, pirated videos, pirated software, stolen cars, drugs, money laundering and arms dealing have turned Ciudad into a $12–14 billion annual industry. By contrast, Paraguay's official GDP is only about $9 billion.

It took man thousands of years to move faster than the speed of a galloping horse. It then took less than a century to move faster than the speed of a train. From there it was only a few decades to move faster than the speed of sound.

Today, satellites, faxes, cell phones, the Internet and e-mail enable us to send our voices, our images, our ideas and our money at the speed of light. The planet has been reduced to the size of a computer screen and the artificial borders which we once called nations have, for all intents and purposes, begun to evaporate. Long before the new century is over, it seems clear, those borders will serve little or no purpose except for the sake of nostalgia and, perhaps, the retelling of history.

They have already become nonentities for transnational organized crime.
During the final years of the twentieth century—an era when we
have witnessed the disintegration of Communism and the Soviet Union,
the end of the Cold War and our abject failure to raise a democratic,
free-market Russia out of the ashes—we have lived through the greatest
quantum leap in technology since man invented the wheel. Radical
changes in transportation and communication have encumbered governments' ability to exercise controls over the movement of goods, services,
people and ideas. During the final years of the twentieth century we have
witnessed both the concluding stages in the globalization of markets and
the initial stages in the globalization of crime.

We have also coined a new type of money—megabyte bucks—electronic blips on computer screens that are not tethered to central banks or
geography. Money has always been a political force. But never before has it
been so easily energized by criminal activity which burrows inside the
confusion created by the global flood of goods, services, people, ideas and
this new money itself.

For much of the half-century that followed World War II, Italian organized crime was, both in practice and in fact, the state. The Mafia's political power derived directly from the enormous mass of money it was able
to launder, to reinvest in criminal activity, to hand out as bribes and to
accumulate as profits. The Mafia used its money effectively to replace the
government with a body politic designed in its own image. It stands as a
model of corporate efficiency.

It is a model that has been replicated throughout the world.

Latin America's second largest export is cocaine. It accounts for 8 percent of Colombia's GDP, and something around half that in Peru and
Bolivia. It is estimated that the industry employs five hundred thousand
people, covering every aspect of the business from farming to production,
distribution and financial services. For all intents and purposes, drug barons
are the majority shareholders in Latin America Inc. Their economic power,
and hence their political authority, is nothing short of staggering. Take, for
example, Colón, Panama, the world's largest warehouse. Up to $2 billion
worth of goods are stored there at any given time, some 60 percent of
which come from Asia. The Free Zone turns over $12 billion annually.
Yet if the wealth of transnational criminal enterprises were taken out of the
picture, if the drugs, laundered money, counterfeit goods, illegal arms and

other contraband that the Latin American drug cartels move through
Colón—especially the goods they trade with Italian, Russian, Chinese,
Japanese, Nigerian and other transnational criminal organizations—were
simply erased, the government of Panama and much of the rest of neighboring Latin America would promptly go bankrupt.

The picture is just as grim in what used to be the Soviet Union. Today,
organized criminal groups are the only effective government in Russia.
They control 40 percent of all private businesses, 60 percent of the state-
owned businesses and 80 to 90 percent of the banks. They exert executive
control over key economic sectors, such as consumer products—including
two thirds of all alcohol sales, estimated to be worth $1.5 billion a year—
petroleum distribution and pharmaceuticals. By its own estimate, the
Russian Interior Ministry believes the annual black market revenues of
these groups have now topped $18 billion, about the same that Russia was
expected to reimburse its creditors in 1999.

Exactly like the multinational corporations they imitate—and have
become—transnational criminal organizations realize what many politicians have never come to understand, that this is about one and only one
thing: wealth creation.

To achieve that goal, the underworld needs the upperworld.

Consider the analogy of a pot of coffee. A pot needs to be large
enough to hold enough coffee and, at the same time, there must be enough
coffee to fill a pot. Without the professionals—lawyers, bankers, accountants and company formation agents—to prepare the stage for global criminals, they could never function on a global basis as successfully as they do.
And yet, if there were not so much money to be made in global crime,
there would not be professionals to accommodate them.

In that sense, a part of the upperworld needs the underworld, too. A
marriage of convenience, it is much the same with the merger of underworld groups. Both phenomena are based on wealth creation. However,
the globalization of crime differs in one important area. Where the upperworld professionals who service these underworld groups operate within
diminishing boundaries—because those boundaries protect their professional monopoly on services—transnational criminal organizations operate
beyond boundaries because that's where jurisdiction no longer applies.

Law enforcement, as we know it today, is a local remedy to local problems. It is a statement of sovereignty, as represented by government, and

therefore by definition confined by borders. It is the state that says you may not comport yourself in that manner while inside this imaginary line. It is, also, the state that pays the police to enforce the law and punish those who do not comply. Boundaries and budgets rule. As a result, the state winds up with borders that must be respected and neither the authority nor the money to go beyond them. Criminals create wealth by purposely functioning beyond sovereign reach.

In San Diego, the border is inundated by Chinese nationals, smuggled into Mexico by Asian organized crime groups, and from there smuggled into the U.S. by Mexican organized crime groups, using the same routes and methods that the Mexicans perfected to smuggle cocaine into the U.S. for the Colombian cartels.

To the south, in Veracruz, on Mexico's Gulf Coast, a group of French organized criminals, with direct links to traditional Italian and Corsican gangs, ran an international stolen-car ring. They contracted with Mexican gangsters to carjack luxury models, showing a particular fondness for Chrysler Voyager deluxe vans. They also contracted with a Cambodian faction in Florida to steal cars off the streets there. In both cases, cars were shipped to France with newly registered Mexican documents. Bags of cement, lime and plaster were sent with the cars, which suggests that the idea was to couple car theft with the smuggling of heroin inside those bags.

In Ensenada, Baja California, Mexican traffickers and their Southeast Asian heroin-dealing partners—Thai and Laotian—worked out a drugs-by-mail scheme. The gang in Mexico shipped bath products to Thailand, where the envelopes were intercepted by Thai gang members working inside the post office. They emptied out the bath products, refilled the envelopes with heroin and stamped them "Undeliverable—Return to Sender." The envelopes entered Mexico without customs inspection because it appeared that they'd originated in Mexico. Mexican gang members inside the Mexican postal service then delivered the drugs to their cohorts for smuggling into the United States.

Farther afield, in Central Asia's Turkmenistan, two thousand tons of kerosene—an essential ingredient in the manufacture of cocaine—was sold by an organized crime group there to a company in Argentina, which paid for the shipment entirely in cash. That company was a front for the Colombians. Even though kerosene is a non-controlled substance, they were willing to go that far away to hide the transaction's trail. The same company also bought large quantities of kerosene from Polish crime groups, paying for it with cocaine delivered to the groups' agents in Chicago.

In Cyprus, on the Greek side of the Green Line that divides the Mediterranean island into Greek and Turkish halves, more than $1 billion arrives every month from Russia, where it is washed through the nearly eight thousand Russian companies and banks that have been formed there since 1993. Another twenty-two to twenty-five thousand shell companies there belong, mostly, to Eastern Europeans. Once clean, some of that money goes to Britain. On the north side of the Green Line, Turkish heroin is bartered and sold like any commodity, and monies from that market have also been traced to Great Britain. In today's global economy, the city of London is merely one blip on a computer screen away from Wall Street.

In Washington, D.C., the U.S. State Department's Bureau for International Narcotics and Law Enforcement Affairs, which publishes an annual list as part of its International Narcotics Control Strategy Report, points a finger at the most reprehensible drug-money-laundering nations in the world. Among those given "high priority" status by the Americans are the obvious offenders: Mexico, Aruba, the Cayman Islands, Colombia, Cyprus, Nigeria, Panama, Russia, Singapore, Switzerland, Thailand and Venezuela.

Britain is also on the list.

So is Canada.

Until the political will is strong enough, sovereignty will be the rope with which we tie law enforcement's hands behind its back.

In Tel Aviv, the "Law of Return" continues to see an influx of Eastern Europeans claiming to be Jewish who, in fact, are not. They get into the country with counterfeit paperwork—sold openly in Cyprus—and apply for Israeli passports to substantiate their new identity. In a country with no money-laundering laws, these people use the proceeds of crimes to invest in select politicians who may someday influence the disposition of the Israeli government. One group, in particular, is said to be willing to commit $2 billion with just this in mind.

As long as we live in a world where a seventeenth-century philosophy of sovereignty is reinforced with an eighteenth-century judicial model, defended by a nineteenth-century concept of law enforcement that is still trying to come to terms with twentieth-century technology, the twenty-first century will belong to transnational criminals.

Law enforcement could take lessons from these groups, as they open overseas branches to expand established markets, to gain access where they once were forbidden and to create new markets. Almost as if they themselves have learned their lessons at the Harvard Business School—and in some cases they have—transnational criminal organizations approach logistics, personnel and accounting professionally. They research and develop new products. They hire experts to guide them through the complex and ever-changing maze of legal issues, marketing techniques and all things financial. They understand cost flow, reinvestment, franchising, time management and risk management. They have learned to construct and maintain networks of front companies, to negotiate prices, to decide delivery methods, to set schedules of payment and to build into all of this a philosophy that takes into account future market developments.

And, like any sound multinational corporation, they also seek out strategic alliances. Such as the Asian organized criminals who import heroin into Canada, then hand off their drugs to an Italian group that ships them in bakery trucks to New York, where they are distributed by a Puerto Rican street gang.

Like the Mongrel Mob in New Zealand who signed a deal to protect Chinese Triad gang members serving time in jail there. For their services, Triad members on the outside pay Mongrels on the outside with drugs. Relationships formed on the inside are then translated into joint ventures once members of the two groups get out of jail.

Like the seventy Italian organized crime cells active in Germany that deal weapons, traffic drugs and steal cars, and are each tied to Mafia groups in Italy. Some of them have also been linked to Turkish organized crime, which supplies heroin; Colombian organized crime, which supplies cocaine; Russian organized crime, which supplies weapons; and Asian organized crime, which offers them access to a network of Chinese restaurants for money laundering.

While their core activities remain the same—drug trafficking, weapons trafficking, car theft, fraud in all its guises, alien smuggling, counterfeit production and distribution, murder, kidnapping, extortion, money laundering, and the smuggling and sale of nuclear materials—organized criminals flourish in the global markets of transparent borders and meaningless trade restrictions. Unlike their predecessors, they do not limit themselves to single forms of illegal activity, but deal in anything and everything that can make money for them. By broadening their areas of operation and increas-ing cooperation with other groups, the pot of gold at the end of the rain-bow has grown significantly in value.

The man who pulled into the liquor-store parking lot that evening had never been to Harrods.

Nor had he ever been to London.

In fact, England was just about the furthest thing from his mind as he got out of his car, locked the doors, strolled into the shop—chimes sounded to announce he'd come in—and thought to himself it was lucky his wife had phoned to remind him about the wine.

The Vietnamese clerk behind the counter at the far end said hello.

The fellow nodded and glanced around.

The place was overstocked with bottles in all shapes and sizes, with large signs announcing that some of them were on sale, and huge wooden barrels filled to the brim with more bottles.

Eventually the man located a shelf marked *Burgundy*.

The clerk asked if he was looking for anything in particular.

The man said that he needed some wine for a dinner party, but, thanks anyway, he could find it himself. He perused the bottles in front of him, turned momentarily to the next shelf where the Bordeaux was, did some fast arithmetic, decided that would be too expensive, and returned to the Burgundies.

The six bottles he settled on would set him back $78 and change.

The fellow behind the counter loaded them into two bags—explaining that this way they wouldn't be too heavy and break—then rang up the sale.

The customer pulled out his credit card and put it on the counter.

The clerk picked up the card, explained that the store had a special on champagne and motioned toward one of the wooden barrels.

The fellow looked at the champagne.

The clerk swiped the card through a reader under the counter.

After thinking about it for a few seconds, the man shook his head and turned back to watch the clerk put the credit card through a reader on the top of the counter.

When the little receipt churned up, he signed it, took his receipt, took his wine, said good night and went home to his dinner party.

Long before dessert, the number of his credit card, together with the encoded information from the magnetic stripe on the back of it, was e-mailed to Hong Kong. There, data from several hundred other cards—collected much the same way up and down the West Coast of North America—was collated and e-mailed to Malaysia.

Within twenty-four hours, a brand-new credit card, issued in the name of the customer from the liquor store, was bundled along with 199 others and prepared for delivery to a customer in Italy.

A fresh carton of cigarettes had been carefully opened, as had each pack. The cigarettes were dumped out, and the cards stacked inside. The packs were then resealed—made to look as if they'd never been opened—and replaced in the carton, which was also resealed. At Subang International Airport in Kuala Lumpur, the courier taking them out of the country purchased a bottle of whiskey and put the cigarettes in the same plastic duty-free shopping bag. The following day, he walked straight past Italian Customs—no one cared about duty-free goods—and delivered the specially prepared carton of cigarettes to a gentleman in Milan.

Twenty-five credit cards, including the card that otherwise should have belonged to the customer from the liquor store, had been presold to a Russian in Prague. Three days after they were delivered to him, one of the men on the team dispatched to London by the Russian in Prague walked into Harrods and used up nearly all of the $20,000 limit on the man's card.

The designer watches and Hermès scarves that he bought, together with designer handbags, jewelry, more watches, fine leather goods, digital cameras, French perfume and handheld computers—all paid for with the Visa, Mastercard, American Express and Diners Club cards that were in the batch of twenty-five—were packed in team members' luggage and checked on to a regularly scheduled flight to Prague. From there—along with other goods that had been purchased in Paris and Rome and charged to other credit cards controlled by the man in Prague—they were trucked to Moscow. Within a week, all of those items were on sale in specialist boutiques at the Gum department store, across Red Square from the Kremlin.

The credit card company had no choice but to write off their loss. They sent their client a new card with a new number and he never had the problem again. As far as he was concerned, it was just some weird mistake. But investigators at the credit card company knew better. It was fraud on a massive, global scale. Although they hadn't yet discovered the specifics—that members of an organized Vietnamese crime gang were being paid to double-swipe cards by a Chinese Triad society, who made counterfeit cards and sold them to a member of the Camorra Mafia, who, in turn, resold some to a Russian organized crime group—they did take a look at the store where they suspected the first step happened, but could never prove anything. And without at least one culprit, no law enforcement agency anywhere wanted to know.

Anyway, no one was ever certain in whose jurisdiction the crime been committed.

None of the diverse law enforcement agencies that might otherwise have become involved was willing to authorize the cost of investigating a Russian in Prague who'd ripped off some fellow in North America with the help of a gang in Hong Kong and another in Italy.

Where national objectives were once defined by a government's ability to protect its citizens, territory and borders, they are now characterized by law enforcement's inability to defend those citizens and territories from threats outside those borders. Where power and authority were once defined by political polarities, such as East versus West, they are now defined by the control of, or influence over, markets, such as foreign exchange and essential commodities.

Whatever lines once existed between business and crime in many countries have been rubbed away. Take, for example, the former Soviet Union. There being no job security at institutions such as the KGB, operatives who hadn't socked away a nest egg found themselves on breadlines. The assets they possessed were contacts throughout the world, networks of foreign informants and the phone numbers of moles planted in the West years ago.

The operatives who stayed on breadlines were the dumb ones.

With global networks already in place—many of them used for criminal purposes under the guise of Cold War espionage—regearing to function as an organized criminal business became the KGB's pension plan. Some national security threats that should have passed away with the end of the Cold War have been placed on life support by the deliberate overlapping of traditional criminal activity with terrorism.

In New York, Greek criminals showed up with five tons of radioactive zirconium for sale. A critical ingredient in nuclear reactors, it had been smuggled to the West by a Russian organized crime group who used the Greeks as their agents. They also had plutonium and enriched uranium to sell.

In Tokyo, on March 20, 1995, the Aum Shinrikyo religious sect killed a dozen people and injured another five thousand by releasing deadly sarin gas into the subway system. At the time, the group had assets of more than $1 billion in secret bank accounts, $8.25 million in cash, a large quantity of gold bars, a farm in Australia where they'd been testing the gas on sheep and cattle, plus a clandestine chemical weapons factory in Tokyo that was so big it made the group the city's largest private real estate owner. Since then, Aum Shinrikyo has begun recruiting again, and has reportedly signed twenty thousand new members, all of them discontented Russian soldiers stuck on military bases in the far eastern reaches of their country.

As it became increasingly evident that the Soviet Union was in the midst of social and political meltdown and would soon disintegrate, a meeting was held at CIA headquarters in McLean, Virginia, to discuss what looked like the very real possibility of criminal nuclear proliferation. Senior managers were concerned that when the system crashed, former Soviet nuclear scientists would be out of work, and to feed their families they would offer their skills and knowledge to the highest bidders. It was known at the time that countries like Iraq, Libya and Syria were eagerly courting Russian expertise.

Because the CIA already knew who these Russian scientists were, they created a database to track them. They gave each one a number and set up a system so that they would always know who was where. This, the agency felt, was the best way to protect America from the spread of Russian nuclear expertise. And while they were zeroing in on the Russian nuclear scientists, no one was bothering with the biochem scientists or the crypto guys.

Iran began working on biological weapons toward the end of its war with Iraq. To develop "the poor man's atom bomb," they'd been able to purchase strains of bacteria from Canada and Holland, plus the necessary laboratory equipment from the Swiss, Germans, Italians and Spanish. But they'd still not been able to breed the germs into deadly toxins. That is, until the Russians arrived. Within two years their program leaped from the developmental stage to production and the creation of delivery systems.

In Bulgaria, Russians have been hired to teach at a school where graduate-level students from other countries learn how to create and program computer viruses.

In Cali, Colombia, highly experienced Russian cryptanalysts are employed in a telephone company owned by a faction of the Cali cartel, their job being to intercept secure phone calls anywhere in the world made by the Drug Enforcement Administration.

In Britain, police computers are not compatible. The Metropolitan Police computer in London cannot talk directly to the Strathclyde Police computer which cannot speak directly to the Thames Valley Police computer. That has prompted one senior officer to hang a sign on the bulletin board facing his desk that reads, "We're more disorganized than they are organized."

In Ottawa, the Royal Canadian Mounted Police (RCMP) has only just awakened to the fact that many of the computer programs running the Police Information Centre date to 1972 and are, therefore, obsolete. The database, which was designed to handle 60 million requests for information per year, is now handling twice that, making access to it more difficult and more time-consuming for the fourteen thousand police, corrections and immigration organizations in Canada who use it. When it's working, it supplies criminal records plus information on arrest warrants and stolen cars.

In Washington, the computer at the FBI's National Criminal Intelligence Center, a central clearinghouse for law enforcement across the country, is also overloaded. Criminals arrested in one state who should otherwise be identified as wanted in other states often slip through the net because many agencies—especially local police forces—have neither the manpower nor the budgets to upload information into the system.

In all 140 chapters of the Hells Angels motorcycle gang—whose death's-head logo is a registered trademark; anyone who uses it without permission gets sued, the same way Coke and Microsoft and Nike take people to court for such abuses—computers are linked via a coded intranet. When the Los Angeles chapter does a deal with the Mexicans to deliver methamphetamine to a Chinese gang in Seattle, within a few hours of the deal being made, every chapter around the world has been informed and told to stay away.

The Republic of Niue is a two-hundred-beers airplane ride from anywhere.

An uplifted chunk of coral rising out of the middle of the Pacific Ocean, Niue is a protectorate of New Zealand, which is twenty-four hundred miles to the southwest. There are no beaches, there is no continental shelf and the weather can be rough. A minuscule self-governing member of the British Commonwealth, Niue is home to eighteen hundred people who are struggling just to survive. They would like the rest of the world to think of Niue for skin diving. At least one senior law enforcement officer in Hong Kong thinks of Niue as "bird shit, telephone sex and money laundering."

The birds were there before the people. The telephone sex came much later, imported by the Japanese, taking advantage of technology and the international telephone payment system. Someone in Tokyo looking to get turned on dials a number and winds up having his ardor routed through an exchange in Niue, where the local phone company receives a share of the outrageous fees charged back to the poor guy on the other end of the line by the telephone sex company in Japan.

Niue is also into Internet domain names. All of its Internet addresses end in ".nu," so anyone who pays a fee to the government there will be granted the right call their Web site something like "whats.nu" or "isanything.nu" or "nottoo.nu."

Next stop appears to be Internet gambling. Customers sitting in front of their modem-linked PCs can play roulette or poker in cyberspace, with their losses—and presumably their winnings, too—racked up on their credit cards by a company somewhere on the planet duly compensating the host nation for the right to be a casino.

Again, those eighteen hundred Niuean souls have to eat.

The big banquet, however, turns out to be the murky world of off-shore shell companies. Since 1994, Niue has been licensing international business corporations (IBCs). For a start-up of around $1,000, anyone can get the right to incorporate a company in any language, including Russian written in Cyrillic. Those IBCs are permitted to use any suffix that any other company anywhere else in the world can use—such as Ltd., Inc., GmbH, SA, NV, whether or not the company does business in Britain, the U.S. and Canada, Germany, the French- and Spanish-speaking worlds, or the Netherlands. To the list of suffixes add A/S, AG., B.V., and Aktiengesellshaft, rendering the IBCs' names virtually meaningless. It is impossible to decipher from the company's name what it does or, for that matter, where it does it. At the same time, it allows a company to pretend that it does something and is somewhere that it doesn't and isn't.

No minimum authorized share capital is required. An IBC is exempt from all local tax and stamp duties. Nor is there any requirement to hold general meetings or file annual reports. To maximize security of assets, IBCs are permitted to transfer domicile, plus reacquire and reissue shares for cash in any currency or any other form of consideration. Those shares can be bearer or nominative and, for really good measure, other companies can be listed as directors, meaning that there is absolutely no way anyone can ever find out who actually owns the company.

By charter, there are only a few things that an IBC cannot do. It is not permitted to carry on business with any residents of the island. Nor is it permitted to own property there, except for an office. In other words, the government of Niue will take your money, but they don't want you moving into the neighborhood or marrying their daughters.

But Niuean IBCs aren't about meaningful relationships. They're about total secrecy and absolute anonymity, and in some sense, about deception. Which are exactly the kinds of services a money launderer would pay for.

The United Nations got upset enough about Niue to put it on a list of countries where the possibility of money laundering was a real concern. The U.S. House of Representatives got upset enough about Niue to republish testimony from Washington attorney Jack Blum, a noted authority on money laundering. To wit, "The International Business Corporation, a corporation with anonymous ownership which can do no business in its country of incorporation, has no legitimate place in the international arena. IBCs are now the central tool of money launderers."

The Asia/Pacific Group of the Financial Action Task Force, an agency of the G-8, whose sole concern is global money laundering, is worried about Niue; as are the Australian Federal Police, who confirm, "We are monitoring developments in Niue and remain concerned that the establishment of an offshore register will lead to exploitation by criminal groups"; as is New Zealand's Serious Fraud Office, which convinced the government to send a representative to the island to try to explain the dangers of an offshore industry; as is the U.S. Department of State's Bureau for International Narcotics and Law Enforcement Affairs, which admits to being "very worried" about Niue's offshore industry; as is the Office of the Controller of Currency of the United States, which thought of Niue as the latest "flavor of the month" in the offshore money-laundering business.

The island's affairs, and cases related to them, are also allegedly being looked at, to varying degrees, by law enforcement in the U.S., Canada, Europe and the Far East.

Although IBCs formed in Niue can be bought over the phone from company-formation agents in central London, no one at the Commonwealth Office seems the least concerned. Adding to everyone else's growing anxiety, however, is the latest dish that the government of Niue has brought to the buffet—banking licenses. For under $20,000, you can buy your very own Niue-authorized financial institution, which, as one brochure touts, "provides access to the international credits market, as well as to the international mutual funds market and the securities market, [and] allows the bank to conduct FOREX transactions and, with minimal expense, to solve problems of liquidity."

At least three company-formation agents easily located on the World Wide Web offer such banks for sale and list branch offices in Moscow and St. Petersburg.

Because organized criminal groups have come to understand that there is no reason to rob banks when they can own one, Russian "businessmen" are believed to have bought several thousand IBCs and banks registered in Niue.

2

GETTING CONNECTED

Mafia is a process, not a thing.

—JOE BONANNO, *A Man of Honor*

THE THING ABOUT MOBSTERS IN THE LATE 1950s WAS
that you could count on them to be consistent. They were predictable. In
those days, five crime families ruled New York—Gambino, Lucchese,
Colombo, Bonanno and Genovese—and they, in turn, were overseen by a
Commission. Nothing happened without the others being kept informed.
When the Bonannos shipped heroin into Montreal to smuggle it into the
States, the other four stayed away from Montreal. When the Gambinos
ran a tax-fraud racket on Long Island, the other four stayed away from
the scam. When a family negotiated an alliance with hoods in Buffalo or
Detroit or New Orleans, the other four stayed away from Buffalo or Detroit
or New Orleans.

It was a gentleman's business, orchestrated by men who were anything
but gentle.

Every now and then, however, there'd be a falling-out and two or
more of the families would "go to the mattresses." One bunch of idiots
would start shooting at another bunch of idiots—civilians and family
members, namely wives and children, were unconditionally off limits—and
as bodies littered the streets, the New York Police Department would take

an unofficial step back. They'd let the bad guys kill one another until the Commission enforced a truce. The NYPD would then count the bodies—someone would inevitably declare in the press, "As far as we're concerned that's twenty-two less gangsters for us to worry about"—and pack them off to the morgue. The badfellas would return to being goodfellas, and everyone would wait patiently for the next time. There was an order to this, a coherence that somehow made sense. It became part of the myth. The stuff of *Godfather* movies.

That's the way it was in the days when being a mobster meant being predictable.

The man who changed his name from Salvatore to Charlie and from Lucania to Luciano, and who once survived such a brutal assassination attempt that forever after he'd be known as "Lucky," was proclaimed by *Time* magazine as one of the most important figures of the twentieth century: "He downsized, he restructured and he used Standard & Poor's as much as Smith & Wesson to change forever the face of organized crime."

Born in Sicily in 1897, he emigrated with his family to the Lower East Side of New York when he was nine. A childhood crony of Al Capone, he dropped out of school at the age of fourteen—still in the fifth grade—to hang out full-time on street corners. He and a bunch of other teenage Italian hoods had formed a gang they called the Five Pointers and were soon regularly getting arrested for shoplifting and muggings.

It was while terrorizing local Jewish kids that he met one who stood up to him. Meyer Suchowljansky, a skinny Russian-Polish émigré five years his junior, refused to hand over any of his pocket money. Single-handedly, he defied the Five Pointers, and out of that bravado a lifelong friendship was born. Within a few years the two of them—now with their new names, Charlie "Lucky" Luciano and Meyer Lansky—were mocking Prohibition by running whiskey from Canada into New York.

Eventually Luciano hooked up with the Giuseppe "Joe" Masseria crime family, where he developed easy relationships with a diverse group of other thugs—notably the Neapolitan Vito Genovese and the Calabrian Francesco "Frank Costello" Castiglia—and in them found men who shared his philosophy that business was more profitable than ethnic pride. At the same time, he spurned the old traditions by maintaining his friendship with

Lansky, and even extending his circle of Jewish friends to include Benjamin "Bugsy" Siegel and Louis "Lepke" Buchalter.

"Americanized men such as Charlie Lucky," wrote Joe Bonanno, "marched to a different drummer. Luciano never imbibed the true spirit of our Tradition. In his personal life, for example, he was not a family man. He was a bachelor who conducted his business out of a suite in the Waldorf Astoria under the name Charles Ross. . . . Luciano was essentially a loner."

In April 1931, after a protracted war between the old-school eastern Sicilian godfather Masseria and the old-school western Sicilian godfather Salvatore Maranzano, the loner saw profit in confusion and conspired with Maranzano to kill his own boss. In return, when Maranzano divided New York into five families, he rewarded Luciano by naming him head of one of them. Luciano then appointed Costello as his underboss and promoted Genovese into a position of responsibility. For good measure, Maranzano crowned himself *capo di tutti capi*, or "boss of bosses."

The comfy world of American organized crime might have stayed that way for a long time, had Luciano not fancied Maranzano's crown. In September 1931, Charlie Lucky and some of his pals—including Siegel and Lansky—knocked off Maranzano. He then solidified power by holding the crime world's first authentic "convention" at the Blackstone Hotel in Chicago.

There, Luciano proffered his vision of a "National Crime Syndicate." He wanted to divide the United States and Canada into twenty-four regions and oversee the regions with a ruling commission. Seven men would sit on a board of directors, made up of the boss of each of the five New York families plus the bosses of the Buffalo and Chicago mobs. They'd arbitrate disputes, set broad policy, establish a workable code of honor that reflected life in America—for instance, only the Commission could approve an assassination—and enforce the council's mandate with a crew controlled by Umberto "Albert" Anastasia and Lepke, known as "Murder Incorporated."

When the other members approved, La Cosa Nostra (LCN) was invented.

Fate now provided two twists: the Twenty-first Amendment to the Constitution on December 5, 1933, and Japan's sneak attack on Pearl Harbor on December 7, 1941.

The repeal of prohibition cut deeply into the syndicates' cash flow, forcing the LCN to look elsewhere for income. That took them into drug trafficking. And that put Thomas Dewey on their backs. In 1936, as U.S. Attorney for the Southern District of New York, Dewey declared war on the gangsters. To get Charlie Lucky, he presented a dramatic three-week case against him for controlling prostitution. No fewer than forty weeping women took the stand to shock the jury with the horrors Luciano had subjected them to. The jurors fell for it. The judge sentenced Luciano to thirty to fifty years in Clinton Prison at Dannemora, New York—a place otherwise known in the underworld as "Siberia."

While Luciano was inside, Pearl Harbor was destroyed and World War II happened along.

Legend has it that he was approached by the Office of Strategic Services, precursor of the CIA, to recruit the Mafia in Italy as local intelligence operatives for George Patton's Seventh Army Sicilian landings. A variation on the story is that the U.S. Navy needed Luciano to defend the home front after a troop ship was blown up in New York Harbor. The navy worried that longshoremen of Italian origin could sabotage the American war effort. They wanted him to guarantee their loyalty. Promising stevedore allegiance would have been easy for him, because many of the docks were under mob control. Asking Luciano to put them in touch with someone in Sicily was also possible. But cutting him in on the plan for the landings stretched the imagination. Besides the fact that no one in Washington would have trusted him with security clearance, Mussolini had long since purged much of the local mafiosi. That said, as soon as the war was over, Luciano appealed to Dewey—then governor of New York—and was granted executive clemency on the grounds of "patriotic services" to the nation. Whatever that means. Still, Luciano was released from jail, then deported to Italy.

Normally, Vito Genovese would have been next in line to succeed Luciano, but he'd been accused of murder and forced to make a hasty exit to Italy. That left Frank Costello to take Luciano's chair on the Commission. Unfortunately for Costello, Luciano's power did not come along with the seat. No sooner had Luciano unpacked in Italy when he decided it was time to pick up where he'd left off. In October 1946 he flew to Cuba to partner Lansky in his dream of turning Havana into the capital of the underworld. He lived there, on the quiet, until February 1947, when he was arrested because of Frank Sinatra.

The Commission had a five-year renewable mandate. Having missed their meeting in 1946, Luciano convened the group in spring 1947 under the guise of a dinner to honor Sinatra. Among those for whom attendance was mandatory were Lansky, "Joe Adonis" Doto, Bonanno, Costello, Anastasia and Joe Profaci. Vito Genovese was there as well, having just been exonerated of murder.

If Luciano saw Cuba as his return to control of the Commission, Genovese saw it as his first step in moving Costello aside and taking back what he believed was rightfully his. Oddly, so many gangsters heading for Havana didn't set off any alarm bells. It was the gala for "Old Blue Eyes" that made the papers. When the U.S. Justice Department read that Charlie Lucky was there, it got the State Department to threaten the Cubans that if they didn't stick Luciano on the next boat for Italy, America would embargo medical supplies destined for the island. So Luciano was hastily returned to the old country.

Over the ensuing years, he built the world's premier drug empire, shipping opium from Turkey to Lebanon, extracting the morphine there, then bringing that to Italy, where it was converted into heroin. He contracted with French Corsicans to move the product to Montreal, where Carmine "Lilo" Galante—who ran the city as underboss of the Bonanno family— was in charge of smuggling it across the border to other LCN members in Buffalo and Detroit.

In May 1950, Estes Kefauver, a Democratic senator from Tennessee, opened a series of hearings on organized crime in interstate commerce. At one of the first congressional hearings ever to be televised, Kefauver told the public, "Modern crime syndicates and criminal gangs have copied some of the organizational methods found in modern business."

After listening to the testimony of more than eight hundred witnesses— including Costello, Anastasia, Lansky, Gaetano "Tommy" Lucchese and Adonis, all of whom denied knowing anything about the Mafia and unblinkingly exerted their Fifth Amendment rights to say nothing more—Kefauver drew several conclusions. He determined that there was a nation-wide crime syndicate known as the Mafia; that it had international ramifications which appeared most clearly in connection with the narcotics trade; that its leaders were found in charge of the most lucrative rackets in their cities; that there were indications of centralized direction and control, although leadership appeared to be in a group rather than in a single individual; that these groups had kept in touch with Luciano since his deportation; that they did business with one another and regularly got together to discuss new opportunities; and that the Mafia acted closely with many persons who were not of Sicilian decent.

Kefauver opened a lot of eyes. Curiously, his sternest critic was the very man whose life had supposedly been dedicated to fighting crime, J. Edgar Hoover. Besides refusing to cooperate with the Committee, the director of the FBI actually tried to undermine it. And on every possible occasion, he staunchly maintained his long-standing position: "There is no persuasive evidence that a national crime syndicate exists."

In 1956, President Eisenhower signed into law the Narcotics Control Act, drastically increasing penalties for drug trafficking. Deeply concerned for their own burgeoning interests, Costello assembled the regular five-year meeting of the Commission. They met on October 17 at the home of Joseph Barbara, a Canada Dry soft-drink distributor who, in real life, controlled mob activities in Northeast Pennsylvania. His eleven-room house, built in the late 1940s for the then-whopping sum of $250,000, was a long stone building with second-floor rooms under gabled roofs at both ends. There were also five outer buildings on his nearly fifty-acre estate. It was well secluded in wooded hills north of the Pennsylvania border, fifteen miles or so along the Susquehanna River to the west of Binghamton, in the town of Apalachin, New York.

At that meeting, the Commission members talked about the new law, about heroin and about how Charlie Lucky would keep them supplied as long as they wanted to be supplied. They talked about how they could count on Meyer Lansky's connections in Cuba to help smuggle drugs into the United States through the southern route and about how Bonanno's Canadian connections would maintain the northern route. But most of all, they kept asking themselves whether they really wanted to be in the drug business. Apparently Frank Costello and Carlo Gambino were both wary of getting involved in any federal crimes that might force Hoover to take action against them.

The group stayed at Apalachin for two days and absolutely no one took any notice.

Seven months later, someone tried to kill Costello. He was just about to walk into his apartment building on Central Park West one evening when a man stepped out of the shadows and shot at his head. Costello was only grazed. The failed assassin was arrested—it was Vincent "The Chin" Gigante, who, thirty years later, would become head of the Genovese family—but when Costello refused to identify him, Gigante walked.

Vito Genovese led Costello to believe that the hit had been ordered by Anastasia. That made sense to him because he and Anastasia had been at odds. What he failed to realize was that Gigante's day job was playing chauffeur and bodyguard to his nearest rival, Vito Genovese. Instead of fighting back, Costello slowly began to withdraw and slipped into retirement. Over the next several months, two of Anastasia's top advisers got knocked off.

Meanwhile, in Italy, the attempt on Costello, the two murders and Costello's departure from the scene did not escape Luciano's notice. He wanted to make the Italians understand that, despite such hiccups, the LCN organizational model worked in America, and would work for them too. So he called a four-day meeting of the boys. It was held October 10–14, 1957, at the Albergo e Della Palme, in those days Palermo's plushest hotel. Some thirty "godfathers" attended. Most were Sicilian. But Bonanno and Galante were there, representing New York and Montreal, as were members of the Magaddino family, which ran Buffalo, and at least one member of the Priziola family, which ran Detroit.

On the evening of October 12, the group moved down to the port, to a restaurant that, in those days, was called Spano's. There, Luciano laid out his master plan for the universe. He explained to his Italian partners how their American cousins had benefited from having a Commission, argued that a similar body to manage the Sicilians' affairs would insulate them to a greater degree against internal warfare, and spelled out how the two ruling councils could then establish ground rules for joint ventures. He said he wanted both organizations to have a similar structure so that his Sicilian chums could join hands with his American chums and, in effect, create for themselves a heroin stranglehold over North America.

These were radical ideas. Getting everyone to agree required a lot of explanation. It also created a lot of argument. So much so that the dinner at Spano's is said to have lasted twelve hours. While the Sicilians came to see how such a confederation would be the most economical way for them to gain leverage in the U.S. markets, the Americans weren't as readily convinced. The last thing they wanted was to have their strings pulled from Sicily, even if it was evident that Charlie Lucky himself would be chief string puller.

Interestingly enough, by then, Luciano had moved his heroin production out of Italy and into France. On the advice of his Corsican-smuggler partners, he'd shifted manufacturing to Marseilles, where, the Corsicans assured him, they could exert their influence on his behalf. The move created what would come to be remembered as "The French Connection."

In the end, through the sheer force of Charlie Lucky's personality, everyone agreed. The dinner at Spano's elevated him to chairman of the Sicilians' Commission, which was dubbed La Cupola, the dome.

One of the people who attended the four-day Albergo convention was Tommaso Buscetta, then an up-and-coming star of Palermo's Porto Nuova family. Some eighteen years later, Buscetta would turn his back on his oath of *omertà*—the honored code of silence—and testify against his fellow mafiosi. It would be the first death throe of the octopus that Luciano had created.

"It was the responsibility of the Commission," he explained in an appearance before a U.S. Senate subcommittee, "to rule on disputes between families that cannot be resolved by the family bosses. It is the responsibility of the Commission to rule on the execution of a Man of Honor. Once the commission has decided to kill someone, the Commission decides who is to carry out its decision, and is empowered to choose its executioners from any family. Organizing the murder is, therefore, the exclusive doing of the Commission."

There is nothing to substantiate the claim that a murder was actually plotted at the Albergo. Only one source claims it was. Clare Sterling, in a book documenting the rise of the Mafia octopus, bases her assertion on a quoted comment by Luciano to the effect that "Albert was really off his rocker." She also contends that two hit men were then dispatched from Sicily with the contract.

Not so.

The target on Albert Anastasia's back had been drawn in America, long before that meeting in Palermo, and the artist with the crayon was Vito Genovese.

On a Friday morning in November 1957, just after ten, Anastasia and at least one bodyguard walked into the Park-Sheraton Hotel on Seventh

Avenue at Fifty-fifth Street. They stopped for several minutes to speak to some people Anastasia knew, then made their way to the barbershop at the other end of the lobby—the same lobby where, ironically, gangster Arnold Rothstein had been gunned down in 1928. Although Anastasia was early for his appointment, Tony, who worked chair number four and always cut his hair, motioned for "Don Umberto" to sit down. Two other customers were having their hair cut. One was waiting. The manicurist was sitting alone at her table along the wall.

The police report of the incident notes that Anastasia took his place, loosened his tie, leaned back and shut his eyes as Tony put a steaming hot towel over his face. The owner of the shop, Arthur Grasso, dragged a short, round stool up to the side of chair number four so that he could talk to Anastasia. The bodyguard fell into chair number five, also expecting a haircut.

That's when two men stepped into the shop from the lobby.

Both were wearing wide-brimmed fedoras and green aviator sunglasses. The younger of them—widely believed to have been the New York–based thug "Crazy" Joey Gallo—got as close to Anastasia as chair number three. The other man, possibly Joey's brother Larry, hurried to the door that led out to the street. Without warning, both started shooting. One bullet hit Anastasia in the back of his head and lodged in the left side of his brain. Another hit him in the left hand. A third pierced his hip. A fourth entered from the upper left side of his back and went down, penetrating his kidney, lung and spleen. Within seconds, both shooters were gone.

A photo of Anastasia's barely covered bloody corpse ran on the front pages of New York's evening newspapers that night, and on the front pages of the Saturday morning editions as well.

The image became one of the most familiar of the decade.

Anastasia, as "Lord High Executioner," had been responsible for as many as five hundred hits. With him out of the way, Vito Genovese was taking over.

He gathered together the other New York family bosses at the Livingston, New Jersey, estate of Ruggerio Boiardo, a member of his own crime family. The meeting, which started at noon on Sunday, November 10, lasted until five on Monday morning. They covered Anastasia's death, ratified Carlo Gambino's elevation to the head of Costello's gang and

despite other topics still on the agenda—especially Genovese's ennoble-
ment as head of the Commission—adjourned, agreeing to meet again later
that week. Because Genovese wanted as many out-of-state family bosses as
possible to attend his investiture, he needed someplace inconspicuous and
big. Someone suggested they phone Joe Barbara to ask if they could come
back to Apalachin.

Such an extraordinary convocation of the Commission was unprece-
dented. What's more, Barbara wasn't well, having recently suffered a heart
attack. Still, he told his friends that they'd be welcome, reserved dozens
of motel rooms for chauffeurs and bodyguards—explaining that they were
for Canada Dry salesmen—ordered two hundred pounds of steak from
his butcher and prepared his house for what was planned to be a two-day
conference.

At around noon on a drizzling Thursday, November 14, as gangsters
from all over the country drove through rural, normally quiet Tioga
County, Sergeant Edgar Croswell of the New York State Police was on
routine patrol.

One black limousine might never have caught his eye.

But thirty of them heading up McFall Road to the Barbara property
was too many to ignore.

Apparently Croswell had heard about the motel reservations and the
order at the butcher's for steaks. He definitely knew that Barbara was a suspect in three killings. So he called for backup—he didn't get much, only a
few officers—and set up a roadblock to keep any cars from driving off the
estate. He then got out of his own car, walked up the path and, literally,
knocked on Barbara's front door to ask what was going on.

Believing that this was a raid, a cry of "the cops are here" sent everyone scurrying. Some of them fled through the woods, their dapper clothes
taking a beating, their expensive shoes filling with mud. Others tried to
drive away, only to find themselves stopped at the roadblock. Even some of
those who made it out the other side of the woods were rounded up as
well.

Under questioning, every one of them told Croswell they'd come to
pay respects to their sick friend Joe. The fact that they all happened to be
there at the same time—and from as far afield as California, the Midwest,
the Southwest, Cuba and Puerto Rico—was just a how-about-that kind
of coincidence.

Although reports vary, it is generally accepted that among those caught in Croswell's net were Genovese; Gambino; Gambino's nephew Paul Castellano; Tommy Lucchese; Joe Profaci; Lilo Galante; Sam Trafficante from Miami; Gerardo Catena and Anthony Riela from New Jersey; Frank Majuri and Louis LaRasso, also from New Jersey; Russell Buffalino from upstate New York; John Scalish from Ohio; Frank deSimone from Los Angeles; Jimmy Civello from Dallas; Jimmy Colletti from Philadelphia; and Tony Accardo and Frankie Zito from Chicago. Some of those who escaped included Stefano Magaddino, Joe Zerilli of Detroit, James Lanza of San Francisco and Sam Giancana, the Chicago gangster who would, during the 1960 presidential election, be the crime link between John F. Kennedy and Frank Sinatra.

One of the people who claimed to have escaped was Bonanno. He denied getting arrested, although he admitted that he was in town that day. Anyway, his name appears on the police reports.

How many gangsters were actually there has never been established. A Senate investigation set the number at fifty-eight, which is how many were officially rounded up. Robert Kennedy, at the time a Senate lawyer, insisted that over one hundred were in town, which probably included bodyguards, chauffeurs and anyone else whose name ended in a vowel.

Years later, Croswell would say there were sixty-three, of whom fifty had criminal records, thirty-five had criminal convictions and twenty-three had served time in jail. Croswell claimed that the mobsters had more than $300,000 in cash between them, and were dressed just like he'd imagined mobsters would be, "in expensive dark suits wearing white fedoras." He was also quick to admit that none of the gangsters had any reason to panic. "If they'd asked us to leave, we would have because they weren't breaking any law by having a picnic."

Known forever as the Apalachin Crime Convention, it is considered a seminal moment in the history of organized crime.

As a direct result, when Robert Kennedy became Attorney General in 1961, he announced that organized crime was a priority of his brother's administration. It also eventually forced J. Edgar Hoover to concede to Congress, "La Cosa Nostra is the largest organization of the criminal underworld in this country, very closely organized and strictly disciplined." Edgar Croswell deserves the credit for that. But it is what Apalachin exposed that really matters—a textbook model of organization, established rules of discipline, a long-term vision of international alliances and a corporate philosophy that criminals should regularly meet to discuss their affairs and seek out joint ventures.

For that, today's transnational organized criminal groups need to thank Salvatore Lucania.

Carmine "Lilo" Galante had just finished lunch at the long table on the patio at the rear of Joe & Mary's storefront restaurant on Knickerbocker Avenue in Brooklyn. A stifling hot Thursday—July 12, 1979—it was 2:40 in the afternoon when he lit one of his characteristic cigars and sat all the way back in his chair.

Born in 1910 in Castellammare del Golfo, on Sicily's northern coast, due west of Palermo, Galante moved to New York as a very young child, where he was arrested the first time at the age of eleven for robbery and assault. A few years later he hooked up with Bonanno, who also came from Castellammare, and began making a reputation for himself as a small-time tough guy stealing trucks and running booze.

When he was twenty, a robbery went wrong and a policeman was shot, earning Galante a twelve-and-a-half-year sentence. After Galante's parole in 1939, Bonanno—now in firm control of his own family—brought him back into the gang. Four years later, Galante murdered Carlo Tresca, editor of the New York–based anti-Fascist Italian newspaper *Il Martello*. The contract had been put out by Vito Genovese as a favor to the man who'd given him protection in Italy, Benito Mussolini. Although Galante was never charged, he was rewarded for the murder when Bonanno promoted him to *capodecina* (captaincy) within the family. A few years later he was promoted again, this time to underboss, and assigned to manage the family interests in Montreal.

Through a Canadian gangster named John "Johnny Pops" Papalia—who controlled southern Ontario from his base in Hamilton under the supervision of Stefano Magaddino, boss of the LCN family across the border in Buffalo—Galante was introduced to a small-time Calabrian-born crook in Montreal named Vic Cotroni. A friendship grew, and after a time Galante brought Cotroni into the Bonanno family. When Galante was tasked with moving Luciano's heroin through Canada, Galante empowered Cotroni to reopen what had once been an old bootleg trail.

In 1963, mob soldier Joe Valachi turned informer and appeared before a U.S. Senate subcommittee investigating organized crime. It was the first time a Mafia soldier had ever violated *omertà,* the first time anyone had ever revealed the inner workings of the empire and the first time the term *La Cosa Nostra* was used publicly. After months of testimony, interviews and depositions, Valachi provided enough evidence to indict twenty-four Mafia members, among them Galante.

The world Galante returned to after his release from prison in 1974 was an unfamiliar one. Luciano was dead and Bonanno had been forced into retirement in Arizona, which essentially meant he was alive but powerless. Although he was now considered to be the head of the Bonanno family, Galante felt he needed to reinforce his authority, and did so by inundating the eastern seaboard with heroin. Within two years, the "boss of the bosses," Carlo Gambino, died. So now, to send out the message that he was the force everyone would now have to reckon with, Galante embarked on a killing spree, eliminating several rivals in the race to succeed Gambino. He even—bizarrely—dynamited the doors off Frank Costello's tomb.

The amount of heroin Galante was importing, the fortune he was earning, the power he was taking, the way he was increasingly relying on Sicilians—soldiers imported from Italy to cut the Commission out of his business—and the killings he was perpetrating made the other bosses extremely nervous. They saw Galante as a greedy man who showed open contempt for what they thought. They urged him to stop the killings. He answered with the warning "Who among you is going to stand up to me?"

A clandestine session of the Commission was called to "rethink" Galante's position.

A few days later, the sixty-nine-year-old boss of the Bonanno family finished lunch at Joe & Mary's restaurant. Just as he lit his cigar, a blue Mercury pulled up to the curb in front of the restaurant. Three men wearing ski masks jumped out. They stormed through the restaurant and appeared on the patio. Two of them had pump-action shotguns.

Later, the coroner placed the cigar back in Lilo's mouth before taking photographs of his corpse.

Many gangland murders prompt only a cursory response from the police. Galante's turned out to be different. Not because the cops shed tears for him, but because when they lifted up the rock that was his murder, they found an unexpected universe of maggots underneath. Within two days, the FBI launched what would become, at least to that point, the largest investigation in its entire history. But it had taken the Bureau several years to get to the point where they were even in a position to do that.

Valachi had confirmed what the second meeting in Apalachin had revealed, that organized crime was indeed alive and well in America. Hoover had reluctantly come to accept that. But the FBI's director, like so many of his right-wing cronies on Capitol Hill, was still going through a weird sort of denial. More concerned with the war in Vietnam and the nightmare scenario of Russian bombers suddenly appearing on Dew Line radar scopes, they were writing off organized crime as nothing but "a domestic problem," and then only in America, Canada, Italy and, to some extent, Japan.

It would take Hoover's death in 1972, Richard Nixon's resignation in 1974 and time for the turmoil that followed both to settle before a fundamental rethinking of the FBI's philosophy could bubble to the surface among its policy makers.

That controversy is remembered today as "the head versus tail argument."

"It was a huge debate and it was awful," recalls former FBI agent James Moody, who retired as the Bureau's organized crime chief. "When I first came on the job, agents would be assigned to look after people by name. Some of the names may have already been identified as LCN members. If you weren't sure about a certain individual, you had to find out if he was an LCN member. Once you established he was, you had to keep track of him and find everybody he was associated with. Then you had to determine what it was he was doing and if it was illegal. If it was, you worked up a case against him. It was very difficult because you weren't investigating a crime, you were looking first at an individual and then trying to find a crime."

The FBI got to the point, he says, where they knew just about everything about everybody associated with the LCN, from the name of some bad guy's dog to the measurements of his second girlfriend. "We had a tremendous amount of intelligence. But that's all we had. Not many people were going to jail. The ones who were might be LCN members, but they were the low-level guys. We were taking out the weakest guys, and they were replacing those individuals with somebody smarter who was saying, I'm not going to do what he did. It was like culling a herd. We were taking out the weak ones and making the herd stronger."

Younger agents agreed. But many senior agents held their ground. "In the end, some FBI supervisors lost their careers over it. They were so insistent on hanging on to intelligence that they were removed from their position. It took time but we started changing. We restructured ourselves. We went after the top men knowing that the guys replacing them were not as knowledgeable or as sophisticated. It took a long time, but we finally admitted that going after the tail didn't work."

Prior to the Galante killing, the FBI did not specifically investigate drug trafficking. If they stumbled across it, that was one thing, but their main target was organized crime. Now, looking into Lilo's death—thinking heads not tails—they noticed Sicilian mafiosi living in New York. The more Sicilians they saw, the more heroin they saw. Eventually, they concluded that the two were not mutually exclusive.

The link that joined the two was a network of pizzerias stretching across the industrial Northeast and into the Midwest. Within a year or so, they were able to establish that the Bonanno family—now headed by Salvatore Catalano—had franchised the distribution of heroin to the Sicilians through these pizzerias and, at least in the beginning, were also using the restaurants to launder money. In fact, with heroin on the menu, there was so much money being put through the tills that the LCN soon had to find other ways to wash their profits. They managed it by carting tens of millions of dollars in cash to investment houses and banks in New York and from there, sending the money to Italy and Switzerland.

The scheme would have made a great film.

When former fish broker Sal Amendolito lived in Milan, he was involved with a guy named Sal Miniati who smuggled currency out of Italy and into Switzerland for wealthy Italians. When Amendolito moved to the States, Miniati got in touch to say that some clients were building a large resort with American investors, all of whom just happened to run pizzerias. He wanted Amendolito to help get $9 million in cash to Switzerland. Because U.S. law requires that any cash deposit over $10,000 be reported to the Internal Revenue Service, Amendolito had to open accounts in a dozen banks. Slowly feeding a few hundred thousand through them, he consolidated the balances in four other accounts before transferring it to Miniati in Switzerland. But $9 million in cash turned out to be unmanageable. Unable to squeeze that much into the original twelve accounts, he looked beyond banks to financial investment businesses. When he arrived at Finagest, carrying four small suitcases packed with cash, they suggested he try Conti Commodity Services in the World Trade Center. There, they referred him to the Chase Manhattan Bank downstairs. An officer at that branch suggested he find a bigger branch. In the end, he wound up leaving the money at Chase headquarters a few blocks away, where it was credited to a Finagest account held at Credit Suisse in Lugano.

This process being too haphazard for his taste, Amendolito started smuggling cash to the Bahamas. As the amounts increased, he opened an account in Bermuda. Finally, he gave up and couriered cash directly to Switzerland. Along the way, he succumbed to temptation. When someone in Sicily discovered money was missing, Amendolito vanished.

He was immediately replaced by Antonio Cavalleri, a banker who managed a Credit Suisse office in the alpine village of Bellinzona. Through Cavalleri, the group created Traex, a company supposedly dealing in property and raw materials. Over the following few months, Swissair unknowingly flew $10 million out of New York for deposit into a Traex account at Cavalleri's bank.

Just as the gang was really getting its act together, Italian Customs stumbled across a suitcase at Palermo Airport containing $497,000. That led to the discovery of five working heroin laboratories in Sicily. The Italians mentioned it to the FBI, and the Bureau now started identifying players in the States.

That's when Franco Della Torre moved to New York. Representing Traex, he opened an account with stockbrokers Merrill Lynch and, during the first four months of 1982, washed $5 million there. Next he opened a Traex account with brokers E. F. Hutton and, making eleven cash deposits in under ten weeks, washed another $7.4 million. Hoping to avoid undue scrutiny, he opened a second E. F. Hutton account, this one in the name of Acacias Development Company, and a further $8.2 million was funneled through there in ten weeks. By the time Amendolito resurfaced in 1983— arrested in New Orleans for fraud—the FBI were on to Della Torre. By this time, too, the Bureau had realized they needed help that could only come from Italy.

"We decided to reach out to the Italian authorities," Moody continues, "to establish a working relationship with them in order to investigate this group. But the Italian government was corrupt. Period. Hands down.

It went all the way to the premier. Italian law enforcement was corrupt. Period. Hands down. The legal system was corrupt. Period. Hands down. We had to keep looking around until we could identify certain individuals we thought we could work with, both law enforcement officers and investigative magistrates. It took a long time and a lot of effort but eventually we thought we'd found the right people. We invited a dozen or so to the United States, sat down with them and worked out a cooperative agreement to investigate the Sicilian Mafia."

In October 1982, at the FBI training school in Quantico, Virginia, senior FBI managers met with Italians representing the National Police, the Carabinieri and the Guardia di Finanza. Also present were senior supervisors from the DEA, the Royal Canadian Mounted Police and the Australian Federal Police. The contacts made there were soon reinforced by a second meeting, this one in Ottawa. Three men who attended both were Italian magistrates Giovanni Falcone and Paulo Borsellino, and a young Assistant U.S. Attorney working out of New York named Louis Freeh.

Although their missions at home were intrinsically different because the nature of the beast they were hunting was different—in the States, the LCN was a law enforcement problem; in Italy, the Mafia was entangled with the state—Falcone and Freeh developed a close personal friendship. Through that, a bridge of mutual trust was built which would ultimately lead to the Mafia's first near-fatal setback.

With support now assured from Italy, a beleaguered team of prosecutors in New York, headed by Freeh's boss, Rudolph Giuliani—then the brash young U.S. Attorney for the Southern District—created a joint task force to take apart this heroin empire. At the same time, in Italy, Falcone was turning Tommaso Buscetta. Following in Valachi's spirit, Buscetta talked for ten weeks, giving the Italians all the ammunition they needed to raid hundreds of addresses in Sicily and arrest 364 mafiosi.

Although a few of the men on the American wanted list were in hiding, including Della Torre and a Swiss jeweler named Vito Roberto Palazzolo—who would be named as the gang's primary laundryman and who would, many years later, reappear in a very unexpected place—Guiliani's task force still arrested twenty-eight people in four states.

The "Pizza Connection" trial charged twenty-two of them for their part in smuggling 750 kilos of heroin into the U.S. with an estimated street value of $1.6 billion. It lasted seventeen months and featured fifty-five thousand FBI wire taps, most of them in Italian. All of the defendants were found guilty and the five Mafia ringleaders were sent away for twenty to forty-five years. The case also embarrassed Merrill Lynch, E. F. Hutton and Chemical Bank in New York, Handelsbank in Zurich and, especially, Credit Suisse in Bellinzona, marking the first drug-trafficking investigation in which the Feds had been able to follow the money. More significantly, it was the first time law enforcement saw how two otherwise independent groups came together in a joint venture.

Noted William Webster, a former head of both the FBI and the CIA, "This was the beginning of our real awareness of the international character of organized crime."

Now, suddenly, a lot of people were realizing that if it can happen once, it can happen twice.

Pablo Escobar was born in Medellín, Colombia, in 1949 and grew up poor. When he died in a hail of bullets in Medellín the day after his forty-fourth birthday, he was one of the richest men in the world.

He'd been a minor smuggler, dealing mostly in goods stolen out of warehouses along the Panama Canal, until he drifted into the cocaine business. He and his childhood friend Jorge Luis Ochoa Vasquez established an import-export company called Sea-8 Trading in Miami, then pioneered smuggling routes into the U.S. Before long, Carlos Enrique Lehder Rivas was brought into the group.

The man who prophetically described cocaine as "the Third World's atomic bomb" understood that any business needs cash flow and reinvestment to survive. While Escobar was courting the press to feed his ego, and Ochoa was trying to move into Europe, it was Lehder who set up money-laundering schemes that built a huge financial base and turned the group into what the Medellín cartel would eventually become—the most powerful drug-trafficking organization on the planet. Escobar made sure it would be remembered as the most violent, too. Over the years, he blew up an Avianca airliner and assassinated four Colombian presidential candidates, a Supreme Court judge and two dozen lower-court judges. In 1992 he orchestrated a bombing campaign against government officials and rival gangs, set off three hundred devices and killed as many people. The following year he sent his men off on a rampage and murdered 178 local policemen.

But then there was so much money at stake that when he was originally arrested by the Colombians, he bargained with the government to avoid
extradition to the United States. He offered, in exchange for protection from
the Americans, to personally pay off the Colombian national debt.

It's worth noting that Pablo Escobar was never extradited.

Gilberto and Miguel Rodriguez Orejuela grew up in Cali, in the heart
of Colombia's agricultural region. Gilberto, born there in 1939, was a phar-
macist by trade who once owned the Chrysler Motors franchise for
Colombia. Miguel, five years his junior, was a lawyer.

They started by moving cocaine into New York in the early 1970s,
then expanding to L.A. and Miami. For a while, their taste for gratuitous
violence surpassed even Escobar's. The two cartels were killing ten to fifteen people per day. But the brothers were smarter than Escobar and
brought a more sophisticated vision to drug trafficking.

Despite being known as the Cali cartel, it was never a cartel in the
same sense that Escobar's group was. Its proprietors had the vision to distance themselves from the retail side of the business, give up smuggling and
see that their future was in wholesale. Cali was more like a main holding
company that franchised out small parcels to a network of independently
owned outlets. Because anybody with collateral in Colombia can become
a drug dealer, the Cali cartel subcontracted to the mini-cartels. Aspiring
traffickers merely had to fill out a very detailed form which listed all their
relatives so that the brothers knew who to kill if someone tried to betray
them, then come up with enough cash or collateral to pay for the shipment up front. The brothers continued to buy directly from the producers,
but they sold on to these smaller groups, letting other people worry about
the transport, marketing, sales and money laundering. If cargoes were intercepted, it wasn't their product. If cash was confiscated, it wasn't their
money. The deck was stacked in their favor, structured to guarantee that
they couldn't lose. And yet as many as three hundred mini-cartels rushed
into business with them.

Almost as soon as Escobar was taken out, the Cali cartel was racking
up annual profits of around $7 billion, more than three times as much as
General Motors.

While all this was going on—while the Medellín and Cali groups were
monopolizing the U.S. cocaine market—the center of European heroin
traffic moved from Marseilles to Amsterdam. Increased drug competition

in New York then forced the LCN to shift some of their operations to Chicago, Los Angeles and Miami.

By now, the Mexicans had also entered the heroin business and quickly claimed a one-third market share of North America.

Challenging Mexico, producers in the "Golden Triangle"—Burma, Thailand and Laos—turned their attention to the United States. They were relying on various Asian organized crime groups to handle their distribution, including Thai, ethnic Chinese and Vietnamese groups who'd established a presence in the States following the war in Southeast Asia.

Not wanting to be left out, heroin producers from the "Golden Crescent"—Pakistan, Afghanistan and Iran—also offered product to U.S. distributors. Much of it was carefully staged in Canada, stored there by Pakistani traffickers for as long as three to six months until appropriate distribution contacts could be established, then driven south across the border. Nigerians were bringing heroin home to Lagos, dividing shipments into smaller parcels and using mules to bring it directly into the States. Meanwhile Lebanese traffickers were setting up a base in Canada. Couriers would fly out of Toronto and Montreal to the Middle East, pick up their drugs and transship back through Canada to the U.S.

Drugs created anarchy—in law enforcement, on the streets and within the traffickers' gangs—plunging the United States into an era of lawlessness that would make the days of bootlegged whiskey and Prohibition seem tame. Worse, the narco-economy bolstered so much of the Third World that attempting to dismantle it today would mean risking plunging the planet into global economic chaos and depression.

All too quickly, America became cocaine saturated. But as the epidemic spread, the Feds racked up a proportionate share of successes. With more traffickers to arrest, they arrested more traffickers. With more product to seize, they seized more product.

While Escobar and the Orejuelas—and everyone else in the trade— wrote off the arrests and seizures as the price of doing business, it didn't take a degree from Harvard to spot greener pastures in Europe. Cocaine prices were much higher there, demand was increasing, borders were porous and very few of Europe's national police forces ever talked to one another. Although Escobar already had a minor presence in Spain, which was natural because of the shared language, he was astute enough to understand that anyone trying to force his way into the European market would be stepping on Italian toes and that the Italians' response would be violent. So, instead of barging in full speed, he went in search of a partner.

According to Italian sources, in 1987 Escobar dispatched an Italian-speaking Colombian named Edgar Procopio Hernandez Pinzon as his emissary. Pinzon was under instructions to contact certain Sicilians and to secure their permission to set up cocaine laboratories in Europe. In exchange, Pinzon was to offer them easier access to product for their already established distribution routes. Clearly, Pinzon had some success, because by the time he was arrested a year later, the Colombians had begun producing cocaine on two windy and otherwise deserted Italian hilltops. In one lab, near Savona, technicians were installed with their wives and children so that neighbors would never suspect that this was anything but a working farm.

Before shutting both labs down, Italian customs intelligence officers took an interest in a U.S.–based Colombian named Honorio Huertas. The way they tell the story, Huertas had brokered a meeting between his handlers in Medellín and an Italian Mafia group—the Camorra is usually cited—plus one American LCN family. The subject of the meeting was said to be the ground rules for future cooperation between the groups. Huertas was subsequently arrested by DEA agents in Miami on an Italian warrant. How fruitful his meetings were has never been fully determined.

Hooking up with the Mafia taught the Colombians a lot about smuggling. When one of their chemists discovered how to mix unrefined cocaine paste with cellulose to produce cardboard-like boxes, an Italian front company was set up to sell cardboard to a Colombian front company who filled the boxes with ordinary goods that were then shipped back to Naples, where the cardboard was dissolved to produce unrefined cocaine paste. The Italians also taught the Colombians about money laundering. The cartel opened Universe Gold Enterprise and Symar Joyeros Mayoristas in Panama while the Mafia formed Aurea International Trading and Eurocatene in Italy. Cocaine cash was smuggled out of the United States, washed through banks in Switzerland, Spain and Mexico, then sent to Italy, where Aurea and Eurocatene used it to buy gold bars. They shipped the gold to Universe and Symar, who sold it on with false invoices to front companies in Cali. The gold was then sold on the open market and the laundered proceeds were deposited against sales receipts.

In fact, the DEA had already stumbled on to Symar, but their investigation was halted when Panama's president, General Manuel Noriega, personally intervened. The scent was picked up again in 1994, after Noriega's departure from Panama, and the Italian police put the ring under surveillance. That was the year this Mafia-Colombian collaboration moved fifteen tons of gold, such a vast amount that for a while they accidentally depressed the world market price.

After three months of watching Aurea and Eurocatene—during which time a ton of gold a month, worth nearly $35 million, was shipped to Panama—the Italians shut down both companies. They arrested eight people, including five Italians, two Panamanians and Gustavo Upegui Del Gado, the Cali cartel's gold expert.

Giovanni Falcone always believed that no matter what deal the Colombians swung with the Italians, it could never be a marriage, just an engagement—that any arrangement would have to be entirely on Italian terms. He'd seen firsthand that organized crime in Italy controlled nearly 20 percent of all commercial activities and had interests ranging from drugs and murder to jeans and real estate. He'd investigated the Mafia's control over half of the financial holding companies in the country, 20 percent of the construction industry and about a quarter of the food distribution business. He knew that despite substantial crackdowns, the Mafia continued to reach into every aspect of national life, wielding influence in every town throughout the country. In Rome, Milan and Naples, at least half the shops, bars and restaurants were paying protection money. In Sicily, especially in the capital city of Palermo, all of them were.

There was no doubt in Falcone's mind when he proclaimed, "The Mafia will never enter into a deal in which it can't keep the upper hand." And yet he foresaw all sorts of alliances about to happen: "Crime syndicates are going to become the biggest beneficiaries of a free Europe." Falcone warned, "There should be no frontiers for justice."

And yet his words went unheeded.

Escobar's initial partner was the Palermo-based Madonia family. Their first joint venture was a six-hundred-kilogram shipment of cocaine from Colombia through Spain to Italy. But until Trans Americas Ventures Associates went into business half a globe away in La Jolla, California, no one quite understood the extent to which Escobar and the Mafia had gotten into bed together.

Operating out of a modern redbrick-and-glass-fronted office building facing the Pacific Ocean, the company was set up to be a financial counselor.

At least, that's what it said on the front door. And in a very real sense, the company did counsel its main client in financial matters. That client was the Medellín cartel, and the company's counsel was how to launder the gigantic amounts of cash they were collecting off the streets of Southern California.

On the cartel's behalf, Trans Americas opened leather-goods shops in Houston, Miami, Fort Lauderdale, Chicago and New York to import merchandise from Colombia. The shops created a legitimate paper trail which was used to justify getting drug money into the banking system. For each ton of leather that was actually imported, paperwork was forged to show twenty tons. The Colombians were so happy with the way Trans Americas ran their sink that they asked them to expand, first to Canada, then into the Caribbean, then to Europe. Dozens of dummy corporations were set up as part of the laundry cycle, including a wine-export company and an animal-rights group, both based in Italy. Over a three-year period, from 1989 to 1992, Trans Americas washed more than $53 million of the cartel's money across North America, through Europe and back into bank accounts controlled by the cartel in Colombia, Panama, Switzerland and the Cayman Islands. They also effected cash pickups in Britain, Holland, Belgium and Italy.

While this was going on, Pinzon continued to make new friends in Italy, not just with the Sicilians but also with the Camorra and the 'Ndrangheta. The Cali cartel opened talks with all three Italian groups, too. What none of the Colombians knew was that Trans Americas was staffed by the DEA and financed under the code name Operation Green Ice.

Undercover agents took careful notes for three years, until they could coordinate one momentous, simultaneous swoop across three continents. On September 28, 1992, police from eight nations—America, the United Kingdom, Canada, Colombia, Costa Rica, Spain, Holland and the Cayman Islands—arrested more than two hundred people, including 112 in the States, three in Britain, four in Spain and thirty-four in Italy. First prize was Jose "The Pope" Duran, a thirty-eight-year-old Colombian cartel kingpin who'd been arrested in Rome. Described by the Italian police as the world's most important cocaine distributor, he had dossiers in twenty different countries under twenty different aliases. Additionally, fifteen money-laundering front companies were raided and $54 million in cash was seized, along with three quarters of a ton of cocaine. One of those companies, an import-export firm in Mantua, Italy, was "managed" by an eighty-year-old woman, with no business experience, named Vera Romagnoli. Millions of dollars had passed through her company on the way, eventually, to Colombia.

Thousands of files were also confiscated on both sides of the Atlantic, among them, computerized records taken out of a Cali cartel office which detailed their worldwide money-laundering. Other documents identified a Mafia-Colombian joint venture in drug trafficking along the French Riviera and a money-laundering joint venture in Germany. As a direct result of Green Ice, the Central Operational Service of the Italian police and the Internal Security Service of the Interior Ministry arrested the Mafia's number-two man in Sicily, plus a *capo* in the Camorra, three Sicilian brothers who'd come to be called the Mafia's private bankers, the Camorra's chief laundryman and, in May 1993, Michele "The Crazy One" Zaza, overall leader of the Camorra. He was nabbed, along with ten members of his gang, on the French Riviera, where they'd invested $1.3 billion in hotels, stores and small industry. Another forty suspects, all tied to Zaza, were taken into custody in Italy, Belgium and Germany. Also arrested were four men directly connected with Salvatore "Toto" Riina, head of the Corleone clan and *capo di tutti capi.*

Riina had been on the run for over twenty years, long enough for the Italian authorities to claim they didn't even know what he looked like. Their last known photo of him was said to be for his state identity card, taken thirty years before. The truth has since come out that he'd been living all the time with his wife and children in the hills around the village of Corleone and that he clearly could have been found if the authorities had looked hard enough. After all, when they needed to find him, they did.

But it was Duran's arrest that truly startled law enforcement.

The coalitions Pinzon had forged for Escobar had been reinvented by Duran for the Orejuela brothers. It confirmed everyone's worst fears, that both of the major Colombian drug cartels had orchestrated workable strategic alliances with various factions of the Mafia. The Colombians had effectively franchised their European cocaine and money-laundering interests. At the same time, they'd set their sights on establishing themselves as franchisees for Italian heroin in the Americas.

In March 1992, the Mafia assassinated Salvatore Lima, an intimate political ally of Italian Premier Giulio Andreotti. Lima also had equally close ties to the Mafia, to the extent that he was in their pocket, and as Giovanni Falcone advanced deeper and deeper into their territory, there was no doubt that he was making a lot of Sicilians very apprehensive.

Falcone was a man obsessed with ending the Mafia's thirty-five-year post-war reign of terror. Around 1990 he'd uncovered the Cassa Rurale e Artigiana di Monreale, a bank based in a small town near Palermo that had been laundering Mafia money for nearly twenty years. Lima had ties with that bank. Later, pundits would say that as Falcone closed in on the bank, Toto Riina worried that Lima was the weakest link in the chain. From him, Falcone would be able to follow the money to Andreotti. He'd been on the Mafia's payroll since 1968 and owed his entire political career— seven times prime minister—directly to them. Rather than allow Lima any opportunity to save his own skin by confessing all to Falcone, Riina decided he had to be eliminated. Credence was given to that supposition when, in May, just two months after Lima's murder, the Mafia hit Falcone. He was driving in an eighty-mile-an-hour motorcade on the *autostrada* outside Palermo. A remote-controlled mine exploded under his armor-plated car. Falcone's wife and three bodyguards were killed instantly with him.

Initially the media explained it away as revenge. They reported that the Sicilians got Falcone because he'd put some three hundred mafiosi in jail. Then a more complicated theory emerged, that Falcone's success in Sicily had earned him a promotion as head of an anti-Mafia super-agency. Once in that job, Falcone might be too difficult to kill and impossible to stop. The media didn't know at the time that Andreotti had a very keen interest in making sure that never happened.

But Falcone's murder was a major mistake.

The Mafia not only seriously misjudged the nation's patience with their gratuitous violence, but the murder galvanized public opinion against them and created a backlash. The government immediately ordered the roundup of fourteen hundred convicted mafiosi, many of whom were enjoying relaxed privileges such as house arrest or bail. At least two hundred of them were returned to prison. Politicians on Riina's payroll were unable to contain the police, and raids across the country captured more than four thousand people who were then charged with criminal activities. Soldiers were dispatched to patrol Palermo's streets. The sledgehammer approach knocked the Sicilians so far off course that before very long nearly five hundred mobsters were willing to denounce their once cherished code of silence and exchange information for leniency. What's more, the Mafia now had to contend with Falcone's successor, Paolo Borsellino. In July, they compounded their original mistake by murdering him and his five bodyguards.

By this point, nothing could save Riina.

The magistrate who succeeded Falcone and Borsellino went after the Cassa Rurale e Artigiana di Monreale. That inadvertently prompted the murder of Mafia businessman Ignazio Salvo, who'd been especially close to Lima. But it also brought to justice other Sicilian businessmen and three bank executives. Just as Falcone had known it would, the money trail from the bank brought the authorities right to Andreotti's front door and, eventually, to Riina's too.

It turns out, ironically, that Falcone's death was not because he'd discovered the Lima-Andreotti-Riina union, but because he was linked to evidence he was gathering about the Mafia-Colombian alliance. One of the last cases he'd worked on involved that six-hundred-kilo cocaine shipment from Escobar to the Madonias. Falcone discovered the Sicilians had paid for it with heroin and that several Madonia soldiers had been sent to work with the local Mafia in Philadelphia, presumably to supervise distribution of that heroin on behalf of the Colombians.

A reasonable assumption is that Falcone alerted the Americans to this, which would account for the fact that within hours of his murder, six FBI agents were on the first flight from Washington to Italy to help in the investigation. Within a year, Andreotti had been thrown out of power and Riina had been tossed into jail. Hardly two years after that, Colombian cocaine had surpassed heroin as the Mafia's primary source of revenue.

Yet it was another event during the Green Ice years—decidedly less dramatic and therefore almost completely unnoticed—that would have even greater consequences than those four murders.

The number-three man in the Cali cartel was a very violent character named Jose Santacruz Londono. An engineer by trade, and on the DEA's most-wanted list since 1980, he'd earned a reputation as a master smuggler by shipping cocaine from Guatemala to Miami hidden in crates of frozen vegetables. In 1990, he dispatched one of his advisors to Luxembourg.

A man on a mission, Jose Franklin Jurado Rodriguez was a professional money manager with a degree from Harvard who'd already set up Santacruz's personal money-laundering cycle. The way he'd designed it, cash was deposited in a Panamanian bank, wired from there to banks in Britain, France, Holland, Italy, Germany, Monaco, Hungary, Finland and Luxembourg, then returned to Colombia, funneled through companies owned by Santacruz, his family and his friends.

Now, in Luxembourg, this most trusted emissary got arrested.

And in his pocket, he had an airline ticket to Moscow.

3

DETOUR THROUGH THE IN-BETWEEN WORLD

I am a law-abiding citizen. It is the law that makes me a criminal.

—AKWESASNE WARRIOR

THE PIZZA CONNECTION AND GREEN ICE CONFIRMED that the Achilles heel of the drug cartels was their need to get huge amounts of cash into the legitimate banking system. If they could manage that—the first and most awkward step in the money-laundering process—they could then spin that money around the world, in and out of secret banking jurisdictions and across borders, eventually bringing it out the other end freshly washed, looking exactly like legitimate income.

The most widely used method to prevent organized crime groups from doing exactly that is suspicious cash-transaction reporting, which requires banks to take notice of cash being deposited that might be of illegitimate origin. The result is that banks and other financial institutions protect themselves from legal retribution by overreporting. In response, traffickers hire lawyers and accountants to represent their interests, thereby creating a state of "plausible deniability." As long as a banker can convince himself the cash isn't suspicious—my client isn't a drug dealer, he's a lawyer—nothing has to be reported. The problem is therefore built into the solution. What's more, it's up to the banker to define the word *suspicious*.

The United States, uniquely, went one step further right from the beginning by requiring all cash transactions over $10,000 to be reported. And the sum is aggregated annually. If someone pays his dentist four times a year with $2,500.25 in cash, because the total exceeds $10,000 in a twelve-month period, the dentist is obliged to file a report.

Realizing that loopholes allowed certain businesses to wire dirty cash out of the country undetected, Congress armed law enforcement with geographical targeting orders (GTOs), requiring money/wire remitters in specific areas—such as New York, where the Colombians had established a huge laundering enterprise—to file reports for sums as low as $750.

Cash transaction reports in any amount are compiled by the Internal Revenue Service, then sent to the Financial Crimes Enforcement Network (FINCEN) outside Washington, where analysts look for trends. Not only does FINCEN possess the most detailed database in the world, its effectiveness is apparent. Analysts have traced assets in the West belonging to Iraq, Libya and Iran, and also financial arrangements put into place linking certain suspects to the World Trade Center bombing. And yet obligatory cash-transaction reporting is not the universal model, for two reasons.

First, it is an extremely expensive operation to mount and to maintain. Unless the political will to do something about drug cash coming into a banking system is all-powerful—which, arguably, it is not in Canada, Britain, France, Germany, throughout the Caribbean and just about all of the Pacific—there will never be a commitment to the necessary funding. Second, instead of solving the problem, more often than not it simply displaces it. Rather than deposit cash in the U.S., traffickers often smuggle it out, for deposit in jurisdictions with few or no reporting requirements.

With so much known about that first step in the money-laundering process, a small group of DEA agents in Atlanta set about trying to find out more about the next step. Operation Dinero was designed to get inside the Cali cartel's money-laundering strategy. But opening a bank and offering it to the cartels as a sink was such a radical notion that when they first proposed it, the various bureaucrats who would have to approve it immediately said no. It had never been done before. And anyway, no one knew how to go about doing it.

Still, the DEA team in Atlanta persisted. Over the course of fifteen months, they planned, briefed and cajoled the Treasury, the Justice Department and federal banking regulators. They secured the necessary permissions and funding, then went in search of a banking haven from which to operate. The island of Anguilla—a thirty-five-square-mile sandbar in the Leewards—turned out to be ideal. It was close enough to Venezuela and Colombia for the traffickers, and had the added benefit of being a self-governing British crown colony. That meant, if need be, the agents could always turn to British colleagues for help.

Next, they went in search of a bank. Through various contacts, they located a man in California who'd bought a Class B banking license in Anguilla—the kind that allows private, secret banking—but hadn't gotten around to using it. After making him an offer he couldn't refuse, they wound up owning his license. They established undercover identities for the agents who would be the bank's officers, outfitted an office in Atlanta and opened a one-room office on the island, complete with a plaque on the wall and an answering machine that forwarded calls back to Atlanta. They set up subsidiaries in Singapore, the British Virgin Islands and the Isle of Man. They established related offshore accounts at banks in Anguilla, Panama, BVI, Man, Switzerland and London. They then printed brochures, stationery and business cards, and at the end of July 1994, put out the word that RHM Trust Bank Ltd. was open for business.

On the very first day, someone with connections to the Cali cartel called to arrange a money pickup. Within twenty-four hours the DEA's bank had accepted half a million dollars with instructions to wire the money around the world. Within a week, the agency had laundered over $3 million.

Legitimate accounts were discouraged, which is why, during the entire forty banking days they were in business, RHM serviced only six clients. But all six were tied directly to the Cali mob. Most of the money that came into the bank was routed by the undercover agents, on instructions from their clients, through Europe—mainly Britain, France and Italy—before being brought back to Colombia or Panama.

Sometime in late October–early November, a request came in to the bank from one of its clients to arrange a money pickup in Rome. Bill Malarney, the DEA agent supervising the sting—whose undercover guise was William Rice, vice president of RHM Trust Bank Ltd.—phoned the DEA's attaché in Italy, John Costanzo, about making that collection.

Costanzo, a native Italian speaker, assumed the part of Vicenzo, a freelance laundryman with contacts in Anguilla. Vicenzo's cell-phone number was passed on to RHM's client. A week later, a man on the other end introduced himself as Mario and explained that he needed someone to take delivery of 1.32 billion lire, approximately $760,000. Vicenzo said he could handle that, and a meet was arranged at the Palombini Bar in the Eur section of Rome. Surveillance teams from the Servicio Centrale Opportivo of the Italian National Police were put into place so that everything could be taped for evidence. But the man who showed up was not the man who'd originally phoned. He was eventually identified as Mario DiGiacomo. The money was hidden in an electronically controlled trap in the trunk of his car. He turned it over to Vicenzo's representatives—undercover Italian cops—and Malarney transferred it through the RHM Bank to Colombia.

The Italians, looking at DiGiacomo, were now able to establish that the Mario who'd rung Vicenzo was actually a heavyweight trafficker named Pasquale Claudio Locatelli.

Born in 1952 in a tiny village near Bergamo, some twenty-five miles northeast of Milan, Locatelli was running a small-time stolen-car ring and receiving stolen goods when he discovered that there was real money to be made in drugs. It didn't take much for him to establish a connection in Morocco—that sort of thing is not difficult for anyone willing to risk going there with a pocketful of cash—and begin bringing hashish and marijuana back through Gibraltar and Spain into France and Italy. While doing that, he hooked up with some guys in the Camorra who were interested in his ability to transport product. They too were bringing drugs through Spain and France, so Locatelli added their shipments to his and, in a sense, became their moving van. Through them he met Colombian cocaine brokers and set up a connection for himself, through Morocco and Gibraltar.

While building his transport and trafficking businesses, Locatelli noticed that both of his new best friends—the Camorra and the Colombians—had mountains of cash that needed to be laundered. To accommodate them, he set up a string of shell companies in Gibraltar and Switzerland which formed the basis of a complex washing cycle. He continued selling those services to them, until he had so much of his own money going through the laundry that there wasn't any room left for anyone else.

Arrested in Marseilles in 1990, Locatelli was convicted for trafficking and sentenced to twenty years. But he had a friend with a helicopter and made a daring escape from prison, although not before getting into a shootout with the cops and killing one of them. Back in Italy, he got into another shootout, this time with the carabinieri.

Easily convinced that life was safer in Spain, he moved to Málaga. There he oversaw his interests in supermarkets, a car-rental agency and other cash businesses, through which he laundered drug money. Locatelli also set about trying to buy a bank in Europe which would give him access to the international banking community. But his real power lay in his ability to import huge amounts of drugs. He sold some to the Camorra, and moved the rest to France, Romania, Croatia, Spain and Greece. He also shipped drugs to Canada, where he soon became the major supplier for Pierrino DiVito and his two sons, a Montreal drug-trafficking family.

In one operation, Locatelli air-dropped nine tons of cocaine onto a ship off the coast of Nova Scotia. Unfortunately for him, the ship foundered in rough seas and five tons of it sank to the bottom. In another, he lost a ship when it was intercepted by a NATO warship in the Adriatic laden with arms, including ten thousand Russian-made machine guns plus enough ammunition to go with them. He'd been actively evading the United Nations' embargo of Croatia. Later, the Italian police would realize that Locatelli had traded drugs with the Camorra, who, in turn, passed them along to a Russian organized crime group in exchange for the weapons he was selling in the former Yugoslavia.

By the time he contacted Costanzo, believing that he was speaking with someone who could launder money for him through Anguilla, Pasquale Locatelli was a career criminal and highly successful trafficker with a major reputation that stretched across two continents. Although he was only on the fringe of the Mafia and never a full-blown member himself, he certainly had enough contacts within it to service his needs. That made him all the more dangerous. And as soon as his name came up in Operation Dinero, it elevated the bank sting from an undercover operation out of Atlanta to an international manhunt led by the DEA in conjunction with law enforcement in Italy, France and Canada.

Everybody wanted a piece of Pasquale Locatelli.

Needless to say, he was not an easy man to find, and it took the Italians quite a while before they finally located him. Then, Málaga presented them with a number of difficulties. The city itself was small, populated only by regular residents and tourists, meaning that a bunch of Italian policemen couldn't just walk around without being noticed. What's more, operating in Spain meant that they had to secure permission from the Spanish national police—and also the police in Málaga—raising the possibility that word could leak back to Locatelli. After all, an international warrant had been issued for his arrest, and yet there he was in Spain, living with impunity. He'd obviously paid off some important people. The Italians therefore didn't know whom they could trust.

They proceeded carefully, securing the permissions they needed from the Spanish, crossed their fingers that Locatelli wouldn't be told, and dispatched two officers to watch him as best they could for three months. Those officers reported back that Locatelli had twenty-five to thirty people working for him in Spain, that he was operating with thirty to forty different cellular phones to keep his communications secure and that every few days he would disconnect some of his phone numbers, rotate others, give phones away, and start again with another bunch. It was very tough to intercept his calls, but every now and then they got lucky, like the one where he bragged that he had two thousand people working for him around the world.

In Rome, the Italians still hope he was only bragging, because they've never been able to identify more than fifty.

Locatelli had a wife and three kids at home in northern Italy—they were separated—and a woman he lived with in Spain, with whom he had another child. Apparently, he kept sending her to health farms in the States, which left him time for a twenty-four-year-old French girlfriend on the side. The Italians identified her as the daughter of Marc Fivet, a dealer involved with the DiVito family in Montreal.

And that's about the time Locatelli disappeared. He left Málaga, and no one knew where he'd gone. The only lead the Italians had was his attorney, a short, robust man named Pasquale Ciola, who lived in Bari, the heel of the boot that is Italy. They knew that Ciola was directly connected to Locatelli's arms dealing in the Balkans, and that he was the go-between with Locatelli's businesses in Italy. To find Locatelli, they had no choice but to focus on Ciola. Before long, they picked up a phone conversation in which they heard Ciola tell Locatelli that his son was going to Spain. Immediately, special agents of the Servicio Centrale Opportivo, along with a team of electronics technicians, were dispatched to Spain to coordinate the search. Ten other agents set up a command post in Rome. Yet more agents in Italy planted a radio beeper under Ciola Junior's car, and three teams in three

unmarked, specially equipped cars—with one Italian officer and one DEA
agent in each—were put on Ciola's tail. One of those unmarked cars was a
Porsche that the Italian police had confiscated from a drug trafficker.

They watched Ciola Junior load up his car—with his wife, child and
a friend, who turned out to be a magistrate who also had connections to
Locatelli—then head north through Italy, west through France and into
Spain. For two days, three cars chased after him as he drove to Spain, sometimes as fast as 130 mph. They didn't know exactly where he was headed,
and at one point, they lost him. In a panic, they convinced the Spanish
police to send up a helicopter to locate him, which they did thanks to the
radio beeper.

Instead of going to Málaga, Ciola Junior took his family and friend to
Marbella, where they vacationed for four days. The surveillance teams sat
in the shadows, waiting. Ciola Junior didn't seem to be in any hurry. The
surveillance teams soon decided that Locatelli wasn't there, and grew des-
perate to find him.

When Ciola Junior packed up his family and friend, put them in the
car and started driving home, the surveillance teams couldn't believe it. But
then suddenly, almost as if he'd been trying to shake someone off his tail,
he turned north to Madrid and inadvertently led the cops to a restaurant
called the Adriano, where Locatelli was waiting.

Before lunch got started, the Spanish police arrested Locatelli and Ciola
Junior, raided Locatelli's headquarters in Málaga and arrested another four
people there, including DiGiacomo.

At this point, Malarney in Atlanta decided to take a shot at Ciola
Senior. Everyone on the team warned him it was too late, that by having
arrested Locatelli first, the lawyer would be on his guard. But Malarney
argued that Ciola didn't know about the bank's connection with Locatelli's
arrest and felt it was worth at least one fax. His note to Ciola simply introduced RHM and, on the advice of a mutual friend, invited the lawyer to
use the bank's services. It was a real sucker punch and Ciola fell for it. He
faxed back saying he wanted to do some business.

It came just in time, because word from Washington was, close the
bank and end Operation Dinero.

Accordingly, the team in Atlanta moved toward the takedown, coordinating simultaneous arrests in the U.S., Canada and Italy. Ciola was among
the first to get busted. Locatelli spent time in a Spanish cell, awaiting extra-

dition to France, where, in early 1997, he was thrown into prison for the rest of his life. If he ever does get out somehow, there are warrants with his name on them in Italy, Greece and Canada.

The Canadians arrested the DiVitos—father and sons—and Marc Fivet, who claimed that he'd been working for the French police all along. It turns out that the French had corroborated that to the Italians, but no one ever bothered informing the Canadians. The Italians were subsequently able to identify the Colombian brokers supplying Locatelli and other people working for him all over Italy.

The final score for Operation Dinero was $110 million seized and more than one hundred people arrested.

The official story, the one that Washington puts out for public consumption, is that RHM Bank became too popular too fast, and that by having washed as much as $12 million for their six clients they'd arrived at the limit where they were becoming part of the problem. That by December 1994, Operation Dinero had accomplished what the RHM Bank had been set up to do. That the DEA had gotten a good look inside the Cali cartel's financial network and, having managed that, it was time to shut it all down.

The official story, the one that Washington puts out for public consumption, is not the whole truth.

That autumn, as the bank sting got up to full speed, the DEA's undercover agents inadvertently stepped on some important toes. At first, no one in Atlanta realized it. But by November, the people who owned those toes were quietly complaining that maybe the RHM Bank should go away.

If Malarney and his fellow agents know who they annoyed, they're not saying. It is possible, because that's the nature of these things, that they don't know. But they plainly got in the way of something important. The obvious candidates are the CIA and the Defense Intelligence Agency (DIA). The obvious reason is that someone, somewhere, was mining a vein the agents in Atlanta had tapped into. It's not Locatelli. And it's not the bank clients tied to the Cali cartel. No, the targets were people on the periphery, minor players in Operation Dinero, but nevertheless people important enough to another agenda that someone was able to shift the government's priority away from a money-laundering investigation to interests with national security ramifications.

Under U.S. law, intelligence agencies are specifically forbidden to work in tandem with law enforcement. That doesn't mean they don't, it just means they're not allowed to get caught doing it. RHM came close to compromising an intelligence-gathering operation, which explains why the Justice Department suddenly decided they were laundering too much money to justify the results they were hoping to achieve.

Enter here a place called Akwesasne.

Translated to "the land where the partridge drums"—in this case *drums* meaning *flaps its wings*—it is fourteen thousand acres stretching from Cornwall, Ontario, and Massena, New York, along twenty-five miles of St. Lawrence River channels and twenty islands, to just north of Vermont. It encompasses territory that the Americans and Canadians jointly recognize as New York State, Ontario and Quebec. But that's not the way the St. Regis Mohawk Indians see it.

One of the six tribes that make up the Iroquois Nation, they believe that the Jay Treaty of 1794, agreed by the United States and Great Britain, ceded to them a sovereign nation. They do not consider themselves citizens of either Canada or the United States. They believe that theirs is one nation inside two other nations. For them, Akwesasne is an "in-between world."

Three governing bodies operate on the reservation, which is home to around eleven thousand Native Americans. The St. Regis Mohawk Tribal Council is the political authority recognized by the Americans, south of the border. The Mohawk Council of Akwesasne is the political authority recognized by the Canadians, north of the border. The Mohawk Nation Council, which is not recognized by either, claims all of Akwesasne as one geopolitical territory. As such, they insist on the right to move across the U.S.-Canadian border without any controls, transporting goods across the border without paying taxes.

Questions of native people's land rights in general, and St. Regis Mohawk sovereignty in particular, are complicated legal issues, hotly disputed and all too often overtaken by emotion. In the most simplistic terms, the Mohawk are allowed to purchase otherwise taxable items in the U.S. without paying tax for personal consumption on the reservation. Trouble brews when those items are then sold—as if the reservation were one big duty-free shop—to non-native people, or when those items are transported off the reservation for sale elsewhere.

Taking advantage of this gaping hole in the border between the U.S.

and Canada, organized criminal groups annually smuggle more than $1 billion worth of goods through Akwesasne. Law enforcement officers on both sides are charged by their own governments to deal with this and are permitted, by law, to go onto the reservation. However, there are very good reasons why they are often reluctant to do so. Huge painted murals pepper Route 37, which runs east-west through the reservation, showing Mohawk braves wearing headdresses and covered in war paint, warning "NO FBI," "CUSTOMS STAY OUT" and "WARRIOR SOCIETY TERRITORY."

There is such a thing as the Tribal Police. But the sixteen to twenty-three officers who make up the force are really just neighborhood cops and not at all equipped to cope with the various connections some of their fellow tribesmen have to organized crime. Especially the Warrior Society. This militant hard core, numbering around two hundred to two hundred fifty, are pledged to the armed self-defense of Akwesasne. Funded almost entirely by drug trafficking, smuggling and other criminal activity, they stockpile enough weapons on the reservation—including automatic weapons, large shotguns, M14 rifles, AK-47s and Russian-made rifles—to inflict serious damage to any force short of the 101st Airborne Division.

Extensive public attention was drawn to the Warriors and the St. Regis Mohawk's cause in 1990 when they demonstrated against plans by the town council of Oka, Quebec—thirty miles west of Montreal—to extend a nine-hole golf course into a pine forest. That land was considered by the Mohawk to be a sacred burial ground dating back to the first quarter of the eighteenth century. Several claims had been laid by the tribe for reversion of rights to the land, all of which had been regularly denied by various governments. What began as a simple protest turned sour four standoff months later when a hundred-man SWAT team from the Quebec Provincial Police stormed the Mohawk's camp. Firing rifles, and throwing tear gas grenades and smoke bombs, they were met by Warrior Society return fire. A police officer was killed. For the next seventy-eight days—in full view of seven hundred journalists, armed police officers, plus a detachment of soldiers from the Canadian Forces—the Mohawk defended their rights to the area. Inside the camp, around thirty Warriors were dressed in army-issue camouflage with chest webbing, with AK-47 rifles and thirty-round banana clips, .357 Magnum pistols and RPK machine guns. At one point, word spread that they also had a 50-caliber machine gun. With them were twenty-two women and children.

Negotiations were begun, then broken off, then begun again several times. Toward the end, Warriors demanded amnesty for all their previous crimes, full recognition by Canada of Akwesasne sovereignty and a seat on the United Nations. It wasn't until soldiers in full battle gear took up positions surrounding the building where the Warriors were holding out that they finally surrendered. Some 150 Mohawk were arrested, but only thirty-seven were charged, and then, only two were ever convicted.

The following year, the Warrior Society was one of twenty-one groups to share a $250,000 human rights award named after and presented by Libyan dictator Colonel Muammar Gadhafi. That same year, a sale of nine hundred weapons was made to a group inside the tribe. Investigators eventually traced some of those weapons to drug traffickers, armed robbers and street gangs across Canada who used them in robberies, assaults, and attempted murders as well as at least seven deaths. The year after that, the Warriors purchased three hundred weapons, one of which was eventually tied to four killings. Two years later a sale to St. Regis Mohawk of two hundred automatic weapons was uncovered.

Recalling their stand at Oka, the Society has mounted a gigantic sign on the side of the longhouse at Akwesasne.

It reads, "Warriors 1 Canadians 0."

Putting the importance of Akwesasne into perspective requires a brief look at the business of reservations.

That means casinos.

America's first high-stakes Native American gambling parlor belonged to the tiny Seminole tribe in south Florida. Born in 1979 as a bingo hall in Hollywood, not far from Fort Lauderdale, it was such an instant success that the tribe soon challenged the state ban on gambling by installing video poker and video slot machines. Everything lay in their claim of sovereignty. The courts upheld it, and today the Seminoles operate a bunch of casinos, turning over around half a billion dollars a year. Pretax profits are apparently about $120 million a year, which is the same as after-tax profits, because the tribes don't pay tax.

The floodgates having opened, there are now nearly two hundred tribes in twenty-eight states sharing in the $5 billion Indian reservation gambling boom. But gambling is one of those industries that attracts strange bedfellows, and the idea of Indian sovereignty being a back door into legalized gambling has not gone unnoticed by a whole slew of strange bedfellows.

According to the California Department of Justice, one of the Seminoles' early partners was linked to Sebastian Larocca's crime family in Pittsburgh, who, in turn, was linked to the Genoveses. It now appears that some of the seed money for that first bingo hall may have come from people controlling Meyer Lansky's funds. Though this was categorically denied for years by the Seminoles, Chief James Billie finally acknowledged in 1999, "There might be some semblance of truth" there.

The man in the middle is said to have been the late Stephen Hennington Whilden, a Harvard-trained Nixon White House lawyer who was general counsel to the Seminoles when they first brought in gambling. He is said to have been the one who set up the meetings with the Lansky people. He is said to have been the one who first realized that the Indians were sitting on this fabulous asset called sovereignty. His line was, tribes reserve sovereignty except where it is expressly abrogated, and therefore the tribes can do things on their land because they are a sovereign nation.

"Wherever you've got jurisdictional confusion," notes Alexis Johnson, a New Mexico attorney who has been one of the most vocal opponents of Indian reservation gambling, "you get 'the guys' surfacing. They understand how confusion works for them, how chaos is their friend. The government can't figure out what the straight line is on how to bust these guys, so they don't get busted. These are not poor Indians running casinos across the country, these are mobbed-up Indians."

As Johnson sees it, gambling is the engine that satisfies all comers. It's an easy way to generate revenue, to create jobs in impoverished tribal economies, to say that money is being made on tribal grounds. But there is a natural relationship between gambling and organized crime, just as there is a natural relationship between gambling and politics. They ride together. Indian casinos, he contends, allow the mob to run a gambling business in a country where gambling is supposedly controlled and limited to Las Vegas and Atlantic City. At the same time, gambling provides the tribes with money to buy political influence.

"You can't run a casino without all kinds of ancillary businesses," Johnson continues. "You've got to have all kinds of people who understand how to run the floor, how to find the employees who are discreet, how to get the employees that have been buffed up and run past a couple of other regulatory bodies, how to get the limousine services to work, how to get the buses to work, how to get the comped guys here and there, who can go to whose network and launder the money, who can take the casino skim to Las Vegas or the Bahamas or the Caymans. The whole thing. They need to set up an entire mechanism. All you have to do is look around to see who has that mechanism in place, who knows how to do that. Certainly not the Indians."

Although the Seminoles are believed to have divested themselves of their earlier partners, they have expanded their operation offshore and own a stake in the Lightning Casino on the Dutch Caribbean island of St. Maarten. Ironically, one travel agent in the Caribbean offers a nighttime gambling package tour to the Lightning Casino—complete with $50 worth of chips—by boat from the nearby island of Anguilla, home of the now defunct RHM Bank Ltd.

According to Florida's *St. Petersburg Times,* allegations were made in a 1995 federal lawsuit that cash was regularly being transferred by the Seminoles from the Hollywood bingo hall to the Lightning Casino. The implication was that this wasn't seed money for an investment; it was, presumably, money laundering. The people involved with those ship-ments to St. Maarten denied that the boxes they were transporting there contained cash. Nevertheless, St. Maarten is one of the more nefarious money-laundering islands and a well-established transshipment point for drugs. It is also home to the Santapaola crime family, whose godfather, Benedetto, is in jail for life in Italy for his role in the assassination of Giovanni Falcone. This is not to say that there is any relationship between the Seminoles and the Santapaolas. But it does worry some people that wherever these tribes set up gambling operations the mob shows up nearby.

Recently, the Lightning Casino applied for a license to open an Internet gambling site. The request was rejected by the Dutch Ministry of Justice. Apparently they didn't like some of the management involved. In response, the Seminoles started looking for another Caribbean base to set up an Internet gambling site. St. Kitts has been mentioned, yet another island with a money-laundering/drug-transshipment–organized crime repute. There are already several dozen Internet casinos up and run-ning on the World Wide Web, scattered all over the world, including one named after singer Kenny Rogers. Another appears to be based in Australia, although it may not be. After all, what you see in cyberspace is not always what you get.

The first Indian internet casino was established by the Coeur D'alene tribe in Idaho, and their Internet bingo game is said to be worth $45 million a year. Recently it came to light that the St. Regis Mohawk are looking for someplace to run an Internet casino. The state of New York would claim that it's illegal for anyone within the state's jurisdiction to gamble that way, but claiming illegality and enforcing state law in cyberspace are two very different things. The beauty of such an operation is that it doesn't take more than a dozen people to keep it running twenty-four hours a day. Also, because money is electronically transferred between players and the casino, it can be banked anywhere, without the government ever finding it. In 1999, Internet gambling revenues were hovering in the $500–600 million region. By 2002, one estimate suggests, they will reach $10 billion. By 2005, that figure could easily double, and double again two years after that. The criminal potential in all of this is staggering, to the point that it easily satisfies the wildest dreams of any organized crime family.

"Indians are cover," insists Johnson. "Indians are a geopolitically significant description. Cross out Seminole. Cross out Mohawk. Just talk about stuff. What Indians resemble is transnational stuff. Geopolitical stuff. What do they look like? They look like tax havens. They look like the on-shoring of an offshore concept. They look like law enforcement breakdowns and we know, axiomatically, they involve jurisdictional conundrum and jurisdictional confusion. Most tribal leaders aren't as smart as the real bad guys, although there seem to be some. Look at the political liaisons, and the lobbying and the lawyering, that's how the deals get brokered. There is always a non-Indian involved somewhere."

Back in Akwesasne, his name was Larry Miller.

A stocky, chain-smoking, sunburned middle-aged guy with silver hair, Miller was a Las Vegas–based businessman who had a slot-machine business and also owned the Massena Club, a nightclub on the edge of the St. Regis Mohawk reservation. His relationship with the tribe was anchored in his friendship with a fellow named Tony Laughing, who, the year before the incident at Oka, was running Tony's Vegas International Casino at Akwesasne.

There'd been a heated debate that split the Mohawk on whether or not to allow gambling. The success of the Seminole bingo hall had created a huge bandwagon, but jumping onboard did not please everyone. At one point, the pro-gambling forces at Akwesasne—supported by the Warrior Society—got into a nightmare of a gun battle with the anti-gambling forces. It was a firefight reminiscent of the war in Vietnam, complete with automatic weapons and tracers marking night skies. On another evening, when police came onto the reservation to close Laughing's casino—claiming he was in violation of state and federal laws—armed Warriors lined up to stare down the police. Laughing later admitted that he'd purchased the assault weapons they'd used to protect his business and subsequently made several donations to the Warrior Society.

Among Laughing's Mohawk chums were L. David Jacobs, chief of the St. Regis Mohawk from 1988 to 1994, who turned out to be his partner in a reservation-based extortion ring; and John "Chick" Fountain, a retired New York State trooper, who left the force in 1983 with twenty-one years' service to run Fountain Financial Security Services—an armored-car cash-delivery business—and the Northern Currency Exchange. Among Miller's partners were the Tavano brothers, Lewis and Robert Sr., with whom he shared the slot-machine business and a company called LBL Importing—as in Larry, Bobby and Lewis —which imported and distributed cigarettes to Indian reservations.

Robert Tavano had once been chairman of the Niagara Falls Republican Party. But in 1976 he was convicted of insurance fraud after stealing $400,000 worth of premiums from the county, and served seventeen months of a five-year sentence. When he got out, he started a travel agency. Louis Tavano also had an arrest record. He'd been nabbed in the 1970s on gambling charges, along with the local godfather, Stefano Magaddino. The case was thrown out because the judge ruled the federal wiretaps were illegal. It nevertheless established that through Magaddino, Tavano had a relationship with the Johnny "Pops" Papalia crime family in Ontario: the same Johnny Pops who introduced Carmine Galante to Vic Cotroni.

Louis Tavano also had a business relationship with the Seneca tribe of western New York State, and to a Buffalo-based company that used to be called Emprise. Now known as Delaware North—and by its chairman's insistence, totally clean of its previous reputation—Emprise was in the coin-operated concession business at sports facilities, such as racetracks. In 1972, the company was busted on racketeering charges, having fronted for several organized crime figures. There were allegations that Emprise had links to the Detroit mob. There are allegations that Tavano had connections with Detroit. From there, the allegations lead to Las Vegas gambling interests.

Reenter Larry Miller.

Understanding the geographic advantage of Akwesasne, Miller couldn't believe his luck when the Canadian government decided they could prevent young people from smoking by dramatically raising the tax on cigarettes and tobacco. From 1984 to 1993, federal taxes on cigarettes in Canada rose from 42 Canadian cents to $1.93 per pack. Provincial taxes also drastically increased. In response, Miller and his cohorts set up an elementary scam. Cigarettes were exported from Canada tax-free and shipped in bond to warehouses on the U.S. side of the reservation. Invoices were drawn up to preclude any U.S. tax obligation. Then the cigarettes were smuggled back to the Canadian side where, despite high markups, they were still cheaper than cigarettes with the government tax added.

The simplicity of the ruse and the ease with which the cigarettes could be taken back into Canada not only encouraged the smugglers, but made many of them multimillionaires. Profits were running as high as $500 per case, which translated to $500,000 per truckload. In 1989, around five hundred thousand Canadian-manufactured cigarettes were legally exported tax-free to New York State. Within four years, that figure had risen to twenty billion. By then, one in three cigarettes being smoked in Canada was contraband.

A large portion of the cigarettes Miller and Co. were exporting tax-free to the States was a brand called Export A. Its customer base was Canadian and never very significant in the U.S. The reason so many were crossing the border was because Miller had been introduced to the right people by the Tavano brothers.

To handle this massive export flow, parent company RJ Reynolds of Winston-Salem, North Carolina, set up a subsidiary of RJR-MacDonald of Canada—owners of Export A—called Northern Brands. The parent company then appointed one of its own senior executives, Les Thompson, specifically to market cigarettes to Akwesasne. Thompson's major clients were Miller, the Tavanos, Laughing and Fountain.

Miller would later claim that the Tavanos also introduced him to Stan Smith, executive vice president of RJR-MacDonald; that in several meetings with Thompson and Smith, the word *smuggling* was frequently used;

and that RJR-MacDonald knew full well that the cigarettes they were selling to him at Akwesasne were being brought back illegally into Canada.

As profits poured in, Miller bought himself a corporate jet so that he
could conveniently commute between his homes in Massena and his
homes in Las Vegas. He also started spending time in Moscow.

And this is where the plot thickens.

According to an Royal Canadian Mounted Police affidavit, Miller paid
$22 million to buy the Beverly Hills Casino near Red Square. Movie Star
Chuck Norris is listed as an investor in that deal.

With many cigarettes now crossing the border, Miller's business in
Akwesasne soon got to the point of being nearly out of hand. As Miller
claimed at the time, "You could stand on the river and watch them load
the boat with cigarettes stacked up above their head, right out in the daylight." In fact, his business reached such a frenzied point that smugglers
were even bringing American cigarettes into Canada, stamped with the
U.S. surgeon general's health warning instead of the Canadian government's
health warning. Eventually, Prime Minister Jean Chretien realized he had
no other choice but to cut the cigarette tax, which dried up a lot of trade.
But not all of it.

Reacting immediately, Miller held a meeting at the Sonora Lodge, on
the Campbell River in British Columbia. His guests were Louis Tavano,
Les Thompson and, supposedly, Stan Smith. His bill at the fly-in-only
resort, where rooms can start at C$1000 a night, is said to have come to
C$310,000. And again, Miller later claimed, the word *smuggling* was fre-
quently used. Since that meeting, and for the next two years, Northern
Brands sold tax-free Export A's to Miller, through two companies in New
York State, one of which was LBL Importing Inc. Papers filed with U.S.
Customs by those companies stated that the cigarettes were on their way
to Estonia and Russia. Instead, they were stored in one of several prefab
warehouses that dot the reservation along the river, until they could be
moved north.

In the warmer months, moving cigarettes north meant ferrying them
by boat across the St. Lawrence, usually at Cornwall Island. In the winter
months, they were taken by snowmobile. Once on the other side, the
Akwesasne gangs handed off the contraband to non-native organized
crime gangs—including Asian and biker gangs such as Hells Angels—who,
as wholesalers, distributed the goods to the black-market outlets.

Before long, Miller diversified into alcohol, in a mirror tax-dodge scam. He and the others shipped whiskey into Akwesasne from several out-of-state locations, mainly Maryland and Virginia, but also from as far away as California and Oregon. By the end of 1998, one wholesaler in Santa Barbara had shipped half a million cases of alcohol to Akwesasne, about $24 million worth.

Laughing, who'd already collected convictions for illegal gambling and resisting arrest—including an assault on U.S. Customs inspectors—was so blatant about this smuggling operation that he once allowed a Canadian television news crew to film it. He later declared that he and six other Mohawk sold six hundred thousand cases of tax-free liquor to Canadians in 1994 alone, making an average profit of $13 per case, which comes to $7.8 million.

Needless to say, federal, provincial and state law enforcement do what they can, but except for the occasional very large bust, it isn't much. The Canadians estimate they seize less than 5 percent of the goods going through Akwesasne. The Americans, hardly more optimistic, say at best they get 10 percent. In late March 1996, the RCMP arrested 170 people after a series of raids aimed at putting a dent in Akwesasne smuggling. They nabbed St. Regis Mohawk, members of a Montreal-area chapter of Hells Angels, organized Vietnamese criminals and Chinese immigrants. They also seized $15 million worth of liquor, cigarettes, cars and other property. It was their biggest bust to date. The following night, smugglers were crossing the river again.

A year or so later, a joint task force of RCMP, tribal police, the U.S. Border Patrol, the New York State Police and U.S. Customs raided several locations on the reservation. This time, they hit right at the heart of the Miller-Tavano-Laughing-Fountain cabal. Announcing that they'd cracked a $700 million smuggling ring—one agent described it as "bigger than Al Capone"—they charged twenty-one people with conspiring to defraud the U.S. and Canadian governments. Included were Miller, the Tavanos, Laughing, Fountain and former chief Jacobs. The two governments also seized alcohol, cigarettes, cash, two of Fountain's armored cars, three of Miller's boats, two of Miller's homes in Massena, five other homes, parcels of land in Las Vegas and a pickup truck.

Jacobs was charged under the Federal Racketeer Influenced Corrupt Organizations (RICO) statute with running the tribe as a criminal enterprise. In partnership with Laughing, who was also charged under RICO, the two had been extorting tribal businessmen with gambling interests. Jacobs also admitted that he took $3,000 kickbacks from Larry Miller for every tractor-trailer load of contraband that Miller moved through the reservation, earning around $200,000. Additionally charged with smuggling and money laundering, he copped a plea. So did Laughing. His profits on liquor and cigarette smuggling were said to be in the area of $550 million. Faced with so much evidence against him, Laughing agreed to serve eight years and pay a $500,000 fine. The Tavano brothers pled guilty for their role in smuggling and the laundering of $50 million. So did Fountain, through whose company much of the money was being laundered. So did Larry Miller, who accused RJR-MacDonald of providing him with information on what brands of cigarettes were selling in Canada, and therefore cooperating with him in an illegal activity. He admitted to moving about six thousand cases of Export A cigarettes a week, but swore, "The tobacco company knew that the cigarettes they sold me would be smuggled."

At first, RJR denied it. Then they refused to comment on it. By December 1998, they'd seen the writing on the wall, or, more accurately, indictments coming down from the grand jury, and caved in. U.S. Attorney Tom Maroney announced that Northern Brands International admitted to aiding and abetting others in the avoidance of U.S. excise taxes—specifically taking responsibility for twenty-six truckloads of cigarettes that they'd falsely claimed were destined for Estonia and Russia—and agreed to forfeit $10 million, in addition to paying a $5 million fine.

Tony Laughing likes to do television interviews from jail. He fancies himself a star and deliberately comes across as quirky and funny. But beneath the surface, he's a dangerous man with dangerous connections.

"I did everything they said I did," he's been quoted as admitting, "and I did more. And when I get out of here I'm going to do it again."

There is some concern that he may well still be doing it. In early 1999, an American television journalist investigating Akwesasne found himself in a confrontation with the Warrior Society. At one point, they threatened to hold him captive. What could have turned into a major incident luckily didn't, and after a few very uncomfortable hours, the journalist was released. Not thirty minutes later he received a call on his cell phone from Laughing—from inside a federal penitentiary—apologizing for the incident.

It seems that Tony Laughing is kept informed about everything that goes on at Akwesasne, is still a force to reckon with there and has been for a very long time. At least some Russians think so. And therein may be the reason that the U.S. government shut down Operation Dinero.

Besides cigarettes and alcohol, plenty of Southeast Asian drugs have been coming through the reservation. Landed in Vancouver by Asian organized crime groups, they are transported across Canada by various outlaw motorcycle gangs, delivered to Akwesasne, taken across to the U.S. side, then handed off to organized crime groups, including other outlaw motorcycle gangs and Asian traffickers.

There is also a thriving market in weapons going in both directions across the border, and being warehoused on the reservation. One story has it that semiautomatic weapons purchased in the U.S. are smuggled across the border, where they are converted into fully automatic weapons, then brought back onto the reservation. Another story has it that there is an IRA weapons connection with the reservations, although investigators who have looked into it have never been able to prove it.

Counterfeit U.S. $100 bills have been showing up at Akwesasne since 1994, the source of them originally being organized Lebanese criminals. It seems they'd passed the notes off to street gangs who used them to purchase weapons at Akwesasne.

There is brisk trade in Cuban cigars, both real and counterfeit; Iranian carpets, which are on the U.S. embargo list; various prohibited agricultural products; animals and skins; and stolen vehicles.

Cars stolen off Canadian streets are driven through the reservation to U.S. ports such as Newark, New Jersey, where they are loaded onto ships bound for the former Soviet Union. There is a definite Russian organized crime connection, which has only really taken hold in the past few years.

"When we send these Native Americans to jail," explains Jeremiah Sullivan, the special agent in charge of the U.S. Customs office in Buffalo, New York, which has responsibility for the U.S. border area that includes Akwesasne, "they interact with all sorts of criminals. They meet members of Russian organized crime groups and traditional organized crime groups. Whoever they interact with in prison, they do business with as soon as they get out."

He says that, in many ways, the service those St. Regis Mohawk smugglers have on offer is really no different that any ordinary moving-van business. "They get paid for carrying boxes. In some cases they may not even know what's in the boxes. Anybody who needs someone to smuggle something knows about them. There's a lot of interest out there in what the St. Regis Mohawk have to offer. One smuggler in Oregon, on the other side of the country, once told us, 'All roads lead to Akwesasne.'"

They certainly seem to, from as far away as Moscow.

A U.S. federal law-enforcement informant in a major car-smuggling investigation told investigators that he'd been approached by some former KGB officers now involved with a Russian organized crime group. They wanted him to find out what security was like from Buffalo to the Vermont border, what resources the Border Patrol had, what resources U.S. Customs had, what resources the Canadians had and how often active patrols came through.

And roads definitely lead to Akwesasne from as far away as Fujian Province in China.

The Chinese refer to the United States as "Gold Mountain," a promised land where many people hope to join relatives already established there and begin a new life. Recruiters in Fujian working for Asian organized crime gangs offer just that possibility. For a 10 percent down payment of the total fee—which has been running at a staggering $47,000—anyone signing on to make the grueling trip is provided with counterfeit documents that will get them out of China and, eventually, into Canada.

The most popular port of entry is Vancouver, where the aliens—following a prepared script—ask for political refuge. Canadian Immigration officers, following set procedures, provided them with dates for a hearing. The aliens are then moved by the gang—referred to as "snakeheads"—to safe houses in Toronto and Montreal, where they are stored like packaged goods in a basement until nightfall. They are then trucked to the Canadian side of the reservation where Mohawk guides get the people to the U.S. side, always at night and often under hazardous conditions.

From the south side of Akwesasne, it is a seven-hour van ride to New York City. In certain instances, aliens have been asked to pay installments of their overall fee at every staging point. If they can't, or if their relatives back home don't wire the money on time, they are abandoned. In other cases, any monies due once they reach New York are paid off, with interest, through forced labor in garment industry sweatshops, restaurants or brothels. For many, it is not only an expensive and dangerous adventure, it ends in failure. For some, it ends in death. Granted, it may only be a small percentage who get caught, but those who do are thrown into jail and eventually deported. Or, as has happened all too frequently, something goes wrong, like the time the rubber raft transporting a load of Asian aliens sank in the St. Lawrence and some of the group drowned. Or the time when an elderly woman died of hypothermia. Or the time when a mother accidentally smothered her eight-month-old child while hiding it under a blanket.

Less frequently, there is the arrest of a snakehead. On one occasion, the Border Patrol realized they'd captured the same man for the third time. Each time, he'd produced different identification bearing a different name. He was taken to court, where a judge demanded $35,000 bail. Under police escort, the man insisted on being driven to his motel room, where he produced enough cash to be set free. He hasn't been seen since.

The big money in alien smuggling goes to Asian organized crime. The Mohawk guides are sometimes paid as little as $50 per person. At other times they may earn as much as $500 to $750 per load, transporting anywhere from eight to twenty-four aliens. But then, the way they see it, they are simply moving packages.

It took a yearlong investigation on both sides of the border to seriously disrupt this particular group. In December 1998, thirty-five people associated with it were arrested, with warrants issued for another twelve. Of those arrested, twenty were ethnic Chinese, eight were Mohawk. The ring was believed to have been bringing 150 aliens through the reservation a month and in operation for at least two years. Using the $47,000 figure that was released in a press conference by the U.S. Justice Department after the bust, that would mean the gang brought thirty-six hundred aliens into North America and made $170 million doing it. At that same press conference, the Immigration and Naturalization Service drew a map of the various routes used by the gang. Not all of the aliens, it turns out, traveled on the most direct itinerary. Some were flown from Fujian to Taiwan or Hong Kong and on to Vancouver. Others were taken via

Germany, France, Morocco, Greenland, Cuba or Brazil before being put on a flight to Toronto or Montreal.

Unfortunately, it's not just illegal aliens from China who are coming through the reservation. More sinister is the traffic in terrorists. The Canadian Security Intelligence Service—Canada's equivalent of the CIA—has admitted, "Most of the world's terrorist groups have established themselves in Canada, seeking safe haven, setting up operational bases and attempting to gain access to the USA."

Over the past few years there have been several terrorists caught there. In January 1996, for instance, two vans came across the border on the western end of the reservation. The Border Patrol just happened to have officers in the area and they stopped one of the vans. Inside were an Algerian, three Pakistanis—who were all Canadian citizens—and one Lebanese gentleman who turned out to be a suspected terrorist. The Border Patrol informed the FBI, who took charge of the five and drove them off somewhere. No one involved with the original arrests has ever heard about the incident again. And the not-to-be-attributed story from the FBI is: "It happened . . . but, well, it didn't happen."

Over the summer of 1998, three Egyptians with ties to a terrorist organization were picked up by a roving patrol on Route 81 north of Syracuse, having come through the reservation with counterfeit visas that have since been traced back to the British embassy in Cairo. Around the same time, it is known that law enforcement officers on both side of the border spent three panic-stricken weeks searching for a box that was believed to have come through the reservation and into the United States. The best any source will reveal is that it contained some type of "NBC"—nuclear, biological or chemical weapon. If it happened, no one seems willing to say whether or not they ever found it.

Rumors have also circulated that the triggering device for the World Trade Center bomb came through the reservation.

If the rumor is true, no one seems willing to admit it.

Then again, no one seems willing to deny it, either.

"There is always a Larry Miller type, a non-Indian, involved somewhere," Alexis Johnson continues. "Laughing and Fountain are the worker bees. They're part of a network. To understand what's going on throughout the country, you've got to understand the lawyers and the lobbyists. There are some very serious people behind the Indians, because this is about big, big money. To have created the jurisdictional breakdown that we see today, you've got to have a serious legal infrastructure in Washington, D.C. The Indians couldn't have pulled it off on their own. What's the probability of the RJR episode just having been a bunch of Indians doing their thing? The answer is some function approaching zero."

None of it could have happened, he says, without the tribal veil of sovereignty. "That's used to say stay away, don't look at us, we get to do what we want because we say so. It's a mask for the Larry Millers of the world. He gets to hide behind the Anthony Laughings and David Jacobs whom he can trot out as Indians. Miller can then do whatever he wants because he's doing it in something that resembles an island in the stream of North America, a tax haven, a jurisdictional confusion zone, a jurisdictional breakdown zone, a place of great confusion, and a duty-free shop. It's about transshipment. It's Isle of Man-ing going on in New York. That's what Indianness is in the U.S. today."

Coinciding with the various busts at Akwesasne came the news that the St. Regis Mohawk were attempting to move their casino rights away from Mohawk ground down to the Catskill Mountains, ninety miles north of New York City. The tribe wants the U.S. Department of Interior to take the land in trust for them, which would make the 235-acre tract next to Monticello Raceway in Sullivan County official Mohawk territory, with all the sovereignty that implies, simply for the purpose of opening a casino there. One of the companies getting into the deal with the tribe is based in the Bahamas, which means no one can be totally sure who's involved and precisely where the money has come from.

Scoffs Johnson, "Do you really think the idea of a land trust is the Indians? Come on, this is Washington lawyer talk. A bunch of guys sat down and tried to figure out what to do. They looked at a map and said, what's America's weakest point? Tribal grounds. Lansky's guys figured out this tribal breakdown a long time ago."

So did a few people who popped up in Operation Dinero.

Within days of RHM's opening, a courier delivered a corporate check in the amount of $676,353 to be deposited into the account of a Cali cartel laundryman named Luis Eduardo Velez-Arias. It had been drawn by a company in Fair Lawn, New Jersey, called Compulinx Inc. and was signed

"Natalya Kaminer." A records check reveals that the officers of Compulinx Inc. were Gregory and Natalya Kaminer and that they were associated with two other companies, Janus Electronics and Calimont Capital Corporation, both of which appeared to be owned and/or managed by Betty and Benjamin Marcovitch. DEA documents suggest that the agency had long suspected the Kaminers of being involved with money launderers in New Jersey and that the Marcovitches had previously cropped up during investigations in New Jersey, New York, Miami and Colombia. Betty Marcovitch is Colombian, her maiden name being Rios-Valencia. The other three are of Russian birth.

On the same day that Velez-Arias's representatives took delivery of that check for $676,353, Benjamin Marcovitch—who claimed he was an oil company executive—deposited $666,040 in cash in a Compulinx account at the Citizens First National Bank of New Jersey in Ridgewood, New Jersey. The bank duly filed a cash transaction report with the Internal Revenue Service. Within a few weeks, FINCEN analysts noticed that it was the seventh CTR accredited to Marcovitch in two years. When questioned by bank officials, Marcovitch is said to have explained that the money was owned by Calimont Capital, an import-export business, and that he was the chief executive officer of Calimont Capital.

Five more deposits quickly followed, totaling just under $460,000.

FINCEN's analysts then noticed that Kaminer, during that same five-week period, had also been the subject of cash transaction reports for several deposits. The first was for $187,000 put into a Compulinx account in New Jersey, followed by a second for $71,380 and a third for $457,464 put into the New Jersey Compulinx account. In addition, he'd deposited four cashier's checks of less than $10,000 each drawn on banks in Montreal.

Investigators subsequently established that a large number of phone calls had been placed from the Marcovitches' Manhattan apartment to numbers in Bayonne, New Jersey, belonging to Anthony Gallagher. A convicted felon who, at the time, was operating a check-cashing service, Gallagher had ties to the Genovese family.

Needless to say, an association that links Russians to La Cosa Nostra, and also involves a Colombian, piques serious interest. And the closer the authorities looked at the Marcovitches, Gallagher and the Kaminers, the more their interest grew.

On September 30, 1994, a cashier's check arrived at RHM Bank Ltd.

to be deposited into the Velez-Arias account for $995,100. It was drawn on the First National Bank of Northern New York in Massena. Five days later, a second cashier's check for $304,551 arrived, also drawn on First National. This was during the time when Chick Fountain, through Fountain Financial Security Services and his Northern Currency Exchange, was shipping "truckloads" of Laughing's and Miller's cash from Massena to Canada. This was during a time when the Royal Bank of Canada became so suspicious about the amount of money coming out of Akwesasne— reliably believed to have been $250 million over a fifteen-month period— they took it upon themselves to notify the RCMP.

Investigators then located a fax which purported to be a copy of a bank wire transfer written in Russian. It translated to reveal that on August 10, 1993, $100,000 was wired from the Promstroj Bank in Russia to an account in New York, on behalf of Calimont Capital. From that, investigators were able to locate another Marcovitch company, this one called Privat Capital Inc. No one will say what they found when they looked into Privat Capital Inc., but the suggestion is that here, again, they unearthed links to Akwesasne. However, a secret DEA "briefing paper" on Operation Dinero notes that the agency, the FBI and the IRS had all been investigating a sophisticated money-laundering operation in the New York area headed by two individuals of Russian extraction who were laundering millions of dollars in the northeastern United States and Canada. It goes on, intriguingly, to say, "The New York targets have extensive business dealings within Russia and one is supposedly a former KGB operative who is using his connections within Russia in the money laundering scheme."

And all this time, Tony Laughing was busy "managing" things at Akwesasne. And Chick Fountain was busy moving money. And Larry Miller was going back and forth to Moscow to oversee "business interests" there. Records from a midtown Manhattan hotel also reveal that meetings took place between "representatives" of the Marcovitch-Kaminer side and "representatives" of the Laughing-Fountain-Miller side. In other words, certain people knew one another on a first-name, face-to-face basis.

When the crunch came and RHM was taken down, the Marcovitches and Gregory Kaminer were arrested in Montreal. They waived extradition and were charged—the Marcovitches on four counts of money laundering and two counts of conspiracy, Kaminer on four counts of money laundering and one count of conspiracy. But unlike other people caught in the Dinero sting, these three were not charged federally. Instead—and unusually—they were charged in New York under the laws of the State of New York. What's more, they waved their right to a jury trial. That, in and of itself, is not rare, but where complex financial dealings are concerned, defense lawyers often prefer to take their chances with a jury, whom they can more easily confuse, than with a judge, who might understand what the machinations were all about.

So the case was heard in New York before one judge and, despite what the DEA and the district attorney's office believed to be a mountain of evidence against them, the Marcovitches and Kaminer walked.

All three were found not guilty on all counts. The evidence against them and the trial transcripts are sealed. And will stay that way for a very long time.

That pleases certain people in Washington.

People with slightly bruised toes.

Because the exact nature of the relationship between the Marcovitches, Kaminer, Tony Laughing, Chick Fountain and Larry Miller—and/or anyone else at Akwesasne—is almost certainly the reason why the RHM Bank sting was shut down.

4

THE MAFFIYA

We Italians will kill you, but the Russians are crazy.
They'll kill your whole family.

—JOHN GOTTI, *mafioso*

In the beginning, the Maffiya created driver's licenses.

They came to New York, huddled masses yearning to be free, what few belongings they owned tied with rope into old suitcases and wooden crates. But it didn't matter what they could carry in their arms, because in their minds they carried their future. They were doctors, physicists and biologists. They were chemists, sociologists and geologists. And each of them, as they waded ashore, counted on that to help them make their way.

Filled with hope, they arrived in Brighton Beach, Brooklyn, where the ones who had come before had settled but, one by one, had learned the hard way that in the New World their old-world diplomas didn't count. Their university degrees were not even a minor curiosity.

They were forced to turn to what is sometimes referred to as "entry-level immigrant" work—jobs that have always been open to the newest arrivals, like waiting tables and cleaning offices and driving taxicabs. But to get a job as a cabbie, they needed a driver's license. The problem there was that many of them had never owned a car back in Russia, and didn't have a license.

At least not until the Maffiya found out there was a market for them.

Traditionally, Russians are good at many things, but they are absolutely superb at counterfeiting. Years of Soviet oppression taught them that if they wanted something, they could either wait for officialdom to get around to it—which often meant it never happened—or they could forge whatever official documents they needed and assure themselves of getting it eventually.

Masters of bureaucratic circumvention, a few ingenious wise guys soon got into the driver's license business. Bathed in the spirit of their newfound capitalism, they produced their own absolutely perfect copies of Russian licenses—heavy cardboard, 5¾ inches by 4 inches, folded down the middle, red on one side, salmon pink on the other, with just enough room on the pink side for a photograph, a name, an address and a date of birth written in by hand, with plenty of official-looking stamps banged on top of that.

They were perfect copies. Although, in the end, that hardly mattered, because no one at the New York State Department of Motor Vehicles knew a real one from a phony one anyway. Clerks there simply exchanged the bogus Russian licenses for valid New York State licenses. Which is how the Maffiya put so many doctors, physicists, biologists, chemists, sociologists and geologists behind the wheels of New York City taxicabs.

Popular belief has it that Russian organized crime arose out of the ashes of the former Soviet Union, a consequence of chaotic social, political and economic transformation.

Not true.

The implosion of Communism merely let the genie out of the bottle. Organized crime was one of the best-kept secrets of the Soviet era. We in the West never had a printed program to tell us who the players were because the Soviets had always refused to admit their existence. But once that genie popped out of the bottle, it headed West with the fervor and passion formerly reserved for the wildest dreams of the Red Army's strategic planners.

Bred to flourish under the command economy of the old system, the criminal element had trekked through a seventy-five-year apprenticeship, mastering every necessary skill—refining corruption, extortion, black-market trading, blackmail—to circumvent the state and beat the system. Criminals survived under Stalin and persisted under Khrushchev, but they thrived under Leonid Brezhnev, who unofficially empowered them because the Party needed them to manage the black markets. Where central planning was failing the state, he saw them as the safety valve, bringing them in as full partners in the fraud that was Communism—an essential element to keep the masses under his thumb. But in tacitly endorsing thief power as the engine of the underground economy, Brezhnev and his cronies inadvertently created a subculture of entrepreneurs who dominated the post-Brezhnev years the way heroin commands a junkie.

Mikhail Gorbachev couldn't control them.

Boris Yeltsin never tried.

When the country disintegrated under the weight of its own ineptitude, no mechanisms were in place to deal with the crisis. The intense rush of Western business to get in there, to take advantage of commercial opportunities, only served to exacerbate the problem.

"Like everything else in Russia, criminality is an emerging process," says Matty Maher, now a consultant on global organized criminality but previously director of international operations for the DEA. "It has become entrepreneurial too. But they are not yet as structured and ordered as the Colombians, Italians or even the Mexicans. While the forces in Russia are focused more on survival than stopping criminals, the criminals in Russia are struggling to develop an infrastructure that will support more sophisticated levels of criminality. Ironic, no, that criminals are building their infrastructure and the Russian government isn't. In a way, that becomes our responsibility. The Russian government is dressed for a banquet, but the only thing on the table is peanut butter and jelly. We have to teach them how to cook."

Communism vaporized and the only people left standing were KGB operatives implanted in the capitalistic West, and empowered criminals. They were the ones who stepped in to take over. By the time privatization rolled around—a euphemism for plunder—the two groups had hooked up. They were the only ones with the money to pay for state industries. They were the ones who also had the business skills to milk those industries dry.

Maher continues, "Something like seventy percent of the commercial activity is today conducted with barter. A company supplying cement is paid in tires because that company was given tires by another company building apartment houses. Another company pays for steel with oil. And the company who gets the oil uses that to pay for food. So the economic foundation of the country does not support the free exchange of currency. In doing things by barter, you not only defeat the tax system, you expose the country and its whole economic and political system to corruption. The people who wound up with all this black money looked for ways to hide it and to reinvest it in something which would return a larger profit."

They found that first in state industries, then in the government. Once they owned those two, they owned the nation. By the time Boris Yeltsin climbed to the top of that tank in front of the Moscow White House to defy the Communists in their final hours, it was probably already too late. There were already three thousand criminal organizations spread across the eleven time zones that make up the nation. Within two years, that figure had doubled. At the millennium, there are nearly twelve thousand groups, boasting membership of perhaps more than one hundred thousand.

In the most general terms, Russia has been consumed by a four-headed monster.

First, there are the *vory v zakone,* the criminal version of Boy Scout troop leaders. The term translates to mean "thieves professing the code," but for the sake of the media the *vory* have been dubbed "thieves-in-law."

Molded out of pre-1917 Revolution traditions, they are a fraternity of organizers—Fagans, if you will—who inspire criminal acts and take a cut. They are the troop leaders who motivate their scouts to rub two sticks together, then hog the campfire.

Almost without exception, the *vory* do their apprenticeship in prison. The respect they command is in direct proportion to the time they serve. And that's where they're awarded the title. The initiation ceremony is formal, and many of them traditionally wear tattoos, kind of like Boy Scout merit badges. They also have a set of rules to live by. But theirs is hardly a code of honor.

"The old-time Mafia used to talk about honor," explains Roger Urbanski, director of foreign relations in the Office of Investigations at U.S. Customs. "There's none of that with the Russians. They have no honor. Just seventy-five years of let's beat the system."

Rather than a code, it is perhaps closer to a Masonic pledge of brotherhood: fellow thieves-in-law are to be treated exactly like family, supported and protected; they must earn their livelihood exclusively from criminal enterprise; they must never cooperate with the authorities; they must preach their code to younger thieves who, in turn, must be willing to take a fall for an older thief; they must fulfill all promises made to other thieves; when differences arise, other thieves must be called in to resolve them; the decision of the arbitrators is final and punishment, which usually means death, must be swiftly carried out.

Estimates vary wildly, but something between fifty and five hundred thieves-in-law are operating today. No one really knows for sure because they don't publish a mailing list, although they do occasionally get together. One well-documented jamboree took place in Tbilisi in 1982. They met specifically to argue the merits of actively seeking more political power. Within a few years, one of them became "politically significant" to Georgian president Eduard Shevardnadze.

The second head of the monster belongs to those former Communist Party members and government officials who saw what was happening, took advantage of their position to salt away fortunes, reinvented themselves in the new age and now steal on an even grander scale.

As most of the bureaucrats in power today once served Communist masters, rising through the ranks of a system in which corruption was a way of life, it's hardly surprising that corruption remains a way of life. Old habits die hard, and then only when they have ceased to serve their purpose. Neither democracy nor capitalism, honesty nor civil responsibility was ever postulated as a suitable alternative. In a nation where the average income is a mere few thousand dollars a year—where, reportedly, one fourth of the population lives below the poverty line—a job offering fringe benefits to double, or treble or quadruple, that figure is something to strive for.

When Russian troops were withdrawn from East Germany, the Bundestag authorized a payment to the Russian army specifically to construct five hundred thousand apartments in Russia so that those troops would have somewhere to live. Approximately three thousand apartments were built. The money for the rest of them has since disappeared.

Then, too, the sheer number of wealthy men in Russia's government more than attests to the fact that civil servitude is a means to financial security. Call it a license to steal, redefined as a privilege of rank.

Category three is ethnic and national groups—Chechens, Armenians, Azerbaijanis and Georgians—who filled the void left by the Communist Party and, literally, became the criminal-state.

In 1993, two Chechens were murdered and dismembered in a luxury flat in London's West End. The hit men were two visiting Armenians. It all had to do with illegal arms shipments—the foreign relations of a criminal-state—and who had the right to sell what to whom. Clearly there was a lot more at stake than just a few rifles, because the dead men, both mere pawns in this game, left estates in excess of $2 million.

Finally, there are the so-called organized crime groups that are really just loose-knit conglomerations of criminals. They may be referred to as the Maffiya, because that's a convenient term to describe a criminal orga-nization, but they are not at all like their Italian cousins. There are no pyra-mid organizational structures, no family ties to unite them, no Commission to oversee their activities. Instead, these groups are more like collections of friends and associates who band together for certain crimes, going their own way for others. As a group they may target a specific industry, or just hold on to a specific territory. They term they use is "zones of influence."

Typical is Solntsevo.

Sometimes known as Solntsevskaya, sometimes translated into English as "the Brigade of the Sun," they originated in a large Moscow neigh-borhood where they monopolize prostitution, drug trafficking, political corruption, extortion and murder.

On March 1, 1995, assassins killed journalist Vladislav Listyev, the Tom Brokaw of Moscow television news. He'd just taken on the job as head of the country's main public TV station and announced that one of his first acts would be to suspend advertising on the channel. His contention was that the advertising industry had been infiltrated by criminal organiza-tions—to wit, Solntsevo—and that before commercials came back to his station, he was going to get them out of the business. So they whacked him. The following day, Boris Yeltsin was quoted as saying, "The merging of the Maffiya with commercial structures, administrative agencies, interior ministry bodies, city authorities, nowhere else in Russia do the authorities turn a blind eye to these things as they do in Moscow."

Because this was such a high-profile hit, the police issued composite sketches and, based on those, soon announced with great fanfare that they had two suspects in custody. But the identification of those suspects proved faulty and, rather quietly, they were released. Shortly thereafter, the news-paper *Izvestia* linked the murder to a power struggle within Solntsevo. But such is their power and the depth of their reach inside the tangled and con-fused bureaucracy that is government there, no one has ever been charged with the crime. Then again, for the eight-year period between 1991 and 1999, not a single widely publicized contract murder—of which there have been, literally, thousands—was successfully investigated and prosecuted. Simply put, there is no political will to bother with them.

Russia is today a full-fledged mafiocracy.

At least six groups operate from Moscow. The Tstentralnaya, Ostankinskaya and Avtomobilnaya are Chechen and count as many as two thousand members between them. The Solntsevskaya and Podolskaya are Russian, as is the 21st Century Association. There are four main groups in St. Petersburg and apparently nine in Vladivostok. Complicating matters, the groups often break down along ethnic lines, or are based on territorial control, or split along generational divides. Some have links with bureaucracy, others are strictly anchored in specific industries. Chechen groups, for instance, are strongly based in the petroleum business. Kurganskaya have set themselves up as the Murder Inc. of Russian organized crime, offering their professional hit-man services to other groups—including the Mafia and the Colombians—around the world.

As soon as groups such as Solntsevskaya acquired a headlock on Russia's banking and financial institutions, they set up affiliates and branches outside Russia, creating for themselves a magic wand. They wave it and $200–300 billion a year disappears into the secret world of offshore banking.

Flexing their muscle, they actually orchestrated the ruble crisis of 1997. Their carefully planned and sophisticated shorting of rubles and shift into dollars sent the Russian economy nose-diving and created a tidal-wave effect throughout the Western financial markets. The profit they made buying back those same rubles refinanced criminal activities inside Russia and earned them more money, which, once the economy straightened out, they turned into hard currencies for a second sizable profit.

According to the Global Organized Crime Project of the Washington-based think tank the Center for Strategic and International Studies (CSIS), Russian criminals launder about $1 billion a month through Cyprus and another $1 billion a month through Israel. The Swiss are finally, albeit reluctantly, willing to admit to having helped Russian criminal organizations launder $40 billion since 1991. By 1994, Russian organized crime had wired enough money outside Russia to finance its own operations throughout the world.

Law enforcement in Russia is either unable or unwilling to do real battle with organized crime or political corruption. The legal system is equally impotent, so much so that Transparency International, a Berlin-based democracy watchdog, considers Russia the fourth most corrupt country in the world, behind Colombia, Nigeria and Bolivia.

A Yeltsin-commissioned report noted that hardly anyone trusts the police, hardly anyone has any faith that laws passed by Parliament will be enforced and, perhaps most startlingly, that nearly 80 percent of all businesses in the country are forced to pay extortion. With roughly two thirds of the nation's economy under the sway of crime syndicates, even Yeltsin himself has had to concede, "Russia is the biggest Mafia state in the world."

Despite such a concession, when the Duma sent Boris Yeltsin Russia's first money-laundering law in 1998, he vetoed it. When they reworked it and sent it to him again in 1999, he vetoed it again.

In the days when the Party owned everything, its members knew what was for the taking and consequently helped themselves to whatever they wanted. Today, criminals become full partners. A businessman trying to run a small factory might be faced with taxes amounting to 80 percent of his profits. In turn, he defends himself by double bookkeeping, showing tax inspectors the bottom line which shows profits running 10 to 20 percent. Because the university-educated leaders of Solntsevo, and other groups, understand what the government doesn't—i.e., how a free market economy works in the real world—they come onto the factory floor and demand 50 percent of the profits.

The Russian term is *krysha,* roof tax. For the rest of the world, it's just the old-fashioned protection racket.

Not every company succumbs to it, even when the requests aren't particularly subtle. In 1993, Coca-Cola's bottling plant on Solntsevskaya's turf was gutted by a rocket-propelled grenade. But when smaller businesses are targeted and threats are made to the proprietors' family, many business-men convince themselves that paying the Maffiya is still cheaper than paying the Kremlin.

Some people argue that groups like Solntsevo are simply the ultimate capitalists—businessmen, unregulated by law, with no real moral code, whose only aim is to accumulate wealth. Out of that comes the suggestion that Russian organized crime is just a modern version of America's "rob-ber barons"—the Morgans, Goulds and Vanderbilts—suspect entrepreneurs who, in return for being allowed to bilk the system, left a legacy of transcontinental railroads, massive industries and schools, libraries and hospitals. The difference is, the Russians have reversed the process.

They started with massive industries and, in exchange for having pried them loose from government ownership, have taken for granted their right to bilk them. This systemic rape of the nation's assets—gas, crude oil, petroleum products, coal, steel, tin, aluminum, timber, copper, zinc, nickel, cobalt, diamonds, antiquities, weapons and nuclear materials—revolves around the illegal shipment of resources to the West, where they are unloaded at bargain-basement prices.

Typically, a business is set up with a facade of legitimacy, then accepts huge amounts of internationally negotiable goods. Disposition of assets is fraudulently manipulated with double sets of banking and business records. Behind the scenes there are corrupt officials, bent businessmen, and the constant undertone of violent retribution for anyone who doesn't follow the script.

Which is pretty much the way it happened in late 1993, when a young man in his early thirties named Andrei Kozlenok arrived in San Francisco to process precious gems and import diamonds from Russia. Going in with two Armenian partners—Ashot Shagirian and his brother David—he named the company after the initials of their first names, Golden ADA. It was an off-the-rack, golden-calf, archetypal rip-off.

So that everybody knew there were new kids in town, Kozlenok made himself very visible by throwing around a lot of cash. He paid $11 million for the firm's headquarters at 999 Brannan Street—way over the owner's original $6 million asking price—$1 million for a Rolls-Royce and a matching pair of Aston Martins, $1.2 million for three boats, $3.8 million for three homes, $18 million for a corporate jet and $4.4 million for his weekend retreats at Lake Tahoe. He also bought six gas stations in San Francisco and eighteen other properties around Northern California. Then, just in case there was any doubt remaining about the depth of his pockets, he ferried over a $1.7 million Russian Kamov Ka-32 military transport helicopter and presented it as a gift to the San Francisco Police Department. It was, to say the least, a splashy introduction for a diamond merchant to a city that had never been a diamond market. Diamonds are London, Antwerp and New York. But then, Kozlenok's background wasn't diamonds. Whatever money he'd made back in mother Russia came from flogging cognac and tires to Russians and gas masks to Kuwaitis. What's more, according to the FBI, the brothers Shagirian had, only two years before they became partners in Golden ADA, been painting sidewalks.

The source of the company's extravagance was "the closet," more formally known as the National Treasury of the Russian Federation. An enormous labyrinth of huge underground vaults in Moscow and others hidden somewhere deep in the Ural Mountains, they are filled to the brim with precious stones, coins, jewelry, silver, platinum and hundreds of tons of gold. Its precise content and total worth is labeled an official state secret. But that's likely nothing more than an excuse for not having to admit that no one knows.

A man who might have been able to provide a good guess, one of the few people believed to have had access to "the closet," was Yevgeni Bychkov. He'd served as head of the State Treasury and as chairman of the Committee on Precious Metals and Gems. and was a close personal friend of Boris Yeltsin. In his spare time, Bychkov was a father figure to Kozlenok.

It was Bychkov's idea to set up Golden ADA. Publicly, he intended to challenge the DeBeer Corporation's control of the world diamond market. Privately, he was putting nearly $100 million worth of diamonds and, literally, tons of assorted other treasures into Kozlenok's control.

Assets that arrived in San Francisco were quickly turned into cash. For instance, several tons' worth of antique gold was melted down and sold far below its intrinsic value, as scrap. Money was then wired to Russia, Belgium, Liechtenstein, Switzerland and Israel, where most of it has since disappeared. Another allegation, denied by Bychkov, is that those assets paid for his new dacha. One allegation, not denied by anyone, is that those assets paid for Kozlenok's $5 million Bermuda home.

As more and more of the nation's riches arrived in San Francisco, Kozlenok's extravagance increased. He acrimoniously shoved his partners out of the business—they claimed he'd threatened to put a $5 million contract on their heads—and then, suddenly, found himself on the run. He was next seen in Belgium, penniless, insisting that he'd been kidnapped by Russians who'd stolen his interests in Golden ADA.

When the IRS knocked on the door of Golden ADA's office, looking to collect $63 million in back taxes, they found automatic weapons, ammunition, bulletproof vests and explosives. In the meantime, the FBI says that $178 million went through Golden ADA and that they've now been able to trace $40 million of it back to Russia, 10 percent of which, they believe, wound up paying to print copies of Boris Yeltsin's autobiography.

Succumbing to world pressure in 1970, the Soviets reluctantly allowed emigration of Jews to Israel. Many of these people had been trying to get out for years. Now, finally free, they started on a journey that would take them, in some cases through Vienna and in other cases through Cyprus, to the Promised Land. But not everyone wound up in Israel.

Some people got off and settled in Vienna. Others got off in Cyprus. In both cases, Russian émigré communities developed and, before long, they would become extremely significant in the world of transnational crime. Huge numbers also came to the United States, many of them settling in Brighton Beach, Brooklyn.

It was standard U.S. policy in those days not to ask for criminal background checks on anyone applying for refugee status. Two reasons are officially given. One is that the additional paperwork that background checks would produce on the average fifty thousand applicants a year was far too much for Washington to handle. The other is that the delay created by background checks would at best deter applicants from applying, at worst expose them to reprisals when Moscow was informed that they wanted out of the country.

Moscow now says Washington was warned that dangerous criminals might emigrate, pretending to be Jews. But if it happened, those warnings got lost somewhere in the translation. When word spread that the Americans weren't doing background checks, Russians who hardly knew what a Jew was claimed Jewish heritage. Hidden among the thirty to forty thousand Russians who showed up in New York in those early years were hundreds, if not thousands, of Russians who were not Jewish. Some had simply forged papers to get out. Others were refugees from gulags who'd served time for a variety of offenses, some of which were political, many of which were decidedly criminal.

Despite Russian assurances that dangerous criminals would never be permitted to leave—just as Fidel Castro would discover a few years later with Cuba's Mariel boat lift—emigration became an easy way for the Russians to empty their prisons and asylums and export their worst problems to the West.

Over the next twenty years, Russian immigration to the States would come close to three hundred thousand people. When the Soviet system finally shredded into a mass of idealistic rubble, travel barriers were relaxed and hundreds of thousands of non-Jews also emigrated.

Today, Brighton Beach—known to New Yorkers as Little Odessa by the Sea—is the largest Russian community outside the former Soviet Union. Old men play dominoes on the boardwalk, in front of cafés with Russian names and menus only in Cyrillic. Two blocks north, the elevated subway tracks that run above Brighton Beach Avenue keep sunlight away from the entrances to nightclubs and restaurants and food stores with Russian names. Above the storefronts, in scores of one-room offices that face the tracks, Russian names on the windows spell out *marriage broker* and *dating service* and *immigration service*, mostly fronts for prostitution and other frauds that have become cottage industries here.

The D and Q trains that rattle back and forth all day and all night drown out car horns and loud voices, and easily cover the sound of gunfire, which has also become part of the local folklore because it keeps happening, as the murder toll slowly but steadily mounts.

But Brighton Beach is not the only vibrant and important Russian settlement in the States. Russians have settled throughout New Jersey and in Philadelphia, Baltimore, Detroit, Cleveland and Chicago. There are Russian enclaves in Miami, Los Angeles and San Francisco. According to a U.S. Justice Department report on the growing presence of Russian organized crime groups, they are even settling in relatively obscure places, like Lincoln, Nebraska.

And as the Russian émigré population has increased, so has crime.

There is extortion, counterfeiting, loan sharking, and a variety of frauds. They've targeted the health insurance industry by creating hundreds of paper companies to bill the companies for examinations and procedures never carried out, and in one scam stole $125 million. They've targeted Medicaid, selling cheap shoes to patients needing orthopedic shoes, stealing a couple of hundred thousand dollars from the government in a few weeks. They've targeted jewelry manufacturers, in one case scamming gold worth $54 million. One group simply aimed a high-powered scanner out of a window at cars driving by, collected peoples' cell-phone numbers and sold them on to other crime groups. It's known as "phone cloning" and before they were stopped, they'd deciphered eighty thousand numbers.

As one law enforcement officer summed it up, "The Russians just add a zero to anything that anyone else thinks of."

Explains another, senior FBI agent Hardrick Crawford, Jr., "They're experts at perpetrating frauds of all shapes and sizes, very violent, very intelligent and computer literate. They hire ex–intelligence officers who are familiar with the ways of Western law enforcement. They hire computer specialists who can hack their way into any business. They hire lawyers and bankers who are conversant in international law and finance. They hire other business professionals who can manage their assets once their money has been laundered and reinvested in casinos, hotels and resorts."

The problems they then present to law enforcement are totally different from, say, the FBI's experience with La Cosa Nostra.

"Our New York office has long been studying the LCN," Crawford goes on. "We can tell you about a particular *capo* for a crime family, who his aunt was, who his brother is, where his father was born. Now, we look at the Russian organized crime groups and first of all we can't pronounce the name of the organization. When you tell us that the individual came from a certain region in the former Soviet Union, we didn't know that it existed. The difficulties presented by such a scenario are staggering. We're always playing catch-up."

Realizing that so many of these émigrés would have a natural fear of law enforcement—a phobia reinforced on a regular basis under the Communists—the FBI established in 1994 the first of several Russian Squads. The New York Police Department also has one.

They are both predicated on the premise that Russian criminals were more adept at white-collar crime than their LCN counterparts, and that their world would be more difficult to penetrate for all sorts of cultural reasons. The squads advertised in Russian-language newspapers, hoping to encourage locals to come forward with tips and gossip about crimes, to talk about murders, extortion, fraud, drugs and counterfeiting. They reached out to newly arrived Russians, hoping to convince them that America was not like home and that in America, the police would protect them. But Russian fear runs deep. Both squads seriously underestimated the fortress mentality. The results were underwhelming. People were simply too afraid of retribution, too scared to testify at trials, and couldn't bring themselves to trust a state system, especially a federal police force. Even promises of witness protection programs fell on deaf ears.

No one had to remind the Russians of Brighton Beach that talking to the authorities was tantamount to putting their entire family at risk. If they didn't get killed, their children might. Or their relatives back in the mother country would wind up paying for their indiscretions.

No matter what the FBI or the NYPD said to them in their own language, at least in the beginning, the newly arrived Russians opted for survival first, convinced that they couldn't survive unless they lived in a Russian community, and they couldn't live in a Russian community if the local crime bosses suspected them of siding with the authorities. So, as the Russian émigré population increased, so did murders and violence and extortion and prostitution. And the locals stayed silent.

"I've often thought that Russian organized crime guys have seen too many old gangster movies," says Tom Kneir, the deputy assistant director of the FBI's Criminal Investigative Division, "because they pattern themselves after the strong-arm stuff. They're not at all shy when it comes to putting out a message. If someone needs to get whacked, they get whacked. You see some very very sophisticated criminal activity, stock manipulations, the looting of the precious metals, and surrounding it is all that violence. Most of our homegrown white-collar high-level criminals do not resort to violence in any form or fashion. They live by their wit, not by their brawn. But with the Russians, no matter how sophisticated the scheme is, if a message needs to be sent to a witness or to someone who is cooperating with law enforcement, they go with that option."

Simultaneous with that wave of Russians coming ashore in the early 1980s, but absolutely unrelated to it, the state of New York changed the way it collected excise taxes on fuel. They shifted the burden from the retailers who'd been responsible for paying the tax, to the wholesalers who would now owe the tax as soon as they sold the fuel. In so doing, the state inadvertently opened the floodgates for untaxed trading between wholesalers, which came to be known as "the daisy-chain scam." Precisely the sort of swindle that Evsei Agron found especially appealing.

A tiny, balding man with a furry black mustache, his visa papers listed his profession as jeweler, although he told people he was vice president of a Brooklyn health club. The place couldn't have been too healthy, because it was a front for the Colombo family and the scene of a 1982 gangland killing. In a previous life, Agron was a convicted murderer from Russia who'd served seven years' hard time before Leonid Brezhnev emptied out his gulags, allowed all sorts of psychopaths to claim Jewish heritage and shipped them off to the West.

Leaving Leningrad in 1971, the thirty-seven-year-old Agron went first to Germany, where he ran a gambling and prostitution ring. Four years later, he arrived in America to find that Brighton Beach's sidewalks were indeed paved with gold—the hard-earned income of those immigrants who'd come before him—and set about filching his share. He installed himself in an office above the El Caribe Country Club Restaurant on Strickland Avenue in Mill Basin, surrounded himself with a crew of almost five hundred goons, carried a cattle prod under his arm like a swagger stick and oversaw a reign of extortion terror that, by 1980, was netting him $50,000 a week. Among his more celebrated stunts was extorting $15,000 from a man by threatening to murder his daughter at her wedding.

Nowhere near as intelligent as he was ruthless, Agron was, however, smart enough to align himself with Marat Balagula.

A black-marketeer from Odessa, Balagula was thirty-four when he arrived in Brooklyn at around the same time as Agron. But unlike his boss, he had two advanced university degrees—one in math and one in economics—and had already put together a chain of fourteen gas stations. Now, with Agron's muscle and Balagula's intellectual skills, they created a series of fictitious transfers through shell companies. They filed false invoices with the government along with fraudulent tax exemption forms to show tax accumulating on the books of one company, while banking that money in the offshore accounts of another. When the taxman came looking for his share, the company supposedly holding the government's money—known as the "burn company"—turned into smoke. Its address was either a phone booth or a vacant lot.

What made the scheme so attractive was the staggering amounts of money involved. The average fuel tanker holds about eight thousand gallons. Federal and state taxes hover around 40 to 50 cents per gallon, depending on the state. It didn't take before long Agron and Balagula were selling $150 million worth of fuel every month and pocketing $30–40 million a month in unpaid state and federal taxes.

Around the same time, Lawrence "Sal" Iorizzo—a 450-pound independent wholesaler who ran three hundred gas stations on Long Island—had also worked out the daisy-chain scam. But Iorizzo's cash-heavy operation had inadvertently attracted some unwanted attention. A couple of wise guys showed up one day having decided they were going to be his partners. To protect himself, Iorizzo turned to Michael Franzese, an up-and-coming member of the Colombo family. In exchange for taking care of Iorizzo's problem—which was done swiftly and effectively with one menacing visit—Franzese and the Colombos became Iorizzo's partners.

A few months later, Franzese was introduced to three Russian gas wholesalers in Brooklyn—Michael Markowitz, David Bogatin and Lev Persits—who were having problems getting their scam off the ground. To begin with, they were owed some money. Then, they were finding it difficult to arrange certain licenses from the state. Franzese explained that debt collection was a Colombo specialty and, also, that the family had someone inside the state capital who could help with the licenses. It turned out to be, the Russians quickly realized, an offer they couldn't refuse.

Franzese merged the Russians' wholesale business with Iorizzo's retail outlets, took 75 percent for himself—which he then spread around the rest of the Colombo family—and left the Russians with 25 percent. But that wasn't necessarily a bad deal for the Russians, because in four years the scheme managed to defraud New York, New Jersey, Connecticut, Pennsylvania and Florida, plus the federal government, out of nearly half a billion dollars.

As Franzese later testified, "It was not unusual for me to receive nine million in cash per week in paper bags from the Russians and Iorizzo. Our profits ran anywhere from two to thirty cents per gallon, and at one point, we were moving four hundred to five hundred million gallons per month."

Before long, the Russians expanded the joint venture with Franzese and the Colombos to include securities and insurance fraud and loan sharking. They also went into the banking business. Iorizzo had contacts in Panama, where he'd formed several offshore companies, and Bogatin had contacts in Europe. So Iorizzo, the Russians, Franzese and the Colombos pooled some money, constructed a web of offshore shells and bought themselves a bank in Austria. Then someone tried to kill Agron.

In January 1984, a lone gunman walked up to him outside his apartment at 100 Ocean Avenue in Park Slope, Brooklyn and shot him in the neck. He survived. While he was on the operating table, doctors pulled bullets out of him from a previous shooting. Later, he told detectives that he couldn't identify his attacker, and anyway, he intended to take care of the matter himself. Apparently he didn't.

Sixteen months later, on May 4, 1985, while he was walking out of the front door of his apartment on the fifth floor, on his way to the elevator, someone put two bullets in his head. This time he didn't survive.

His bodyguard and chauffeur, an ex-wrestler named Boris "Beeba" Nayfeld—who'd been waiting downstairs to drive him to his daily steam bath—suddenly drove away. When the police caught up with him he told them he just couldn't imagine how anything like that might have happened. The very next day, Marat Balagula moved into Agron's office above the El Caribe and Nayfeld went to work for Balagula.

It wasn't long before Balagula also got connected with Italians—in this case the Lucchese family—cutting them in to collect debts and acquire the proper licenses. It turned out to be a relationship that saved his life.

A fellow named Vladimir Reznikov decided he wanted to be Balagula's partner, strolled up to him one day in a Brighton Beach restaurant, stuck a gun in his head and said that the price for not pulling the trigger was part of the gas-tax action and $600,000 walking-around money. Marat told Reznikov that sounded perfectly fine, then phoned his Italian pals. They took the threat against Balagula personally, got the hit okayed and promptly eliminated Vladimir.

The state of New York then tried to plug the loophole through which the scam worked, by changing the way fuel was taxed. It had no real effect, however, as the Russians and their Italian cohorts reacted by changing the way they ran their daisy chains, switching from gasoline to diesel fuel, which was still being taxed in the old way.

By this time, Iorizzo was also in trouble. He'd first appeared on law enforcement's radar screens in early 1984. As soon as he heard they were closing in on him, he fled to Panama. But in a rare show of genuine support for the United States, the Panamanians sent him home. So Iorizzo spilled the beans on, among others, Franzese. At the age of fifty-seven, he was installed in the witness protection program under the name Lawrence M. Harrison, almost immediately violated his deal by getting back into a fuel-tax scam and wound up being sent away for fifteen years. Franzese was also convicted, also decided to cooperate and gave up several of his former Colombo associates.

Franzese's three Russian partners now decided they didn't need the Italians anymore and struck out on their own. Proving them wrong, the Colombos had Markowitz shot and killed. Persits was also shot, although he survived, permanently disabled. Panicked, Bogatin decided Austria offered a healthier climate than Brooklyn and made a run for it, but the Feds dragged him home, put him on trial, convicted him and shipped him off to prison.

As is often the case where loads of money are at stake, Balagula's scam also, inevitably, turned to mayhem. Everyone was skimming off the top, essentially stealing from one another. It was too big for any one person to control, and anyway, Balagula was too busy juggling all of his businesses and acquired assets. Among other things, he owned a New York mansion decorated in pink marble and his own private island off Africa.

Through two fuel distributorships that he ran—one was called Mallard, the other Energy Makers of America—he dealt with the R & R Cab Corporation. That was owned by Nayfeld and his brother Benjamin, who also shared interests in arms and drug trafficking.

When the cops finally closed in on Balagula, he fled the country, hooking up in Africa with his chum Shabtai Kalmanovitch, a "businessman" with access to a supply of Israeli passports.

Wanted in the United States, Kalmanovitch was widely believed to have close ties to the KGB. One of his main bases of operations was Sierra Leone, where he had enough political clout to wind up owning, personally, most of the nation's diamond wealth.

Together, Balagula and Kalmanovitch imported gas to Sierra Leone, a deal supposedly brokered through a company controlled by fugitive U.S. businessman Marc Rich and financed with a guarantee by the Luccheses. From there, Balagula and Kalmanovitch moved on to South Africa and Bophuthatswana, where they put together other deals. Later Balagula's friends would claim that they lost money on every deal they did with Kalmanovitch. True or not, eventually, the Israelis caught up with Kalmanovitch, accused him of selling state secrets to the Syrians, tried him as a spy and sent him to jail. But he only stayed locked up for a few years, which suggests that some of his reputed KGB connections might, in fact, have had some pull.

On the run again, Balagula got arrested in Germany. Whatever connections he had proved useless, as the Germans sent him back to the United States, where he was tried for a 1980 credit card fraud he'd put together with the Nayfeld brothers. They'd matched counterfeit cards to a list of clients' names stolen from stockbrokers Merrill Lynch and managed to steal $300,000 on the cards before anyone could put a stop to it. The judge sentenced him to eight years.

Then the government put a gas-tax-fraud case together against him—for evading $85 million in federal taxes on nearly one billion gallons of fuel sold between 1983 and 1988—and rebooked his cell for an additional ten years.

The next thing that happened was that the Lucchese crowd, who were still running Balagula's gas-tax scam, heard that the Genovese family also had Russian partners in a gas-tax scam. So Tony Casso, the Lucchese underboss who had been Balagula's immediate partner, set up a meeting with underbosses from the other two families, plus their Russian partners, and suggested everyone work together. He argued that by combining their efforts, they could run a mega-scam across the entire eastern seaboard. That sounded pretty good to everyone else, so that's what happened.

Then the Gambino family came along. Some Russians in New Jersey had decided to set up a scam, gone to the Gambinos and, for the privilege of working in Gambino territory, showed respect and cut them in. So now Casso and the others invited the Gambinos and their partners to sign on. Needless to say, an operation of this magnitude did not escape federal attention, and before long, the FBI and the IRS were also in the business, this time as a sting operation.

By 1992, the FBI and the IRS were working a sting that came to be known as "Operation Red Daisy." Based in Newark, New Jersey, they were able to get inside several fuel distributors and begin picking apart various Russian-Italian joint ventures. The four-year investigation focused on the theft of over $140 million in federal motor-fuel excise-tax revenue and "tribute payments" made by the Russians to their LCN partners, including money that made its way up to Gambino boss John Gotti.

After considering the evidence, which consisted of over twelve hundred taped phone conversations and enough surveillance film to fill a one-thousand-square-foot storage area, a federal grand jury returned indictments on twenty-five people, including fifteen Russians. One of the charges was money laundering, as profits from the scam were hidden in Greece, Switzerland, Latvia, Aruba and the British Virgin Islands.

The biggest fish caught in this particular net was mobster Anthony "Fat Tony" Morelli, convicted of racketeering, extortion, interstate travel in aid of racketeering, money laundering, mail fraud, wire fraud and tax evasion, and sent away for twenty years.

As more and more daisy chains have been shut down, the Russians and the Italians have moved on to cocktailed fuel scams. By blending non-taxed products—such as kerosene, waste oil and toxic wastes—with taxable fuels, they've been able to increase volume on which they can collect tax. The fact that such a mixture is highly polluting and, at times, decidedly dangerous, is beyond their concern. They now also move fuels around interstate, otherwise arbitraging taxes. Buying fuel in New Jersey, where state taxes are lower than in New York, then selling it in New York, can make a 2-to 4-cent-per-gallon difference.

FBI Director Louis Freeh says that there are fifty-four countries around the world that have an active Russian organized crime presence. At the top of the list is the United States, where several dozen groups operate. Nearly as many have appeared in Canada, especially Toronto and Montreal. Russians are also showing up in great numbers in Australia, New Zealand and throughout the Pacific. But after North America, Europe is their main target. And the Europeans are playing right into their hands.

In the past, ethnically defined immigrants have always moved into well-established ethnic communities—the way the Russians moved into Brighton Beach—where their presence naturally took root. That is no longer the case. Furthermore, unlike the massive immigration of the nineteenth century, or even the flood of Europeans into America prior to World War II, this wave is not agrarian in nature. Russians on the move today are educated and technologically competent. They don't need land to farm, just cities with telephones that can accommodate modem plugs.

They have swarmed into Eastern Europe—familiar territory after so many years of Communist occupation—to "recolonize" Hungary, Poland, the Czech Republic and Slovakia. From there they have headed west, starting with the city they knew best, Berlin. Today Russian organized crime groups are operating in Germany with near impunity.

Because of the damage done by the Nazi SS and other secret police organizations, unified Germany legislated wide-ranging privacy rights, placing strict limitations on police search-and-seizure powers. For instance, it has only been within the past few years that police there have been given the right to use wiretaps, and then only under very specific circumstances. The issue remains highly emotional.

"It is as if," one senior German law enforcement official has been quoted as saying, "the Russian Mafia is using computers while we German police are stuck with an abacus."

Cocaine comes into Europe by sea from South America, arriving at Rotterdam, Genoa and Barcelona, with traffic increasing into the Spanish fishing-port region of Galicia. Morocco is Europe's main supplier of marijuana, which is ferried into Gibraltar and Spain for distribution across the rest of the continent. Russian organized crime groups are, however, trying to attract activity into Baltic ports, both to ease importation into Russia and also as a transshipment point for the rest of Europe.

In that regard, the former Soviet Union is the major transshipment point for Afghan drugs coming into Europe, and even though most of the heroin that arrives in the U.K. is manifested in Turkey, Russian criminal activity is staggering. According to Britain's Office of National Statistics, the income of organized crime in the U.K. is so huge—a sum approximated at nearly £8 billion—that since it is not included in the nation's published accounts, those accounts are in fact "a distorted picture of the British economy."

The Russians have come to London and established themselves in neighborhoods like Maida Vale, Swiss Cottage and Hampstead, where once only the British lived. They've invaded the French Riviera, as well, buying up the largest properties, where once only wealthy Brits, Americans and Arabs lived. They've gone to Paris and moved into the choicest *quartiers*. They've bought big villas in Rome as well. And wherever they settle, there is Russian organized crime.

Not all of it is immediately visible. Only some of it is commanded locally. Much of it is run by remote control—men sitting on sunny balconies overlooking a beach somewhere, with cell phones, e-mail and faxes.

After cutting their teeth on the indignities of Communism, in a society where breaking rules and survival were all too often synonymous, life in the West turns out to be dead easy.

The West is their candy store.

5

THE B TEAM

They come from the most disorganized country in the world, how do you want them to become organized just like that?

—former NYPD detective PETER GRINENKO

BEEBA NAYFELD THOUGHT HE HAD A REALLY GOOD IDEA. He'd arrived in America in 1978 at the age of thirty-one, to find that the openness of capitalistic society was like a printed invitation to fraudsters. He couldn't believe the abundance of opportunities; wherever he looked, everywhere, they were his simply for the stealing.

What he hadn't counted on was getting arrested so soon.

Nabbed on Long Island in 1980 for having worked that credit card scam with Marat Balagula, he was charged with grand larceny. But thanks to clever lawyering, he was allowed to plead to petty larceny. It was a first-hand lesson that, unlike in Mother Russia, the American justice system could be beaten.

He served no time.

By 1985, the cops were looking at him again, this time because of the murder of his boss, Evsei Agron. They suspected him of having been involved, and indications are that he was, but they could never prove it, so he walked.

It was just after that, while he was working for Balagula as his *consiglieri*, that his really good idea came to him. He reckoned if the Russians and

Italians could do gas-tax frauds together, they could other business together as well. And when one of the Gambino gang mentioned the word *heroin,* Nayfeld was sure he'd found his niche.

He put together a consortium of ten Russians and six Italians to finance a connection through Eastern Europe, which essentially made Boris "Beeba" Nayfeld the first Russian to form an international strategic alliance with La Cosa Nostra.

Heroin was acquired in Thailand—an easy enough stunt to manage— and shrewdly packed inside television sets. Picture tubes were sheared in half, the drugs stuffed inside them, and the tubes then resealed. Even the wiring was put back in place, making it almost impossible to suspect that the sets had ever been tampered with.

According to the bills of lading, the televisions were destined for Singapore. But they were shipped first to Poland. Oddly, no customs officers along the way ever wondered why these TV sets were taking such a circuitous route. The drugs were off-loaded there, then couriered to New York in three-to-five-pound parcels, where the LCN took over.

With U.S. Customs and the DEA normally looking for drugs to come in from the Orient and South America, it was quite a while before they cottoned on to this route.

Yet word of Nayfeld's huge success had easily reached other Russian gangsters who decided they wanted in. One of them, patently jealous, was Monya Elson.

Another graduate of the Evsei Agron crime school, Elson had also come to America in 1978, but without a criminal history. Nicknamed "Kishinevsky," a reference to the Moldavian town where he was born, Elson worked for a clothing designing and a jeweler before joining Agron's brigade. But he found that as an employee he wasn't feared and because he yearned to be feared—to make a name for himself—he moved to Israel, to try his hand at drug trafficking. Within a few months he was arrested and convicted for selling cocaine, and sent away for six years.

By the time he returned to Brighton Beach in 1990, a lot had changed. Agron was dead, Balagula was in jail and Beeba Nayfeld was now a big shot.

Jealous of what Nayfeld had accomplished, Elson established his own crew—known as Monya's Brigade—and, with some muscle behind him, set about trying to take over Brooklyn. He threatened and extorted anyone he thought had any money. He got into drugs and cosponsored a number of multi-kilo deals with members of the Genovese gang. He ran insurance scams. And he tried to establish himself as a *rukovodstovo,* a sort of godfather who mediated underworld disputes. From his Rasputin headquarters—a gaudy nightclub on Coney Island Avenue where the walls are rose-colored marble and, true or not, customers bragged that there were bulletproof doors in the toilets—he listened to other crooks voice their complaints, then pronounced a settlement in exchange for a cut of their action.

Still, Monya Elson wasn't making the kind of money Nayfeld was making, which was the kind of money he wanted to make.

The longer he sat around watching Nayfeld score big-time, the easier it was to conclude that he could strike a note of fear into anyone who thought they might be rivals and, also, move in on Nayfeld's territory, simply by murdering him.

What he never understood was that his reputation for irrational violence would get in the way of his master plan, because enemies were beginning to line up.

"The problem was," says former cop Peter Grinenko, "Monya was a moron. He only got people mad. He kept pushing people. And sometimes he pushed the wrong ones too far."

In January 1991, Monya pushed Beeba too far.

He ordered a bomb planted under Nayfeld's car, which at the time was parked out in front of a local school. The police later explained that the weather had been too cold and had frozen the detonator. Had it gone off, there is no telling how many children would have been killed.

However, the incident did not go unnoticed by Nayfeld.

Elson next moved on Vyacheslav Lyubarsky. He'd been associated with Elson's Italian partners. But when some drug money went missing, Elson decided that Lyubarsky had switched sides and was plotting against him with Nayfeld. Elson shot Lyubarsky, in early March of that year, but merely wounded him.

This time, Nayfeld responded.

In May 1991, a group of gunmen attacked Elson. Except that they botched the job and Elson lived to play another day.

Round two came in January 1992.

Lyubarsky, his wife, Nellie, and their son, Vadim, were just coming home after dinner when assassins appeared in the hallway and promptly liquidated father and son.

Nine days after that, one of Elson's lieutenants, Efrim Ostrovsky, was rubbed out in Queens by Alexander Slepinin.

Word on the street was that Slepinin worked for Nayfeld and that Elson was the next name on his contract hit list. So in June, Elson launched a preemptive strike and murdered Slepinin.

Two weeks later, another Nayfeld associate, Elbrous Evdoev, was shot, but only wounded.

That particular missed hit troubled Elson enough to resolve that perhaps the weather was better in Los Angeles. It's not sure when he actually moved there, or how long he planned to stay, but Nayfeld located him there and, in November, tried yet again to kill him.

Elson was shot in the arm and driven to the hospital by his associate Leonyard Kanterkantetes. Two days later, someone tried to plant a bomb under Kanterkantetes's car, and was killed when it accidentally went off. Now, dropping out of sight and staying out of sight, Elson didn't reappear until he heard that Nayfeld had hurriedly left the country.

On Monday, July 21, 1992, the police in Brooklyn received word he was back in Brooklyn. Nayfeld, hiding in Belgium, heard the same news.

Five days later, on Saturday afternoon, Oleg Zapinakmine—who was Elson's bodyguard and also his nephew—parked the big new Lexus in front of Elson's home on East Sixteenth Street in Sheepshead Bay, then got out to open the rear door for his uncle Monya and his aunt Marya.

As they stepped onto the curb, a brown car drove up. The Elsons only managed half a dozen steps toward their home before three men jumped out with shotguns, motor still running, and started shooting. Elson was hit in the ankle and the thigh. Marya was shot in the back. Zapinakmine suffered a graze wound in the stomach.

The gunmen fled.

Ambulances arrived and rushed them all to Coney Island Hospital. Marya was in serious condition when they got her into the operating room, but she pulled through. Monya and Oleg were declared stable,and treated, and the pair of them walked out several hours later.

While interviewing the victims at the hospital, the police were interested to learn that Elson was carrying $300,000 worth of watches and gems.

One shotgun was found at the scene. The getaway car and a second shotgun were found a block away. However, none of the victims seemed eager to help the police with their investigation and, because the cops knew who Elson was, none of them spent much time pursuing the possibility that robbery was the motive.

Later that night, the police speculated that this was someone's way of telling Elson he was no longer welcome in Brooklyn.

To reinforce that message, soon thereafter someone killed nephew Oleg and then killed Elson's friend Alexander "Sasha Pinya" Levichitz.

Now Monya decided that Mediterranean weather was even better than California weather.

Word on the street was that he was hoping to find safety among the tens of thousands of Russian immigrants in Israel.

Nayfeld had felt the heat too.

He'd heard that the DEA was closing in on his heroin ring, and worried that Elson might be getting closer as well. So he took himself to Egedem, Belgium, a suburb of Antwerp, and the safety provided by friends.

One of those friends was Rachmiel "Mike" Brandwain.

Another was Riccardo Fanchini.

The Russians had established a community in Antwerp even before they began populating Brighton Beach. It was the home of an international diamond market and a port well known for smuggling, and the refugees who settled there—especially those who arrived in the 1970s and early 1980s—added money laundering to the list of local attractions.

Brandwain had gotten in on the ground floor.

Born in Ukraine, he emigrated to Israel with his family in 1959, when he was ten. He did his military service in the merchant navy, which was when he first saw Antwerp. As soon as he got out, he moved to Belgium and started his hustle.

He dabbled for a while with textiles, but it was thanks to the slow demise of Eastern Europe and the creation of a huge black market by Russian soldiers in East Germany that he really scored. The soldiers stole whatever wasn't nailed down and unnailed whatever was, so they could steal that too. Brandwain strolled into the middle of this with cash and picked mountains of stuff at fire-sale prices—including electronics gear and military hardware—which he marketed through his company, M&S

International. He earned the confidence of senior officers who, when they found themselves with bulging pockets and no knowledge of the Western financial markets, turned to Brandwain to serve as their laundryman.

Operating out of a house on Heren Street, in the heart of Antwerp's diamond district, he had contacts with certain diamond merchants who'd established a money-laundering operation which linked them to diamond merchants in London and Israel. He began by feeding the Russians' money through that. As the black market grew and the amounts needing to be washed increased, he constructed a network of offshore companies, designed specifically to shift millions from East Germany and Moscow and into secret bank accounts in Geneva, New York and Tel Aviv.

When Nayfeld arrived, he found everything he needed to maintain his drug trafficking, including that web of companies surrounding M&S International. Within weeks, a metric ton of cocaine, sourced in Antwerp, showed up in Vyborg, Russia.

Later, Brandwain would publicly deny ever having anything to do with drug trafficking. But it simply wasn't true. Interpol claims that Brandwain was definitely involved in drugs, and arms trafficking as well, and had also discussed murder with Nayfeld and in reference to Elson.

Oddly, it's down to Israeli intelligence to partially defend Brandwain's corner. They say that while Nayfeld was in Antwerp, the drugs were his and that Brandwain was merely the financier who did for his pal Beeba what he'd been doing for years for the Russian army. The situation changed when Nayfeld went back to the States to renew his passport and never returned to Antwerp.

Facing extortion from a Moscow crime faction who'd moved in on M&S International, Brandwain called some friends in the diamond business to help him take over Nayfeld's business. Eight years before, he'd been involved in a smuggling ring with local jewelers. They'd been short-circuiting the tax man by moving gold and diamonds to jewelers in London's Hatten Garden and New York's Forty-seventh Street. British Customs somehow got inside this very closed, very Orthodox Jewish community—who usually conduct all their business in Yiddish—and wound up arresting several people for VAT fraud.

Because the smuggling process is the same whether it's gold, diamonds, dirty money or drugs, resurrecting that earlier connection gave Brandwain a way to move heroin into Britain. And despite the fact that the North

London Jewish communities of Stamford Hill and Golders Green roundly and, with one voice, condemn drug trafficking, Brandwain was able to find a few people to help him move product.

It didn't last long, however. In 1996, a thirty-four-year-old Israeli living in Antwerp was arrested at Ramsgate with fifteen kilograms of heroin hidden under the backseat of his car. He got eleven years for it. The drugs were ultimately destined for the Glasgow market, paid for by a Scottish trafficker named David Santini, who was arrested in a separate incident and sentenced to thirteen years. The Israeli's contact was a Russian Orthodox Jew whom he was to meet in North London. An intelligence operation keyed on him led to the arrest of several other Orthodox Jews, including a man from Antwerp stopped at Dover with ten kilos of heroin hidden in a rental car; an American living in North London arriving from Antwerp at the French side of the Channel Tunnel with heroin and cocaine in his car; and a Talmudic scholar in Israel who'd run a private bank, laundering money through a charity.

Brandwain would have also been arrested had he not been gunned down in mid-July 1998 in broad daylight on an Antwerp street. The contract is believed to have been put out by those people in Moscow who'd elbowed their way in to M&S International and were now trying to get into the middle of his heroin ring.

Nayfeld's other friend in Antwerp, Riccardo Marian Fanchini, had also been on to a good thing when Nayfeld first arrived.

Polish by birth, not Italian, as his name suggests, Fanchini was chairman of Kremlyovskaya, a company that made Belgian vodka and sold it, duty-free, to Russia. While the money was rolling in, he hung out in Monte Carlo and followed the Formula One Grand Prix racing circuit. Kremlyovskaya even sponsored teams for a while, including Jordan Peugeot in 1995, with drivers Eddie Irvine and Rubens Barrichello.

Fanchini and Nayfeld went way back, to the early days in Brighton Beach, along with a third friend, Yakov Tilipman, who now ran Benitexes, the Moscow importer of Kremlyovskaya vodka. In 1987, Tilipman had been arrested in New York in connection with some major jewel thefts. His accomplice was named as Jerzy Bank, who turned out to be Fanchini.

The FBI moved Fanchini high up on their list of suspected Russian organized criminals, and his company was also being looked at as a money-laundering front. But before anyone could shut him down, the Russians repealed the law permitting the importation of tax-free vodka, effectively pulling the plug on Kremlyovskaya. By the time the 1996 Monaco Grand Prix rolled around, Eddie Jordan and the management of Peugeot realized who they'd been dealing with and bailed out.

The Belgians didn't like the way Kremlyovskaya had gone bankrupt, and arrested Fanchini on fraud charges. The FBI also decided they wanted him, and put in their bid for his time once the Belgians were through with him.

In the meantime, Nayfeld's passport ran out.

Fearing that no U.S. embassy or consulate would renew it for him, he snuck back into the United States to do it himself. He managed it quickly, without any hassles, and was on his way to Kennedy Airport with a one-way ticket to London when the DEA grabbed him.

One of the first things he did when he realized he wasn't leaving the country again for a very long time, if ever, was to settle at least one old score.

He informed on Monya Elson, implicating him in heroin trafficking and murder.

Until 1995, the only Russian criminals the Italian National Police had seen were some independent operators trying to pass off counterfeit money, and prostitutes showing up on street corners. In February of that year, word came from the DEA that a man they wanted for extortion, drug trafficking and murder was believed to be living in the country.

It was Monya Elson.

Asked by the DEA to keep an eye on him while they prepared extradition papers, the Italians were equally concerned with the presence of a man like this, mindful of the serious threat he posed. So senior managers at the Italian National Police ordered the elite "Second Office" of the Service Centrale Operativo to target him.

Under the command of a highly driven and supersuccessful Mafia hunter, Dr. Alessandro Pansa, the team operates out of a secret modern fortress of a location in a working-class district of Rome, where heavily armed guards patrol the perimeter gates and strict security inspections control who comes in and who leaves. With the wealth of sources built up over years of pursuing Italian organized crime, Pansa's men launched

"Operation Rasputin," located Elson living in the Hotel Angela in the Adriatic coastal village of Fano and placed him under surveillance.

They knew they could arrest him whenever they wanted to under Italy's "Mafia association laws," which made it a crime to have organized criminal affiliations. It was also evident that he was living in Italy illegally, so even without the DEA's extradition request they could deport him back to the States. But Pansa was an old hand at this, had too many questions and wasn't going to interrupt Mr. Elson's life until he had all the answers.

They listened to him speaking on the phone to Shabtai Kalmanovitch and also to a Russian living in Budapest named Semion Mogilevitch. Little did they realize at the time that Mogilevitch would soon be described in the West as the most dangerous man in the world.

Pansa expanded the intelligence-gathering to determine what Elson was doing in the country and, especially, whether or not he was there on his own.

What Pansa's men unearthed astounded their bosses.

Heavyweight Russian criminals had been operating openly in Italy for over two years, making major real estate investments in Sardinia and laundering money on a massive scale. Others had established export businesses all over Italy to purchase goods for cash, then ship them back to Russia. Still others had shoved a gaggle of highly suspect financial transactions through the Italian banking system. A small group had settled quietly in Italy as early as 1981–82, implanted there for no other reason than to lend logistic support for another group working out of Moscow. And still other Russians—unassociated with the ones living in Italy—were flocking into the country, opening bank accounts, filling them with cash, then wiring the money out of the country, typically to havens like Switzerland, before closing the accounts and never being seen again.

For the Italians, now greatly worried, Elson looked like a minor player.

They knew about his Brooklyn past, and that he often commuted between Israel and Italy. They knew he was shipping furniture to Russia and dealing in gold. They also discovered that beneath the veneer of legitimacy he was laundering a lot of money.

On March 8, 1995, Pansa gave the order to arrest him. They grabbed Elson in Fano and locked him up, hoping to get a lot more out of him than they apparently got. They held his wife for a while, too. And after all the usual rigmarole of extradition, the Second Bureau handed him over to the DEA, which brought him to the States, where he will be a permanent resident at a federal facility until he dies.

Rid of him, Pansa's men moved on to bigger fish, having spotted one whose name appeared in Elson's money-laundering scheme. This was a man they considered to be the biggest of all in Italy.

Yuri Essine had an export business just like Elson's, sending consumer goods, foodstuffs and furniture back to Russia. It's become a typical way of masking tax fraud and, through double-invoicing, capital flight. And he too invested in gold, an obvious way to launder the funds he was stealing through his export business.

But Essine was not the insecure fool that Elson was.

Born in Russia's easternmost port, Vladivostok, in 1951, he'd been a gang member there before moving to Moscow and joining a criminal group called Primorskaya. Over the years, he'd earned a reputation as a cunning and ruthless criminal. When his friend Sergei Timofeyev—nicknamed Sylvester because he fancied himself the Russian Rambo—assumed command of the group, Essine contracted with Kurganskaya to have him murdered, and duly took Sylvester's place.

He'd arrived in Italy in 1994. The Second Bureau found him living with his wife in a huge estate in Santa Marinella, on the coast northwest of Rome. Surrounding him was a ring of Russian nationals, many of them Sylvester's former henchmen and bodyguards, who now protected Essine and helped to run his interest.

Over time, they were able to tie his group into crimes being committed outside Italy, including extortion, kidnapping, arms dealing, alcohol smuggling and stolen cars.

Inside Italy, they linked him to the Mafia, supplying their clubs on the Adriatic coast with Russian prostitutes. He was also extorting an Italian businessman with interests in Moscow, making him pay a *krysha* of $4000 a month. Essine's name surfaced, as well, in connection with two kidnapping cases in Italy, although both victims were Russian nationals. One was said to have stolen $3 million from Solntsevo, and Essine wanted it returned. The Italians later heard on a wiretap that the man had been killed. The second owed Essine a personal debt and he wanted it settled.

Unlike Elson, this man was a major player, not just because he had major crime connections, but also because of his dealings in oil.

In the mid-1990s, there were around forty joint-venture Russian oil companies operating in the U.S., Canada, Europe and the Middle East. Most of them were set up to pilfer the nation's assets and move money out of Russia. Essine's was Globus Trading, which operated both as a buyer and a broker of oil and petroleum products. To handle that side of the business, he brought in Alberto Grotti, a vice president of the Italian oil company ENI. Essine held a 30 percent stake. Grotti secretly had the same.

Together they used Globus to launder money from Russia, through Austria, Great Britain and Switzerland. Globus also dealt in counterfeit currencies, importing forged U.S. dollars from Russia in $30,000–50,000 parcels.

Investigating Globus led the Second Bureau to a forty-nine-year-old former KGB agent who lived in Rome, named Dimitry Naumov. Already deported from France and Austria for his questionable dealings, in addition to being part of Essine's counterfeit currency ring, he also dealt in other sorts of false documents, including passports. He moved some of Essine's oil through his own company, Dimex, and had worked out a scheme to ship $20 million worth of frozen meat to Russia. The paperwork was made to look like a bogus foreign-aid program so that he didn't have to pay European duties.

More importantly, he too had ties to Semion Mogilevitch and was known to be dealing in nuclear materials, particularly the dubious substance red mercury. He'd lived in Vienna and knew the Averin brothers, Viktor and Aleksandr, who were suspected as being senior officers in the Solntsevo. He also knew their boss, the man said to be the head of the group, Sergei Mikhailov.

They now believe that it was in Vienna that Naumov first encountered the Russian businessman Grigory Loutchansky, whose company Nordex had been based there. Loutchansky has also been suspected of dealing in nuclear materials, has been described by *Time* magazine as "the most pernicious unindicted criminal in the world," and apparently wound up owning Dimex.

Not surprisingly, Naumov was an especially interesting link for the Italians because he tied Essine directly into all these other players. What they didn't yet know was just how strong these links were.

Then, in April 1996, for some still unknown reason, Essine and Naumov went their separate ways. And it was an acrimonious separation.

After months of surveillance on the pair, plus thousands of hours of wiretaps on forty different telephones they used, the Second Bureau decided that by arresting Naumov—on charges of illegal weapons and document forgery—they might learn more about Essine, Mogilevitch, the Averins, and Mikhailov.

So, in June, they grabbed him.

During the search of his apartment, they found documents detailing arms trafficking between Russia and Austria, and evidence that pointed to Naumov's involvement with the trafficking of radioactive substances, notably red mercury.

For whatever reason, they didn't hold him very long, and once released, he fled home to Russia. On September 23, ten days after he arrived in Moscow, he was sitting in the bar of the Hotel Tverskaya when two men walked up to him from behind and put eight bullets in the back of his head.

As their investigation continued to broaden, the Italians now came across a name that gravely worried them—Aleksandr Solonik. A former Russian policeman who'd been fired after accusations of rape, he was a hired killer and a charter member of the infamous Kurganskaya Brigade.

The Russians had issued a warrant for Solonik's arrest as the prime suspect in the Timofeyev murder. Shortly thereafter he was identified by a routine police check. A gunfight followed, during which Solonik used a seventeen-round Glock pistol to kill four officers. It took a bullet through his kidney to stop him.

Under questioning, he basically confessed to being a contract killer, but did not go into many details and categorically refused to name his employers. There was a brief trial, he was sentenced to life and installed at Moscow's maximum security Matrosskaya Tishina prison.

He escaped in June 1995.

The story is that his employers, in gratitude for his silence, paid his guard half a million dollars to plant a dummy in Solonik's bunk and help him crawl down a drainpipe.

The breakout added to the Solonik legend that had long been floating through the Russian underworld. Stories abound of him jumping out courtroom windows, of always disappearing just in the nick of time, of two-handed, two-gun shoot-outs, of South American plastic surgery to change his face.

The Second Bureau discovered that he'd been living in Rome for two years, using the name Vladimir Kesov, and that he traveled regularly between Italy and Greece.

They were able to locate an apartment he used; they watched it for two months and, when he didn't show up after all that time, they broke in. They found it stocked with three Kalashnikovs, two small Scorpion machine guns, seven pistols, two shotguns, twenty-five hundred rounds of ammunition, silencers, laser aiming devices, knives, wigs and other disguises. They also found documents indirectly connecting Solonik to Essine. Oddly, the two were acquainted with many of the same women, but the Second Bureau was never able to establish any contact more direct than that.

The Greek authorities were notified and the search for him centered around Athens. They located him living in a large, rented seafront villa—they claim he was dealing weapons and running a string of prostitutes there—and notified the Russian authorities. An elite team was dispatched from Moscow to bring him back, but they arrived a day too late.

On February 2, 1997, Solonik was found wrapped in black plastic garbage bags in the woods twelve miles north of Athens. The thirty-seven-year-old had been strangled from behind with a wire. After two weeks, when no one claimed the body, the Greeks buried him in a pauper's grave.

In the meantime, a woman's body was found, this one only three hundred yards from the villa. It took some time to identify because she'd been chopped to bits, stuffed into a suitcase and buried. It turned out to be Solonik's girlfriend, a former Miss Russia and a onetime student at Britain's Lime House boarding school, nineteen-year-old Svetlana Kotova.

No one has ever been charged with the two murders, nor is anyone ever likely to be. The Greeks put it down to an underworld settling of scores. Sources say that Kurganskaya owed Solonik a lot of money for previous contracts, that they weren't paying him, and that he'd been threatening the very killers who'd hired him to murder others.

In Italy, some investigators who have also looked into this point in a different direction. They claim that the team of Russian police who went to Greece to bring Solonik home was a decoy, and that another team preceded them. It was the first group of cops who extracted revenge for Solonik's killing of the four policemen, and then dismembered Kotova to send a message to others that cop killers—especially when the killer is a former policeman himself—would simply not be tolerated.

The Italians then learned that Solonik had been planning to come to

Rome that same week to fulfill a contract. His target was Yuri Essine. Their attention now refocused on him.

Pansa ordered his arrest and a daring plan was set into motion.

In mid-March, a group of Pansa's men moved surreptitiously into the little ski resort of Madonna di Campino. Essine was holding court there, in the Golf Hotel, celebrating his forty-sixth birthday with a dozen associates.

The police skillfully gathered the intelligence information they needed, putting officers into the Golf as tourists and waiters. On the afternoon of March 15 and throughout the day on March 16, the rest of the team, nearly eighty officers, furtively moved into place. Some of them hid in the next village. Others hid in the hotel next door.

At precisely 4 A.M. on March 17, they invaded all thirteen rooms.

The entire raid lasted fifteen minutes. Essine and his friends were awakened and arrested, their rooms were searched and they were hurried out of the hotel. By 5 A.M., everyone was on their way back to Rome.

Not one of the hotels' regular guests ever realized what had happened.

Globus was promptly dismantled. Grotti would have been prosecuted, but he was already in jail serving a three-year sentence for corruption.

Unfortunately, the wheels of Italian justice ground too slowly, and after a very long time of waiting to come to trial, Essine was allowed to bail himself out of jail. Naturally, he skipped. The Italians don't know where he is—they presume he's back in Russia—but are certain that he's no longer operating in their country. He's since been tried in absentia and found guilty, and will spend the rest of his life in jail if they can ever get him back.

The void left in Brooklyn by Nayfeld and Elson had been more than filled.

A heavyweight had moved in.

Or, at least, a 150-pound guy with bad skin whom everyone believed to be a heavyweight.

Vyacheslav Kirillovich Ivankov also hailed from Vladivostok but was Essine's senior by eleven years, born on New Year's Day, 1940. The shape of his face and the cast of his eyes gave him a slight Oriental look, which led to his nickname, Yaponchik, meaning "the little Jap."

The beginning of his criminal career can be traced back to the early 1960s, when, as a follower of a thief-in-law called The Mongol, he provided muscle for the gang's extortion schemes. His ruthlessness earned him a reputation both inside and outside criminal circles, culminating in his arrest by Soviet law enforcement and a five-year sentence.

It was during that stretch in jail that he became a *vory v zakone.*

When his time was up, he returned to the streets, forming his own gang made up mostly of ex-athletes. But each act of ruthless violence merely called attention to him, and by 1981 he was back behind bars, this time to serve a fourteen-year stretch in a Siberian gulag.

Released after ten years—thanks entirely to political and judicial connections corrupted by other *vory v zakone*—he was picked up at the prison gates by a limo, flown by private jet to Moscow and welcomed home by his friends with a huge champagne reception at the Metropol Hotel. Shortly thereafter, he left mother Russia for Germany. From there, he made his way to New York.

The MVD in Moscow warned the FBI about Ivankov, and based on what the Russian security service was saying, the Bureau labeled him the most powerful Russian organized crime boss in the United States. One line was that he'd been sent to Brooklyn by the men running the Solntsevskaya organization with a mandate to take over their interests there and put rival groups out of business.

Ivankov himself was telling people that a group of thieves-in-law had sent him to America "to bring order here in émigré circles."

The Russian media gave him credibility in early 1993 when they tagged him one of the country's most important thieves-in-law. The American press picked up on that and basically constructed a reputation that suited him. There are various versions of the myth. One has him as a wrestler who was sent to prison the first time for beating up someone in a bar. Another has him running the black market under the Soviet system. Then there is the story that he was sentenced to fourteen years in prison when he committed a string of robberies pretending to be a cop. Yet another has him shipped off to a gulag in 1982 for robbery, forgery, arms trafficking and drug dealing.

"Who sent him over here?" Jim Moody, then the FBI's organized crime boss, shrugs. "Good question. We didn't know who Ivankov was. The Russians told us he was a thief-in-law and that he was in the U.S. We then had to identify where he was, which was quite difficult because he kept moving around and using all sorts of aliases. It took us a while to pin him down. When we arrested him, he had seven passports from seven different countries. I think he may even have had American passports."

But Peter Grinenko, the former New York detective and supervising Russian expert for the Brooklyn District Attorney's office, says the whole thing was nonsense, that Ivankov never deserved the reputation of a major Russian bad guy:

"He was a car thief who got arrested in Russia when he went to the fellow whose car he stole and tried to sell it back to him. And he wasn't sent here to take over anybody's American organization because there is no such thing. Russian organized crime is anything but organized. The key to understanding the Russian Maffiya is to realize that they are not actually a Mafia. They have no defined organizational structures like the Italians. They're individuals who are into scams and shakedowns, individuals who operate in small groups in order to make money any way they can. There is no pyramid structure, there is no central control, there is no Commission. They don't fit the definition of organized crime because they're not organized. They get involved with people they know and use each other to commit crimes. And once they've done that, they rip each other off."

If the FBI didn't buy Grinenko's theory, it was either because they knew better or because it suited their purposes not to. And Moody remains convinced of Ivankov's star status: "He was so important that shortly after he came to the United States, there was an editorial in *Pravda* requesting he be brought back home so that he could get control of the street crime in Moscow. He was an infamous figure in Russia."

He entered the U.S. on a forged passport with a visa—sponsored by a company in New York called Twelve-LA Inc., one of several he hid behind—noting that he was in the film business. Within a matter of months he secured a green card, having paid $15,000 to marry a Russian woman who'd already become a U.S. citizen.

Once they located Ivankov, the FBI put him under surveillance.

They watched as this stocky, powerful man with a stubby gray beard covering acne scars settled into life in Brooklyn with his wife.

They watched as he regularly cheated on her with several girlfriends, as he bought himself a place in Denver and as he set up a string of shell companies. Media Waves was supposed to have been his drug-trafficking front. Slavic Inc. was supposed to have been his money-laundering front. The chairman of Slavic was a Russian hockey star, Vyacheslav Fetisov, who played in the National Hockey League for the Detroit Red Wings. Fetisov has always denied any wrongdoing.

And they watched, with ever-increasing interest, as he traveled to Los Angeles, Miami, Denver and Boston, to Moscow, Monte Carlo and Vienna.

Especially Vienna, where Ivankov met with friends, where he stashed money and where one of his two sons was living.

He also traveled to Belgium, where investigators have since found records of an M&S International affiliate in Moscow having transferred millions of dollars to Slavic Inc., clearly linking Ivankov to both Brandwain and Nayfeld.

Another place he spent a lot of time was Fairfield, New Jersey, where he frequented the Troika Restaurant. Besides his fondness for the cooking, his cell-phone bills, averaging $5,000–6,000 a month, were sent there for payment by the restaurant.

Yet while Ivankov might have somehow managed to fit into the new Wild West that Moscow was fast becoming, he was decidedly out of place, even in Brighton Beach. It wasn't merely his lack of sophistication, it was also his ego. His clothes were much too flashy, an imitation of a man he clearly admired, New York Mafia boss John Gotti. And he all too soon became a too-visible high roller at the Taj Mahal casino in Atlantic City.

To help learn who he was, what he was doing and how they could stop him, the FBI called on the Russian MVD, which sent agents to New York, the first time Russian and American law enforcement had ever cooperated on this level. The Russians analyzed tape recordings, identified photographs and went onto the streets with the American agents to spot some of the people the FBI didn't know. But it wasn't until Ivankov began extorting two Russians on Wall Street that the Bureau could build a case against him.

Alexander Volkov and Vladimir Voloshin had set up an financial advisory firm in New York called Summit International Trading and Investment Corp. Somewhere around late 1994, they received a wire of $2.7 million from someone they knew at Moscow's Chara Bank, a licensee of the Central Bank of Russia. So the story goes, the banker was facing difficulties at home and had been especially adept at making certain that the money he was entrusting to Volkov and Voloshin couldn't be traced. There was a run on his bank and he somehow wound up dead.

The pair in New York presumed they'd just inherited a fortune.

But the assistant director of the bank also knew about the money, and he wanted a piece of it. He stood accused of hiring Ivankov to help collect it.

Ivankov sent word that this was going to cost Volkov and Voloshin $3.5 million. They refused. To make them understand how serious he was, in April 1995 he sent another message—this time in the form of an attack on Voloshin's father in a Moscow subway station. An unknown man beat him to death.

The killing drove the two Russians into the arms of the FBI. They helped the agents come up with a cell-phone number for him—which also identified Ivankov's interest in the New Jersey restaurant—and added it to the list of phones already being tapped.

The bankers' final meeting with Ivankov sort of happened in the main restaurant at the New York Hilton on the Avenue of the Americas on May 25, 1995, except Ivankov wasn't there.

The two bankers were sitting at a table when a number of very large men in dark suits appeared in the exits of the restaurant. Once they were in place, another man approached the bankers and explained, in Russian, that there were only two ways they were going to leave the hotel. One was to get up and go to their car, but in this case, their safety could not be guaranteed. The other was to stand up and walk out with him.

They chose option number two.

He drove them, with the men from the exits, to the Troika Restaurant in New Jersey, where they were held captive for twenty-four hours, until they signed agreements to hand over $3.5 million to Ivankov.

While Ivankov was plying his trade in New York, his brother-in-law, Vyacheslav Marakulovich Sliva, was installing himself in Toronto.

He'd told immigration officials that he was coming to see a friend, and specifically named hockey star Valeri Kamensky, who was then playing with the Quebec Nordiques. Kamensky has since denied knowing Sliva. Whether they knew each other or not, what Sliva didn't say was that he had a criminal record in Russia, because that would have precluded his entry into Canada. His first arrest was in 1961, at the age of sixteen, when he stole a watch. He went away for three months. Two years later, he was jailed for refusing to go into the army. He did four years for that. Then, in 1982, he was arrested for robbery, sent away for eleven years and served nine.

At least, that's what he eventually admitted to.

With those omissions, plus false information he did provide—including his sister-in-law's name where it asked for his wife's, because he didn't have a wife at the time—he was granted a visitor's visa and arrived in Toronto in 1995.

Smart enough to stay low-key in Toronto, Sliva nevertheless became the key to getting Ivankov. It was information the RCMP developed in their wiretaps on him that provided the FBI with the probable cause they used in their affidavits to obtain wiretaps against Ivankov.

From what both forces now heard, it sounded as if Sliva had been sent to Canada by Ivankov and their mutual friends back in Moscow to take over all Russian crime activities in the country. The RCMP says they overheard Sliva make death threats, and also discuss with Ivankov how the two of them intended to divide extortion payments coming in from Russian players in the National Hockey League.

Sliva had targeted a number of them—including Alexander Mogilny, Vladimir Malakhov, Oleg Tverdovsky and Alexei Zhitnick—threatening them and their families with violence if they didn't meet their demands. Presumably several paid. The NHL took its time before admitting that there was a problem. And then, a fifteen-month investigation by the United States Senate suggested that the extortion of Russian players in the NHL was more widespread than the league was willing to 'fess up to. Since then, Senate investigators have spoken about extortion of Russian basketball players in the NBA and Russian tennis players on the professional tour.

The Canadians developed intelligence on Sliva, learned that he'd had been forced to flee Russia after threats had been made on his life there, and easily tied him to a man in Denver who had a long, personal association with Ivankov, a man suspected of being a senior thief-in-law. Despite regular contact between the two, though the RCMP never overheard them plotting criminal activity, the way Sliva did with Ivankov.

Some senior people in the RCMP were convinced that Sliva was the number-two man in the Russian North American organization.

Regardless of his status, even those who agreed with Grinenko wanted him out of the country. But putting together a case against him was never going to be easy, and it certainly wasn't going to be cheap. So the Canadians settled on the most cost-efficient and swiftest method. They arrested Sliva at his high-rise condominium at Finch and Bayview Avenues in July 1997 and charged him with failing to disclose his criminal record on his visa application and being criminally inadmissible to live in Canada.

Sliva professed innocence for at least a couple of days, until he understood that there was no way he was going to be permitted to stay in the country. He agreed to be deported and was promptly returned to Moscow.

It was a better fate than Ivankov's.

In many ways, the same rules that governed life during the heyday of the LCN around the streets of Little Italy—New York City's traditional Italian neighborhood to the west of Chinatown—apply today in Little Odessa by the Sea. Rules that say seeing stuff that doesn't concern you can be hazardous to your health.

Oleg Korataev was forty-four years old, an ex-boxer and an ex-con. Convicted in Russia for robbery and assault, he came to America in 1992 on a visitor's visa, found someone in Brooklyn to marry, which got him his green card, and went to work for the U.S. branch of the organized crime gang he'd known back home, called the Valiulins.

At 3 A.M. on January 12, 1994, after ringing in the Russian new year at the Café Arbat, Korataev walked outside onto Brighton Beach Avenue with a man who took a .38-caliber pistol out of his pocket and shot Korataev in the head, killing him.

Most of the one hundred witnesses questioned by the police said they hadn't seen anything. The few who admitted they had said that they'd seen the man shoot the boxer, go back inside the restaurant, then leave a few minutes later with a woman. But no one in the restaurant knew anything about the murderer, or the woman.

Despite Korataev's reputation for being a brutal enforcer with criminal connections in Brooklyn, Toronto and Russia, everyone the police spoke with that night, oddly, seemed to come from Boston—decidedly outside NYPD jurisdiction—and otherwise suffered from amnesia.

The FBI believes that the contract on Korataev was taken out by a Moscow drug dealer named Dzhemal Khachidze as a warning to Ivankov to stay away from his market.

The message must have been clear enough, because three days later, Ivankov flew to Puerto Rico to meet with several other thieves-in-law, including Khachidze's people, in an attempt to work out their differences. Knowing about the meeting, the FBI not only taped what they could of it, but sorted through everyone's hotel-room garbage.

One of the topics discussed in San Juan, out of Ivankov's earshot, was how to eliminate him.

Reporters from the *New York Daily News* somehow happened onto the summit meeting story and asked Ivankov about it. He denied ever having been to Puerto Rico, claiming that in four years of U.S. residency, he'd never left the country.

But the FBI had enough of his Puerto Rican garbage to prove that he'd been in San Juan for seventeen days that January, and a subsequent search of his apartment uncovered a number of fake passports, all of which had foreign immigration stamps in them.

Now, with Volkov and Voloshin willing to testify, plus the mountain of wiretap evidence that the FBI had accumulated on Ivankov, the U.S. Attorney's office in Brooklyn decided they had enough to pursue a case.

On June 19, 1995, a few minutes after seven in the morning, a small army of FBI agents banged on the door of an apartment in Brooklyn belonging to one of Ivankov's girlfriends. He answered the door and they dragged him out kicking and screaming. Later, they were forced to uncurl his fingers so that they could get his prints.

Needless to say, he was held without bail.

Through confidential informants, the FBI then learned that two of their agents who'd helped to track him down and arrest him were the object of a contract. Ivankov, who was said to be paying $200,000 a month to a pair of "brigades" to protect him, allegedly asked them to liquidate the agents. Affidavits eventually produced in federal court claimed that one of the brigade leaders was a former KGB agent who'd already murdered half a dozen Russians on Ivankov's behalf. The two FBI agents were immediately placed under protective watch.

When he was arrested, Ivankov had a slip of paper in his wallet containing information about a bank account in the Bahamas. But then there was another one, the account where he'd intended to stash the $3.5 million, and that was only just across the Hudson in New Jersey.

He was charged with extortion and conspiracy, and also with fraudulently marrying the woman for his green card. At his trial, Ivankov's attorney insisted that his client was a freedom fighter, a man unjustly framed by the former Communists simply because of his outspoken anti-Communist stance and, especially, because of his devout faith in the anti-Communist Russian Orthodox Church.

The jury didn't buy his story, and neither did the judge. She sentenced him to nine years and seven months on the main two charges and to nineteen months for the bogus marriage. Prosecutors had attempted to get him on the murder of Voloshin's father in Moscow, believing that he'd personally ordered it. But the judge would not consider crimes attributed to Ivankov outside the United States.

"We were kind of surprised when we arrested him," Jim Moody confesses. "Most high-level organized crime guys have a persona about them. They conduct themselves in a certain way. They have some sophistication. They know how to deal with people. This guy was a scumbag. All the way through. That surprised us. No class at all."

Caged in a tiny cell near Lake Placid, New York, Ivankov still protests his innocence and insists that he will neither forget—or forgive—the people who put him there.

When he finally gets out, in his late sixties, the U.S. Government intends to deport him back to Russia. What little remains of his organization today will, by then, be nonexistent. The fear he can spread these days is already minimal. By then it will be hardly detectable.

For some of the agents who helped track him down, he was a cartoon cutout, an exhibitionist who did not understand that by boxing toe to toe with American law enforcement he was only setting himself up for a severe beating. For others, especially the agents who finally took him out, Ivankov was a dinosaur, an old-school thug who didn't understand that, in the New World, the old ways didn't work the way he expected them to.

For Tom Kneir at the FBI, "Ivankov was an idiot. He put himself out there saying, I'm going to show you that I'm the biggest, baddest guy on the block. All he did was make himself a pretty easy target. He stood up in front of everybody and threw out a challenge. So the FBI and the U.S. Attorney's office said, Okay, asshole, you're next."

The Russians who came after Ivankov were anything but idiots.

6

THE FOUR HORSEMEN

There will be no frontiers for crime.
There should be no frontiers for justice.

—Giovanni Falcone

ACCORDING TO GERMAN INTELLIGENCE SOURCES, Grigory Loutchansky was born in Tbilisi, Georgia, in 1946, raised in Latvia, allegedly served two years in prison for embezzlement, became an academic at Riga University, and in 1989 formed a company called Nordex. It is believed that it was paid for with money stashed in Europe by the KGB.

A conglomerate dealing in oil and petroleum products, chemicals, metals, fertilizers and foodstuffs, within five years Nordex was reporting a turnover in excess of $2 billion. At the end of the 1990s that figure is said to be above $3 billion. The company trades within the former Soviet Union as well as operating in several other countries, including the United States, Canada and Britain. One of Loutchansky's business contacts was the tarnished, now dead, British tycoon Robert Maxwell.

Originally based in Vienna, Loutchansky moved Nordex to Moscow—more accurately, the Austrians encouraged him to leave by deporting seventy of the company's eighty employees—where today it ranks in the top ten of Russia's largest private companies. Nordex is also said to be the largest of around three dozen firms active in the West as fronts for Russia's foreign intelligence service, or former intelligence officers who were smart enough to feather their pension funds.

If there is a secret to his success, at least according to what Loutchansky likes to tell people, it's in the high margins that Nordex realizes on trading activities due to the substantial differentials between domestic and world prices. An example might be a deal he managed some years ago in Ukraine.

The Kremlin had cut off oil supplies because the government in Kiev owed Moscow too much money and wasn't making much of an effort to pay it. Nordex bought $120 million worth of oil from Russia for hard currency—the Ukrainians only paid in rubles—and bartered it in Kiev for sugar, wheat and other commodities, which they then turned around and sold to the Russians.

It was a classic middleman's swap, but it is not for commercial tightrope-walking that Loutchansky has attracted attention. He hit the American headlines in July 1995 when he was invited to a Democratic fund-raising dinner with President Clinton at the Hay Adams Hotel in Washington and, rather suddenly, the invitation was withdrawn. To the embarrassment of the Democratic National Committee, *The Pittsburgh Tribune-Review* revealed allegations by the intelligence services—that beneath the veneer of a globe-trotting businessman, he was the planet's most important dealer in black-market nuclear materials.

What's more, he'd already attended an October 1993 fund-raiser with the president, at a time when the National Security Agency was said to have seen firm indications that Nordex was a front for weapons smuggling.

Photos taken at that dinner show Loutchansky with Clinton and a New York real estate investor named Sam Domb, who'd secured Loutchansky's invitation. At one point, Domb denied having known Loutchansky before the dinner. However, the *New York Post* reported that he admitted to them he'd brought Loutchansky along as his guest, hoping to do business with him. While it is not entirely clear if Loutchansky himself ever contributed to Clinton's campaign, he did receive a thank-you letter from the president for his support.

By the time the invitation arrived for the 1995 affair, Loutchansky was already barred from entering England, Canada and Hong Kong—he'd tried and was unable to satisfy immigration authorities about the source of his funds—and is quoted as admitting that he feared he would also be stopped from entering the U.S.

Previous to that, it was conjectured that Loutchansky could have been involved when a huge cache of arms—twenty-seven thousand

Russian machine guns, five thousand Czech pistols and seven million rounds of ammunition—was intercepted en route from Panama to Croatia. No charges were lodged, nor was any evidence ever publicly put forth that either Loutchansky or Nordex was involved. Since then, however, Nordex was tied to the transport of SCUD missiles from North Korea to Iraq. The information stems from a report which alleges that in spring 1995, officials inspected a plane—Loutchansky's privately owned Antonov 124, said to be the largest aircraft in the world—whose cargo of warheads was discovered when it stopped to refuel on its way from Pyongyang to Baghdad.

Loutchansky has also been suspected by intelligence services of being associated with Russian criminal activity—in particular, money laundering. He controls Nordex, and British intelligence sources say Nordex controls nearly forty businesses in the West plus another sixty inside the former Soviet Union.

Following his appearance on the Democratic fund-raiser guest lists, Israeli interest in Loutchansky heightened. Various stories circulated of meetings with high officials in the government. They believe he had once been a senior KGB agent, and at least some of their suspicions were confirmed—that is, as far as his intentions—in a report passed along to them by an American intelligence agency. It is said to have detailed Loutchansky's attempt to buy influence with Boris Yeltsin through several large election campaign contributions.

In fact, *Time* magazine claimed that he has long since bought his way into real power. They connected Loutchansky and Nordex with former Russian prime minister Viktor Chernomyrdin.

Before assuming his post in the Kremlin, they wrote, Chernomyrdin had frequently visited Nordex in Vienna, and those visits were tied to a lucrative commodities deal. After his appointment as head of the government, Chernomyrdin ordered Russian Customs to waive licensing requirements and export fees on a shipment of thirty thousand metric tons of electronics-grade copper, a Nordex deal.

It was further reported by *Time* that, in 1993 and 1994, American intelligence had intercepted some very specific Nordex communications which led them to believe the company was supplying nuclear materials and other bomb-making components to both North Korea and Iran. As a consequence, the State Department pressured the U.S. Export-Import

Bank to scotch a loan that would have backed a joint venture in Kazakhstan between U.S. Steel and Nordex.

Mossad, the Israeli intelligence service, claims to have located Chernomyrdin's Swiss bank accounts and established that his personal fortune—said to be in excess of $5 billion—was built on the back of Gazprom, the Russian oil conglomerate that he once headed, and that, today, ties back directly to Loutchansky.

John Deutch, director of the CIA in June 1997, stated categorically that Nordex was "an organization associated with Russian criminal activity." Added James Woolsey, who preceded Deutch at the Agency, "While we have slain the dragon of the Soviet empire, we now find ourselves in a jungle filled with a bewildering variety of poisonous snakes."

In Vienna, Police Commissioner Peter Stiedl confirms that when Nordex was based there, they investigated Nordex and were particularly concerned about funds in one account that they suspected to be the proceeds of crime. They asked Moscow for information about those funds, the company and Loutchansky.

"That information was never forthcoming," Stiedl says. "We even froze the money and held it because we felt that we could establish probable cause. Four different teams in Russia said they would help us. The first group showed up, said they would get us what we wanted and went away. A second team showed up, but they were totally different people who didn't have any of the information. So we requested it again. By the time we were dealing with the fourth group, it was too late. There was a huge amount of conflicting information, but the Russians never confirmed to us what we needed to know, so we had to return the money."

Loutchansky has always denied any and all allegations against him and his company. He says he does not traffic in arms or drugs, nor does he launder money. He says he is merely a successful businessman who is being victimized by the press. He labels stories tying him either to organized crime or the intelligence services as outrageous and false.

He has frequently been quoted as saying, "None of the statements about links of this group of companies with the criminal world is corroborated by facts or by the results of the numerous investigations which were carried out both by the Russian and foreign secret services, including Interpol."

Which may be so, but in 1995 an eleven-nation, two-day conference was hosted by Interpol and the sole subject of the meeting was Mr. Loutchansky.

The second horseman had also once been based in Vienna.

Sergei Mikhailov didn't get into crime until late in life—it was in 1984, when he was twenty-six—by reporting his motorcycle stolen and attempting to collect on the insurance. It cost him six months.

A sports fanatic, he'd wanted to be a trainer, but somehow sidestepped into hotel management and even worked for a time as a waiter in a restaurant. However, what he learned in jail must have suited him, because as soon as he got out, he gave up working for a living to string together the loose-knit group that would rule south Moscow under the name Solntsevskaya.

When he was arrested again five years later and charged with extortion, the main witness against him suddenly decided he couldn't remember anything, and without that testimony the case was dropped.

In 1993 he was arrested a third time, suspected of killing someone in a casino. Again, witnesses failed to provide evidence.

Around that time, a gang war broke out in Moscow and bodies were being strewn around the streets. Mikhailov left. He first established himself in Israel and was granted a passport on the grounds that his wife was Jewish. One story has since surfaced that the woman wasn't his wife. A second, that she wasn't Jewish. Then he opted for the peace and quiet of Vienna.

Not satisfied with just Russian and Israeli passports, he got himself named Honorary Consul for Costa Rica, a title that came along with a diplomatic passport from Costa Rica. He increased his collection of IDs with papers from Greece, Belgium and Portugal, as a CNN correspondent and as a member of the Kremlin's security detail.

While his business interests have always been cloaked in mystery, by design, it is widely believed that by 1992, Solntsevskaya had gained control of the Russian Exchange Bank and that he and his friends were using that as a conduit to get money out of Russia. Certainly by mid-decade, the Russian banking system had become the world's most important money-laundering sink, snatching the title away from the equally corrupt financial world of Panama.

It is known that Mikhailov got involved in gas and oil deals in Russia, a five-star hotel project in Budapest and bananas in Costa Rica. Along the way, he managed to get himself banned from France indefinitely and banned from the Czech Republic for ten years. It is suspected that hidden behind those businesses—and his persona non grata status—were Solntsevo's extortion rackets, arms and drug trafficking, and money laundering.

Two years after arriving in Vienna, with his name linked by the Austrians to Russian organized crime and to Loutchansky, he left for Switzerland. On June 21, 1996, he purchased a large house in the village of Borex, just outside Geneva, for 1.3 million Swiss francs. He installed his wife and two young children there, and began shifting some of his business interests to Belgium.

He hooked up with Mike Brandwain, and, along with his right-hand man, Viktor Averin, registered one of his main companies there, MAB International—as in Mikhailov-Averin-Brandwain. Through that company, negotiations were opened on several construction contracts. One was for a sewer system in Moscow. Another was for a gas pipeline in Turkmenistan. Whether MAB International was involved with Vyacheslav Ivankov is not clear. There was a relationship somewhere, but it might have been personally with Mikhailov or through Solntsevo as his sponsor.

Regardless of who Mikhailov's silent partners might have been, by this time, Swiss authorities were taking an anxious look at who he was. Because they didn't like what they saw, less than four months after the Mikhailovs moved into their new home, the cops arrested him at Geneva-Cointrin Airport.

Mikhailov spent the next two years in jail, awaiting trial. While he was there, the Swiss ambassador to Russia received several death threats; a Moscow magistrate interrogated him as a suspect in the still-unsolved murder of television journalist Vladislav Listyev; a scandal broke out in Israel over identity papers, implicating Mikhailov, Averin and several others with someone inside the Ministry of Interior who supplied the papers; and his own lawyer got arrested for smuggling letters between Mikhailov and Averin past the jail censor.

It wasn't until December 1998 that the Swiss finally tried him on charges of being the head of Solntsevskaya.

The stage for this drama was Geneva's Criminal Court, an imposing building opposite some tiny boutiques along a narrow and winding street on a hill in the heart of the old city. Emphasizing the powerful reputation of the defendant, a tight security cordon was drawn around the *quartier* with police SWAT teams wearing flak jackets and carrying automatic weapons. Mikhailov arrived every morning in a bulletproof Mercedes, wearing a gray suit and bulletproof vest. He was safely delivered inside the building before being permitted to get out of the car, always handcuffed and always under heavy guard.

Some witnesses were issued bulletproof vests, others were allowed to hide their identities behind screens in another room where they testified by closed-circuit television.

To follow the proceedings, which were held in French, the bulky Mikhailov had an interpreter constantly whispering in his ear.

Two star witnesses were planned.

Only one lived to see the trial.

Vadim Rozenbaum, who was said to have firsthand knowledge of Mikhailov's criminal activities, was murdered in Holland in 1997, only days after his name appeared on the witness list. The second man, Nikolai Oporov, the former chief of the Moscow Police Organized Crime Bureau, received so many death threats that the Swiss took the rare step of granting him political asylum.

Testifying from another room at the courthouse via closed-circuit television, Oporov told the jury that the first time he'd heard Mikhailov's name was in 1987, when Solntsevo was working a small-time protection racket, extorting street kiosks. He tied Mikhailov straight to the leadership of the gang.

So did Geneva's special anti-Russian crime squad, who produced photos and other evidence of meetings between Mikhailov and leaders of various Eastern European organized crime gangs.

So did Swiss police inspector Patrick Scheurer, who testified to finding all those identity papers, plus Mikhailov's various passports, and to tapping telephone conversations in which Mikhailov himself told others that he was running Solntsevo. He also produced evidence that Mikhailov possessed a shell company in the Channel Islands through which he'd laundered tens of millions of dollars.

Robert Levinson, the retired FBI agent and Russian organized crime expert, also put Mikhailov at the head of the gang. He said that Mikhailov controlled two "combat brigades"—assassination squads—who would commit murders in Russia and other countries in Europe, then go to Miami to cool off. He said that under Mikhailov, Solntsevo ran nightclubs in Brighton Beach and in Los Angeles, and had a car dealership in Houston, Texas, all of which were fronts for drug dealing. He told the jury, "The organization was engaged regularly in the extortion of businesses, the distribution of drugs including cocaine, counterfeiting of currency and trafficking in arms."

When the defense put on its case, the picture painted of Mikhailov was as a highly successful businessman—they needed to explain away more than $4 million the Swiss had frozen in his bank account—who exported gas and oil from Russia, bought bells for churches and donated money to orphanages.

One of their star witnesses was former U.S. Attorney General Ramsey Clark, who testified that what Levinson had said was hearsay and would never be permitted in a U.S. court of law.

In all, there were around eighty witnesses, the majority of them called by the defense.

After eight days of trial, stretched over two weeks, the jury was faced with deciding four charges. To the horror of many—and the decidedly shocked delight of Mikhailov—they found him not guilty of belonging to the Solntsevskaya crime group; not guilty of controlling the crime group from Switzerland; not guilty of using forged documents; but guilty of violating the law that prohibits foreigners from purchasing real estate in Switzerland.

The prosecutors had failed to prove their case, mainly because they'd attempted to prove that he was a Maffiya godfather instead of taking the more direct route and aiming at specific crimes. The problem there was, they hadn't found any specific crimes committed in Switzerland, besides the ownership of property. The Russians never provided enough information about him, nor had any other country requested Mikhailov's extradition.

He was kept in jail overnight before being deported on the single guilty verdict. He objected. He wanted to stay in Switzerland. They loaded him onto a regularly scheduled Aeroflot flight to Moscow. He objected to that too.

He wanted to go to Budapest.

Averin was in Budapest.

But Averin was second string.

In the back of his mind Mikhailov must have worried about being killed in Moscow. He'd been out of circulation for two years, young guys had moved up, there was discontent with him among the Solntsevskaya foot soldiers and the streets had become even more violent.

Budapest was where he would be safest.

Budapest was where he could count on the protection of, arguably, the most dangerous man in the world.

Semion Yudkovich Mogilevitch was his friend, benefactor and favorite business partner.

Two years older than Mikhailov, the Ukrainian-born Mogilevitch— today, a three-hundred-pound, balding, mustached man who holds a graduate degree in economics from the University of Lvov—had been able to parlay thin air into a seemingly invincible business empire. And, like Loutchansky's, his protestations of legitimacy also, all too often, fall on deaf ears.

According to several intelligence and law enforcement sources— including the British National Criminal Intelligence Service and the FBI—Mogilevitch is into everything, from weapons to money laundering, from prostitution to art smuggling, from extortion to drugs. There are even some people who claim he is into murder.

Adds one senior FBI agent, "Mogilevitch is involved in more bullshit than you can shake a stick at." Even Mogilevitch's pal Monya Elson has described him as "the most powerful mobster in the world."

Supposedly, he has a headlock on freight passing through Moscow's Sheremetyevo International Airport—the Lucchese family invented that gimmick when they took over Idlewild Airport, long before it was renamed JFK—and is believed to have bought a bankrupt airline from one of the central Asian republics. It has always been rumored that he runs a big part of Eastern Europe's black markets from businesses he set up in the Czech Republic. It is known that he bought one of Hungary's bankrupt armament industries, and that his name was linked to a multimillion-dollar cache of Warsaw Pact weapons which got sold to Iraq. That particular arrangement is said to have included surface-to-air missiles, which brings up the hypothesis that he is linked to Loutchansky's alleged arms dealing and the SCUDs.

In the 1970s, when that first wave of émigrés was allowed to leave Russia for Israel, Mogilevitch was a member of a street gang, working petty thefts and counterfeiting. But he saw opportunity in the exodus, convinced people who were leaving immediately that he could sell their belongings for them and would pay them in hard currency when they got to Israel, collected the goods, sold them and kept all the money for himself.

By his own admission, in an interview with the *New York Times*, he was convicted in 1973, at the age of twenty-seven, of black-market currency dealing. But all he did, he claimed, was buy a small gold coin on the black market for his girlfriend. He served eighteen months.

His next run-in with the authorities, he said, happened two years later, when he was charged again with unlawful currency dealing. This time, his excuse was that he was trying to help an emigrating friend get $2,500 out of the country. He was sentenced to four years.

Whatever the truth of those early arrests, it is clear that he got connected with the right people somewhere along the line, because he was soon dealing in oil and gas. And it is difficult to believe that he could have secured contracts without paying someone off. Much of that business was pushed through a company registered in Alderney, Channel Islands, called Arbat International. There has always been a rumor that the Channel Islands are where Mogilevitch is linked to Ivankov. It is known that there are Channel Island links to Sergei Mikhailov.

Sometime between 1991 and 1993, Mogilevitch also fled the Moscow gang wars, opting first for Israel, where he obtained a passport, then leaving for Budapest, which was just starting to happen. He claims it was because he'd met a woman there and fallen in love. By coincidence, the Hungarians were selling off state industries, the police didn't have a clue about transnational organized crime, he had money to buy muscle, he knew that muscle could buy him respect and he proved that respect could produce all sorts of opportunities. Being married to a Hungarian woman conveniently allowed him legal residence there.

A second company now appeared on the registrar's books in Alderney, this one called Arigon. Among the deals that Mogilevitch is believed to have godfathered are a joint venture with the Genovese to ship toxic waste from the States to Chernobyl; the movement of stolen artworks and religious artifacts through Western auction houses; the purchase of a jewelry factory in Hungary to produce counterfeit money, financial instruments and Fabergé eggs; and the establishment of a chain of nightclubs and strip joints, through which he could presumably push prostitutes and drugs and launder money.

The clubs were called "Black and White," and he opened them in Budapest, Riga, Kiev and Prague. But that world can be a violent one, and the deeper he got into it, the higher he raised the personal stakes. In 1994 a Frankfurt brothel owner was killed, along with twelve of his prostitutes. Suspicion fell on Mogilevitch, the murders being a grisly warning to any groups thinking of moving in on his patch. A German television crew went to Budapest to interview him about it and claim to have been apprised of what awaited them if they didn't leave town immediately. They left.

Shortly thereafter, Mogilevitch was involved in a shoot-out in Budapest, said to have been an attempt on him by a rival gang, either to revenge the killing or to muscle in on his clubs. He was not charged in either case.

In May 1995, Mogilevitch traveled to Prague, where Viktor Averin was hosting a birthday bash at the Uhaluba Club. Just before going to the party, someone tipped off Mogilevitch that during the evening he was going to be murdered. Mogilevitch turned around and went home, but not before calling the police. They raided the party and interviewed all two hundred guests. They never found out if the assassination story was true. But Mogilevitch thought it was true. And that seriously spooked him. For the next several years he spent most of his time well guarded in Budapest.

Anyway, by 1995 he was on to a new way to make a huge fortune—long distance and by remote control.

A Russian émigré named Jacob Bogatin, who'd been an engineer in a Soviet military research institute, had started a small magnet-manufacturing company near Philadelphia called YBM. A few years before, while buying privatized companies from the government in an end-of-Communism fire sale, Mogilevitch had also picked up a magnet business, called Magnex Rt.

The twain might never have met had it not been for Marat Balagula's fuel-tax scam in Brooklyn. One of the people involved with Balagula had gotten arrested, was tried and found guilty, then allowed out on bail to await sentencing. Instead of sticking around, he jumped. Arrested in Vienna, he was held there for a year until the Austrians decided they didn't have enough evidence against him in a money-laundering scheme related to the Balagula fraud, and let him go. Rather than return to Brooklyn, where warrants were piling up, he made his way to Poland, where he wheeled and dealed and wound up owning a bank—he called it the First Commercial Bank of Lublin—which he set up as a money-laundering sink for any crime group willing to pay his fee.

Mogilevitch knew that man, who happened to be Jacob Bogatin's brother David. Consequently, Jacob Bogatin also spent time in Budapest.

The plot Mogilevitch then hatched was one worthy of someone with an economics degree. He took a shell company called Pratecs, floated it on the Alberta Stock Exchange—where there was little or no due diligence because little or no information was required—and folded YBM and Magnex into it. Behind the scenes, Mogilevitch reversed shares into Arigon and Arbat and set up a string of shells in Hungary through which he could use the newly created YBM Magnex to launder money.

Starting life as a penny share, they cooked the books of Pratecs for months, then brought it to the Toronto Stock Exchange, where it fast became one of the darlings of the TSE 300. At one point, around March 1995, word came from London that someone involved with the company was under investigation. Shares were suspended. The company then issued this rebuttal: "The allegations were aimed at two companies in the UK and the attorneys of these two companies. The companies are in no way related to YBM or its subsidiary, Arigon. However, because the companies are owned by an employee and a former director of Arigon, and the companies' monetary affairs were handled by the same solicitors that Arigon used in the past, it had put Arigon also under scrutiny."

Such double-talk seemed to satisfy the powers that be in Toronto.

Further double-talk satisfied the investors. The company announced that while producing magnets in Hungary, it had discovered a residue power called neodymium, which, when added to crude oil, significantly cut refining costs. They then explained how they were buying crude oil on the spot market, treating it with neodymium, and making a lot of money selling it to the government of the Ukraine under a long-term contract. The best thing about this, the company said, was that the more magnets they made, the more powder by-product they had for their oil interests.

They might as well have been selling snake oil.

Market analysts could see that since its inception, YBM Magnex's net sales had quadrupled, net income had jumped by a multiple of nine and earnings had increased by a multiple of five. With hordes of brokers touting the shares to fund managers, the stock took off. It moved up to $10 and then, between the summer of 1997 and March 10, 1998, hit a high of $20.15. The company was now valued at $1 billion.

In the midst of the excitement, YBM Magnex acquired Crusteel Magnetics in Sheffield, England, and the following year, two other magnet firms in Lancashire. The three were joined together into YBM's British subsidiary, Crumax Magnetics. But also along the way, the company's auditors, Deloitte & Touche, didn't like the fact that there were all sorts of strange things going on and that, in certain cases, there was no paperwork to back up accounting entries. According to its own accounting, YBM's turnover had risen from $90 million in 1996 to $138 million in 1997. But then, YBM's version suggested their main market for magnets was the U.S. Deloitte discovered that YBM shipped most of their magnets to Russia and the Ukraine. They were refusing to sign off the 1997 accounts. Rumors abounded and warning signs—with the benefit of hindsight—were conspicuous. Several large blocks of shares were discreetly sold by people inside the company.

By Tuesday afternoon, May 12, 1998, the stock had slipped from its all-time high and was hovering around $14.35. On Wednesday morning, May 13, at precisely 10:30, some sixty officers of the Organized Crime Strike Force—composed of agents from the FBI; IRS; Customs, Immigration and Naturalization Service; and State Department—working out of the U.S. Attorney's office in Philadelphia, walked into the company's Newton, Pennsylvania, headquarters, presented their search warrants and proceeded to cart away tons of documents and computerized records.

Exactly twenty-three minutes later, the TSE halted trading on YBM Magnex. And just like that, shareholders were looking at $635 million of worthless stock.

Just before Pratecs went public, the British had become curious about a man named Konstantin Karat, whose name appeared as managing director of Arigon Ltd. Looking at Arigon, they suspected the company was laundering money through London. They were able to connect Karat, Arigon and Arbat to Mogilevitch and laundered funds back to him. But the people apparently doing the wash for Mogilevitch were not Russians. They were a pair of English solicitors.

Officers at NCIS compiled dossiers on Mogilevitch, Arigon, Arbat, Karat and the solicitors until December 9, 1994. At that point, believing they had indeed uncovered criminal activity, they passed along a "development package" to the Southeast Regional Crime Squad (SERCS) for further investigation. Officers on SERCS's money-laundering investigation team promptly focused their attention on the relationship between "Moguilevitch"—spelled that way in the development package—and the small firm of London solicitors known as Blakes.

The two partners at Blakes were Adrian Bernard Churchward and

Peter Blake-Turner. They'd been the ones to set up Arbat and Arigon for Mogilevitch in Alderney. They'd also set up other Channel Islands companies for him, including Createbury Ltd. and Limegold Ltd. On closer inspection, it turned out that Mogilevitch and Churchward were linked with a company called Pendosi and, closer still, through Churchward's wife, Galina Vassilyevna, who was the mother of Mogilevitch's son. A police report also concluded, "There was no money laundering identification system in existence at Blakes."

With additional intelligence developed through contacts in Hungary, Russia, the Czech Republic, Austria, the United States and Canada, the SERCS team became increasingly convinced that Mogilevitch was running an organized crime group that dealt in extortion, prostitution, arms dealing and drug trafficking. They'd also come to believe that the solicitors were washing some of Mogilevitch's criminal profits through accounts they controlled at the Royal Bank of Scotland on Lombard Street.

Overall, SERCS officers spent five and a half months investigating the three men and their business interests in several countries. One conclusion they drew was that, because money was banked in the solicitors' client accounts, none of the transactions were being scrutinized by the money-laundering reporting officer of the Royal Bank. He'd taken the attitude that solicitors were regulated by the Law Society and that it was up to the Law Society to look into clients' accounts and their use as conduits for dirty money. In this respect, officers at the Royal Bank was hardly unique. They knew their clients and, like so many bankers still do, had every excuse for wiping their hands of the matter. What's more, banks have also discovered that when they do take the time to question lawyers about their clients' accounts, the answer customarily forthcoming is that that information is protected by client-attorney privilege. Which is why lawyers' clients' accounts make for near-perfect money-laundering sinks.

The SERCS officers eventually concluded that, over the course of three years, as much as $50 million had been moved through the solicitors' client accounts for Mogilevitch. They came to believe that Arigon was Mogilevitch's private holding company, while Arbat—which, among other businesses, ran a funeral parlor in Moscow—was the laundry. Neither company appeared to be trading, but money was moving through Arigon, then into and out of Arbat and the funeral home.

The problem they now faced was exactly the same that the police in

Vienna faced when they looked into Loutchansky's money, the same problem police investigators all over the West face whenever Russian or Eastern European money is involved. They need to prove, beyond a reasonable doubt, the criminal origin of the funds. And without information coming from police in the East, that is extremely difficult.

With patience and what relationships they'd been able to build on a cop-to-cop basis with the Moscow police, the officers constructed a convoluted but nevertheless interesting scenario.

A man known to the British police only by his last name, Mysinkov, had been operating an advanced-fee-fraud scam—bilking the Moscow city government out of $3.2 million with 111 contracts for sugar—using a company called Perigey. That money was showing up in the Pendosi and Createbury accounts, but disappeared from there. When the British cops asked the Moscow cops to put them in touch with Mr. Mysinkov, they were informed that he'd died in unknown circumstances and that, just prior to his death, his wallet and passport had disappeared.

Back in London, the SERCS team had reason to believe that the targets of their investigation were, if nothing else, handling stolen funds, although they couldn't identify specific crimes. Based on that, they made applications for warrants to search the solicitors' office and homes.

Churchward, his wife and Blake-Turner were arrested on May 16, 1995, and the searches carried out. All three were then released on police bail, awaiting evidence from Russia that could be used in a British court. According to the police, the search produced "extensive intelligence relating to financial transactions conducted by the Mogilevitch Organization." They were also able to ascertain that the Royal Bank of Scotland held just over $2 million in three separate Arigon accounts.

They now moved against Mogilevitch and Karat. Warrants for their arrest were issued and the funds were seized. In the meantime, the Russian authorities didn't appear to be in much of a hurry to help SERCS. The Moscow police had passed their request on to the prosecutors' department, and that's where the paperwork sat, awaiting a decision. Officers from SERCS and NCIS tried to move things along, stressing to their Russian counterparts that time was of the essence. But to no avail. They asked again about the Mysinkov case. They were told it was closed. They used what political pull they could to get the paperwork on the Mysinkov matter. The answer came back it's all gone.

In the absence of any evidence, the charges of conspiracy to handle stolen goods against Churchward, his wife, Blake-Turner, Mogilevitch and Karat were withdrawn. The only way left open for the SERCS team was to pursue a prosecution for what they decided would be a minor money-laundering offense. And under Britain's 1993 money-laundering laws, the clause they might have used only applied to new clients. So that was not pursued either.

The money sitting in the Arigon accounts was unfrozen and legal costs were awarded to the Churchwards and Blake-Turner. No application for costs was made by anyone else. A phone call from Mogilevitch himself came in to someone at NCIS, though. The officer wasn't there at the time and Mogilevitch left a message asking why he was being chased by the British police when he was nothing more than a legitimate businessman trying to earn a legitimate living. At least according to the officer at NCIS, the call was not returned.

Officers at NCIS who worked on the intelligence-gathering side of what came to be known as "Operation Sword" described Mikhailov and Averin as "thugs" who depend on Mogilevitch's business skills.

When Mikhailov got locked up in Switzerland, they say, Averin ran scared and headed straight for Budapest, where Mogilevitch could protect him. Back in Moscow, the Solntsevo foot soldiers were unhappy that Mikhailov was still getting his share of the profits while locked up and unable to earn any money for the group. The man who was supposedly the paymaster for the combat teams was named Arnold Tamm. And he allegedly cut off payments to Mikhailov. Mogilevitch is said to have stepped in and was funneling money to Mikhailov, and also to Averin, through the Channel Islands companies.

While this was going on, the officers say, Mrs. Mysinkov came to see Mogilevitch about her husband's money. She'd been told that Mogilevitch had done her husbnd a favor by allowing him to launder his advanced-fee-fraud profits through Pendosi and Createbury, and now that her husband was dead, she wanted the money back. Apparently, she was met at the airport in Budapest as she got off the plane, told in no uncertain terms that the money now belonged to Mogilevitch, and was bundled onto the next plane home.

There is also a strong belief around the intelligence services that the Hungarians have always been well aware of who Mogilevitch is and what he does—how could they not be?—and allowed him to live there because they'd come to an understanding with him.

It was the "devil you know" syndrome. In exchange for his get-out-of-jail-free card, Mogilevitch had pledged to the government that he would not commit crimes in Hungary and also that he would personally keep out other, more violent and therefore less controllable groups.

The deeper the NCIS investigators burrowed inside Arigon and Arbat, the more they unraveled about Pendosi and Createbury to solve the mystery of the Mysinkov money. His $3.2 million had been wired from a Lithuanian bank to a Hungarian bank, and from there to accounts held by a Swiss bank at Chemical Bank in Buffalo, New York. Six days later, the sum total was wired out again to several accounts in Europe, including one they believed to be controlled by Mikhailov and another they believed to be controlled by Averin. They also traced money from the Channel Islands to accounts in Philadelphia that appeared to be controlled by Josef Bogatin. That's how they stumbled across YBM.

Needing to know more about YBM, British officers traveled to the States and, accompanied by an FBI agent, drove to the company's headquarters in Hatboro, Pennsylvania. What they found at the given address was an old school, with tiny offices where classrooms had once been. A piece of paper was taped to a door that looked as if it led to what used to be the cafeteria. In handwritten letters, it read "YBM."

They knocked, but no one was there.

Because it was all so obviously suspicious, they kept an eye on the company and its banking relationships with the Channel Islands, until word came that Pratecs was being listed on the Alberta exchange and that YBM was being folded into it. Horrified British investigators now sent a stern warning to the exchange officials in Alberta. They explained the connection to Mogilevitch and outlined the prospect of him being permitted to float Pratecs—which would mean that he'd be floating YBM, Magnex Rt and Arigon—and that if he got away with this he'd be out of control, and that the next step would be his purchase of a bank. At that point, they argued, he might also be beyond reach.

Security officials at the exchange asked for evidence.

The officers at NCIS tried to make them understand there was a difference between intelligence information and evidence—especially evidence that could be presented in court—and that they only had intelligence. But, they insisted, their information was sound. They urged the Canadians to realize, "The directors of this company are connected to Russian Organized Crime and indeed the main individual, Semion

Mogilevitch, is considered to be the leader of Russian organized crime in Hungary and the Czech Republic."

Even the FBI pitched in with their fears: "Semion Mogilevitch runs an extensive prostitution operation out of the Black and White Nightclubs in Prague and Budapest. Foreign law enforcement agencies have documented Mogilevitch's prostitution operation as the centerpiece of his operations in Europe. Arigon is a central element of the Mogilevitch Organization."

In Alberta, exchange officials turned a deaf ear, and Pratecs was floated.

Operation Sword produced 545 files of records and 1,325 exhibits, including a record of every financial transaction conducted on behalf of Mogilevitch and other Russian organized crime figures by Churchward over a five-year period.

The SERCS's final report concluded, "Mogilevitch is one of the world's top criminals who has a personal wealth of $100 million. He is a target of Law Enforcement Agencies and Security Services in several countries and as a result of the effect of his financial impact on the City of London he clearly falls in the category of an NCIS core criminal."

If nothing else, the officers had the minor satisfaction of closing down every company they found to be controlled by Mogilevitch. Bank accounts were also shut. And on August 10, 1995, an order was signed by the Home Secretary forbidding Mogilevitch's entry into the United Kingdom. A similar ban on entry has also been posted in the United States.

In the days following the raid on the YBM Magnex headquarters, it was discovered that Arigon had resurfaced in the Cayman Islands under the name of United Trade Ltd. Forensic accounts were brought in and their report, on file with the Alberta Court of Queen's Bench in Calgary, describes a tangled web of mysterious bank accounts, unexplained money transfers and unusual transactions, all indicating that money laundering had been taking place. Documentation to support the transfer of millions of dollars, the report says, was nonexistent. The relationship between YBM Magnex and a Bahamian subsidiary, United Trade, was highly suspicious because the bank account didn't seem to be under corporate control.

They wrote about "several transactions effected by United Trade involving the movement of substantial amounts of money though bank accounts controlled by United Trade. These transactions . . . have several indicia of money laundering."

United Trade also shows up associated with millions of dollars moved around various bank accounts in Eastern Europe, and all sorts of suspicious trading. There were indications that oil, wheat and magnets had been moved in and out of companies, most of them associated in some way with United Trade, but there was insufficient documentation to explain what it was all about.

The accountants found that Mogilevitch controlled a company in Budapest called Technology Distribution, which was the sales agent for United Trade. Woven around that was a web of other companies, at first glance independent of him, but ultimately all connected back to him through various interrelationships, such as shared addresses and shared directors. By having signature authority on various bank accounts—namely Technology Distribution's and United Trade's—it was then child's play for him to move product and money through all these companies and effectively make everything disappear.

Since the fall of YBM Magnex:

Crumax Magnetics was forced into receivership.

NCIS and SERCS were left to conclude that YBM Magnex had been created for one single purpose, "to legitimize the [Mogilevitch] criminal organization by the floating on the stock exchange of a corporation which consists of the UK and USA companies whose existing assets and stocks have been artificially inflated by the introduction of the proceeds of crime."

Both the FBI and the RCMP have alleged that there were links from Arigon back to Brandwain's old group in Brussels. U.S. Customs also suggested that the link exists and that it ties Mogilevitch into everything Brandwain was doing, including narcotics trafficking, money laundering, extortion, murder and the smuggling of stolen auto parts into the former Soviet Union.

And a man named Tamas Boros died.

On July 2, 1998, a car bomb, said to contain as many as twenty sticks of dynamite, exploded in the middle of a shopping district, killing Boros and three innocent bystanders. He'd been a well-known restaurateur in Budapest, owned a nightclub and was said to be cooperating with Hungarian police in an investigation of Semion Mogilevitch. No one has been charged with the four murders.

Israel's "Law of Return" is set in stone.

One of the founding pillars of the Jewish state, it guarantees the Diaspora that any Jew, from anywhere in the world, regardless of his country of birth, will be welcomed "home" and automatically provided with citizen-ship. Looking at how some Russians abuse that law today, it seems almost naive of the founding fathers to have enacted it quite the way they did.

In the earliest days of the state, 1949–50, there were somewhere between eight and nine hundred thousand Jews in Israel. Since then, there have been three main waves of Russians coming to Israel. In the 1970s, the immigrants were high-profile intellects and dissidents, rejected by the Soviets for their political views. And they were easily absorbed into Israeli society.

In the late 1970s and early 1980s, there was an influx that included many Russians from Georgia, and inside that group were some professional criminals. They ran extortion, gambling and prostitution rackets, but there was no one group, or even one person, that seemed to be in charge.

Then came the 1990s.

In the final decade of the century, over eight hundred thousand Russians have arrived in Israel. How many of them are really Jewish is anyone's guess. In many cases, they only stayed long enough to get their passport, then left and have never come back. It was this third wave that brought the Mogilevitches and the Mikhailovs and the Loutchanskys. It was this third wave that proved an Israeli passport was not just a window into the United States, it was an open back door.

Of course, not all of those non-Jewish Russians left the country. Police in Tel Aviv have drawn up a list of thirty local residents they believe to be organized criminals and only one is definitely Jewish. The problem with putting labels like that on people is that in Israel—a country where emo-tions about everyday, ordinary things already run strong—the issue of Russian immigration and organized criminality is emotional in spades.

A senior Israeli police intelligence officer explains, "Some people left Israel a long time ago because all they ever wanted from us was citizenship. Others never came back because we've been able to embarrass them. The ones who stayed did so because Israel does not extradite its citizens. That may be changed one day, but as of now, an Israeli can be indicted by a for-eign court and, in certain instances, can even be tried in Israel under that indictment. But they are not extradited. It essentially gives some of these Russian organized criminals a free pass to commit crimes outside Israel."

Decries one Russian Israeli, "If you took the same things said about us in this country and said them about Jews or blacks or any other ethnic minority in any other country, you'd probably be arrested."

As true as that might be, a 1997 investigation into how some Russian immigrants had avoided their obligatory Israeli military service uncovered a network of organized criminals, sixty-three of whom had entered the country with forged documents.

Still, politicians tread on such thin ice at their peril. As citizens, each of these recently arrived Russian immigrants votes. As their numbers have increased, so has their real political power.

Enter here the fourth horseman.

Gregory Lerner arrived in Israel as part of the third wave in 1990, at the age of thirty-nine, became a citizen and took the Hebrew name Zvi Ben-Ari.

A former journalism student at Moscow University, he'd supposedly hawked black-market razor blades to earn a living in the mid-1970s. By 1982 he'd worked his way up to fraud and had served two years in prison.

But by the time he got to Israel, he was telling people that he was a banker who'd been running a company called Lomus International. He said that under the Soviets, he'd been given government backing to establish commercial banks, that in 1988 they'd advanced him seventy million rubles in the form of a three-year loan, but in 1989—along with the first signs of the social and economic changes that were about to happen—some of his backers tried to call in his loan.

Again, this is his version of the tale.

While he was on a business trip to Austria, he said, the KGB set him up by raiding his offices, taking away all the paperwork that mentioned the loan and substituting in its place paperwork that did not mention the loan.

By 1992, he was living in Switzerland, running an import/export company. That's when the Swiss arrested him on a warrant from the Soviets and deported him back to Moscow.

It was the first and only time the Swiss ever honored an extradition request from the Soviets.

Back in Russia, he stood trial for embezzling funds, stealing his employees' salaries and taking bribes. When he left jail eighteen months later, he headed straight back to Israel.

Over the next few years, he went about building an empire of shell companies scattered around the world that, on the surface, appeared to justify the wealthy lifestyle he was living. By maintaining visibility, he created an aura around him that fooled a lot of people, including the press, which often referred to him as "Israeli millionaire Zvi Ben-Ari." At one point, a survey of Russian immigrants in Israel named him among the four most popular of their own. Eventually his name surfaced in the papers as a possible candidate for a Knesset seat. Secretly, the Israeli police suspected that Lerner had bought his way into Israel's Russian-language press. But they were never able to prove it.

What they now knew for sure, however, is that Lerner was connected to Solonik and also to Ivankov. The story they tell—one that remains unconfirmed by the FBI—is that the Bureau's wiretaps on Ivankov's phones in Brooklyn caught him talking to Lerner on several occasions. And that, after listening to conversations with, literally, thousands of people, Lerner is the only person who ever dared talk to Ivankov as an equal.

If it's true, it says something about Lerner.

If it's not, it says a lot about the image that Israeli law enforcement has of him.

In 1995, Lerner founded the Israeli-Russian Finance Company, in partnership with Russia's Promstroi Bank. Once he'd managed that, it was only a matter of time before the Bank of Israel finally granted him a limited permit to handle security transactions. That happened at the end of November 1995, but with the proviso that he could only deal in overseas funds controlled by nonresidents.

In other words, they didn't want him to become an Israeli banker. It was, at best, naïveté, at worse, sheer stupidity. In this day and age it doesn't matter where the bank physically is—it can be on the moon—as long as there's a way to wire money to it.

Although Lerner was never far from their radar screens, a formal investigation into his banking affairs was only opened by the Israelis the following year after a man purporting to have been his former partner field a complaint against him in Russia. The man claimed that Lerner had defrauded him. With help from law enforcement in Britain and the United States, the Israelis were able to take close looks at all those shell companies Lerner had sprinkled around the globe. There were companies in Panama, throughout the Caribbean, in Mauritius and Luxembourg.

But the one that caught everyone's eye was in Cyprus.

It was a bank.

Vienna has, since the end of World War II, been the historical pivot point between Russia and Israel. But secret banking, the availability of worthless shell companies and good weather prompted the Russians to make Cyprus their "bus station" into Israel.

Limassol has become a Mediterranean suburb of Moscow, St. Petersburg, Kiev and Tbilisi. What used to be an inexpensive fishing village has, thanks to the Russians, now joined the list of the world's fifty most expensive cities. Where once Saturday nights saw a few thousand drunk British package tourists raising hell, now there are twenty thousand Russians with offshore companies and laundered money in their bank accounts, Greek lawyers who speak Russian making themselves available as facilitators, and forged identity papers on sale to anyone with cash to pay for them.

In Cyprus, Russian birth certificates that show a Jewish mother can be purchased for under $5,000. Papers that show a Jewish name cost a little bit more.

Across the fence, still patrolled by United Nations troops, that cuts through Nicosia and divides the island into Greek and Turkish halves, the north side has also been washed with a wave of Russians. There are said to be 150,000–200,000 living there, some for the weather, others for the "safe passage" on offer, because Northern Cyprus is not recognized by, nor does it have extradition treaties with, any other country, except Turkey. No matter who you are, if the police in Istanbul don't want you, no one can bother you in Northern Cyprus.

And from either side, it's only a few hours on a plane to Israel.

The shell companies Lerner was using in his elaborate money-laundering scheme all revolved around that bank in Cyprus. Money coming out of Russia was going through the various shells to manipulate their balance sheets and eventually coming back through Cyprus.

What's more, the bank in Cyprus was being made available to Italian organized crime and the Colombian cartels to wash their money.

Lerner had become the mobs' banker.

At the same time, he was helping himself to more than his fair share, particularly of the monies he was procuring through his Promstroi Bank partnership in Russia. Contracts were forged, then used to back loans from other Russian banks, which upped the balance sheets of his Israeli-Russian Finance Company, which helped to keep the Bank of Israel from looking at Cyprus.

Money needed to be brought into Israel—but by now, it looked spanking clean—because other Russian organized criminals were paying him to do their bidding there.

They needed him to buy influence.

There are some politicians who say that influence cannot be bought outright in Israel. There are others who maintain that it can. Lerner proved that, if nothing else, it's fairly easy to rent it.

Although campaign contributions to political parties are not permitted within nine months of an election, there are very few conditions restricting contributions to individual candidates. Anyway, in a society oriented toward cash—as the entire Middle East traditionally is—it's little wonder that in recent elections men like Lerner have offered bribes to politicians. When one party refused his cash outright, he volunteered to pay for its political broadcasts. That too was refused.

Although the story was initially denied, it now turns out that that Soviet dissident turned Israeli Trade and Industry Minister, Natan Sharansky, accepted $100,000 from Lerner. Sharansky insists the money was passed along to an organization that sponsors Russian Jews looking to emigrate to Israel.

It later came to light that Lerner also made approaches to, among others, former prime minister Shimon Peres.

The case opened a very sore point with Israeli police intelligence. A senior officer laments, "Political infiltration is a strategic threat to any nation. It is all the more critical in a country like Israel, where coalition governments are so fragile. We know of instances where certain Russian criminals actually debated whether or not to work their way into one of the two main parties or to target one of the smaller parties."

As early as 1996, Israel's chief of internal security, Moshe Shahal, had publicly raised serious questions about the nation's political safety. He claimed, "Elements of the Russian Maffiya are effectively trying to control Israel." He based his assessment on the political ambitions of fifty different organizations—likening them to American-style crime families—that the security services had identified. These groups, he believed, were branching out from prostitution, gambling and extortion to drugs and politics. "The gangsters are now trying to buy and influence politicians."

Shahal was widely criticized as a cowboy firing from the hip and insulting the sensitivities of Israel's Russian population.

One story floating around Israel is that organized Russian criminals are planning to spend in excess of $1.5 billion—some have put the figure as high as $4 billion—over the next few years to secure political power.

If Shahal is right, as there is every reason to believe he is, the ramifications are enormous.

For example, Israel does not have money-laundering laws. The reason why goes back to the Law of Return and the need the founding fathers perceived to remove all the bureaucratic stumbling blocks facing immigrants wishing to import capital. In other words, Jews seeking refuge in Israel should not be impeded by laws that would prevent, or even delay, them from being able to arrive with their assets.

"Anyone can bring money here," the police intelligence officer goes on, "put money into the banking system and no questions are asked. It makes Israel a prime vehicle for laundering dirty money. There is a feeling, now, that money-laundering laws will have to be implemented. Russian organized crime has a huge stake in preventing us from making changes. Now consider that coalition governments in Israel often hang on very thin majorities. A few votes either way by a minority party can have disproportional influence over the entire population. And yes, there is clear evidence that certain Russian immigrants have been seeking just that disproportional voice."

The single thing that currently keeps the Russians and others from turning Israel into one of the world's major sinks is that the economy is not large enough to accommodate the sums of money they would want to put through it. The problem is that as the economy has grown and, in the absence of money-laundering laws, drug trafficking has grown too.

There had been a few drug cases before 1995.

In a notable one, a ton of cocaine had been shipped from Venezuela to St. Petersburg. The drugs had been hidden in cans labeled as meat and the final destination had been Belgium. The shipment was discovered and the case has, ever since, been used as an example of the link between Russian organized crime and the Colombian cartels.

According to one Israeli source, however, the Russian involvement in the case came from Israel and had the backing of former KGB operatives. The Israelis tried to pursue it, but they could never get any evidence out of Moscow. The only compensation the Israelis could muster was that the drugs were never destined for Israel.

But the game changed in 1995 when heroin began showing up in the country.

Asian heroin, known as "rock heroin," comes into Israel from Holland. Turkish heroin comes in through Lebanon. At the same time, a marijuana problem developed in the Sinai Peninsula, and coke now arrives in worrisome quantities from Latin America.

Russian-Israeli organized crime is suspected to be at the heart of it, but that doesn't necessarily mean that any of the traffickers are living in Israel.

Lerner was arrested by the Israeli police on May 12, 1997, at Ben Gurion Airport, just as he was stepping onto a plane for the United States. He had $50,000 in cash on him plus two satellite telephones. At his various homes—he owned six villas and three apartments—they found a further $400,000 in cash, an unlicensed rifle and forged passports.

They wanted him for fraud and bribery. They wanted to discuss with him the murder of several Russian bankers and the attempted murder of a senior banker at Promstroi Bank. And they also wanted him because the Russians were accusing Lerner of having stolen $85 million from them.

He spent ten months in jail, most of them denying his guilt. While he was stuck there, more than 120 investigators worked on his case. They interviewed three Israeli government ministers and seven members of the Knesset. By that time, they'd built a strong enough case against him that he agreed to a deal.

In exchange for a guilty plea to thirteen charges, including fraud and attempted bribery, the prosecutors dropped their investigation into murder and attempted murder, fined him 5 million shekels ($1.4 million) and sent him away for six years.

It makes him the only one of the four horsemen temporarily out of circulation.

Concludes the police intelligence officer, "The fact that criminals not living in Israel were able to get someone inside the Ministry of Interior to facilitate passports for them, the way Mogilevitch did, shows how inefficient our warning systems are. This is not really about Russian immigrants and street crime, this is about upper-level organized criminals. This is about men who are connected to each other through culture, language and businesses, who are always looking for new opportunities and enterprises. They don't have a sense of humor. They see everything as black or white, friend or foe. There is no gray. They have no fear. They have no shame. Only Lerner is here."

The others are alive and well in the rest of the world.

7

BANKING IN NEW YORK

I want to offer a big deal to Proctor & Gamble. I want to make deter-gent soap. The name will be "Mogilevitch." Mogilevitch guarantees that this washes everything, from underwear to money.

—SEMION MOGILEVITCH, to the *New York Times*

B ILKING THE SYSTEM HAD BEEN THE NATIONAL SPORT of the Soviet Union.

When Communism disintegrated and a fledgling, quasi-democratic, kind-of-capitalistic Russia slowly tried to extract itself out of the quick-sand that had been life under the Soviets, the people carried with them into this new world their cynicism, their deep-seated distrust of all things official and their well-honed instincts for self-preservation.

Privatization was strictly a Western concept. Corruption was what they understood. Their right to steal was inalienable.

They'd learned their lessons well in the rigid world of the forced econ-omy. Standing on-line for hours to buy whatever might be at the end of that line was how they'd paid their dues. Now, in the sudden freedom of the 1990s, it was as if the rules had vanished with their rulers.

Everything was for sale.

And anything that couldn't be bought could at least be filched.

Companies, overtaxed and burdened by extortion, produced docu-ments to show that they were importing something. In order to pay for the goods, they needed to transfer money out of the country. Like contrails in the sky marking the paths of high-flying jets, there are, these days, literally thousands of money trails coming out of Russia. That the corresponding goods never arrive back in the country surprises no one.

One of the most popular destinations for this mass capital flight is Great Britain. In addition to modern financial facilities provided throughout the city of London, Britain offers fashionable real estate to live in, expensive private schools for Russian children, art and antiques to be bought at auction, elite shopping and lax money-laundering laws.

By 1995, the influx of Russian capital had become so great that the city of London Police set up a specialized Financial Investigation Unit specifically to look at capital flight. Since then, they've carried out an average of fifteen major investigations per year. The crimes they look at average $3–4 million, and while not all of those crimes involve Russian-sourced money, most of them do.

The Russians easily took advantage of London as a pivotal point linking Moscow with the Channel Islands, the Caribbean, Cyprus and Israel. A few years ago the Russian financial newspaper *Kommersant* noted, "Tens of millions of dollars have left the former Soviet Union, specifically bound for Britain."

By now, the figure is into the tens of billions.

In one case, British police intelligence officers had indications that three people in England had laundered $50 million for a Russian organized crime group. But intelligence information is not the same as hard evidence which can be presented to a jury, and no prosecutions resulted.

In another case—this one still ongoing—a police constabulary fraud squad noticed two Britons living in a rural part of the country marketing promissory notes on behalf of a former Soviet state-owned industry. The men were approaching various European banks looking to discount the notes. Initially, investigators believed they were either dealing in forgeries, or that the notes behind the trades were somehow fraudulent. But the notes were real. And the scheme turned out to be very sophisticated.

Among the earliest transactions, one had a face value of $2.7 million and was purchased by a major British bank. Another, worth $5 million, was taken up by a British-based company which appears to be legitimate, although investigators aren't totally sure. A third, for $4.3 million, had been sent through Britain to a subsidiary of the main company in Russia. Another, for $8 million, was picked up by a major Swiss bank. The funds these men received were then moved into overseas accounts. For their efforts, records showed what looked like commissions ranging from $30,000 to $80,000 per transaction.

That's when a second circuit appeared. This was money coming out of St. Petersburg and going into a British company which purported to be in a very specific industry, while in reality, it turned out to be nothing more than someone's back bedroom.

Soon there was a third circuit. Money was being moved through a Moscow–Antwerp connection. Police were able to trace $200,000, but have yet to find out anything more about it.

Next, a British–Cyprus link came to light. Payments of up to $500,000 at a time, plus several of $30,000 and at least one of $170,000, have gone through there. One theory is that this was a circuit designed specifically to handle the two Britons' commissions.

Following that, additional monies came into a British company controlled by the two men. There were payments from a foreign bank in the City of London for $165,000; from a Swiss Company for $500,000; from a company that may or may not exist—police still aren't certain—for $500,000; from one of several Isle of Man companies apparently controlled by one of the two Britons, for $180,000; and from a company in Moscow, which may or may not represent a legitimate business dealing, for $160,000. Some of this money left the British company for distribution elsewhere, notably $5.9 million which was purported to be payment to a U.S.-registered company that, police claim, does not exist.

More promissory notes continued to appear—including one for $11 million and another for $25 million—which were picked up by a company in the Middle East seemingly linked to the two Britons. One of the two has further associations with a second company in the Middle East, which in turn has associations with a company incorporated in the United States but which has bank accounts in one of the Baltic states. Police have traced nearly $6 million going through that link.

They've also uncovered an "arrangement" between the formerly state-owned company in Russia and a foreign company which is linked to one of the two Britons, and records there indicate movements of $8 million.

Enter now a U.S.-based businessman associated with both men in Britain and a man in Moscow whose name appears on the privatized company's contracts. It is believed that several payments have been made directly to accounts in the States which the first man has then invested on someone's behalf in legitimate American business ventures. By the time this money is deposited back into the bank accounts of whoever it is in Moscow authorizing the systematic pillage of that particular company, the income arising from those investments will appear perfectly clean.

Lucy Edwards is a slight woman with dark hair who was born in Leningrad in 1958 with the name Lyudmila Pritzker. One night when she was nineteen, she went to a club, met an American merchant marine named Brad Edwards and, within a matter of days, married him. That got her out of the Soviet Union.

She moved with her husband first to Illinois, then to Colorado. They had a daughter, but the marriage broke up in 1988. She then made her way to New York and found work with the Bank of New York (BoNY) as a teller.

That was the same year that BoNY bought Irving Trust, an old, established Manhattan-based financial institution that had been actively pursuing business in Eastern Europe. Because timing in life can count for so much, within a few years, the native–Russian speaker Edwards was working in the bank's newly formed Eastern European Division.

Money was hemorrhaging out of the former Soviet Union by the ton, and banks around the world were racing eastward to soak up as much of it as they could. BoNY was especially aggressive. They courted business wherever there were Russians with money to court, and raided other banks to take business away from them. For Russians in business back home, all this was like being a saloon keeper in the Wild West when all the cattle drivers rode into town. It was a wide-open seller's market. British and American banks, especially those with offices on both sides of the Atlantic, held a special attraction because it made the task of moving money out of Russia and into the West all the easier.

With so much money flying around—and so much money to be made by banks that could provide the right services—Russian-speaking bankers holding work permits in London and New York were at a premium.

One of the managers Edwards now reported to was a Russian-born woman, three years her senior, named Natasha Gurfinkel. She was also married to a Russian, Konstantin Kagalovsky, who was just taking up his post as his country's representative to the International Monetary Fund. Kagalovsky and his financier chum Mikhail Khodorkovsky shared business interests in a Russian bank called Menatep, and Kagalovsky was, for a time, vice chairman of that bank. But Menatep got itself into financial trouble, which was quickly compounded by its interest in the totally crooked European Union Bank of Antigua.

Paperwork filed at the time suggested that EUB was an offshore subsidiary of Menatep. EUB's majority shareholder seems to have been Alexander Konanykhine, a man apparently wanted in Russia on charges of embezzlement—it is said he stole $8.1 million from the Exchange Bank in Moscow in 1992—and who was, at the time that the charter was granted in Antigua, in prison in the States for having violated his visa conditions. Nevertheless, the government allowed EUB to open its doors. Or, better put, to open its Web site.

In reality, the bank didn't exist in Antigua, or anywhere else for that matter, just cyberspace. Its only presence was on the Internet.

The bank was chartered to open accounts, take deposits, take orders for credit cards and wire money anywhere in the world twenty-four hours a day. Its Web site pitch read, "Since there are no government withholding or reporting requirements on accounts, the burdensome and expensive accounting requirements are reduced for you and the bank."

Naturally, EUB claimed to maintain the strictest standards of banking privacy, reinforced by the claim—somehow made with a straight face—that Antigua was a serious financial center with serious penalties for anyone violating its serious banking-secrecy laws. Shortly after EUB went on-line, the Bank of England warned the U.S. Federal Reserve Bank that while Menatep was denying any involvement in EUB, Konanykhine had asked the Antiguans to keep Menatep's involvement in EUB a secret.

Among the many things not publicly disclosed was that EUB's computer server, which effectively was the bank, was located in Washington, and that the man operating the computer server, who was effectively the banker, happened to be in Canada. How much money was ultimately funneled through the bank—washed by Russians for other Russians and, as well, for some of their Latin American drug-trafficking friends—is not known. Nor will it ever be. Because one day in mid-1997, just like that, someone unplugged the server. That was the last anyone ever heard of the depositors' money. Upwards of $12 million disappeared.

By his own admission, Khodorkovsky was a director of the European Union Bank, but "only for one week in 1994." According to one well-placed source, business links have been traced between Khodorkovsky's Menatep and another now largely defunct Moscow-based financial institution called Inkombank. Both Menatep and Inkombank are said to have had "active relationships" with BoNY.

It turns out that Inkombank was one of several clients brought to BoNY by Natasha Gurfinkel. She wrenched it away from rival Republic Bank. It was a much heralded coup, and by 1995 Inkombank was BoNY's largest generator of fee income, making BoNY the most important clearing bank in Russia for domestic transactions. It was later alleged that Republic had filed at least one suspicious-activity report about Inkombank with federal regulators and wasn't terribly upset to see Inkombank take its business elsewhere.

With all this going on in the background, Edwards and Gurfinkel surrounded their working relationship with a natural friendship. Edwards saw in Gurfinkel a woman educated in the States who was starting to live the American dream of success and wealth. Gurfinkel saw in Edwards an associate who had the energy, the drive and the skills to help her turn BoNY into the major player in Russia.

Within a year of taking on her new assignment, Edwards remarried. She'd met a recent arrival in the States, Peter Berlin, a molecular physicist from Moscow. A slim, bearded man, he was living in New Jersey, trying to set up an import-export company. It is unclear what his immigration status was when he got to the States, but by marrying Edwards—who was an American by virtue of her first marriage—Berlin was able to obtain U.S. citizenship.

The two lived in New Jersey. Berlin worked out of their apartment, which was the registered address for his company, Benex, while Edwards worked her way up the ladder at BoNY. Before long he was brokering sales of electronic goods to Russia. While running this phase of his business, it is believed, he was asked by some of his clients to provide false invoices on the back of which they could move money out of Russia.

He had the means of facilitating the movement of funds.

His wife had access to a bank that could be used.

The couple left New Jersey for a new house in Narrowsburg, New York, a few hours north of Manhattan, along the Pennsylvania border. It was only years later that reports would surface to suggest they'd already worn out their Garden State welcome. Allegedly, in 1992, Edwards was arrested for theft in a New Jersey department store and pleaded guilty. Apparently, she was arrested a second time for the same offense two years later and again pleaded guilty. Berlin has also been arrested, reports say, having been nabbed for shoplifting in 1993. Charges against him were said to have been dropped.

What happened next seems to be that, in the very early months of 1996, Benex International opened an account at BoNY's Wall Street headquarters. Six months later, a company called Becs International also opened an account at the BoNY branch. Bank records are said to show that Lucy Edwards was listed as a Becs employee and had a signature authority on the account.

Unaware of her involvement with Becs and/or Benex—none of that came to light until late 1998, although BoNY admits it should have prompted questions immediately—the bank promoted Edwards to vice president and assigned her to its London offices, specifically to seek out new Russian business. Also by this time, Berlin had moved into an office in the most unlikely of financial centers, Forest Hills.

A short ride from both La Guardia and Kennedy Airports, Suite 612 at 118-21 Queens Boulevard is one room which had been leased to a company called Torfinex Corp. It was also home to General Forex Corp and Tofex Corp.

And that's where they all might be today—Edwards and Berlin, commuting between London and Forest Hills; Gurfinkel and Kagalovsky, moving on to the next stage of their trek through the American dream—had it not been for a scam in Canada and a kidnapping ransom in San Francisco.

Britain's National Criminal Intelligence Service was investigating the YBM Magnex scandal, trying to unravel Semion Mogilevitch's offshore empire. One of many shell companies they'd stumbled across was called Benex. At first glance, it looked like just another empty shell through which money flowed. Benex was using an account at the Bank of New York, which didn't seem out of the ordinary either, because shell-company accounts pop up all the time at legitimate banks. But when the NCIS officers took a much closer look, they couldn't believe what they saw.

The amount of money going through the account was staggering.

During just one six-month period, for instance, no fewer than ten thousand transactions had moved $4.2 billion!

The Brits alerted the Americans and dossiers were opened at the Manhattan District Attorney's office.

Around the same time, the Russian police had asked the FBI for help in a kidnapping case. A $300,000 ransom had been paid to secure the release of a Russian named Edouard Olevinsky. The Bureau traced the payment through the victim's bank in San Francisco. It had also gone through accounts at the Bank of New York and the Sobin Bank in Moscow. That didn't raise any suspicions either, at least not until they heard about "unusual transfers" coming through accounts held at BoNY by Peter Berlin that were also, according to one source, "popping up elsewhere." Presumably that means either Olevinsky's bank in San Francisco, Sobin Bank in Moscow, or both.

A dossier was soon opened at the U.S. Attorney's office for the Southern District of Manhattan.

Suddenly two U.S.-based investigations and one in Britain became the largest international money-laundering inquiry in history.

As this was just taking off, sometime around the end of 1997, the Department of Justice Asset Forfeiture and Money Laundering Section, in conjunction with the U.S. Attorney in Boston, launched a suit to recover $7 million in money-laundering proceeds from four foreign banks. The government claimed that from 1985 to 1987, a man named John E. Fitzgerald—principal laundryman for a New England marijuana-smuggling cartel—had deposited this money in accounts held by the traffickers on the Caribbean island of Antigua. Fitzgerald had already pleaded guilty to moneylaundering offenses and a U.S. court had already ordered the money in those accounts to be forfeited to the United States. Shortly thereafter, according to the Justice Department, one of the named banks—Swiss American Bank—had transferred $5 million out of the traffickers' accounts and into an account held by the government of Antigua. The remaining funds had also been moved, into accounts held by SAB itself.

The other banks named in the Justice Department's attempt to reclaim this money were the Swiss American National Bank of Antigua, the Swiss American Holding Company SA of Panama and Inter-Maritime Bank of Geneva.

Even though a federal judge dismissed the case against the four banks for lack of jurisdiction, alarm bells were now starting to sound. Inter-Maritime, officially known as Bank of New York–Inter Maritime, was the brainchild of a mysterious man named Bruce Rappaport. And he was someone a lot of people had been interested in for a very long time.

Described by the *New York Times* as "a Swiss banker who has had brushes with governmental investigators," he started Inter-Maritime in 1966. The bank now employs around ninety people. Considered small by Swiss standards and minuscule by global standards, its core business has always been private banking and investment management. It is said to manage assets in the low hundreds of millions of dollars. And while some of those assets are known to come from Russia, that, in and of itself, might not mean much. After all, it could hardly surprise anyone that financial institutions in Switzerland might be involved in helping Russians hide money.

Born in Haifa—then Palestine, now Israel—in 1923, Rappaport popped up regularly in Washington gossip back in the 1980s in connection with the Iran-Contra affair. It was said he'd been in the middle of a $10 million payment from the Sultan of Brunei to Colonel Oliver North, but that North had never received the money. Rappaport sternly denied any involvement. His name also came up in relation to the BCCI scandal. Apparently he'd had business dealings with a Middle Eastern shipping magnate who'd been financed by BCCI.

It must be said that Rappaport has never been prosecuted for any crime. Still, conspiracy-crazies continue to see his fingerprints on suspect deals around the world. Much of that probably stems from the fact that so little is publicly known about him and his business affairs. The two things most people can agree on are that Rappaport was a golfing partner of the late CIA director William Casey—that in and of itself keeps conspiracy theorists plenty busy—and that Rappaport has also maintained longtime relationships with government officials in Antigua.

Whether those relationships in Antigua are based on banking or real estate is mere conjecture. There is no denying that Antigua has thrived for several years as a Russian money-laundering haven. The government there is said to have once granted Rappaport a near monopoly on the local fuel-oil market. More recently, they manifested their affection for him by appointing Rappaport as Antigua's ambassador to Russia.

It has also been suggested that both Menatep and Inkombank had business relationships with Rappaport. But that he might have banking interests in Antigua—the same island where Konstantin Kagalovsky and Menatep had a relationship with the European Union Bank—is obviously just a coincidence.

Trying to pull all the facts together into a coherent case that could be taken to court—and suffering from the all-too-usual territorial squabbles between the Manhattan D.A.'s office and the nearby U.S. Attorney's office—investigators were able to determine that at the heart of their inquiry were at least eighty-seven thousand electronic transfers that had accounted for the movement of $15 billion. Some of them appeared to involve Russian companies evading taxes. Some of them appeared to link Benex with Russian organized criminals.

The New York Police Department, the Federal Reserve Board and the Comptroller of Currency were now also taking an interest in this. Before long, investigators were looking at banks and various financial relationships in more than fifty jurisdictions.

It was soon clear to everyone involved that in order to unravel this, full cooperation would need to be forthcoming from all of those jurisdictions, including—and especially—Russia. However, as one agent on the case notes, "None of us would care to be hanging by our thumbs waiting for that day to happen."

Almost certainly still unaware of law enforcement's interest in their business, the Gurfinkel-Edwards team worked well, playing on the fact that they were both Russian and both, in their own way, connected. The two women mined sources that other foreign banks had left untapped. Before long, one observer said, they were dealing with clients that other foreign banks had already turned down.

At the same time, Edwards and Berlin were also busy with their own agenda. They are said to have approached an American diplomat in Russia, looking for help in purchasing a former defense factory that they wanted to convert to civilian use. But just as the FBI was getting interested in that aspect of this case, intending to use the diplomat as an undercover operative, the *New York Times* broke the story of the enormous sums being washed through BoNY. And that ended any chance of getting inside this part of the Edwards-Berlin association.

For more than a month, from the middle of August 1999 until early

October, it was a front-page story, and it moved very quickly. Edwards was dismissed from BoNY. Gurfinkel resigned. Konstantin Gurfinkel denied any wrongdoing—everybody involved did the same thing—and the IMF grew concerned. Press reports suggested that some of the money funneled through BoNY had been IMF funds originally intended to keep the Russian economy afloat.

Edwards's and Gurfinkel's offices at BoNY were searched, documents removed and sealed. Their homes were searched as well. When British police raided Berlin's London apartment, they reportedly found business stationery imprinted with both Benex and Bank of New York logos.

When Berlin's office in Forest Hills was raided, four new companies came to light—Lowland Inc., Becs International LLC, Valcom Solutions Inc. and Intermedia Enterprises. Two of the original four companies based at that address, and at least one of the newly uncovered companies, had relationships with BoNY.

Police also discovered that the man named as a director of Torfinex, Aleksey Volkov, was a director of Sinex Corp., Sinex Securities and the Sinex Bank, a shell company granted a banking license in July 1996 by the highly suspect offshore Pacific Island jurisdiction of Nauru.

The first charges finally came down in early October. A federal grand jury in New York indicted Edwards, Berlin and Volkov. But none of this was for money laundering. The three were charged with running an illegal wire-transfer business in New York.

Not surprisingly, while all this was going on, the Bank of New York was making every effort to tell the world that they had been cooperating and would continue to cooperate fully with the investigation.

At this point, the chief culprit seemed to be Mogilevitch. Reuters now reported that in July, just before the Bank of New York scandal broke, he'd successfully sued a Hungarian television station for quoting the American media in labeling him one of the most dangerous criminals in the world. When the scandal hit the international press, Mogilevitch apparently decided that he didn't like the Hungarian weather anymore and returned to Moscow.

One story around Washington has it that the State Department—which never officially denies or acknowledges such things—put pressure on the Hungarians to do something about his presence there. The Hungarians were told that their continued harboring of Mogilevitch put relations with the U.S. at risk. Among other things, Budapest is home to a

U.S.-funded college for European law enforcement officers. For whatever reason, rather than extradite Mogilevitch to the States, Hungary permitted him to leave. Whatever he might have left behind—funds, businesses, associates—is still not clear. In any case, evidence seemed to suggest that Mogilevitch's links with Benex were just the tip of the iceberg. Many people were also speculating that he was somehow tied in to Inter-Maritime and possibly even to Rappaport himself.

But this was before anyone started drawing horseshoes.

If you draw a big letter U—just like a horseshoe—it's easy to see how this all played out.

At the top right, place the name Semion Mogilevitch. Under that, coming down the right side, as if connected through Benex, put the name Peter Berlin. Under him, toward the bottom of the horseshoe, goes his wife, Lucy Edwards. Sharing the bottom with her is her former boss, Natasha Gurfinkel. Rising up along the lower left side is Gurfinkel's husband, Konstantin Kagalovsky.

They're the obvious ones.

Now the names really become interesting.

Kagalovsky, as Russia's representative to the International Monetary Fund from 1992 to 1995, has been politically linked to a pair of former Russian prime ministers, Viktor Chernomyrden and Yevgeny Primokov, plus the two men who are said to have been the architects of Russian reform, Anatoly Chubais and Yegor Gaidar. Put their names in one group on the left side of the horseshoe, just above Kagalovsky. Come up another notch, and add the names of a pair of men with whom the previous four are all politically linked. These two are the éminences grises of Boris Yeltsin's presidency, Boris Berezovsky and Roman Abramovich.

Berezovsky is the multimillionaire businessman who, it has always been said, bankrolled Yeltsin since the beginning. Among his holdings are several Swiss-based financial-services companies, one of which handles the overseas financing of Russia's state airline, Aeroflot. In early 1999, an arrest warrant was issued in Moscow against Berezovsky, in connection with allegations of laundering money through the Aeroflot accounts. Charges were subsequently dropped. There have also been suggestions of financial links to Inter-Maritime and personal ones with Rappaport.

Abramovich, a man in his early thirties, is in the oil business and has direct ties to various Russian companies, including the second largest oil producer in the country, Yukos. Also count among the officers of Yukos Mikhail Khodorkovsky and Konstantin Kagalovsky.

Interestingly enough, Yukos hit the headlines just before the BoNY scandal did, when Khodorkovsky was accused of watering down the shares to bilk investors. He supposedly sold off most of Yukos's assets to offshore shell companies, which he and his cohorts allegedly control, in the Bahamas, the Isle of Man, the British Virgin Islands, Ireland, Cyprus, the Marshall Islands and, believe it or not, Niue. In the summer of 1999, Khodorkovsky was a guest on Primakov's private plane as they traveled together to the United States.

In addition to being one of Yeltsin's closest advisers, Abramovich is particularly close to Yeltsin's daughter, Tatyana Dyachensko, and is said to be her chief financial adviser. That ties him, as well, to Tatyana's husband, Leonid Dyachensko, who has had several well-publicized—possibly even dubious—business dealings with Berezovsky.

An oil trader by profession, Dyachensko—who accompanies his wife on regular lavish shopping sprees in Switzerland, where the couple are believed to pay for everything with a credit card in the name of a Swiss company with connections to BoNY—has since been named as beneficial owner of a $2 million bank account in the Cayman Islands.

The account is held in the local branch of the Bank of New York.

Furthermore, Dyachensko is linked to the Siberian Oil Company, otherwise known as Sibneft, which appears to be controlled by Abramovich as general director with Berezovsky as his silent partner.

The story there, more sinister than the rest, begins in the mid-1990s when the Kremlin decided to sell off control of the state-owned Omsk oil refinery. The director general of the refinery was very vocal in his opposition to the sale, and a week before the shares were put on the auction block, he was found floating facedown in a local river. The sale went ahead and Sibneft walked away with the shares. Sibneft then channeled its oil sales through a company in New York called Belka Energy and a company in Russia called Runikom. Dyachensko is widely believed to be behind the New York company.

So the horseshoe that starts with Semion Mogilevitch on the right side comes through the Gurfinkel-Edwards connection and then directly into Boris Yeltsin's family and circle of friends.

By coincidence, around the same time Congress was impeaching and trying Bill Clinton in the Monica Lewinsky affair, the Duma was debating the impeachment of Boris Yeltsin. Is it also by coincidence that Yeltsin was willing to work out a compromise, sources say, where he would have stepped down in exchange for immunity from prosecution for any and all unspecified crimes that might have been committed by anyone in his family?

The legislators refused. And in the end, Yeltsin—gambling that the impeachment effort would fail—stayed put and won.

These days, any accusations that tie the BoNY scandal to the Yeltsin inner circle put Kremlin spin doctors on overtime. When the allegations were first raised, they said this was a plot by Western media moguls, other Western businessmen and, especially, certain—albeit unnamed—Western politicians to discredit Russia. They then wheeled out the head of Russia's Central Bank to dismiss money-laundering charges as "far-fetched," although, to their chagrin, he later estimated that $1 billion a month leaves Russia.

Yeltsin himself continues to insist that all this has been invented specifically to humiliate him.

Oddly, his denials came on the back of legislation passed by the Duma which would have otherwise created Russia's first money-laundering statute. They'd written a law at the beginning of 1999 and Yeltsin had vetoed it. That autumn, they sent him a fresh version.

And he vetoed it a second time.

As pressure mounted on the Russians to act, they eventually did. While Russia was attacking Chechnya—which, if nothing else, served to keep money laundering and Yeltsin relatives off the front pages at home—prosecutors reluctantly embarked on a fishing expedition of Russian banks.

Little came of it.

By this time the Swiss were concerned that banks in their country were harboring some of this money. Still smarting from their initial denials of, and subsequent display of filthy hands from, Holocaust funds that had lain dormant in Swiss banks since the end of the war, they too embarked on a fishing expedition for dirty money.

Theirs was more ordered than the Russians' because they'd had a lot more practice at it.

Before long, part of the Swiss investigation centered on a Russian named Lev Chernoy, who had apparently "taken over" Russia's aluminum industry and was a partner in a Geneva-based company. Swiss prosecutors wanted to know more about Chernoy's business dealings, specifically with Boris Berezovsky. In turn, they suspected that Berezovsky had transferred $200 million in hard currencies out of Aeroflot accounts and into Switzerland. Both Chernoy and Berezovsky are said to have had close dealings with the Bank of New York.

All of this more than fills up the horseshoe. But the problem with horseshoes is that they don't connect at the top.

To make a horseshoe into an oval, you need to draw a curve from the top left—where the Yeltsin family and their political chums reside—to the top right, where Semion Mogilevitch heads this list.

Some people suggest that one candidate for having his name up there—the missing link, as it were—could be Grigory Loutchansky. He is believed to have had numerous dealings with Boris Berezovsky, is reported to have had a long standing business relationship with Chernomyrden—at least while Chernomyrden was head of the former state industry Gazprom, Loutchanksy allegedly facilitated deals and, the presumption is, capital flight through his Austrian-based Nordex—and is believed by law enforcement around the world to have done arms deals, notably surface-to-air missiles for Iraq, with Mogilevitch.

It has also been suggested that Loutchansky may have had legitimate business dealings with Inter-Maritime. Again, Loutchansky continues to insist that he is a legitimate businesssman.

In Geneva, Inter-Maritime officials steadfastly deny laundering money for Russian mobsters. While BoNY has held a 28 percent stake in Inter-Maritime since 1996 and, at one point, Rappaport owned nearly 8 percent of BoNY, they add that Rappaport's holdings have been reduced to below 5 percent. They insist that Rappaport's role is that of non-executive chairman; that he has some supervisory responsibilities but does not refer clients to the bank; that he has never brought business to the Bank of New York; that he is not involved with the day-to-day affairs of the bank; that neither he nor the bank has anything to do with any of this.

Rappaport also issued a statement insisting that he had no personal or professional dealings with any of the people or any of the companies named in reports of the affair.

Further clarification of Rappaport's business dealings with Russian nationals is hindered by his inaccessibility. Further clarification of Inter-Maritime's business dealings with Russian nationals is hidden behind Swiss banking secrecy, which, one official reminds an inquisitor, is written in stone: "Even if I wanted to tell you, which I don't, I'm not permitted to. It's illegal."

In October 1999, the U.S. House of Representatives Banking Committee called hearings on the BoNY scandal. Among the people asked to testify—because the Committee believed he had "material knowledge of these matters"—was Bruce Rappaport. He declined.

Since then, Lucy Edwards and Peter Berlin have been arrested in the U.S. and have pleaded guilty to several charges, including money laundering.

Enter here a new and even more worrying connection.

While investigating Yuri Essine and his export business, Italian authorities took an interest in Russian activities along the Adriatic coast. In particular, they wanted to know more about a possible Russian organized crime link with Italian organized crime in the city of Rimini.

A beach resort with a small pleasure-boat port at one end and a main promenade lined by hotels, apartment houses and fish restaurants, Rimini is also filled with nightclubs and travel agencies, many of them displaying signs out front written in Cyrillic.

Rimini turns out to be a city that nearly lost its way in the tourist battle against more fashionable resorts, so a few years ago the powers that be stumbled onto a gimmick. They promoted themselves to the Russians. They courted tourists from throughout the former Soviet Union—perhaps naively thinking that the average Russian could afford an Adriatic holiday—and wound up with a lot more than they bargained for.

Russians began arriving in droves. In fact, planeloads of Russians arrive every week. But these aren't tourists who sit on the beach and eat ice-cream cones. These are Russians on a shipping trip. They step off their chartered flights and are bused directly to a wholesale leather-goods market just outside of town. These are Russians carrying wads of brand-new $100 bills—they pay for everything in cash and ship purchases by the planeload back to cities across Russia.

Some of them may be legitimately working for an import/export business. But most of them are not.

The Russians who have invaded Rimini are believed by the Italians to be part of a huge money-laundering circle. They say it starts with drugs sold in Russia. The cash from there is washed through Rimini's leather wholesalers, who, it must be said, are more than happy to have this influx of cash and, in turn, tend to bank it in nearby San Marino, safely out of reach of Italian tax inspectors. The goods shipped back to Russia are sold in the new markets there by front companies and the profits generated are then reinvested in drugs.

That's one of the things that the Yuri Essine investigation revealed.

And while looking into this Russian-Italian connection, the Italians stumbled across a company called Benex.

Russian-Italian joint ventures ring alarm bells all over Italy.

These days, Benex and the Bank of New York and the possibility that the highest level of Kremlin players are somehow involved in this new game ring alarm bells that can be heard all the way back to the United States.

8

REMAPPING THE EARTH

The more open the world becomes, the more vulnerable people become to those who have organized and have weapons, information, technology and the ability to move.

—WILLIAM JEFFERSON CLINTON

THERE ARE MANY DIFFERENT KINDS OF MAPS OF THE EARTH. As kids in school we all knew the pull-down kind that hung just above the blackboard. It showed the United States in the very center of the world and the British Empire in pink so that everyone could plainly see how the sun never set on it. That's how we learned that the planet is divided into political boundaries.

Sometimes there was also a terrain map, with the continents in relief, so that we could trace the range of the Rocky Mountains from Colorado up to Alaska and then from Colorado down through Mexico and along the west coast of South America, almost to the very tip.

The older we got, the more complicated our maps got, like a great circle polar projection, which demonstrated that an airplane ride from Los Angeles to London takes you over Canada and not straight across the Atlantic via New York, the way it looks on that pull-down map at the top of the blackboard.

But it took classes in economics and geology and stuff like meteorology to get to maps of global relationships—plate tectonics or climate, vegetation or population—maps that divided the planet into languages, religions, standards of living, standards of education, sources of energy, mineral production, available transportation, actuary tables, public health or species of animals. Whatever the subject, somebody somewhere could draw a map of the world and assign colors to it to differentiate the haves from the have-nots.

Someday, someone will do that for transnational organized crime.

The colors will define spheres of influence.

But as soon as it's drawn, the map will be obsolete.

Austria shares borders with eight countries. The only other nation in the world that has more contiguous neighbors, besides Russia, is Germany. It borders on nine.

Now, if you redrew that map on the blackboard, shoving Austria and Germany together with most of their neighbors—forming a sort of Hapsburg Empire minus Spain—you could color that in bright red to show that, during the 1990s, this was the center of the transnational criminal empire. During the final decade of the century, this was where all the gangs came together.

A year after the Easter 1990 meeting at the City Club, Italians and Russians returned to Vienna, this time checking into the Marriott Hotel. And this time, the Austrian Ministry of Interior had been tipped off. They put agents into the hotel. But the Austrians didn't have legislation in place permitting them to do proper surveillance. They couldn't bug the rooms. So they were never able to establish who was there—people registered under false names—and specifically what was discussed.

However, as a direct result of that meeting, both the Austrian National Police and Vienna Police demanded new legislation that would permit them to carry out the proper surveillance of such meetings. They'd been fighting the politicians for years to get new laws. It was the Marriott gathering that cinched it for them.

Over the next few years, similar meetings were held around Europe—notably in Warsaw, Berlin and Prague—but they were irregular, the participants kept changing and intelligence was difficult to collect. When the European press cottoned on to the idea that mobsters were having conventions, meetings seemed to pop up everywhere. Sightings were reported in Gyoengyoes, Hungary, and in Beaune, France, and in the middle of the Mediterranean on chartered yachts, far from prying eyes. In a few instances, the Russian newspaper *Izvestia* even listed the topics that were being discussed—casino gambling in Moscow, relations with non-Russian gangs and murder—as if they were there covering the events.

No fewer than two dozen European crime-group conferences have been accounted for by the press over the period 1991–1999. Most of them took place. But a few of them probably didn't, at least not the way they were reported. It is highly unlikely, for instance, that Ivankov and the head of the Sicilian Mafia, Toto Riina, cohosted a meeting in a tiny rural French village, as one paper had it. There could have been some sort of meeting there, but Riina had been in hiding for decades and, in all probability, wouldn't have dared to leave Sicily, while the Brooklyn crowd would never have been permitted to cut the LCN out of the loop by going directly to Riina.

That said, during a homicide trial in France in the mid-1990s, in order to place the defendant at the scene of the crime, the police were forced to reveal two meetings which had taken place, both of which they'd surveilled. They claimed there were Russians, Italians, Colombians, Turks, Yakuza and Sun Yee On Chinese Triad. Accepting that it happened the way the French police said it did, a group like that could have discussed all sorts of criminal activity—the permutations are frightening—but it's a sure bet that, at some point, they talked about narcotics.

The global drug market in the 1990s proved more than big enough for everybody. By cooperating with one another, groups minimized their risk, eliminated competition and maximized profit. The Russians and Colombians formed strategic drug alliances at meetings in Vienna in 1991 and again in 1995. Subsequent conferences took place in the Caribbean, where the two groups continue to meet regularly on the islands of Aruba, St. Vincent and Antigua. One agreement has the Colombians bartering cocaine for distribution inside Russia, in exchange for whatever commodities they need. In a few instances, that's been Afghan heroin, which the Colombians market in North America. More often, however, it's surplus Soviet military equipment, especially helicopters and light aircraft, which the Colombians use to fly drugs around the world.

Further discussions have focused on the Russians' capacity for moving money around the world. Colombians have now started shipping drug cash back to Mother Russia for laundering. Deposited in Maffiya banks, the money is wired through centers such as Cyprus before being brought into the Western financial capitals—Zurich, London, Frankfurt, New York— and finally bedded down in the Caribbean. Intelligence sources believe that Russian-controlled Colombian drug money comes through the city of London to the tune of several million dollars per week.

The Russians and the Italians have also started doing joint ventures. When they sat down in Warsaw a few years ago to meet with Colombians and a group of smaller Eastern European traffickers, one result was a Russian marketing concession of Italian-refined heroin to gangs in Bratislava. Another was cocaine—paid for with heroin by the Italians— shipped from Peru to Moscow and from there to Poland.

Maintaining the relationship, two Russian-Italian-Colombian meetings took place at the Vienna Marriott. The first was in May–June 1994, the second the following year. Among the people known to have attended both are Sergei Mikhailov, Viktor Averin and a man named David Sanikidze. That second meeting happened just after news of Ivankov's arrest in New York. At some point, either before the Colombians arrived or after they left, the Russians discussed Ivankov's fate. If he was acquitted, worrying about his successor was moot. But if he was found guilty, they all had their own interests to protect. It was decided, in the event of a guilty verdict, that Sanikidze, a Georgian businessman, would go to New York to take over.

In all, the Austrian police have recorded some fifteen conferences in the city, mixing and matching groups: Russians from Moscow have met with Poles and Czechs; an Italian group from Milan has met with Russians and Hungarians; at the end of 1998, a delegation from the Ukraine showed up to speak with some Sicilians.

"They come to Vienna," explains Michael Sika, director general of the Austrian Interior Ministry and an expert on transnational organized crime, "for the same reason that spies came to Vienna during the Cold War. It's geographical. Austria is neutral turf. This is where the KGB met with the CIA. There is a certain tradition. They meet here to discuss deals in other countries, and by deliberately not committing crimes in Vienna, they hope to avoid police attention."

They come as businessmen. No fedoras. No violin cases. No obvious shoulder holsters. Just a lot of men in suits with attaché cases, looking more like accountants than anything out of Al Capone's Chicago.

"Take the Italians as a good example," says Sika. "Local police pressure has forced the Sicilians to seek new markets, to look further into Europe. They're especially prevalent now in Germany and the Czech Republic, where they do money laundering, prostitution and drug trafficking. Organized crime needs an ethnic base. Italian organized crime, in particular, only exists in countries that have a firm Italian community base. We don't have that in Vienna, so they come here to meet, not to commit crimes."

There are, he says, three types of so-called organized international criminal groups:

"The first is a Mafia, a group with a strong hierarchy and structure, with central control and discipline, with technical experts, legal experts, business experts. Then there is a quasi-Mafia, a group based on a family structure, such as the Camorra or Hell's Angels. Finally, there are groups like the Russians. No real structure. They cooperate for only one or two crimes, then go their own way. And when they form these alliances with other groups, that's the kind of entity they create."

Which, he insists, is precisely what makes them both so dangerous and so difficult to police.

"When the crime is over, they disappear. They form another alliance for the next crime. Conspiracy used to be cooperation of two or three people for a long time. This definition no longer holds, because the conspiracy is only just long enough to do a crime. That's why I don't call this organized crime, we call it professional crime. It's fluid, always moving. The Sicilian Mafia and the Camorra are static. The Yakuza is static. The Russian gangs are static. But the alliances they form are fluid."

Even though the Austrian police knows that these alliances are being formed in Vienna, Sika unhappily concedes that there is very little they can do about it.

"It's no crime for them to meet here. It's true that conspiracy to commit a crime in another country is a crime in Austria. But proving it is the problem. The conspiracy is hatched in Vienna, but the crimes are committed in Germany, the money is sitting in the Cayman Islands, the Italians are in Sicily and their Russian partners are living in Hungary. The only way to stop that is through solid international cooperation among police."

He notes that while Austria has a very good relationship with the Italian police, they find it impossible to have the same with Russians, Czechs, Hungarians and Slovaks.

"Whenever you deal with police in the East, there is always a lingering suspicion about them. I wouldn't say they're all corrupt, although the Russians are and the Czechs can be. Hungary is better than Slovakia, but neither are great. Police officials change too often. It's difficult to know who to trust, difficult to build up any sort of long-term relationship, because a year later those people have been moved on to another job. We have real problems establishing genuine trust."

It was long believed by law enforcement in the English-speaking world that Vienna's main appeal was as a money-laundering center. The presence of the infamous *sparbuch*—a bearer passbook savings account that guarantees anonymity—helped to create just such a reputation. And the Austrians' staunch refusal to end *sparbuch* fuels the fire.

The Financial Action Task Force—the anti-money-laundering advisory established in Paris by the G-8 group of nations—has reproached Austria for not doing away with it. The European Union claims that Austria is in breach of its money-laundering rules by maintaining it. A few years ago, the Italians staunchly objected as they watched traditional Mafia money move from Switzerland and Liechtenstein to less obvious financial centers, such as Vienna and Salzburg. In a formal report, the Anti-Mafia Commission in Rome complained, "Austria absorbs illegal money from all over the world like a sponge."

But *sparbuch* remains, although some banking rules have been updated. Banks are now obligated to report sums over 200,000 schillings ($15,500); *sparbuch* is only available to Austrians—needless to say, there are ways around that—and cash deposits in excess of 100,000 schillings have to be explained to a banker's satisfaction.

There is no doubt that *sparbuch* continues to be used to some extent by criminals, but its too cumbersome to be a primary device. To open fifty or sixty accounts—which is what it would take to put large sums through the system—would be difficult, if not impossible.

That's why Russian groups and Italian groups have formed Austrian companies. There are literally thousands of them on the register. On close inspection, none of them show any business activity. They're used for nothing more than moving money into the Caribbean or just next door to Liechtenstein and Switzerland.

That's why Asian organized groups have opened restaurants. There are 550 Chinese restaurants in Vienna. Police report that out of those, perhaps fifty have enough customers to sustain a regular business. The other five hundred appear to have no legitimate source of income. The money coming through the tills belongs to Asian organized crime groups, and increasingly, to Russian and Italian groups who are paying the Asians to wash their money.

As Vienna Police Commissioner Peter Stiedl puts it, money coming through Austria these days is no longer black, it is gray.

"That's become a real problem for us. The crimes that produce the funds are not committed here, so investigating them is difficult. In 1989, when the Communist governments of Eastern Europe crumbled, many people who had access to funds brought them to Austria. Some of that money was quickly moved out of the country, but it wouldn't have mattered what happened to it because we had no mechanisms prior to 1992 to freeze accounts, no way to get inside those accounts. We knew the money was here but didn't know the source of it. That's been changed. However, it's still difficult for us to do anything about this gray money because there is almost no police cooperation with anyone in the Eastern bloc. If someone commits a crime in the former Soviet Union, we need information about that crime. Someone has to tell us that the funds here have been created by a crime. But we can't get that information out of the Russians. So there's not much we can do from our end about the money here."

To guarantee that the welcome mat will always be out, the groups have created what might be called a *Pax Viennoise*. And it is clearly visible. Along the Danube in Budapest, there are sixty to seventy organized-crime-related homicides a year. In Vienna, over the five-year period from 1994 to 1999, there have been three.

Achmedov Hodscha was a fixer. He combined a talent for being at the center of Russian activity in Vienna with good connections back in Moscow. It put him in a position to do favors around Vienna for other Russians. But he was never tied in to the big guys. He was a petty player who found he could earn a living as an exporter of spare auto parts and a smuggler of prostitutes. He sent the spare parts to the Czech Republic and Slovakia and brought the women in from Rumania and Bulgaria.

He had to pay his suppliers in Eastern Europe 10,000 deutsche marks for each woman he "bought" from them. His clients in Vienna fronted him.

In 1994 they paid up front for nine women. The people in Eastern Europe gave him extended terms. He jilted them both. There was no way he was ever going to get away with it, and it's amazing he ever thought he could.

On the night of September 19, 1994, the thirty-four-year-old was in front of his house when he spotted some guys coming down the block. He must have recognized them, because he ran to his car and tried to get it started. They put eleven shots through the window with a machine pistol. The killers—whether they were acting for his Austrian clients or the Eastern European suppliers—were never caught.

It was nearly two years before the next one.

Israel Laster was a hustler. Born in Poland in 1928 and very much a part of the old Russian community that lived around Mexicoplatz, he dealt in whatever he could: sometimes arms, sometimes counterfeit goods, including currency. He had a police record and was well known to the cops, but he wasn't connected to anything major. He was strictly small-time.

On June 16, 1996, he was shot by a Bosnian man who'd pretended to be a house painter. At first, the gunman told the police that he'd killed Laster because Laster hadn't paid him for painting his apartment. It didn't sound right to the murder squad. They suspected that the Bosnian had been hired by an organized group outside Austria, possibly because of a weapons deal that somehow touched on the former Yugoslavia. But the Bosnian never said anything else.

Exactly three weeks later, just two days after Ivankov was convicted in Brooklyn Federal Court, two men murdered David Sanikidze. The figure-head front for Orbis, Georgia's state airline, Sanikidze owned a company called ABV which, among other things, owned hotels in Russia. He also controlled a construction company in Vienna, developed real estate in Florida and was a close personal friend of Georgian president Eduard Shevardnadze.

He was Ivankov's business partner in several criminal activities, although he was never thought to be a *vory* himself. A man with contacts in high places, he had access to people that Ivankov never could have met and provided him with something that he could never have otherwise had—respectability. Both stashed shell companies and money in Austria. Sanikidze was also a surrogate father to one of Ivankov's sons who lived in Vienna.

At first, the police were certain that organized crime was behind the killing. They learned about a deal in France that was worth $170 million. Money had been transferred to New York for Ivankov and Sanikidze. But another group claimed they were owed a part of it and demanded their share. It's possible that when it wasn't forthcoming, they looked to the two principals to get it. With Ivankov out of circulation, Sanikidze became the prime target. So the motive was business.

The two men arrested for the shooting had another story. A fellow named Richard Dzhavakhadze was the chief of security at Sanikidze's ABV Hotel in Tbilisi. He'd been on the take, big-time. Sanikidze caught him at it and demanded to be repaid. When he wasn't, Sanikidze ordered his murder. In May, the contract was carried out in Moscow. One of the two men who killed Sanikidze was Richard's son, Popov. So the motive was straight-forward revenge.

But the second man—the one there with Popov—had his own reasons. He was Grigory Oniyani, the brother of a powerful Georgian gangster who just happened to be Sanikidze's primary rival. So the motive was business too.

The press heralded the case as a wake-up call, to remind politicians that organized crime was a reality in Austria. At the same time it put men like Mikhailov and Averin on notice that, even in the safe city of Vienna, they weren't totally safe.

"They can never be safe anywhere in that business," says Max Edelbacher, chief of the Serious Crimes Squad of the Vienna Police. "But they appear to be safer here than elsewhere. They come for two reasons. Eastern Europeans have traditionally used Vienna as a staging post between Moscow and Tel Aviv. And they come here because of our banking secrecy. We found that more than forty percent of the suspicious cash transactions reported by our banks involve funds from the Eastern bloc countries. But they are generally careful not to commit crimes here. The Russians in Vienna don't even work extortion of other Russians, the way they do in Brooklyn. They use Austria to launder their money and for recreation."

He believes that transnational organized crime groups generally migrate in three stages. Initially, they introduce themselves into a country, bring money, set up businesses and buy real estate. Next, they move soldiers into the country to protect their businesses. In the final stage, they try to take over the local organized crime groups and impose their will.

"We may be in the second stage in Austria," he goes on. "So far they like the hospitality, they like the banking conditions and they're trying to stay invisible. But we've observed that the leaders are leaving Austria and going to the south of France. That has created a vacuum for younger groups to move in. They're doing joint ventures with the local Austrian criminals, bringing in girls for the brothels and smuggling aliens. They also smuggle art. They steal it in Poland and the Czech Republic, get it into Vienna, then sell it throughout the rest of Europe. So far, they're staying quiet. We are starting to see some minor operational disputes here. If they lose control, or if other groups try to elbow their way in and turn the rest zone into a crime zone, then everything will change. But if the murders don't escalate, and they haven't so far, then that means somewhere a deal has been struck."

Sika agrees. "The Russians buy property here. Not just in Vienna but throughout the country. They come here because this is a pleasant country. They come here because it's safe for them. And the reason it's safe for them is because they don't commit crimes here."

He says that Mikhailov still has connections in Vienna. Viktor Averin is believed to be living full-time in Budapest, but his family is in Vienna and he apparently spends weekends there. Mogilevitch maintains connections in Vienna as well.

"He is a dangerous and important man," Sika confirms. "We believe he is protected by the Hungarians and by the Russians. He doesn't come here often, as far as we know, but if he did come to Vienna, he wouldn't be arrested. There is no international warrant for him at this time."

In Germany, Russian criminals are responsible for one third of all crimes. They deal in drugs, arms, prostitution, computer fraud, extortion and auto theft. Working out of Berlin, they launder money through more than two hundred gambling parlors they own or control. They smuggle illegal immigrants across borders and radioactive materials too.

Surrounding all this is an extreme level of violence. "Crimes are being committed with a brutality that we have not seen before," says one German law enforcement official. He adds, not for attribution, "We're five to ten years behind the criminals. We're only starting to put in place means to come to grips with them now."

When the Kremlin agreed to pull Russian soldiers out of East Germany, those same soldiers decided they suddenly faced a bleak future. The command and control element of the army had all but broken down and without the state to help feed their families, many of them took the opportunity of their final year or so in Germany to build a nest egg. They quickly put together a huge black market in everything they could steal, from cigarettes to Kalashnikov rifles. From there, they branched out to stolen cars—BMWs and Mercedeses taken off the streets of Berlin at night, loaded into military aircraft and delivered within hours to their organized crime partners in Moscow, who just as quickly sold them to the only people in Russia who could afford such luxuries, other organized criminals. While all of this was going on, the German police could do little more than watch. Surveillance cameras were set up outside Russian bases. They saw the cars being driven onto the bases and then being air-freighted out, but without legal authority to enter the Russian bases, they were helpless. Of course, they tried setting up roadblocks to prevent the cars from entering the bases. But the Kremlin officially objected every time they tried to seal off a base, and the business flourished. The problem was not solved when the Russians finally closed those bases. Many of the soldiers, now well connected to organized criminal groups, simply moved east, establishing operations in Hungary, Poland, Slovakia and the Czech Republic, where Russian ties to the former Communist states were still very strong.

Now, instead of relying on military immunity, they live in the former Soviet satellites, protected the by long-established corruption of the political and legal system. Compounding matters, there is more money involved and, thanks to improved communications and ease of travel across the German border, the systematic bilking of the country is rife.

Expensive autos are still regularly stolen off German streets and raced across the border, mainly into Poland, where they are either sold for cash, which is fed back into drug trafficking and arms dealing, or traded for young girls who are smuggled back into western Europe—Germany and Holland are prime targets—and held as white slaves for prostitution.

The world has never been so small.

Russian gangs run prostitution rackets in Paris, cooperate with Colombian cartels to launder money through *bureaux de change* and are

believed to have invested with some Italian gangs in businesses along the
Riviera. Asian organized criminals are using their traditional base in
Holland to ship amphetamines to groups in Australia, which include
Lebanese, 'Ndraghenta and Romanian. Czech mobsters have forged alliances
with criminals in the Middle East to assure a constant supply of heroin,
which they then move through Austria into Germany, France and, increasingly, Britain. Some of these same Middle Eastern criminals—usually
Lebanese—have become middlemen, linking Eastern European criminals
with Balkan drug-trafficking organizations.

Once, drugs from Turkey, Afghanistan and Pakistan traveled freely
through the former Yugoslavia, trucked in and out on the way into Western
Europe by Turks and their ethnic Albanian partners. Slobodan Milosevic
put a stop to all that. Not because he wanted to keep drugs out of what's
left of Yugoslavia, he just wanted to keep out the Turks' and Albanians'
drugs. Cutting them off meant choking the currency supply that the
Kosovo Liberation Army was using to pay for their weapons. And anyway,
there were plenty of other criminal gangs who'd pay handsomely for such
transshipment privileges.

Closing the Balkan route forced the Turkish and ethnic Albanian traffickers to sidestep Serbia and move through Bulgaria, Romania, Hungary
and into the Czech Republic. From there, heroin is divided into parcels
destined for Switzerland, Germany, France and Great Britain. The hard
currency these gangs earn in the West is spent in the East on weapons. They
buy from Russian organized criminals and Abkhazi separatists in northern
Georgia, or do deals directly with them, swapping heroin for weapons.
Whatever it takes to assure the traffic of arms back to the Balkans.

Closing the Balkan route also opened a trafficking highway through
Macedonia and into Albania, then across the Adriatic to Bari. That's where
the Kosovars have joined with traditional Italian organized crime groups
to trade drugs for arms. Along with heroin, the two groups smuggle illegal
Albanian aliens into Italy, and non-Albanians too—Kurds, Pakistanis and
Sri Lankans—who only get brought along because they've paid the
Kosovo Liberation Army the money they need to buy the heroin which
starts the cycle.

Slovakia has been turned into a transit territory. The size of the shipments coming through was highlighted in early 1998 when Colombian-
grown marijuana was seized. Originally shipped from Panama to Florida,

it was loaded onto a container ship bound for Bremen, Germany, and trucked from there to Bratislava. The load weighed thirteen metric tons.

Meanwhile, the Serbs continue to finance their activities through counterfeiting currency which they feed into the world's financial markets through a reported two hundred private banks and currency-exchange offices under their immediate control. They also allow other groups, notably the Mafia, to launder $1.5 billion a year through those same sinks. They have also reportedly opened up the Balkan route to Middle Eastern organized crime groups who now have a way to get marijuana up to Slovenia and, from there, easily into Austria.

War, bloodshed and political instability are good business for transnational organized crime. Then again, these days, so are peace and prosperity.

Bulgarian criminals steal luxury automobiles to feed Russia's black-market car salesmen with product. They are then often paid with drugs that are cultivated throughout the former Soviet Union. Polish gangs do exactly the same thing. One report notes that the average life expectancy of a new Mercedes in Warsaw is under three months.

In Switzerland, at the beginning of 1998, Federal Prosecutor Carla Del Ponte—who has relentlessly pursued dirty money in Switzerland, to the great annoyance of Swiss bankers—claimed that Russian organized crime had stashed more than $40 billion in the nation's banks. At the same time, the Swiss identified ninety companies plus more than 680 Swiss and foreign nationals living in the country as having direct links to Russian organized crime. From Switzerland, those companies and individuals can be connected to Russian and other organized criminals throughout the world.

In the United Arab Emirates, planeloads of Russians arrive on charter flights almost every day of the week, mostly at Sharja, and are then bussed into Dubai, where they swarm like locusts through the gold market, wearing money belts stuffed with crisp new $100 bills, buying up just about everything they see.

In Britain, there are direct links between Russian organized crime and prostitution, illegal immigration and fraud in international football transfer fees. Extortion of British companies operating in the former Soviet Union has become an accepted business expense. Kidnapping of businessmen in places like Chechnya has become all too common. However, from the criminals' point of view, it serves a double purpose. Gangs take the payoff money, then come back to sell the company protection against kidnapping.

In Thailand, criminals cooperate with ethnic Chinese gangs to smuggle illegal aliens out of Asia and into the United States, Canada, Germany, France and Britain. They claim to have a success rate near 90 percent, and even station their own agents at the arrival side to facilitate immigration controls. It is believed that one particular Thai group has used the LCN in North America, traditional Italian groups in Europe and the Yakuza in Japan to collect debts for them. Illegal aliens who can't pay are then forced into either prostitution or heroin trafficking.

In New York, where Chinese gangs have decided they need help distributing drugs outside their ethnic neighborhoods, there have been street-level alliances with other groups, including the LCN. A recent DEA estimate suggests that while Asian opium production is up, heroin shipments coming into the United States from Asia have declined. The assumption they make is that the Asians have simply opened new markets. In a sense, they're right. A foreign intelligence service with a strong interest in tracking Asian heroin says that the traffickers are sidestepping the DEA by joining forces with the Colombians. They ship raw opium to the cartels, who refine it in the jungles, then franchise out to the LCN and the Mexicans for sale in North America.

Cooperation between Chinese law enforcement and Western law enforcement has improved slightly over the past few years, but then, since the "goldfish fiasco," it could only get better. In 1988, the Chinese tipped off the Americans about a huge heroin consignment bound for San Francisco. The drugs were stuffed inside dead goldfish and controlled by a local Wo Hop To Triad society. The gang leader, William Mui, was arrested. In return for the favor, the Americans told the Chinese about Mui's associates in China. The Chinese arrested Wang Zongxiao and shipped him off to California to testify against Mui. For a few weeks, it actually seemed as if the two countries were building a firm law enforcement friendship. That is, until Wang's lawyer convinced him to defect and ask for political asylum. It has taken the Chinese a very long time to trust Western law enforcement again.

Vietnamese gangs have carved out a niche for themselves running massive cigarette-smuggling businesses in Germany and France, where there are strong ethnic communities. The original source of the cigarettes was Poland and Hungary, where many of them were manufactured under license, and some were simply counterfeit. As the Vietnamese expanded

their operation and required more product, they began importing cigarettes from the United States, shipping them to Rotterdam, then smuggling
them into the markets. Their profit comes from cheating on the excise
duties. Their de facto license to operate was granted by the larger Eastern
European gangs, who feel contraband cigarettes are too small a business to
be concerned with. German police indicate that, in the wake of increasing
violence against Vietnamese street sellers from small gangs trying to elbow
in on their pitch, they have turned to one of the Chechen organized crime
groups for protection. One estimate out of Belgium suggests that of the
nearly one trillion cigarettes that are exported annually to warehouses
in Antwerp and Hong Kong, some 30 percent—that's three hundred billion—go missing. Black markets thrive in Britain, Spain and Italy.

As Asian gangs have moved west, traditional Western gangs have moved
east. Nigerian criminals are settling in Japan, marrying local women so they
can't be deported and doing deals with Yakuza gangs, which see them as
partners in typical advanced-fee-fraud schemes.

In Australia, the same Lebanese gangs trafficking in Europe have had a
presence since the 1970s. Originally importers of heroin and marijuana
from the Syrian-controlled Bekka Valley, there is evidence that they failed
to do deals with the Chinese, were rebuffed by the Vietnamese gangs
and have finally settled into partnership with the Colombians. The
'Ndrangheta has also had a long-standing relationship with Australia. So
have Romanian gangs. They once tried to get into the heroin trade, were
stopped from becoming importers and have had to settle for a role as
resellers. They also work social security frauds. The Yakuza are there, seeing
Australia and New Zealand as investments worth cultivating.

In spring 1999, Australian police wound up an eight-year undercover
operation and broke up what they described as the nation's biggest-ever
drug ring. They arrested 135 people and seized enough chemicals to flood
the Pacific with $200 million worth of heroin, amphetamines, cocaine and
marijuana. Operation Phalanx coordinated the efforts of sixteen police task
forces, shut down three operating drug labs, identified a dozen already
dismantled labs and took out a huge chemical-storage facility. The major
players were native Australian, but the bust emphasized that the group had
working alliances with other organized crime groups in Vietnam, Hong
Kong and Amsterdam.

And, of course, the Russians have landed in Australia as well.

"They're crawling all over the Pacific," notes one senior Australian Federal Police official. "The Russians are here, using this country as a base. But Australia is not unique, because they're everywhere. They've invaded the Pacific and managed to do what the Japanese during World War II had only dreamt of."

As the globe shrinks, the danger posed by transnational criminal groups increases proportionately. The world has never been so dangerous.

Atomic weapons, which have been remapping political boundaries since 1945, are now remapping the transnational criminal boundaries.

During the 1990s, there have been fifteen hundred to two thousand incidents of nuclear materials known to have been offered for sale. The figure depends on who's counting and what criteria are being used. But by everyone's count and by any yardstick whatsoever, given the intricate and complex nature of nuclear physics, it is indisputable that almost no one in this market has a clue what he's dealing with. Technological ignorance runs rampant. It is that fact alone which explains why, thank goodness, all but a handful of the materials offered for sale have been absolutely and totally useless to anyone attempting to manufacture a nuclear device.

Putting aside—but not discounting—the obvious health hazards to the population of idiots running with radioactive materials in jam jars, there are three very basic and extremely disquieting concerns. The first is, the number of incidents of trading in illegal atomic materials continues to increase each year—in some years more than doubling—while the quality of materials offered for sale has been improving. This is an ongoing dilemma of unmistakable danger. There is no such thing as a minor nuclear bomb. The second is, with each incident, the odds shorten on an educated seller meeting an educated buyer. The third is, unlike other crimes, you only hear about the trade in nuclear materials when the bad guys fail. When—not if, but when—the bad guys finally succeed, it may not make the papers until after someone lights the fuse.

Four incidents, all of them during 1994, demonstrate how excruciatingly close they've already come.

In May, sixty grams of radioactive powder, which included one fifth of an ounce of weapons grade plutonium—that's Pu-239 at 99.75 percent purity—was found in Tengen, Germany. It was in a lead canister, hidden in the garage of Adolf Jaekle, a fifty-two-year-old businessman who got caught only because he was under investigation for counterfeiting. It later came out that he'd reportedly been guaranteed up to $100 million from a rogue state—speculation centers on Iraq and North Korea—to purchase enough material for a bomb.

In June, 0.3 grams of weapons-grade uranium—that's U-235—was discovered in Landshut, Germany. In a sting operation, the police also seized a small quantity of enriched uranium tablets. They arrested one German, four Slovaks and a Czech.

In December, 2.72 kilograms of near-weapons-grade uranium— U-235 enriched to 87.5 percent—was found in Prague. Acting on a tip, Czech police stopped a Saab driven by a Czech scientist and found the material in two metal containers on the backseat. American investigators were able to help the Czechs trace it back to a ten-kilogram theft of enriched uranium from a Russian nuclear research center at Obninsk. Buyers who were known to have been approached included a Nigerian crime group who'd offered heroin in exchange for the uranium, Spaniards rumored to be linked to the Basque terrorist organization ETA, and North Koreans. The operation fell apart when the sellers offered the uranium to a German undercover agent at $200,000 a pound. It was the largest amount offered to date on the black market. A few arrests were made, but the smugglers and their suspected Russian organized crime partners are still at large. At least one of the criminals had promised his contacts in the Czech Republic that he could guarantee delivery of five kilos a month of this material, and forty kilos immediately.

The fourth, the odd one out, took place in August. A steel suitcase arrived at Munich Airport off a Lufthansa flight from Moscow. It contained twenty ounces of radioactive material, three fifths of which was near-weapons-grade plutonium—sometimes referred to as "weapons capable"— Pu-239 at 87 percent pure. There was also two hundred grams of lithium—Li-6—another necessary component in the manufacture of a thermonuclear device. It was announced at the time that three men, caught up in an undercover sting, had promised to deliver up to nine pounds of material. But the operation took place on the eve of national elections in Germany in which law enforcement and nuclear trafficking were an election issues. It is now clear that the German government manipulated this one to bolster votes.

Still, two salient points came out of it. The first is the message sent to the rest of the world, that radioactive materials are readily available. Explains David Kyd at the International Atomic Energy Agency (IAEA), "The Russians said it didn't come from them. And this stuff is not easy to fingerprint. It's not easy to know the origin of fissile material. The German official explanation was inadequate. German security agents were waiting at the airport. That's just too slick. But even if it was a hoax, it opened eyes. It was a wake-up call and has had a salutary effect."

The second is the nationality of the three men arrested. Two were Spanish and one was Colombian. Even though he was a doctor by profession, the moment you mix Colombians into the equation, somewhere, somehow, there is a connection to cartels and drugs.

"One of the real problems with nuclear materials is that they are not easy to detect," Kyd continues. "Contrary to public opinion, there's not a lot of radiation that comes off a nuclear device. Any group of terrorists competent enough to know how to set off a device will know how to shield what little radioactivity comes off of it."

He's often said that if he were a nuclear trafficker, he'd hand off his materials to a drug dealer. "I'd contract it out to the drug lords and let them move it. Look at how much drugs cross our borders. If you're talking about a bomb, you need grapefruit sizes of plutonium. If it's uranium, a bowling ball size will do. One or the other would be just as easy to hide in a bale of marijuana."

Nuclear trafficking is still in its infancy. But there might be some comfort in knowing that, in most instances, the goods offered for sale are useless. Uranium pellets enriched to 3–4 percent are of no interest to Iraq, Iran, Syria, Libya, North Korea, Pakistan, India or South Africa, among many others. Research quality, which is enriched to 20 percent, doesn't hold much attraction either.

There have been some cases of criminal groups brokering "dual-use" materials, which are nonradioactive metals that have industrial applications but which are also found in atomic weapons. And these have created some interest. But it is "the big-bang stuff" that really opens wallets. Anything available at more than 80 percent would get looked at by everyone in the market because it can be used as feedstock in the enrichment process. Anything enriched to over 90 percent is what makes a bomb.

According to the IAEA, the Iraqis have been using a 1940s process in their bomb-development program. The blueprints are available to anyone for free at the patent office. It's a messy and inefficient process. And even if they somehow acquired weapons-grade plutonium, they wouldn't automatically have a bomb. But they'd be a lot closer with those materials than they would be without them.

Saddam Hussein had already gotten pretty far at the time of the Gulf War. The CIA discovered just how far thanks to the human shields he'd installed at his Tuwaitha nuclear research center. As soon as they were freed, the Agency bought their clothing and, through forensic testing, established the presence of highly enriched uranium.

It takes around twenty-five kilos of uranium enriched to 90 percent to build a bomb. And where uranium is concerned, it's an easy process to hide. A plutonium device only needs eight kilos of highly enriched materials, but it's a much more complex process, and more easily detected because of the unmistakable shape of the building where it's being done. Saddam is reasonably believed to have already spent in excess of $10 billion and still hasn't gotten a bomb for his money. No one doubts that he is willing to spend a lot more.

In recent years he's shifted slightly, not so much looking for materials at any price but going in search of people who can speed up his development and manufacturing processes. What's more, the risk of detection is higher when dealing in the black market for uranium or plutonium than it is when dealing in the employment market for out-of-work Russian physicists. If he were to put another billion or so on the table for experts and materials—a sum he could certainly afford—it probably wouldn't take the world's organized criminals very long to start looking at ways to get their share.

But then, Saddam is the one who originally created the awareness among intermediaries that sellers could find buyers. On both sides of the Gulf War, the call was answered by subcontractors and freelancers who now thrive in Europe. And in Japan, too, where affiliates of U.S. companies have attempted to sell nuclear materials. The market there has not escaped the attention of the Yakuza, who, like their Russian organized crime counterparts, have also explored the lucrative possibilities on offer.

The marketplace has created joint ventures.

Russian organized criminals, mainly working out of Vladivostok, met with Yakuza members in an effort to find and steal weapons-grade materials in the Pacific region that could then be offered on the black market to the highest bidders. The Russians have the contacts in the Middle East. The Yakuza have their own people inside industries based in Japan.

So have the Aum Shinrikyo. When police searched their various premises after the Sarin nerve-gas attack, documents were found at the cult's "Science and Technology Agency" detailing uranium enrichment. Highly technical and marked "Internal Use Only," the documents dealt mostly with specialized experiments using lasers to enrich uranium. They were sourced back to a Japanese heavy-machinery company. It was also discovered, through information obtained in other documents, that an Aum member was on the staff of the Kurchatov Institute, Russia's most prestigious nuclear physics laboratory.

As the market in what is sometimes referred to as "the poor man's equalizer" has expanded, criminals feeding it have grown more sophisticated and peripheral markets have grown up too. Prime among them is the market for "red mercury."

Touted by some as an essential ingredient in pure-fusion weapons, the Russian-invented substance has also come to be known as a magic potion that can do anything, including be used as a shortcut to creating a nuclear device. It just depends on how much the guy who's buying wants to believe the guy who's selling.

Around 1990 or so, a story circulated that Soviet scientists had come up with a powerful new explosive. The version lauded as the official one noted that it was, "red and semi-liquid, of pure mercury and mercury antimony oxide, irradiated for up to twenty days in a nuclear reactor. It can then yield enough energy to fuse tritium atoms."

That would be a nuclear bomb. Except that many physicists are very skeptical that a compound of pure mercury and mercury antimony oxide would be sufficiently stable to be used as an explosive. And anyway, apparently no one of genuine repute has ever seen the stuff. At least, not anyone with certifiable qualifications to know what it is and what it can do. According to the FBI, every time they've looked into it, they've either found a small amount of low-grade nuclear material—which clearly wasn't red mercury—or hot air.

In other words, despite the description on the label, there is no evidence that red mercury exists.

But that's never stopped organized criminals from selling it to purchasers who want to believe they're buying the real thing. The Austrians have recorded several incidents of red mercury sales, a significant one matching a Russian seller with a Saudi government official. By the mid-1990s, red mercury was showing up all over the Pacific. It first showed up in Hong Kong and Macau, then quickly spread to all the major Australasian markets.

Interestingly enough, a certain folklore has grown up with it. One theory is that red mercury was invented by the Western security services. The idea was to bait a net and see who they could catch in it. Another theory is that the Soviets cooked it up because they needed the money. A more likely rationale is that some scientist theorized it was possible and some organized criminal decided, I can sell possibilities. And the reason that's more likely is because that's what happened. Word got out that red mercury could solve the most worrying problems of bomb designers in the Third World, and deals were done. The going price was $300,000 per kilo.

Even without red mercury, there is enough unaccounted-for fissile material that once belonged to the Soviet Union to turn much of the developed world into an uninhabitable moonscape. Perhaps as many as one thousand sites within the USSR's former borders still house enriched uranium and plutonium. But no one knows how much is there, or even how much used to be there. It seems the Soviets couldn't be bothered keeping detailed records of such things. And anyway, what remains of the records they did keep is, today, in disarray. It would take decades to work out the true extent of what's missing, that is, if anyone ever bothered. At the moment, no one is.

If the submarine base at Murmansk is any indication, then nuclear accounting, storage, inventory controls, maintenance and security at other sites is not just seriously inadequate, it is near nonexistent. What's left of the Soviet nuclear fleet is rusting away with fuel reactors still onboard. Some years ago, two Russian naval officers simply walked into the base, sawed through a padlock on a door at Fuel Storage Area 3-30, and walked out with four kilos of fresh submarine fuel—U-235 enriched to 20 percent. It was six months before they or the fuel rods were found.

In May 1993, Lithuanian police, acting on a tip, searched the basement vaults of the Joint-Stock Innovation Bank and found twenty-seven wooden crates of beryllium. Valued in the open market at around $600 a kilo, the cache of 4.4 metric tons was officially worth $2.64 million. Used in missileguidance systems and precision optical equipment, beryllium is known to physicists for its ability to reflect neutrons. That means it is also used in nuclear bombs. Sort of a fuel additive, beryllium helps to create a bigger explosion with less fissile material. What the police didn't know was why it was in the bank vault, and who'd put it there.

What they did know was that, suddenly, all previous bets were off.

Up to this point, doomsayers were warning that because Russia's atomic stockpile was so easy to pilfer, it was only a matter of time until enough nuclear materials to build a bomb fell into the hands of the Maffiya and terrorists. Authorities in Moscow and Washington were, understand-ably, anxious to pour scorn on those kinds of statements. They insisted that safeguards were being put into place to protect the atomic stockpile, and that anyway, the only cases to date involving the theft of fissile materials involved non-weapons-grade and were managed by amateurs.

Typical was the butcher in St. Petersburg who had a relative working at a plant with access to uranium-235. The relative put some in a jar and took it home, and the butcher tried to sell the stuff at the local street mar-ket. But that was one jar's worth. This was 4.4 tons.

The mystery took years to unravel, but basically came down to this: a man said to be connected to Russian organized crime was able to buy it from a former Soviet factory where the workers were starving because they hadn't been paid. The purchase was made in the name of a karate club in Moscow. They had it shipped to a laboratory in Vilnius, while waiting to sell it to a Russian in Austria. At the lab in Vilnius, someone realized that included in the beryllium was 19.8 pounds of highly radioactive cesium. One of the more deadly by-products of nuclear fission, cesium has a black market that would have paid around $800,000 for that much. So the cesium disappeared.

The Russian in Austria was paying $2.7 million for the beryllium, hav-ing pre-sold it to a Swiss company with an address in Italy for $24 million. That company had a client for the beryllium with "interests" in North Korea. The police in Vilnius killed the sale. When Interpol heard about it, they went to see the Swiss company's office in Italy. But they'd moved and left no forwarding address.

Working on a tip from a discontented member of an Italian organized crime gang, prosecutors in Italy dismantled a Mafia ring in 1998 that was offering a cache of nuclear materials for $170 million. For sale were bars of uranium weighing 1.33 kilos, controlled by the 'Ndrangheta. It is believed they were brought into Italy from Zaire, where the Russians had originally shipped them in 1972. It is believed there were several potential buyers in the Middle East. Only one of the seven bars has been found. Among the fourteen people arrested was a member of the Santapaola family, the same clan operating out of St. Maarten in the Caribbean, where Russians meet Colombians and the Seminole Indians have an interest in a casino.

Perhaps even more chillingly, at the end of 1998, a U.S. federal court indicted Saudi terrorist Osama bin Laden on grounds that he "made efforts to obtain the components of nuclear weapons."

Over the past several years:

Police in Tanzania arrested a man with radioactive cesium.

Police in Romania arrested two men in possession of eighty-two kilos of non-weapons-capable uranium. In unrelated incidents, they arrested seven people offering to sell seven kilos of uranium and strontium-90; four others trying to sell four kilos of uranium-235 and uranium-238; several more attempting to sell 4.5 kilos of uranium tetrachloride; five Romanians with 2.6 kilos of uranium; and three more with three kilos of uranium pellets.

Police in Switzerland arrested a man with low-enriched uranium. Acting on information obtained in that case, police in Turkey then arrested eight people with another 1.13 kilos of the same material. In unrelated incidents, they arrested an Azeri with 750 grams of uranium; seven Turks with twelve kilos of weapons-grade uranium; and five people in connection with twenty-two pounds of uranium discovered in Istanbul.

Police in the United Arab Emirates arrested a man in Dubai offering to sell three kilos of red mercury.

Police in Poland arrested a man coming into the country from the Czech republic with eleven small containers of strontium-90. In an unrelated case, they seized eight kilos of radioactive americium-241 and cesium-137.

Police in Hungary arrested four Slovaks with 1.7 kilos of depleted uranium in a fruit jar on their way into Austria. In unrelated incidents, police discovered twenty-six kilos of various radioactive materials in the trunk of a car; arrested two men with 4.4 kilos of fuel rods stolen from a reactor in Russia; and confiscated two kilos of uranium fuel rods.

Police in Tehran arrested five Iranians for being in possession of uranium.

Police in Bulgaria arrested a group of Russians and Ukrainians in possession

of "materials of strategic value," some of which were radioactive. In unrelated incidents, Bulgarian police found four lead capsules containing
radioactive materials on a bus going to Turkey; and arrested six Bulgarians
carrying nineteen containers of radioactive material.

Police in Slovakia arrested three Hungarians, four Slovaks and two Ukrainians
with 18.4 kilos of radioactive material. In unrelated incidents, they
arrested four people trying to smuggle in one kilo of non-weapons-grade
uranium.

Police in Italy arrested a man after he'd murdered a victim who couldn't pay
for five grams of plutonium. The nuclear materials were never found.

Police in India arrested four people trying to sell 2.5 kilos of uranium extracted
from ore.

Police in Germany discovered a flask of radioactive material sitting in a rail-
road station. In unrelated incidents, they arrested a Polish man for trying
to sell one kilo of uranium; a Zairian man for smuggling in 850 grams of
uraninite; and confiscated 800 milligrams of uranium coming in from the
Czech Republic.

Police in South Africa reported that 130 barrels of enriched uranium waste
was missing from a storage facility.

Police in Canada reported that non-radioactive isotopes worth $350 million
were brought into Toronto by a Swedish-Russian joint venture, for
smuggling into the United States.

And, in a slight twist, police in Russia arrested two Lithuanians for smuggling
uranium-238 into Russia.

If anyone doubts how much stuff there is out there, more than five
hundred metric tons of U-235 and 300 tons of Pu-239 have been extracted
from dismantled Russian warheads and are stored somewhere in Russia,
waiting to be disposed of. Enough material to create sixty thousand nuclear
weapons, that's only what they've recovered through disarmament agreements. This is not their regular stockpile. The Russians have, incessantly,
denied that any of their weapons-grade, or even near-weapons-grade,
materials have turned up in the West. They have, however, admitted that
quantities of highly enriched uranium have gone missing inside Russia.
But they conveniently ignore the residue from the collapse of the Soviet
Union.

Nearly five thousand scientists got stuck in Kazakhstan. They are
unable to earn a living because the Russians don't want them back and

there isn't much for them to do in Kazakhstan, and it only takes one to hire himself out and bring his own nuclear materials along. Life in Ukraine for ex-Soviet physicists isn't much rosier. But then, no one has to go that far to find dangerous merchandise. When the Russian military pulled out of East Germany, they left behind a whole pile of atomic junk.

Not long ago in Washington, seventeen of Russia's most senior military officers were asked how they rated the chances of "nuclear migration" to a Middle Eastern country. In other words, on a scale from one to ten, how likely was it that some country in the Middle East would soon come up with the technological know-how and the source materials to build a nuclear device.

All seventeen said, "Ten."

9

CONNECTING IN CALI

There was this guy, there are others.

—Homicide Detective BILLY AHERN, NYPD

VLADIMIR BEIGELMAN FANCIED HIMSELF A CONTENDER. At thirty-six, the dark-haired, husky Russian with a thick gold chain around his neck was a man intent on making the right connections. Always on the prowl for the next scam, he was a man looking for a way to break into the big leagues, a man convinced that with the right connections he wouldn't be a contender all his life, he could become a player, and being a player meant money.

His pal Oleg Zapinakmine had the right connections. He was Monya Elson's bodyguard. And after Nayfeld attempted to kill Elson on that Saturday afternoon in July 1993—when Elson, his wife and Oleg all lived to tell the tale—Monya and Oleg became just like father and son. Being friends with Oleg gave Vladimir a line to Elson, and because Elson had heavyweight connections with the Genovese family, he saw this as his line to the Italians.

But before Beigelman could milk that connection, Oleg's luck ran out.

On September 24, 1993, while getting into his car, which was parked right in front of his house in Brighton Beach, the twenty-five-year-old Zapinakmine noticed one of his tires was flat. He bent down to take a closer look. He never saw the man with the gun who came up behind him and put a single bullet into the back of his head.

Understandably, Oleg's death shocked Beigelman. Although, in a harsher light, he decided it didn't necessarily shut the door to the Italians. There might still be ways to get connected through Elson. In the meantime, he had a steady earner with the Colombians.

They'd rented a big house for him in Mill Basin, an up-market neighborhood where many Russians, newly arrived and stuck in Brighton Beach, aspire someday to be. Not far from King's Plaza, just north of Brooklyn Marine Park, the house had a private dock along a small inlet which leads into Jamaica Bay—waterfront access that made smuggling easy. And they were paying him enough in cash to live better than he'd ever lived before. So now, with Larissa expecting their second child, keeping the Colombians sweet—at least until something better came along—was a worthwhile ambition.

The Colombians, too, were pleased with the way things were working. At least he thought they were. After all, when he started complaining about the Ford Aerostar van they'd bought for him, they promised, albeit reluctantly, to get him a better one. But just as suddenly as Oleg's murder, it looked like his luck was running out as well. Vladimir never had to do much to earn his keep with the Colombians. His contact, Enrique, merely asked him to hold on to a couple of thousand kilos of coke whenever they landed it, stashing it safely in his house until one of them came to pick it up. The problem was, somewhere along the line, a few hundred kilos went missing.

They accused Beigelman of stealing it. He accused them of stealing it. The quarrel got worse. The Colombians cut him off. They said they would never give him any more work. They threatened that he was in serious trouble if he didn't come up with the coke, or at least the money to pay for it. He continued to protest his innocence. They stopped paying his rent. Bills piled up. He blamed them.

He'd hustled all his life and knew that he could always, somehow, find a way to make a living. Ducking and diving was what he did best. But now, the combination of Oleg's death and the missing drugs had thrown a serious monkey wrench into his game plan.

Enrique had promised to make it all right again. But until Thursday night, December 2, 1993, when a call came in to Beigelman's home, he didn't know if or when his luck would ever change for the good again.

It was a quarter to nine. Larissa Beigelman answered the phone. A man with an Hispanic accent asked, "Where's the Russian?" She handed the phone to her husband. Vladimir didn't speak for very long, a couple of minutes at most, before hanging up and saying to Larissa, "I'll be back in a little while. I'm going out to Queens to get a new car."

This was a good sign.

He fetched his keys, tossed a blue down winter coat on top of his dark jeans and his Hard Rock Café "Save the Planet" T-shirt, stepped into his white, green and blue track shoes, put on his New York Giants cap and grabbed a pair of driving gloves.

He did not take his wallet.

He did not take his gun.

Leaving his wallet home might not have mattered and Larissa might not have noticed, but it was strange that he didn't slip his gun into his pocket because Beigelman always carried a gun whenever he left the house. Maybe he didn't bother taking it this time because all he was going to do was pick up a new car, because he wasn't expecting any problems, because he thought to himself, if Enrique is giving me a new car it means we're back in business together.

The drive from Mill Basin to the meeting point in the middle of Queens took around forty minutes. Two Colombian teenagers were standing on the sidewalk, waiting for him, right where they were supposed to be. They instructed him to park the van there and leave the keys in the ashtray, explaining that they would take him to the new car and come back to pick up this one.

He did what he was told and walked around the corner—with one kid on each side of him—into the 9200 block of Fifty-sixth Avenue.

The neighborhood is residential, made up mainly of apartment houses, although toward the middle of the block there's a playground behind a chain fence. They were on the playground side. And just as they got to a streetlamp, two other guys came up to them.

If Vladimir Beigelman hadn't figured it out yet, he was never going to.

The shooter fired from only eighteen inches away.

Billy Ahern is built like a halfback, compact enough so that you know he can move well, big enough that so that you know you don't want to get in his way.

Brought up on Long Island, he joined the New York Police Department in the early 1980s and by December 1993, after a dozen years on the force, he'd just about seen it all—street-gang warriors, stickup men, stickup children, con men, child abusers, hookers, knife slashers, bank robbers, rapists, muggers, husbands who beat up their wives with their fists, wives who slam their husbands to death with hammers, drug dealers, murderers—but mostly drug dealers and murderers.

Starting his shift that Friday morning, doing general detective work at the 110th Precinct in Corona, Queens, the talk was about how a Russian had gotten dusted the night before. The neighborhood was Colombian, so a white man's body on the sidewalk was worth talking about.

He heard that a call had come into the precinct at 10:20 P.M. saying someone had been shot. Uniformed officers arriving at the scene found a Caucasian male in his mid-thirties, 170 to 180 pounds, lying dead on the sidewalk, shot numerous times. Detectives showed up a few minutes later and counted five bullet holes—one in the man's left cheek next to his nose, one in the left side of his nose, one in the left side of his neck and two in his left shoulder. From the stippling around his eyes, they could tell he'd been shot at very close range.

Ahern would later remark, "They definitely wanted this guy dead when they shot him."

Surprisingly, the street was not covered in blood. In fact, the crime-scene photos show there was very little blood. Apparently, when your heart stops as abruptly as Beigelman's did, blood stops flowing just as quickly.

The detectives who searched the body couldn't find any ID—no wallet, no credit cards, no driver's license—nor could they find any car keys. But the dead man's pockets weren't turned out, which said to them that the motive probably wasn't robbery. Not that robbery was ever much of a possibility. A dead white guy in this neighborhood, shot the way he was shot, had all the signs of a drug-related murder.

There was a second baseball cap not far from the body, a blue scarf nearby and a few witnesses.

One of them was an off-duty cop. He told the detectives, "There were two males, possibly Hispanics, twenty years of age, running from the scene. Also a dark-colored car. Two male Hispanics confronted the victim, shots went off, the dark car came up, one of the male Hispanics jumped into the car, the other ran off on foot." He said one of them threw something into the yard. It turned out to be the scarf. Thinking the gun was wrapped inside, he picked it up. But it was empty.

Other witnesses put four people at the scene—the two guys who walked with Beigelman, the shooter and someone with the shooter. They said that one of the two guys walking with the victim jumped into the car—identified as a dark Buick Grand National, which is known for being very fast—while the other ran down Fifty-sixth toward Ninety-third Street. The shooter and the guy with him just disappeared.

The only thing the detectives could safely conclude was that they didn't know for sure who went where.

Someone did say that the victim had gotten out of a van which was parked around the corner, so the detectives walked around the corner and found a Ford Aerostar with keys in the ashtray. First, they ran a check on the license plate. It turned out to be registered to a false name with a false address. Then they called for a drug dog, who sniffed his way through the van and discovered false walls built into the panels where drugs had once been hidden. Eventually they had to rely on fingerprints to ID the victim, which took several hours. Much later that night, once they had a name and address for him, officers drove to Mill Basin to notify his next of kin.

Larissa took the news badly. The detectives tried asking her questions. She refused to speak. No matter what they said, she would not cooperate. And shortly after the murder, she moved away.

But Ahern didn't know anything about her when he showed up for his shift that Friday. All he knew was the morning scuttlebutt, that some Russian had been whacked the night before in a Colombian neighborhood. It sounded to him like just another dead drug dealer, hardly enough to marshal a lot of police enthusiasm. Yet the detectives dealing with it still had to go through the motions of filling out the appropriate forms, so the lieutenant in charge of homicide—knowing that Ahern had worked on cases with the Drug Enforcement Administration—asked him to make some phone calls, to find out if they knew anything about Beigelman.

Ringing the Manhattan office of the DEA, Ahern told them who he was and what he wanted, mentioned the victim's name and heard the agent on the phone shout out to other guys in his office, "Hey, the Russian's dead."

The agent then explained that they'd just started working a case on Beigelman, based on information from a DEA office outside New York.

His name had popped up because he was purportedly sitting on a multi-kilo shipment. By coincidence, a few nights before, they'd actually installed a pole camera to watch his residence.

Ahern passed the information back to his lieutenant. Deep down, he had a gut feeling that, given time, this was a case he could solve. But all he'd been asked to do was get on the phone. Anyway, he had his own cases to worry about. So this one was duly shoved into the recesses of his mind under the heading of someone else's unfinished business.

For the detectives working the Beigelman murder, there were never any indications of who did what or why. The witnesses' statements were too vague. And the off-duty cop who'd been interviewed at the scene was never spoken to again. The file was officially sent away to gather dust on December 21, 1993. The only published record of the murder appears to have been in New York's *Newsday* newspaper. A small box in the December 4 issue was labeled, "The homicides by gunshot reported by city police during the 24-hour period ending at 6 P.M. yesterday. The Toll: 3."

Those murders were:

6:26 A.M. Friday. An unidentified man found burned beyond recognition, apparently after being shot to death on West 163rd Street, Manhattan.

11:16 P.M. Thursday. Joseph Bascardi apparently bleeds to death after being shot by a man robbing his Bayside deli.

10:19 P.M. Thursday. Vladimir Beigelman of Brooklyn shot to death at Ninety-second Street and Fifty-sixth Avenue, Queens.

Normally, that would have been the end of the story. As Ahern later explained, "A guy dealing drugs is dead and if you can find the guy who did it, you do the community a great service because you lock him up and get two off the streets for the price of one. Nobody gives a fuck about dead drug dealers."

In NYPD jargon, those murders are referred to as "misdemeanor homicides."

Someone in "time management"—some faceless man in a gray suit with a slide rule, presumably working out of a windowless office in the back alleys of police headquarters—decided that there should be a general rule for these things and settled on four days. That's how long a New York

City homicide detective can devote to any one murder. Except in rare circumstances, either the case gets solved in four days or it gets dumped. The only reason the Beigelman murder didn't meet the four-day rule was because the folder sat on desks a couple of weeks longer than it should have.

Needless to say, the four-day figure wasn't plucked out of thin air. Most murders which get solved do get solved within four days. But then, most murders are committed by people known to the victim, so the cops don't usually have to look very far. It turns out, however, that perhaps as many as 80 percent of the murders that don't get solved within four days are written off simply because the detectives don't have enough time to do what they need to do. They have to move on because other cases are piling up. That's why, a few years ago, some senior officers wondered what would happen if an elite team were given enough time to do whatever they had to do. And by late March 1995, Ahern had moved from the Corona precinct to one in Jamaica, Queens, where a homicide lieutenant named Phil Panzarella was running a Cold Case Squad.

Known to his men as "Sundance," Panzarella is legend around the NYPD for his photographic memory. He and his team of seasoned homicide investigators were assigned to search through the archives for unsolved murders—crimes long since forgotten, with witnesses long since moved away and forensics long since lost—to reopen them and, ultimately, to solve them. Panzarella offered the newly arrived Ahern a ton of cases to choose from, but on March 30, 1995, Ahern elected to reopen the Beigelman murder.

After getting the records up from archives and going through them in minute detail, he phoned a DEA agent he'd worked with on other cases—a highly experienced, six-foot-two-inch, 210-pound street narc named Brian Crowell. They'd met back in 1991 when Ahern was dealing with one of his first homicides. A Colombian woman in Queens, a real estate agent, had been murdered in her office. In broad daylight, the shooter had boldly walked in, filed past several people sitting at their desks, gone up to her and blown her away. During the course of that investigation, Ahern stumbled across Crowell, who'd been targeting restaurants and money remitters through which the Colombians were laundering drug cash.

Later, Ahern would say about Crowell, "Ninety-nine percent of the people are talkers. Only one percent are doers. Brian is a doer."

And Crowell would say about Ahern, "Billy knows a lot of those guys hanging out on street corners, who they are, where to find them, how to talk to them. He knows what he's doing."

Ahern reminded Crowell that the DEA had recognized Beigelman's name the morning after the murder and asked him to run it through their system. It didn't ring a bell to Crowell. At least he didn't recall anyone called Beigelman popping up in any of his cases. But that wasn't surprising, because he wasn't dealing at that level. His team was targeting Colombian cell heads, guys at the top of each sales and distribution team, guys who oversaw assigned territories.

When Crowell first got into the business, Colombians only dealt with Colombians. Then they started handing off to Dominicans, but only at the street level. Now he was seeing cell heads dealing directly with Dominicans, who, in turn, had achieved significant influence in New York's cocaine trade. They not only controlled entire neighborhoods, such as Washington Heights, but they'd found a niche for themselves in transport too, staging shipments in the Dominican Republic.

A Colombian-Russian link was, nonetheless, out of the ordinary.

Crowell ran a check and reported back to Ahern that Vladimir had been a bagman who'd been set up in Mill Basin—in what the trade calls a mid-level stash house—for the purpose of receiving two to three thousand kilos of coke at a shot. He said that a DEA office out of state had made Beigelman's name, address and phone number, had come up with a pretty good idea about what and who he was involved with and, based on that, had set up a surveillance camera. He noted that they even had footage of Vladimir leaving his house on the night of his murder.

The initial contact with Beigelman's wife had failed, so Ahern tracked her down to Brighton Beach, hoping to reach out to her. He explained that he'd been assigned to look into her husband's death and that he was genuinely interested in finding the perpetrators. She responded tersely by giving Ahern the name of her attorney. That struck him as odd, and she wouldn't elaborate, except to say that from her experience with the detectives who'd originally investigated the case, she wasn't interested in cooperating. Turning now to the lawyer, Ahern convinced him to set up a meeting. And on April 4, just five days into this investigation, Larissa, her lawyer, Ahern and Crowell sat down together in the lawyer's Manhattan office. The two cops assured Larissa that they were only interested in finding the people who'd murdered her husband, that they knew about his drug dealing and that they had no interest in any involvement she might have had.

After making their pitch, Ahern and Crowell left the room to give the wife and the lawyer a chance to talk. Five minutes later the lawyer invited them back in and announced that she would cooperate.

Larissa began by telling them a lot of things they already knew, although hearing it from her confirmed it for them. Next she said that shortly before her husband's death, he'd had gotten a call from Colombia arranging a pickup for two to three hundred kilos. The two guys who came for the stuff—the same two who always made the pickups—later claimed it never happened. Beigelman insisted that the Colombians had ripped it off. Finally she admitted that Beigelman had gotten involved with the Colombians through her. In those days, they were living in New Jersey and he was a low-level hustler working gas-tax frauds for the Russian mob. She had a job in a clothing store where she became friendly with a Colombian woman who also worked there. The two couples started going out to dinner. It was the Colombian woman's boyfriend, Enrique, who connected Beigelman to the cartel. During the course of their friendship, Enrique got into trouble and was locked up in New Jersey for dealing drugs. Bailed with money wired from Cali, the minute he was out, he jumped. Around that time the Beigelmans had moved to Brooklyn.

Back in Colombia, Enrique went to his boss and told him he knew a white guy who was married with a kid who was looking to get connected. Enrique's boss liked what he heard about Beigelman, knowing from experience that white couples were inherently less suspect than Latinos. He said, set it up, making Enrique "Beigelman's rabbi"—the guy who oversees the deal, makes sure it works and gets held responsible if it doesn't. When the two pickup men—who happened to be Enrique's cousins—complained about missing two to three hundred kilos, Enrique immediately shut off shipments and payments to Beigelman. But he still found himself in trouble with his own boss. He was kidnapped and held hostage, and made to understand—in no uncertain terms—you put it together, it's your problem. Using what little credibility he had left, Enrique convinced his boss that he could resolve everything by going to New York. His boss agreed. Left unsaid was what would happen if he failed.

If there ever was a code of honor among thieves, as professed in fiction and films which romanticize the golden age of the Mafia, it certainly doesn't exist where the Colombians are concerned. Before going into business with any Colombian national, the cartel bosses insist on knowing where the employee's family lives. They may try to reach out to a guy who steals money or the dope from them and demand a meeting. They may be benevolent enough to ask once what happened. But when their patience runs out—and historically it's on a very short fuse—they go for the family. Consequently, they don't often get ripped off by their own. Nor, for that matter, do many of their own dare to testify against them.

With more than just his own neck on the line, Enrique headed for New York. But the outstanding warrant in New Jersey meant he couldn't fly direct. Instead, he traveled first to Mexico, came across the U.S. border at Tijuana and, once in the States, made his way to Brooklyn. He slept at the Beigelmans' house for almost three weeks. Later, Ahern and Crowell would see from phone records that he regularly reported in to his boss in Colombia.

During Enrique's visit, Beigelman reminded him about the van. He said it just wasn't up to his standards and that he wanted something nicer. Enrique promised to correct that problem as soon as they resolved the matter of the missing cocaine. For the entire time he was in New York, Enrique tried to get in touch with his cousins. But he never managed it. And Beigelman refused to put Enrique in touch with them, all the time insisting that he didn't have anything to do with the missing drugs and that he didn't want to have anything to do with them. Enrique returned to Colombia in November, after consoling Beigelman that as soon as everything was squared away, they'd set him up again.

With that story fresh in their minds, Ahern and Crowell turned to the out-of-state investigation where Beigelman's name had first appeared. The officers handling it had an informant whom they were willing to share. At the beginning of April, Ahern and Crowell traveled to see the informant. He admitted to knowing the Russian, confirmed Larissa's story, identified Enrique and added that he'd even had a conversation with Enrique about the murder.

He maintained, "Enrique told me, Beigelman caused me a problem. Somebody had to go. He was the most likely candidate. Better him than my cousins. So he went."

By July, Ahern and Crowell were still trying to identify Enrique's cousins. Separately, Ahern was having difficulties locating the off-duty detective who'd been at the scene. That's when a Colombian gang war broke out in Queens.

A group called Los Tusos was shooting it out with a group known as Mono's Crew, a band of thugs named for their drug-dealing leader. Bodies were dropping on a daily basis. One day the 110th Precinct would have two. The next day the 108th would have three. Then the 115th would have one. Then the 110th would have two more. Word on the street was that the leader of Los Tusos used to work for Mono, that the two had a falling-out and that this would go on until one side eliminated the other.

Although there were some people left standing at the end, it went on for months, and cleaning up the mess cut into a lot of police time. Ahern was no further along in collaring the people who'd killed Beigelman, except that the name "Chino" kept popping up. His contacts were telling him they didn't know if Chino was involved but Chino took a lot of contracts and Chino was a real bad guy—so bad, in fact, that nobody seemed willing to identify him. But just after Christmas, Ahern learned that Chino was the leader of Los Tusos.

Based on information obtained during the gang war, Ahern was able to get a plate number for Chino's car. Knowing where he was likely to hang out, Ahern and two other homicide cops—Joey Miles and Rueben Martinez—climbed into an unmarked van and, on the long shot that they might get lucky enough to spot Chino's car, headed out on the streets.

The long shot not only paid off, but against all odds, it happened within thirty seconds.

Chino drove by.

They followed him until he pulled over. The cops in the van also pulled over, a safe enough block behind. At least, they thought it was safe enough. Chino and two others got out of their car eating Chinese takeout and, almost too casually, started walking towards Ahern and his partners.

Chino got to within one hundred feet, and was now staring at the three cops.

Ahern announced, "We've been made."

One of the others asked, "What do you want to do?"

Ahern answered, "We take them."

They didn't know if Chino and his pals were armed. Nor did they have time to worry about whether arresting Chino might somehow compromise the murder investigation. The three bailed out of their van, guns drawn, screaming, "Down on the ground . . . down on the ground . . ." taking Chino and his two pals by surprise, at the same time shouting on their radio for backup.

Squad cars from all over Queens responded with sirens blaring.

Less than a minute after the takedown began, Chino and the other two were cuffed and in the process of being carted away.

Born in Medellín, Colombia, twenty years before, Juan Dairon Marin Henoa, a.k.a. Chino, liked to brag that as a teenager he'd killed people on assignment for Pablo Escobar and that once he'd reached majority—when he could be tried as an adult for his crimes—he skipped the country. In the States, he freelanced, working for anyone who'd pay him, which, since the demise of Escobar and the Medellín cartel, meant the Cali crowd.

Normally, kids like Chino stay quiet. At least the smart ones do. But Chino clearly wasn't the brightest child on the planet, and as soon as he and Ahern sat down to talk, Chino suffered a case of verbal diarrhea. He admitted to doing several hits in New York—eleven in all—and when Ahern asked why, Chino shrugged. "Because I had contracts."

Ahern got him to account for each of those eleven murders, going into detail about how much he was paid, who paid him and even which gun he used. For the record, it was a .9mm Glock, a favorite of Colombian hit men because the barrel can be removed and thrown into a river somewhere, a new barrel can be put on it and, effectively, it becomes a new gun which is untraceable to the last hit. Ahern also asked how each of the eleven victims died. Chino said they'd been shot in the head, because "I shoot you in the stomach or in the chest, you might live. I shoot you in the head, you're dead."

Ironically, after confessing to all of those murders, Chino swore he didn't know anything about the Beigelman murder. He did, however, know a lot about the gang-war killings, and readily gave up three names. Ahern hunted those three down, arrested them and, under questioning, they gave up five more names. After grabbing them, he had eleven people behind bars. Yet none of them would admit to knowing anything about Beigelman.

There was, however, a common thread running through their stories. The Apollo Bar on Corona Avenue.

The gang members told him that was where they used to muster up, meaning that when a hit was contracted, the fellow holding the contract—a guy like Chino—would go to the bar to ask if anyone wanted to come out with him. He'd negotiate a price, averaging around a couple of thousand dollars per man, and recruit a crew.

Word on the street is that the contract on Beigelman went for
$70,000, although there are some people who contend it might have gone
for ten times as much. While it's true that in the world of Colombian
drugs, killing a white guy costs more than killing a Colombian—which
can be arranged for a measly few grand—the one sure thing that can be
said about the fee is that however much it was, it didn't last long. The guys
who take these contracts are all alike. Chino, for example, picked up several hundred thousand dollars in murders in 1995, and yet, Ahern notes,
"He spent everything on drugs, cars, girls, guns. Didn't have a cent left.
Nothing. Didn't have a pot to piss in."

Knowing that the Apollo was the "employment agency" piqued
Ahern's interest because it was only five blocks from where Beigelman had
been murdered. He and Crowell guessed that someone there might know
something, so they started making the rounds, asking questions.

And their hunch paid off.

One Colombian barfly admitted, "I was hanging out on Roosevelt
Avenue and two guys came by and asked me if I could take them for a ride,
'cause I had a car. So I said sure, they got in and told me where to go. I
wanted to know why they wanted to go there and they said, 'cause we just
shot somebody and we want to make sure he's dead. They get to the block,
it's lit up like a Christmas tree with cop cars, and that's how the hit men
knew they'd done their job."

Another came up with a name for the fellow who'd picked up the
contract. Someone else suggested word had come directly from Cali that
Beigelman needed to be killed because he was an undercover DEA agent.
That was the cover story, the line they invented to make it easy to find a
crew and someone to pull the trigger.

Informants at the bar also bandied about four nicknames. Ahern and
Crowell were able to put photos to the nicknames and last names to the
photos. But the fourth man on that list, they were assured, was dead.

The problem here became separating real names from phony names,
because these guys changed their names all the time. One day someone
was Juan Gomez. The next day he was Manny Garcia. The day after that
he was Jose Gacha. Dealing with addresses was no easier. These guys lived
in one room with three pairs of pants, two shirts, one pair of sneakers and
a paper bag to carry their clothes when they moved to a new location,
which they did every few days. Finding the dead guy was a little more

straightforward. The DEA located a death certificate for him. "Otherwise," Ahern warns, "I wouldn't believe he was dead."

Even though all this was going on, Ahern had still not given up looking for the off-duty cop who'd been at the scene, earning his nickname from Panzarella as "the Energizer Bunny." When Ahern finally located him, the off-duty cop shrugged: "I told the cops at the scene, I'm available. If you need me I'm in. But no one ever bothered to call me after that."

It turned out they'd gotten his name wrong.

More importantly, the off-duty cop added, "I can ID these guys."

On March 6, 1996, eleven months after Ahern and Crowell first interviewed Larissa, and two and a quarter years after the murder, they got a major break. A phone call came in from Florida from a DEA agent who had locked up a guy who was talking about a Russian getting killed in New York. Ahern was on the next plane heading south.

That man admitted to knowing the shooter, plus the names of the other guys on the crew. He ID'd the two who met Beigelman around the corner and confirmed that the fourth guy was dead. From what he heard in Florida, Ahern was no longer sure he knew who'd picked up the contract. But whoever it was, he still wanted him. Even more so, Ahern wanted the guy who'd put out the contract—Enrique's boss.

Back in New York, on March 21, Ahern and Crowell and two other cops went to a location in Queens and arrested Neil Matos, a kid whose street name was Baby Face—one of the two who'd walked Beigelman to his death. At the time of the murder, Matos was just thirteen years old.

When Ahern informed Baby Face that he was under arrest for a murder in 1993, Matos coldly responded, "What took you so long?" He admitted it was his baseball cap and blue scarf that were found at the scene, and confirmed the names of the others.

At this point, Crowell left Ahern to get on with the case alone, returning to his regular duties at the DEA, where today he's still out on the street, giving cell heads a lot to worry about.

With Baby Face locked up, the shooter was easy to locate. The name Ahern had for him appeared on the system. His current address was listed as a nearby federal prison. Concluding that the shooter wasn't going anywhere for a very long time, Ahern decided first to hunt down Baby Face's partner. Matos claimed he too was already in jail. But if he was, Ahern couldn't find him, at least not under the name he was using in 1993. Then

Ahern stumbled across an informant who gave him the name of the money man in the States who'd paid for the hit. He too was already in federal custody on other charges.

Baby Face's partner has still not been found. The shooter was charged with three other contract murders. And there is still some doubt as to who, exactly, picked up the contract. Enrique was in Colombia and his cousins—who'd almost certainly stolen the two to three hundred kilos—were somewhere in hiding. The U.S. Attorney's office in New York was, however, planning to put a number of people away for life.

The odd one out was Baby Face. He was treated as a juvenile and placed on probation. Shortly after his eighteenth birthday he was arrested for crack distribution, treated this time as an adult, and is back in jail. His only lament seems to be that he never got paid for his part in Beigelman's death.

The fate of Enrique's boss is a different matter.

The out-of-state DEA investigation that originally connected Beigelman to Enrique's cousins in turn connected the coke he was storing to a rising-star drug baron in Colombia named Juan Carlos Ramirez Abadia.

Known as Chupeta—Lollipop—because of his boyish looks, he was raised in a middle-class Colombian family and trained as an industrial engineer. He learned the drug business under the tutelage of brothers Ivan and Julio Fabio Urdinola Grajales, who ran the North Valley cartel, a sort of subsidiary of the Cali cartel. By the early 1980s, Chupeta, who was born in 1963, was already starting to see where the organization's weaknesses were and to postulate a suitable strategy to compensate for them. He recognized how the Urdinolas' joint venture with the Italian Mafia had turned them into Colombia's primary heroin traffickers. Slightly further afield, he noticed how the Medellín cartel was beginning a minor flirtation with the Mexicans.

One of the traffickers associated with Escobar in Medellín was a Honduran named Juan Ramon Matta Ballesteros. Through contacts, presumably in Spain, he'd befriended a Mexican trafficker named Alberto Sicilia Falcon. When Ballesteros introduced Falcon to his friends in Colombia and Falcon returned the favor by introducing Ballesteros to his friends in the Guadalajara cartel, they did what new friends sometimes do—they went into business together. The deals that followed, however, were minor. Ballesteros supplied small amounts of product for the Mexicans to smuggle, even though the Mexicans weren't terribly interested in trafficking coke and Ballesteros wasn't terribly keen on running drugs through Mexico. They didn't need each other. The Mexicans had marijuana, a product they were very adept at handling, and the Colombians had the Caribbean, an efficient, cost-effective and well-established thoroughfare into the States. Another Medellín cartel member, Gonzalo Rodriguez Gacha, also took advantage of Ballesteros's friendship with Falcon. Again, not because it was a necessity but because Gacha—who relished his nickname, "The Mexican"—happened to love all things Mexican.

For much of the 1980s, these early ties were little more than a hobby and never anything like a serious, big-money business connection.

It was almost ten years before the Cali cartel upped the stakes. Because the Caribbean was becoming too dangerous, the Orejuela brothers negotiated a relationship with Juan Garcia Abrego, the trafficker who controlled much of the border with Texas through his Gulf Cartel, who was ensconced just across the Rio Grande from Brownsville in Matamoros, Mexico.

But in between Ballesteros's deal and the Orejuelas' deal, the pact that bridged the way from hobby to business was Chupeta's.

In the mid-1980s, he'd come to deduce that the future of Colombian trafficking was no longer in running a business like a major international oil conglomerate—having a hand in every stage from desert oil wells to gas-station forecourt retailing—but to consider the operation itself as a commodity and, taking a lesson straight out of the McDonald's Hamburger School of Business, move into franchising.

It was a lesson he learned the hard way. In 1987, Chupeta was in charge of running cocaine in tractor trailers across the U.S. for the Urdinolas. To minimize suspicion, he hired Jamaicans to drive the loads, a radical departure from the golden rule, which had always been, Never trust anyone except another Colombian. When a half-ton shipment was busted in Loma, Colorado, the Urdinolas insisted he pay for it. So Chupeta started a sideline business for himself. He decided it was better to take a smaller profit by wholesaling to someone else—thus guaranteeing much-needed cash up front—in exchange for minimizing his risk. The most obvious candidates were the Mexicans, because smuggling anything and everything across the U.S. border was what they did.

He brokered a relationship with the Juarez cartel, then paid a retired Colombian air-force pilot upwards of half a million dollars to fly thirteen hundred pounds of coke in a King-300 to an unpaved airstrip in Chihuahua, Mexico. Initially, he agreed to pay his Mexican partners around $3 million per shipment for their services. Then they demanded 35 percent of the take. Before long, they were insisting on half.

Chupeta might not have liked the percentages, but he gave the Mexicans drugs to sell on their own account because they paid up front and minimized his risk. The strategy worked so well that he soon branched out to do similar joint ventures with the Guadalajara cartel.

At the time he ordered Vladimir Beigelman's death, Chupeta had opened the door wide enough for the Mexicans to control all coke sales on the West Coast and to begin moving east to secure strongholds from the Rockies to Chicago. In doing that, he'd become one of the five most powerful cocaine traffickers in the world, ruling a mini-cartel with as many as two hundred franchised agents. By his own admission, between 1987 and 1995 he smuggled at least thirty tons of coke through Mexico into the United States. By their own calculation, the DEA says the figure could be two or three or four times higher.

It was just after the hit on Beigelman, but in no way related to it, that a series of events occurred that were beyond Chupeta's control and that changed his life.

Conceding to pressure from the United States, the Colombian government finally cracked down on the Cali cartel. As a consequence, civil war broke out among the traffickers. Both Urdinola brothers went to jail, although that didn't stop either their trafficking or their attempt to move in on the wounded Cali cartel. Chupeta was forced to take sides and wisely chose Cali. The Orejuela brothers also wound up in jail, although that didn't curtail their drug trafficking or impede their ability to ward off the Urdinola takeover. The infighting left a void.

Chupeta was there to fill it. With the remains of the Cali cartel crumbling around him, he emerged relatively safe, the best and brightest of the younger generation.

One of the senior Cali members, Jose Santacruz Londono, had also been put in prison, but at the beginning of 1996, he escaped. In early March, the Colombian police found him in Medellín and, under the rules of engagement for someone resisting arrest, they killed him. That was followed by a brutal two-day crackdown in Cali by the national anti-narcotics squad.

Now Chupeta was thrown into a panic, fearing that he too might be accused of resisting arrest. Under the allegedly corrupt regime of President Ernesto Samper—whose election campaigns are widely believed to have been financed by drug money—the Colombians had created an generously lenient system of surrender. Chupeta opted to make it work for him, and ten days after Londono's death, he gave himself up to government prosecutors in Cali. Nine months later, he was condemned to twenty-four years in prison, the stiffest sentence yet to a Colombian drug trafficker.

But in Colombia, twenty-four years doesn't mean twenty-four years.

It was quickly reduced to thirteen.

Charity was administered based on his surrender and an agreement to forfeit assets worth perhaps as little as 10 percent of the money he'd made drug trafficking. Like the brothers Urdinola and Orejuela, Chupeta is almost certainly still in the drug business, running his interests with mobile phones from his cell.

But in Colombia, thirteen years doesn't mean thirteen years.

In 1997 he turned against his partners, outlined for the Colombians how his Mexican franchise operation worked and contended that it never could have happened without a thoroughly corrupt Mexican government. The following year he turned state's witness again, this time testifying before a Mexican judicial panel, accusing several senior officials with ties to former Mexican president Carlos Salinas de Gortari of having been on his payroll—among them, Mexico's former deputy attorney general for narcotics matters and a former commander of the judicial police. Chupeta even went as far as to insist that no drugs moved through Mexico without their permission.

Apparently that was good enough to cut the thirteen years down to seven or so.

But in Colombia, seven or so doesn't mean seven or so.

He could be out, with most of his assets still intact, in under five.

Billy Ahern and Brian Crowell would love to see him brought to the States to stand trial for the murder of Vladimir Beigelman. But that's not going to happen. Anyway, Chupeta—the player who made it into the majors by franchising his drug business like hamburger stands—probably wouldn't even recognize Beigelman's name.

10

THE NEW MELTING POT

The traditional Mafia is saying, we're watched, but we can fly in Russians who are not known to the authorities and get them to some heavy lifting. They're able to function because we don't know who these guys are.

—former FBI agent BOB LEVINSON

MIAMI WAS WHERE THEY DECIDED TO GET together. The weather was good. They had friends there. They had business there too.

It was 1993.

Ivankov traveled down from New York. Mikhailov and Averin flew in from Vienna. Essine came in from Italy and Sergei "Sylvester" Timofeyev flew in from Moscow. A few other minor players were there. No one ever published the attendance list, but notable by his absence was Monya Elson. He would have come, except they didn't invite him.

This was the meeting where they decided that Essine would have exclusive control over Italy, and where Ivankov and Mikhailov—with Averin in tow—divided up their interests in Moscow's most important hotels. Ivankov claimed a full-third share. Mikhailov agreed, taking a third for himself. The rest would go to the others.

This was the meeting where Sylvester told the others about his own meeting in Moscow the year before with a representative of the Cali cartel, about how a man had flown in from Peru with instructions to set up a connection. After hearing that, the others decided they needed to set up future meetings with the Colombians, and the Italians too.

This was the meeting where they decided that Vienna would be declared a crime-free zone.

This was the meeting where they decided to murder Monya Elson.

Except that Elson—furious at having been excluded—hit first. He had Sylvester gunned down in Moscow.

In the days before drug money, Miami had far fewer banks than it does today. Then, suddenly, there were oceans of drug money. Then, suddenly, there were more banks in Miami than any other North American city except New York. And nowhere else in the world has the natural alliance of drugs and money manifested itself in quite this way, ripping the soul of the city away from the United States and transforming it into the capital of South America. Walled estate by walled estate, security camera by security camera, marina by marina, golden-reflective-glass-fronted bank by golden-reflective-glass-fronted bank, white-powder foreign aid built Miami.

The LCN had colonized the south way back in the days of Lucky Luciano, because the weather was better than up north, because Meyer Lansky was using it as a staging point for Cuba and the Bahamas, and because airplane travel was creating business opportunities in real estate and the leisure industry. By the 1960s, even the five New York families had developed strong, traditional ties with Miami. They were well ensconced when the Colombians arrived in the late 1970s and the early 1980s. Yet, as the Latinos waded ashore, they were greeted with silence.

In the past, whenever one group moved into another group's neighborhood, there were the usual stern warnings, and if those warnings weren't heeded, there were gunshots. But in Miami, as those oceans of drug money washed over the entire peninsula that is South Florida, it was almost as if the long-established LCN guys didn't mind.

In the late 1980s and early 1990s, the Russians arrived. And again, there was silence. And again, it was if neither the LCN nor the Colombians cared that new kids were setting up on the same block. Those people in law enforcement who understood what such silence meant now started to get extremely nervous. Rightfully so. The Russians knew the LCN from New York. The Colombians knew the LCN from the Caribbean. It was now just a matter of forming stronger bonds between the Russians and the Colombians, which wasn't difficult because the Colombians were a one-crop shop—if you wanted to deal serious amounts of cocaine, you had to do business with them—and the former Soviet Union was just sitting there, crying out to be exploited as one of the world's foremost cocaine markets.

Anyway, Miami is the perfect melting pot for gangsters.

The international airport is the main hub for Latin America. You can get anywhere south from Miami. Because it is also a main hub for North America, you can get away north from Miami as well. You can get to Europe easily from there, and the Orient too. It is also the feeder point into the Caribbean and the world of offshore banking.

The Port of Miami is one of the largest and busiest in the western hemisphere. Nearly nine hundred thousand full-size cargo containers move through Miami every year. A nightmare for U.S. Customs, it is categorically impossible for them to inspect even a fraction of those. So drugs easily sail in and drug cash easily sails out in the same containers. Whatever tiny percentage winds up getting seized is written off by the drug barons as the price of doing business.

Telephone and satellite communications are as good in Miami as anywhere in the world, and with so many banks vying for business, finding a crooked banker is only slightly more difficult than opening the Yellow Pages. In fact, judging by the precedent set by the BCCI affair in the 1980s, there's no need to bother with the Yellow Pages. Inventing a bank is actually easier.

Drug traffickers were bringing mailbags full of money into the BCCI office in Miami. To cover the arrival of all this cash—which the bank could never have otherwise explained—managers there created a nonexistent branch in the Bahamas. The cash deposits were then logged onto the books of the nonexistent branch. Next, the managers in Miami filed appropriate forms with U.S. Customs to import that cash from the Bahamas to Miami. Once those were filed, the cash was deposited in another Miami bank, representing a shipment from the Bahamas branch. That the branch never existed, except on the hard drive of a computer in Miami, says a lot about how banking in Miami has sometimes worked. It also speaks volumes about the kind of world we've created for ourselves—where any banker in any corner of the globe can log any transaction onto the books of any bank in any other corner of the globe, without ever leaving his own office. Then

too, in the world of Miami banking, the Yellow Pages is only worth bothering with if it's closer than the nearest modem.

"The same the thing that attracts tourists to Miami is the lure for the
criminal element," notes Hardrick Crawford Jr., Assistant Special Agent in
Charge of the FBI's Miami field office. "The weather is great. The beaches
are great. It is the gateway to the Caribbean. At the same time, it is an
uncontrolled and uncontested market. You have the LCN and the Russians
and the Colombians here, and cocaine flooding in by the ton. Using Miami
as a hub, it's easy to supply a willing market in Europe, Canada and the rest
of the United States."

Unlike New York, he says, where geographical boundaries have been
clearly defined, there are no staked-out political subdivisions in Miami.
"They all see Miami as an open geographical arena."

Nor are there any real conflicts between organizations. "The cocaine
wars in the Miami area in the 1980s were a result of Colombian organizations having violent shoot-outs with one another. These shoot-outs even
extended back to Colombia itself. The various criminal organizations, particularly the Colombians, learned that it was counterproductive for them
to be shooting at one another, and thus they became more organized and
less confrontational. Today they all see Miami as a free market. They've
decided there is plenty for everybody. There's a lot of money to be made.
They've decided there's no need for violent conflicts which only draw the
unwanted attention of the media and of course, state, federal and local law
enforcement. Instead, they get together."

Bob Levinson couldn't agree more. He worked with Crawford at the
FBI in Miami and by the time he retired from the Bureau in 1998, he was
recognized as one of the most knowledgeable experts on Russian organized
crime in Western law enforcement. Today, in private practice, he
is arguably one of the most respected experts on Russian organized crime
in the country. "South Florida is palm trees, open territory, nice people, nice
beaches, and the bad guys all want a piece of that. They also see South
Florida as a place to invest money and a good place to live. So a variety of
criminal organizations have built bases of operations in Miami. But what we
started seeing while I was still working for the Bureau were alliances
between Russian organizations and traditional LCN. And this is a very
alarming trend because before this, everyone was just operating on their
own turf. No one bothered anybody. There was a mutual respect. Now,

alliances are being formed. It means that where the Russians can't get something done, the Italian-Americans groups will go for it, and vice versa."

As an example, Levinson cites that group of Georgians who have set themselves up as enforcers. "The Kurganskaya is running around New York and Miami doing the dirty work for some of the Italian-American organizations. The traditional Mafia is saying, we're watched, but we can fly in Russians who are not known to the authorities and get them to some heavy lifting. They're able to function because we don't know who these guys are. That's what's going on now. And I think that's significant."

Over the years the FBI has painstakingly documented a great deal of migration between New York and Miami, New York and Los Angeles, Miami and Los Angeles, and back and forth to those cities from Toronto as well. They've also watched Russians making the commute between Miami and San Francisco, which they believe is the link between the U.S. and Far Eastern Russian money and people. They've surveilled couriers who bring money which has been collected from extortion payments in San Francisco and Los Angeles to New York, stop there for a few days, then travel on to Moscow and St. Petersburg. They've also surveilled Russian criminals who operate in San Francisco, coming to Miami to cool off.

The principal center for Russian organized crime in the Far East is Vladivostok, which used to be a closed city and which now has at least four formal organized crime groups. Many of the people who normally operate out of there have been seen in the United States, setting up joint ventures along the West Coast. These same people have formed drug trafficking alliances with the Yakuza and alien-smuggling alliances with Asian organized groups in China. But the bulk of their proceeds are laundered in the U.S.—the cycle starts in San Francisco and Los Angeles and, more often than not, at some point the money and the mobsters, too, pass through Miami.

The FBI isn't alone in its anxieties. Other U.S. law enforcement is just as concerned, as are the Canadians, the British, the French, the Germans and the Italians, all of whom have active-duty law enforcement officers stationed in Miami. This isn't a liaison desk job. These are investigators who work alongside U.S. law enforcement to protect their own national interests in a critical part of the world. No country can ever hope to understand its own cocaine and money-laundering problems—and by extension the Caribbean and South America—without first coming to grips with Miami.

This growing disquiet over organized criminals getting together was precisely why an ad hoc collection of Miami-based law enforcement officers also decided to get together. A small clique from the DEA, the FBI, the Immigration and Naturalization Service, the Metro Dade Police, the Broward County Sheriff, the North Miami Beach Police and the State Department's Security Branch—which handles passport fraud—began meeting informally in late spring 1994.

The most convenient place for everybody—centrally located, with plenty of parking and totally secure—was a training room at the DEA's Miami Field Division headquarters. After the second or third gathering someone thought it would be amusing to put a flag with a picture of Lenin in the room, and after that they started referring to the venue as "The Odessa Room."

Because they knew one another well and most of them had worked on cases together, they were able to shove aside the usual inter-agency rivalries and openly share information. Like when it was mentioned that a couple of Lithuanian guys were looking to trade Russian-made surface-to-air missiles for white powder.

An undercover sting was developed and played out over two years. Posing as drug traffickers, the agents met with the targets in Miami and in London, trying to sort out a deal. The targets finally came up with a plan to supply their clients with Bulgarian surface-to-air missiles. They could deliver the goods into the United States, and had arranged a way to make certain that no one could ever trace the arms back to the original source. They showed the undercover agents all the paperwork and all the forged signatures they needed to convince their clients that for $330,000, the weapons they were getting were real. The undercover agents kept asking if these missiles could blow an airliner out of the sky. The targets assured them that's exactly what the missiles could do. And both were very quickly locked up.

At other times in those Odessa Room meetings, when the same person's name got mentioned a lot, all of the agents took notice. Which is what happened when they started talking about Leonid "Tarzan" Fainberg.

Born in the Ukraine, Fainberg trained as a dentist before emigrating to Israel. From there he moved to Germany and, in the early 1980s—with an Israeli passport that proclaimed his first name was Ludwig—came to the United States. Settling in Brighton Beach, he worked in a furniture store delivering stuff, tried his hand at running his own furniture store, operated a video-rental shop and then a coin-operated video-game business. By then, fast closing in on thirty, he fancied more action. Miami was happening, so he moved there and opened a discount clothing store. By 1991 he'd been able to hustle enough out of that business, and supplement his income through contacts with the growing Russian underworld, to buy himself a strip club. Porky's was located in Hialeah, not far from Miami International Airport, and quickly earned a reputation as being sleazy, even by Hialeah strip-club standards.

Adding to the intrigue, Fainberg looked the part of Tarzan. Pumped up through steroids and weight lifting, he had a goatee, a blond ponytail and a business card with a caricature of himself as Atlas holding the world in the air with one hand. He knew enough Russians in South Florida back in Brooklyn to assure a constant flow of young Russian girls to work his club. Because his customers were willing to pay for such things, he encouraged the dancers to make contact with the customers, getting them to go as far as they possibly could without actually engaging in public sex.

A flamboyant character, he didn't have much of a record, just some minor stuff that happened from time to time. There were misdemeanors for lewd and lascivious behavior at Porky's, and one case—although charges were never filed—where he acted as muscle for a friend from Moscow who was extorting two Canadians in Miami. They were running a successful bagel shop, the Russians moved in, took over the business and frightened the Canadians back to Toronto. But that was all.

Fainberg's friend from Moscow was, however, scary. His name was Anzor Kikalischvili, and he was a major player. A self-described businessman, he was one of the people always rumored to have been at that 1993 Miami meeting. If he wasn't there, the reputation he's built for himself suggests he should have been. Kikalischvili is known to be a close friend of Josif Kobzon, the so-called "Russian Frank Sinatra." A saloon crooner, Kobzon was the man who went to Israel to bring his friend Gregory Lerner back to Russia. Kobzon is also known to have been tight with Ivankov. Kikalischvili's friendship with Kobzon therefore links him to Lerner and Ivankov. No one is quite sure what sort of friendship, if any, Kikalischvili shared with Fainberg. But when word reached Fainberg that certain people back in Moscow were saying he was too independent, that he was overstepping boundaries, that he wasn't authorized to get into the areas he was getting into, that he was a marked man, Fainberg ran straight to Kikalischvili for protection. And because Kikalischvili got on the phone and quickly made everything right, Fainberg owed him. So when Kikalischvili needed muscle to help shake down those Canadians, Fainberg couldn't refuse.

Sometime after the two moved in on the bagel shop, Kikalischvili was caught on tape telling someone that he was setting himself up in South Florida to be the man in charge. He said it was important to have someone like him taking control of things. And then he bragged, "I already have over six hundred people here." To stop him before he could get anywhere near such a position, the U.S. Immigration and Naturalization Service canceled his visa and stuck him on a list of undesirables.

Fainberg's contact with Kikalischvili seemed typical of the business he was running out of Porky's. And that's why Fainberg's name kept popping up at those ad hoc meetings in the Odessa Room. He was establishing himself as a "facilitator." He was available to help other Russians looking for action in Miami. Intelligence gleaned from witnesses in other cases had it that whenever Russians in New York—and sometimes even as far away as Moscow—said they were heading down to Miami, they were told to look up Fainberg. The promise was that he could hook them up with girls, or dope, or sell them whatever it was they were looking to buy.

Fainberg was the local Welcome Wagon, precisely the sort of character the agents in the Odessa Room wanted to know a lot about.

Through some of the backers he'd lined up to open Porky's, Fainberg had become friends with some local Cubans. One in particular was Juan Almeida. He owned the Fort Apache Marina, a boat-storage-and-repair operation in North Miami Beach, and was known to have connections in Colombia.

Around the same time that Porky's opened, Almeida mentioned to Fainberg that some of his Colombian pals were looking to buy Russian military surplus aircraft. Getting into this game would be pretty good, Fainberg decided, and immediately sent word back to the Colombians that he had all the right contacts. Even if he clearly didn't.

The Colombians were anxious to believe that he did and said they wanted to do some deals. To make them happen, Fainberg began traveling on a fairly regular basis to Russia. Sometimes he went alone. Sometimes he took Colombians along. He translated for them, made contacts for them and helped them buy some bulletproof limousines and six surplus helicopters.

Then, in the fall of 1994, Fainberg opened a supper club called Babushka at 3363 NE 163rd Street in North Miami Beach. It was a cute little place, where he served good Russian food and featured music on weekends. It quickly got to be a hangout for Russians with money or Russians just passing through town who, for whatever reason, wanted to meet Fainberg and felt that Porky's was too down-market. But running two places and working all his scams on the side soon became too much for Fainberg. Word went out that he was looking to hire a manager for Babushka.

When that news was repeated in the Odessa Room, one of the DEA agents sitting there thought about it, saw the opportunity to take on Fainberg, and realized that he knew exactly the man for the job. It was a fellow who once ran the Gem furniture shop on Coney Island Avenue in Brooklyn, the same fellow who'd once given Fainberg a job there.

Mr. Roizis was yet another Russian émigré whose first name got changed along the way. Sometimes he was Josef. Sometimes he was Aron. And sometimes he was Gregory. But his friends always called him Grisha. But back in the old neighborhood, Brighton Beach, they still remember him as "Cannibal."

Born in Russia in the late 1940s, Roizis wound up in a reform school at the age of fifteen after severely beating up a man who'd crossed him. A dozen years later, he took his wife and two young children to Israel, where he fought in the Yom Kippur War. Two years after that, he moved his family again, this time to Brooklyn. He worked as a housepainter, as a salesman and occasionally as a drummer and singer in a nightclub band. But the appeal of making a fast buck was always too much for him, and as a result, he also found himself getting arrested a lot, albeit for minor stuff.

On one occasion, he was taken into custody by police—they say it was for his usual stunt of just being an all-around jerk—and was being booked when a cop made the mistake of referring to him as "a fucking Jew." Still handcuffed from behind, Roizis flew off the bench where he was sitting, knocked the cop to the ground and, literally, bit off the end of his nose. Other cops then beat the crap out of him. But "Cannibal" became a legend in the old neighborhood.

He had that furniture store for a while, which wasn't a bad business,

but it wasn't good enough either, because Roizis had a minor heart condition and—unlike in Russia, where medical bills didn't exist—treatment
in the States required money. There wasn't enough coming in from the furniture business. So he turned for help to someone he'd met while working in the nightclub, Marat Balagula.

He'd seen for years how heroin had lifted other people—namely Boris
Nayfeld and Monya Elson—out of the boardwalk tenements and into pala-
tial houses in exclusive, fancy non-Russian neighborhoods. He asked
Balagula to please set up a connection for him. Balagula duly introduced
him into Nayfeld's consortium of ten Russians and six Italians—their
Golden Triangle heroin connection that moved drugs out Thailand,
through Poland and into the States—which, in 1991, brought in more than
enough to keep Roizis's medical bills from backing up.

But a year was all it was worth. Roizis was off on a furniture-buying
trip in Romania when word reached him that the Drug Enforcement
Administration had busted up his heroin ring. The others had either been
arrested or were about to be. For the sake of his heart problem, he suddenly decided that life in Romania would suit him fine.

Except it didn't. An international arrest warrant was issued for him
through Interpol. In September 1992, once the Romanians realized who
he was, they complied with the warrant, kicked out his front teeth and
tossed him into jail. They eventually notified the DEA that he was available for collection if they wanted him. And that, the Romanians decided,
was the end of that. They did absolutely nothing else. Or, better put,
absolutely nothing at all.

Their excuse was, he's not our prisoner, we're just holding him for the
Americans, so there's no reason for us to spend any of our money on him.
They didn't bother feeding him. They didn't bother giving him his heart
medication. They just left him there to wait.

Roizis's wife arrived in Bucharest in a hurry, which is perhaps the only
reason he survived. She fed him. She medicated him. She also helped get a
DEA agent from the U.S. Embassy in Vienna to show up to interview him.

Understandably, Roizis was now in a total panic for his life. He told the
DEA agent, "I don't care what you're charging me with, just get me the hell
out of here. I'll waive any fight over extradition. Please, just get me out."

The DEA brought him home and, for good measure, stuck him in jail
in Otisville, New York. While he was there, they also worked out a deal

with him. Using his heart problems as a cover for splitting his trial away from the others in the heroin consortium, Roizis secretly pled guilty. Then, just as secretly, he began testifying before several grand juries about everyone he'd ever met and everything he ever knew. He talked about the ten Russians and the six Italians. He talked about Elson. He talked about Nayfeld. He talked about Balagula. By the time he was finished, Roizis had helped to put away some of the biggest names in Brighton Beach. Satisfied, the DEA cut their ties with him.

Now, with Fainberg as their target, they found themselves going back to Roizis, asking if he'd be willing to work for them undercover. The offer from Fainberg was for more than just a job in the Babushka. He explained to Roizis that if he'd invest some of his own money in the restaurant—to pay off back rent, take care of some unpaid bills and finance needed repairs to the air-conditioning system—Roizis could come in as a partner.

The DEA's Miami field division convinced some of the hierarchy in Washington to come up with $70,000 to finance Roizis's investment in the Babushka and, just like that, they had someone inside Fainberg's organization.

The Agency's original plan was to bug the restaurant, standard procedure in an undercover operation like this one. The agents controlling Roizis figured that a few well-placed listening devices would come in handy when it came to dealing with Fainberg and also, given the restaurant's clientele, lead them to a lot of other people. Making this even sweeter, because Roizis was one of the owners, this would be consensual taping, which meant they could wire the place without going through all the red tape of court orders.

It was totally legal. But totally unworkable. They wired Roizis's office and a couple of the booths where some of the gangsters were known to hang out, then set up a system where they could turn the bugs on and off, depending on who was there. Unfortunately, the band was always playing and the place was too noisy. They couldn't hear a damn thing. In the end, they were forced to wire Roizis himself with a little pocket recorder from time to time.

The next thing that happened was that Brent Eaton, the DEA agent who worked the case alongside FBI Special Agent Tony Cuomo, heard about a Russian-speaking DEA agent named Alexander "Sasha" Yasevich. He was born in Odessa, along the Black Sea, and came to America with his parents when he was fourteen. He grew up in Brighton Beach, drove a taxi to put himself through school, joined the Marines and was what Eaton calls "a real rough-and-tumble guy." Fluent in Russian, Hebrew, street lingo and crime lingo, he was, Eaton and Cuomo realized immediately, the perfect guy to bring into the operation.

Sasha agreed, and they hooked him up with Roizis. The story they cooked up was that he was a guy from the old neighborhood, which wasn't a difficult role to play because it was true. In fact, Sasha and Roizis had lived in the same building and had known each other as kids. Sasha also knew Fainberg by sight, but had never met him.

Introductions were finally made on January 27, 1995.

Sasha strolled into the Babushka, sat down, ordered a meal and started eating. Roizis walked by, did a double take and they went through the act of recognizing each other. There were several minutes of all the usual hugging, kissing, shaking hands, then Roizis brought Fainberg to the table to meet his old pal Sasha. The three talked about the old neighborhood and went through all the usual did-you-knows. The undercover relationship took instantly.

Fainberg fast became Sasha's buddy. They hung out together. As confidence grew between the two, Sasha told Fainberg that he dealt heroin and arms. Fainberg told him that he wanted to open up a separate strip club and suggested that if Sasha gave him $150,000 they could be partners and Sasha could launder all his money through the club. He insisted it was a great way to wash dirty money and then explained how he avoided taxes by skimming cash. In fact, they spoke about all sorts of criminal activities and, before long, Fainberg even confided, "Those same people I sold helicopters to, they talked to me the other day and said they want a submarine."

Neither Sasha nor the agents listening to the wire he was wearing could believe it.

Fainberg went on, "They're talking about a big military submarine, with a crew of twenty-five or more, that they can purchase or lease or something for a couple of years. They want to sneak it underwater to Colombia and use it to deliver drugs up and down the West Coast of the United States." He confessed, "It's so big it scares me."

A startled Sasha played his role perfectly, gently encouraging Fainberg to tell him all about it.

Like many crooks, Fainberg had a penchant for cloned cell phones—the ones that work off stolen numbers—so that he didn't have to pay for calls. So the DEA arranged with the Secret Service to get some phones set up that could pass as clones. Every now and then, Sasha—who explained he had a connection—would give a phone to his pal Fainberg as a gift. Those were the phones that he used to call Russia and South America. In fact, he phoned everywhere on them. He couldn't thank Sasha enough for them. And never suspected they were tapped.

As the possibility of a submarine deal developed, Fainberg turned more and more to Sasha for advice. Sasha kept saying that, because he'd been in the military, he had a lot of the right contacts, hinting that he was hooked into military intelligence. He told Fainberg that the best thing they could do was have everything checked out, so that they'd sound really intelligent when they talked about stuff like submarines. He said, that way, they could both make some money out of it. Fainberg appreciated his friend's counsel, admitting that he felt, technically, a little over his head.

Over the course of two months, Sasha was Fainberg's number-one adviser. Fainberg would go off to Russia, then come back and tell Sasha what was going on. He'd ask for more advice. Sasha would promise to check on things with his military contacts, then come back a few days later with an answer. Then Fainberg would go off to Russia again, and come back seeking more advice.

On March 19, 1995, Fainberg introduced Sasha to Juan Almeida.

Ever cautious, Almeida interrogated Sasha for half an hour.

Obviously he passed muster, because Almeida now told him, "Okay. I need you to help us move the submarine from point A to point B. This is very confidential, so you can't tell anyone about it." He said, "My buyers have unlimited funds, price is not a problem, but they do require security because they're going to use this for illegal purposes. They're going to find gold off the coast of the Philippines." Then he laughed and winked.

Sasha never met Almeida again.

The Colombians, through Almeida, had provided funds for Fainberg's various expenses—the middleman was a fugitive, in Florida since 1991, named Nelson "Tony" Yester—and guaranteed that they would arrange to have enough money sitting in Switzerland to make the purchase when the time came. They budgeted up to $35 million for the deal.

By this point the DEA had picked up a lot of information about Fainberg. They knew what he was dealing in—drugs, counterfeiting, prostitution, extortion and car theft. One day, when Fainberg told Roizis that a Russian military plane he'd sold to Colombian coke dealers had been seized by the DEA in Bogota, they added arms-brokering to the list.

They'd also known for some time that he was trafficking stolen cigarettes. But now, when they learned that two of his truckloads had been seized by the police—one in Georgia and one in New Jersey on its way to New York—they decided to cut in some other agencies. They got the Bureau of Alcohol, Tobacco and Firearms involved. They sold Fainberg some untaxed liquor. They got Customs involved too. Sasha introduced an undercover agent to Fainberg, saying that he'd laundered money through him.

Along with Yester and Almeida, Fainberg was shipping coke from Ecuador to St. Petersburg in fresh iced-down shrimp. He talked to Sasha about the deal and told him that the St. Petersburg guys were looking for a ten-kilo sample. Fainberg said he couldn't send it with the shrimp deal, and asked if Sasha would take it over there for him. The DEA immediately nixed it. With hindsight, they regret it. They would have been able to come up with a million ideas to explain how Sasha got there and the drugs didn't. Meeting with Almeida's and Yester's contacts in St. Petersburg would have gotten Sasha more involved in the dope end of the thing.

After a while, with all this other stuff going back and forth, the submarine deal seemed to stagnate. Through Sasha, the DEA had photographs of Fainberg climbing all over diesel subs in Krondstadt and Murmansk. He continued traveling to Russia every month or so, staying for up to a week on each trip, coming back to tell Sasha that he would find a submarine soon. But it just wasn't happening. And by that summer, it came to light that Yester had misappropriated a few hundred thousand dollars. That created a lot of friction.

The undercover budget to keep Roizis in the restaurant business was also starting to run out. What's more, Sasha's home office in Washington was getting testy about him constantly being in Florida, working on this project, when they had things for him to do. So the operation slowly wound down.

Roizis decided that if the DEA wasn't going to support him any longer, he was going to get out, because he just couldn't stick around on his own. The Babushka folded. He moved back to New York. Sasha went back to Washington, although he stayed in touch with Fainberg. Every now and then he'd remind Fainberg that he was always looking for a heroin deal, if one ever came along.

The DEA had settled on heroin because coke was too easy to arrange. On July 3, 1995, Fainberg phoned Sasha to say he might be able to make a heroin connection for him, that is, if he was still looking for some. Sasha said he was. Fainberg told him this was heroin base being sold by Russians. Sasha said he wanted to meet. Unbeknownst to Sasha at the time, Fainberg was under pressure from the Colombians to come up with the misappropriated money. Yester had left the country and was living between Panama and Caracas. Fainberg was also still running back and forth to Russia. He and Yester were supposed to meet in St. Petersburg, so he couldn't make the scheduled meeting in New York between Sasha and the heroin traffickers. It got canceled and never rescheduled.

Fainberg did, however, come up with a submarine. He found a Tango Class diesel submarine in Murmansk and negotiated a price of $5.5 million. The deal would be run through a civilian government agency who'd rule it to be surplus and approve the sale to Fainberg's people under the guise of being for oceanographic research. He later told Sasha that the Russians were giving submarines away because money was so short and the military guys were broke. He also found a retired admiral who, along with his crew of twenty-five, would sail it. Fainberg guaranteed them two years' employment.

The problem now became how to get the sub to Colombia.

The admiral explained that he didn't want to sail across the Atlantic because the boat would need a complete overhaul as soon as they got into port. His idea was to tow it. But a submarine in tow was pretty visible, and someone might be curious enough to wonder what was going on. That prompted several more meetings. Fainberg, the admiral and the Colombians got together in Switzerland to discuss it. The Colombians even flashed their bankbook with the $35 million in it to prove they could afford this.

Apparently, the more the admiral talked, the less enthusiastic the Colombians grew. There were a lot more downsides to running drugs in a submarine than they'd ever imagined. The Colombians had second thoughts, realizing that submarines—even if they're pretending to be research vessels—simply attracted too much attention. So, after a time, they said, Thanks anyway. They decided they'd rather find a surface ship that might be more suitable for the oceanographic-research cover.

When the DEA found out that the Colombians had walked, and mentioned it to some people in other agencies, a senior manager in one of those other agencies sighed, "Too bad. I wish they'd gotten it. They come at us with everything to smuggle drugs. From speedboats to container ships to aircraft of all sizes to balloons to microlites, they use them all. Those get through. They even use semi-submersibles between Colombia and Puerto Rico. Very small, fiberglass, with small engines, virtually impossible to track. Those get through, too. We should have done whatever we could have to encourage them to buy that sub. Just imagine, they could have filled it up with four hundred tons of drugs. We should have let them do that and come at us fully loaded. Because submarines we can find."

As it happens, the entire coast of North America is ringed with special sonar devices specifically to detect submarine penetration. Furthermore, the U.S. Navy has a huge library of soundprints—engine and other noises given off by submarines that are particular to each boat. From the sound-print alone, Naval Intelligence can tell not just the class of sub, but its name and number. The Colombians might not have known that. Fainberg almost certainly didn't. It's possible the Russian admiral could have mentioned it, as someone in his position would know.

Anyway, that was the end of that, at least as far as the submarine was concerned. But Fainberg was still in business. He'd swallowed the bait from Customs and in the fall of that year decided to nurse his sorrow over the submarine by laundering money for them. Sasha had introduced him to an Italian agent who played his part very well, took Fainberg out on a yacht, and filled his head with all sorts of promises about future deals. Fainberg handled the first shipment of cash just fine. But the second time he was handed $45,000 to put through the washing cycle, he helped himself to it. That brought things to a head with Sasha. He berated Fainberg, said that he'd already paid the Italians their share and, "Now you owe me."

Just after that conversation, Eaton and Cuomo learned that some local television people had been shooting an exposé on Russian organized crime, filmed inside Porky's, had spoken with Fainberg and said some things that had frightened him. They'd talked about undercover operations. Fainberg had suddenly begun to wonder about Sasha.

Eaton, Cuomo and their bosses agreed that nothing else could be done undercover, so Sasha was pulled out. But the DEA and FBI still had some scores to settle. In January 1997 they took down Fainberg. It couldn't happen sooner because it took the FBI that long just to translate all the calls and conversations they'd recorded—more than fifteen thousand—and then to make some sense out of them. It was Eaton and Cuomo who personally arrested Fainberg. Yester was gone, but was indicted and is wanted. Almeida hid in for a while in Russia, then just gave himself up.

Unusually for an operation like this, especially with the DEA's involvement, they wound up with no dope and no seizures, but an awful lot of evidence. After hiring and firing at least six different attorneys and, at one point, defending himself, in February 1999 Fainberg finally decided he'd had enough. He settled for a plea bargain, admitted his guilt to racketeering, agreed to testify against Almeida and Yester, and resolved to cooperate with the Feds in their ongoing investigation into Russian crime groups. In exchange, he's been admitted to the witness protection program. They'll change his name and give him an entirely new identity and he'll spend the rest of his life hoping—possibly even praying—that neither the men he's implicating nor any of their various friends ever find him.

11

THE CARIBBEAN CESSPOOL

Just think of them as dandelions.

—BEN SOAVE, RCMP

THE CARIBBEAN, WHICH IS LARGELY A COLLECTION OF former British colonies or current British protectorates, is living testament to the money-laundering cesspool that is the British Commonwealth.

Shame on the British!

The banks are there. The shell companies are there. The Colombians are nearby. The Italians are there. The Russians are there too. Dirty money and drugs have turned the Caribbean into organized crime's version of the warm-water port the Soviet military could never establish.

That bank secrecy is a service many people are willing to pay for is hardly an excuse for its existence. To claim that selling such a service is the sovereign right of any government, as long as no laws are being violated locally—in total disregard for laws that are being violated elsewhere—is downright disingenuous. Most people who hide money are doing so for reasons that at best might be questionable, at worst are blatantly illegal. For a government to shut its eyes to that is, in and of itself, deceitful.

Start, then, with the Cayman Islands. A recent survey suggested that the Caymans, with one bank for every forty-nine residents, holds assets nearing $500 billion, which works out to nearly $20 million for each resident.

In the Caymans, they tell you from the get-go that everything is aboveboard. They say they don't want money launderers and that they reject dirty money. They insist they have cleaned up their act and that they are no longer a sink for the world's drug cash. But none of that is the same as saying there's no dirty money regularly coming into the Caymans. In reality, what they've done by becoming holier-than-thou is skillfully played their "plausible deniability" card. No, our clients are not Russian drug dealers, not at all, our clients are well-established Panamanian lawyers with whom we've been dealing for years.

As for who those Panamanian lawyers are working for, well, that's another matter. They don't do business with money launderers and drug dealers, but they hardly lose sleep trying to find out who the beneficial owner of the money is because that might scare the money away. All they need to do is reassure themselves that they know their clients.

Today in the Caymans, bankers, lawyers and government officials all sing from the same hymnbook: we've sorted out the laundrymen and will not allow dirty money to pollute our otherwise sterling reputation. They claim they have strict anti-money-laundering laws in place and that the bad old days of men with dark sunglasses arriving by private jet carrying suitcases filled with $100 bills are long gone.

In fact, they are right on both counts. They do have strict anti-money-laundering laws. Except that those laws are frequently overlooked. And the days of men with dark sunglasses and suitcases are over. Today the money is wired in from someplace else.

Like many similar songs sung in that part of the world, it is off-key enough that you know they can't carry a tune.

Washington attorney Jack Blum remembers going to the Cayman Islands in 1970 and seeing one dozen to two dozen offshore banks along a beach. "Now that sandbar is a city. And it's all been built on offshore money."

Growth in the Caymans during the 1990s has been spectacular, undeniably due in part to two political phenomena.

The first was the fall of the Soviet Union and the huge amounts of capital that have come to the West. Russian money has poured into the Caribbean. How much of this capital comes from businessmen hiding money from the tax authorities and how much of it is being siphoned out of the economy by organized criminals is impossible to say. Suffice it to say that some of the money laundered in the Bank of New York scandal not only went through the islands, but specifically came through the Caymans. It is, therefore, total nonsense for anyone in the Caymans to suggest that while up to 10 percent of the world's drug money—around $50 billion— is being laundered by the Russians through the Caribbean, none of it washes ashore in the Caymans.

The second, less obvious source of Cayman prosperity was the Chinese takeover of Hong Kong. In fear of what Beijing might do, a great deal of money was shipped out to be bedded down in the Caymans for safekeeping. Some of it was legitimate money. Some of it was owned by Asian organized criminals. But by the time it got to the Caribbean, it was all squeaky clean. What's more, just because it now lives in the Caymans doesn't mean the money isn't still being managed from Hong Kong.

And therein lies one of the anomalies of the offshore world. Money can be in one place, the management of it halfway around the world, the beneficial owner well hidden somewhere else again. Money can be shifted through jurisdictions, manipulated around accounts and brought out in other forms anywhere around the world without anyone ever having to physically be anywhere. In short, the entire offshore world is nothing more than the smoke-and-mirror figment of someone's imagination which manifests itself on the hard drive of a computer.

Welcome to Antigua.

On an island short on natural resources, the government doesn't spend a lot of time pretending that the banks chartered there are legitimate. Since 1993 they've licensed at least a dozen Russian banks, plus as many trust and insurance companies. In 1994, they also licensed the European Union Bank.

As the world's first cyberspace bank, it illustrates only a few of the questions that need to be answered. If a bank exists only in cyberspace, who has the authority to investigate? Whose job is it to police the international financial system? In the end, how will anyone ever bring the perpetrators to justice or recover the money?

The first hurdle is a huge one because before anything else happens, it must be established where the crime was actually committed. The EUB operated on license from the government of Antigua, but not in Antigua. Such a license is, of course, meaningless. A company operating offshore from the offshore jurisdiction is, by definition, beyond the control of the licensing authority. In this case, offshore meant the Internet.

Where is it? And in whose jurisdiction is it? Making a joke out of its own license, under Antiguan law the theft of the EUB's assets was not illegal. So again, where was the crime committed? If anyone ever comes up with an answer to that question, the next two are, who committed the crime and who's going to investigate it?

The *Washington Post* reported that between 1994 and 1996, the government of Antigua authorized the formation of twenty-seven offshore banks on the island, four of them Russian-owned, one Ukrainian-owned. This on an island of sixty-three thousand people. This, too, on an island where the government has steadfastly denied that they encourage or otherwise tolerate money laundering.

Just as it is everywhere else, due diligence is required of Antiguan bankers opening accounts for foreign depositors. That's what it says on paper. It hardly comes as a surprise, however, that when pressed, bankers there admit that due diligence isn't always possible when the depositor is a foreigner. And can be completely ignored when that same foreigner is talking about seriously large deposits.

Hand in hand with the sale of national sovereignty—Antigua and the Caymans are only two of about fifty countries around the world which have gone down that route—is the manifest protection of criminals from the laws of other countries. Another place where it happens is the island that is half Dutch St. Maarten, half French St. Martin.

Both sides of the island are wall-to-wall duty-free zones. Neither side cares much about suspicious cash transactions. And the relatively lax customs formalities, at least on the Dutch side, mean that large amounts of cash are easily brought onto the island. It is well known that Russian cruise ships come into port there every week, and that Russian "businessmen" sail off on those cruises with their Colombian and Italian associates. The Dutch police back in Amsterdam are concerned, but they can't do all that much about it. Nor can the Americans. So the Russians, Colombians and Italians continue meeting openly in St. Maarten, knowing they can rely on the independence of the Netherlands Antilles to keep law enforcement from stopping them. In the meantime, the Russians, Colombians, traditional Italian groups and the LCN are all actively investing in the islands, especially in buying, managing and running casinos.

When Cuba finally reopens, it's a sure bet that the same groups will be there too. In fact, the only thing that is uncertain about Cuba is whether or not there will be any room left for the Italians and the LCN, because the Russians and the Colombians have had a huge head start. They're already there.

Not only are sovereignty, real estate and businesses for sale everywhere in the islands, many of them also flog citizenship. Web sites all over the Internet advertise passports for sale. Many will sell you a Costa Rican passport. Some offer Irish passports. The *Miami Herald* reported recently that as many as three hundred wealthy Russians have bought passports in three former British colonies. Between March 1995 and April 1997, the government of Belize sold 278 "economic citizenships," fifty of them to Russians. During that same time frame, Russians purchased one hundred citizenships from St. Kitts and two hundred from Dominica. At least in the case of the latter, new "citizens" are permitted to choose new names for their passports.

It usually takes fewer than three weeks to arrange and costs $25,000 to $50,000, depending on the quality of nationalization. Citizens then have the right to travel under whatever name they've decided to use for their passport. And with these passports, there are sixty to seventy nations that do not require formal visas, which otherwise would be required of anyone holding a Russian passport.

As an example of how far these matters can be carried, some years ago the Seychelles advertised the ultimate in citizenship. For $10 million the government there was willing to provide an internationally recognized diplomatic passport, plus guaranteed immunity on the island from any sort of extradition requested by any other nation. It was no coincidence that the offer came at a time when the Sicilian Mafia was being ripped apart, limb by limb, at the hands of aggressive Italian prosecutors responding to the murders of Judges Falcone and Borsellino. It was only withdrawn when international condemnation directly threatened business interests in the Seychelles.

Washington attorney Jack Blum remains one of the lone voices in the wilderness to warn ceaselessly about the offshore world in general, and the Caribbean in particular. "There are now $5 trillion in offshore tax havens. There are more than a million offshore, anonymous corporations, designed for the sole purpose of concealing the origin and destination of money. When you have dozens of countries around the world that offer their services and protect your privacy and your secrecy, it's just a question of where you'd like to have your privacy protected. And which flag. And which set of diplomats to argue that the records shouldn't be turned over."

The situation, he says, is very serious now. But down the road he sees how it will become critical. "You can't run the kind of integrated financial system, the kind of integrated trading on world markets that we have, where firms do business around the world twenty-four hours a day, trading every manner of commodity and currency, and still have large chunks of that kind of trading completely outside the realm of supervision. Where we can't be sure that the company's books are real. Where we can't be sure that the assets are really there. Where we can't be sure that there won't come a morning when somebody says, oh well, the money all fled and we have no idea where it went. The collapse of an institution that comes from non-supervision could very well alter the world financial markets. We've been here before. We've had unsupervised banking in some jurisdictions that destabilized a world markets. In the United States we had the lesson of the Great Depression, which caused the imposition of a regulation in the first place. The question is, are we going to go through the whole thing all over again, or do we have enough sense to know that it's time to rein it in?"

He's not speaking just about the banking system, he adds, but about much of the world's economic system. He cites, for example, how much of the world's insurance business is now in jurisdictions that are substantially unregulated.

Such as the Caribbean.

"If you open an insurance company in the British Virgin Islands, no one will supervise whether there are any assets. Should a company like that be allowed to sell insurance? We've had dozens of cases of fraud in the United States where it turned out that the insurer, or the ultimate insurer, was in an offshore jurisdiction and the money was gone. In a major catastrophe, where that money is vitally needed to rebuild facilities, you could have a disaster."

Then, he suggests, look at banks. "Berings Bank had unregulated, unsupervised trading activity in Singapore, which is derivative of market activity somewhere in Japan, which collapses a bank that the Bank of England thinks it has under its thumb in London. That's the kind of problem we can confront and that's why we can't have holes, especially the size of the holes we now have, in the regulatory system."

After that, he points to the tax ramifications.

"You can't run modern government without revenue. In France, the government says to the people, we have to cut your social welfare benefit. In Germany, the government says we can't afford to give you health care, we can't afford to give you retirement. Well, the question is, could they if all of the people paid their taxes? If they're not paying their taxes and the money isn't there to pay the social benefits, and the money isn't there to build the infrastructure to take care of the social problems, you have real political difficulty. In the Third World, it's catastrophic. How will the billion people or so in India take care of their needs for food, water, shelter, education, transportation, if the government of India can't raise tax money? Can Mexico straighten out the corruption in its government bureaucracy, can it build the kind of water and sewage treatment that it needs to make Mexico City livable? Can it solve the air pollution problem in Mexico City? Without government revenue the answer is a flat no."

If current trends continue, he says, and the offshore world thoroughly democratizes, then virtually anybody with a PC will be able to get out from under any and all government controls. "When that happens, the revenue base of both the United States and all of the major countries of Western Europe will begin to evaporate. Right now it's an issue that's not being addressed because of a combination of pressure from the bankers who are making money and the rich who are telling their own government, it's not us, we're doing it for other people."

So the Caribbean is the financial equivalent of a black hole, a colossal force of gravity sucking money into an oblivion we call banking and corporate secrecy.

"Russian organized crime," Blum concludes, "has used the offshore system to great advantage."

So much so, the FBI reports, that they have now socked away enough money just in the Caribbean to self-finance their criminal activities, perhaps forever.

Every now and then, the U.S. State Department or the British Foreign Office sends a delegation down to the islands—oddly, it often happens in winter—to remind the politicians and bankers and businessmen there that they have a responsibility to the world community, that they need to get their own act together, to self-regulate, to clean up what is termed in diplomatic niceties an embarrassment. To placate their guests, the politicians and the bankers and the businessmen agree, and for the next few days pay much lip service to the problem. Sometimes they even institute changes. Evolution, not revolution, they say, to justify the snail-like pace of reform. It's almost as if they need to give the criminals enough time to find a more sophisticated way of doing the same thing.

The people who could solve the problem, Caribbean political leaders, have no incentive to do so. This is how the country earns a living, although, in many islands, the offshore wealth being generated does not necessarily filter down to the people. For all the billions sitting in banks and companies throughout the Caribbean—making some islanders very rich and many governments very corrupt—there is still extensive unemployment, underdevelopment and poverty.

In Britain, Holland and France—three nations with heavy investments in the islands—there is no political will to force change. One reason is because there are no substitute crop programs for banks that are shut. Nor are there alternate jobs for out-of-work company-formation agents. But most importantly, there are simply no votes in it at home. A draconian crackdown on offshore criminality would not feed the poor or pave the roads. It would instead ruin the local economy, threaten the financial infrastructure, in turn destroy the tourist industry and put everyone on the breadlines.

Almost unnoticed is the direct correlation with the money sitting in those banks and the white powder being sold on the streets, destroying our inner cities and killing our children.

When the car bomb went off that day in 1963, no one in the Sicilian village of Ciaculli imagined that this singular, ugly event, which claimed the lives of seven policemen, could possibly mark a turning point in the economic history of the Caribbean. The two places were separated by five thousand miles of seas, by language, culture, tradition, ethnicity and customs.

The intended victim of the bomb was Salvatore Greco, a local mafioso. The men who wanted him dead worked for a rival clan. The death of the policemen was, as far as they were concerned, an unfortunate accident. But the Italian government didn't see it that way. Nor did the people of Italy. They wanted revenge. The government obliged with one of those final-straw, backlash reactions. They decided that, because Sicily had become so corrupt, they would punish the killers and all the other mafiosi for that bomb.

Emulating Mussolini's purge of the Mafia, they made up a list of every-one on the island believed to be involved with crime, and deported them. Most were displaced to northern Italy. Many eventually drifted back to Sicily. The ones who stayed merely carried organized crime with them to Milan and Turino, Bologna and Venice. But some left the country altogether.

Pasquale Cuntrera and his older brother Liborio were born in Siciliana, a tiny village on Sicily's southern coast. So was their friend and cohort Leonardo Caruana. The two families had dominated the village for generations, intermarrying and forming a clan that was held together by blood and tradition. Far enough away to be safe from the Mafia strong-hold of Palermo, the families banded together to terrorize neighboring villages and hold unrivaled power. But in 1951 or so, Pasquale and Leonardo were both indicted on double homicide charges, arson and the theft of some cows. There was never any question but that they would be acquitted. But when they were, for some reason, the two men decided to leave Sicily and wound up in Montreal. Six years later they were granted Canadian nationality.

By the time the bomb exploded in Ciaculli, the families were well enough established that the ones who now left Sicily could come to Canada. But not all of them did. Some chose South America, where there'd been an immigrant Italian population since World War II. The ones who settled in Venezuela found a neighborhood in Caracas that might well have been anywhere in Italy. The language, the tradition, the food and the cafés were all Italian. It was right next to the part of town that would become "Little Colombia."

The Mafia and the Colombians had been doing a *danse macabre* for years. It wasn't exactly as if they were looking to ally themselves, it was that a seller's market in cocaine was developing in Colombia at the same time that the consumer market for cocaine was developing in Europe and the United States. The Colombians were strictly suppliers. The Cuntrera-Caruanas in Venezuela and Canada eased into the relationship as buyers.

Over the next thirty years they became almost inseparable partners in a global enterprise that grew to the point where the family controlled a significant portion of the estimated 4.5–6 tons of cocaine being shipped through Venezuela every month. The Colombians had a buyer they could trust. The Cuntrera-Caruanas had a source of supply they could depend on. Together, they all became fabulously rich.

The family exploited their Venezuela–Canada pipeline and developed a new one between Venezuela and Miami, using that as a gateway into the Caribbean. From there they opened new markets, moving family members around the world to assure corporate growth. They invested in shipping, a casino, hotels, a travel agency, real estate, oil, several produce companies and Ganaderia Rio Zapa, a cattle-breeding ranch in the border region near Colombia that was big enough to have its own airstrip. They apparently have since sold it to the Gambino family.

The historical structure of the Cuntrera-Caruanas as a crime gang is almost feudal. Two families, with lots of brothers and sisters and cousins, who started marrying each other back in Sicily and produced lots of children with lots more cousins for other cousins to marry. That is one reasons they've survived—the cement of loyalty has been mixed with blood. Another reason is that by integrating themselves in other countries, they evolved away from Sicilian criminals, who in time, came to think of them almost as outsiders. The Cuntrera-Caruanas weren't from Palermo and they didn't mix with the New York LCN families. They were deliberately less prone to violence than, say, the Corleonesi under Tito Riina, and deliberately distant from the internal struggles of the other groups. They were patient, clever, low-key—they were operating in Britain for over ten years before the police and Customs got on to them—and moved cautiously into new territories, only taking them over when the time was right.

It was Liborio who opened the branch office in England, from which he ran a heroin and money-laundering ring in Portugal and Austria, and expanded the family's interests to Hong Kong and Japan. Two Caruana brothers— Alfonso and Pasquale—also worked out of Britain for a time. They refined Liborio's money-laundering network, buying a hotel, a travel agency and an import-export business through which to funnel the family's drug money.

But the main reason the family survived, almost intact, was that they'd found their niche early on and stuck with it. They didn't branch out into all sorts of other crimes. They dealt drugs and they washed money, and that was basically it. They were a business enterprise that devoted their energy to establishing new drug routes, setting up deals between their Sicilian and Colombian associates, and washing money for them too. When their Italian heroin-processing plants were shut down, they took it in stride, wrote off the losses as the cost of doing business and started refining in Thailand. At their height they were shipping fifty kilos of heroin a month.

In 1981, they set up a joint venture for heroin with other mafiosi and Thai organized traffickers, marking the first time that the Italians and the Asians had dealt together. Within a year, the FBI later estimated, the Cuntrera-Caruanas were responsible for more than half the heroin smuggled into the U.S. This was in addition to their core cocaine business, plus a sideline in cannabis that couldn't be measured in pounds or kilos. One shipment known to have gone to Canada weighed six tons. Another, bound for the U.S., weighed eleven tons. They transported around $2 million in cash weekly into the States to keep the cocaine supply running smoothly into Canada, masking all of their drug trafficking behind legitimate furniture companies, produce wholesalers, banks and shipping firms.

In 1985, British and Canadian police seized a $300 million heroin shipment moving from London to Montreal. In 1987, the Canadians grabbed a six-ton hashish cargo in Newfoundland. By now, cases were being brought against the family, and they were clearly taking hits. But for some reason, whatever hits they were taking only had a minor effect on the way they did business, and almost no effect at all on the men running that business. Law enforcement couldn't understand why.

The first real hint came in 1987, when a South Florida businessman, John Galatolo, was arrested on cocaine-smuggling charges. He admitted to the DEA that he'd personally brokered a deal for the Mafia to buy six hundred kilos of coke from the Cali cartel. That firmly established the family as cocaine franchisers for Italy. What the police still didn't know was how much further that relationship had developed.

At the start of their alliance, the Colombians tried to restrict the family to their home base. Cocaine could go to Italy, but North America and the rest of Europe was out of bounds. They reckoned they could distribute their own powder throughout the rest of the world. But Europe is a long way from Latin America, and although the Colombians could function easily in Spain, other parts of Europe proved to be a more difficult market. Little by little, they became more and more dependent on their Italian friends.

Finally, in February 1990, when the Dutch police found three tons of cocaine hidden inside a consignment of fruit juice, Pablo Escobar was willing to concede defeat. He understood that he needed Mafia distribution networks throughout Europe, and that no group was better placed to help him than the Cuntrera-Caruanas. The Cali cartel quickly followed suit.

Intelligent investing not only provided the cover of legitimate businessmen, but gave them companies through which they could keep better control over their drug trafficking while, at the same time, easily wash ever-increasing sums of money. Their assets were well diversified and spread out between Britain, Switzerland, Venezuela, Aruba, Italy, Thailand, Pakistan, the United States and Canada. It wasn't until 1992 that an Italian newspaper summed up, for the first time in public, just what the family was.

They labeled them "The Rothschilds of the Mafia."

Just three decades after being thrown out of Sicily, the Cuntrera-Caruana family was a $1 billion multinational corporation worthy of a place in the Fortune 500.

The Caribbean is thirty-seven million people in twenty-eight political entities, sixteen of which are independent states, the remaining twelve being dependent territories. With little more than beaches to sell to tourists plus coffee and bananas to export, they've needed to find ways to survive. Cash crops such as marijuana are faster and easier than catering to tourists' incessant demands. Shell companies and offshore banking are lucrative and don't pollute the beaches. Drugs and money are also two areas where these smaller nations can compete globally against their Goliath neighbors to the north.

The seven entities that make up the eastern Caribbean are key transshipment points for drugs being smuggled into North America. All seven—Antigua and Barbuda, Barbados, Dominica, Grenada, St. Kitts and Nevis, St. Lucia, and St. Vincent and the Grenadines—are independent members of the British Commonwealth. They are also key transshipment points for drugs heading to Europe. It is estimated that as much one third of the drugs being smuggled into Britain transship through these seven islands.

The presence of organized crime groups in the Caribbean is nothing new. Italian mobsters were holding hands with Meyer Lansky when he invented the place. Since those days, all sorts of conferences, committees, joint task forces, joint action groups, associations, economic development boards and other well-intentioned collections of well-minded people have been getting together for years to do something about the Caribbean. But in the end, they are out-gunned, out-financed, out-corrupted and out-lawyered by those people who stand to lose the most if ever the status quo should change.

There is simply too much money at stake to let do-gooders do good.

Aruba is something of an odd man out in the Caribbean. Not because they don't transship drugs or launder money there—they do that in huge quantities—but because it is not a Commonwealth nation. Like St. Maarten, it is Dutch.

Some sixty-eight thousand people live in the 193 square kilometers of land—about the same size as Washington, D.C.—that make up the flat island of Aruba, with few crops, no forests, no woodlands, in fact, no natural resources at all, except for white sand beaches.

It is also one of the rare places in the Caribbean where unemployment is very low. That is thanks entirely to tourism, which is at the very center of the economy, and to oil refining and storage, which also play a significant role.

In between those two is the offshore banking industry.

Heroin and cocaine from Colombia, Venezuela and Surinam are transshipped there on the way to North America and Europe. Money is laundered there through land investments, casinos, resorts and the enormous Aruba Free Trade Zone.

Money laundering was criminalized in Aruba in 1993. It gave the politicians the opportunity that politicians all over the Caribbean seek to tell the American government, which is constantly trying to bully Caribbean nations into doing something about drugs and money laundering, hey look, we're doing something. And there's no doubt that they are putting laws on the books that could have an effect. But they're not enforcing them or otherwise putting a dent in the drug trafficking and money laundering that go on.

The reason why is simple—the very people who could make a difference have no incentive to do so. Those are the bankers, lawyers, accountants and company-formation agents who have the political clout to warrant that their interests in drug trafficking and money laundering will not be disturbed. They have a law, but they still have the casinos, the offshore banking, the shell companies and the Aruba Free Zone.

The Dutch have taken a stand, too, hoping to change things in Aruba, which, some Dutch policemen acknowledge, has always been an embarrassment. But there are plenty of laws on the books in Holland making drug trafficking and money laundering illegal there, and with their own unimpressive success rate at home, it's unfathomable how they expect to do much five thousand miles away.

It is a black market with a neon sign that flashes *corner store*. From de-taxed whiskey and perfume to guns, whatever anybody in Venezuela

wants, even today, they can find in Aruba. Like the moon pulling the tides
on earth, so powerful is the island's draw on its nearest neighbor that in
1983, when the Arubans called in Venezuela's debt, the Venezuelan currency
collapsed. The knock-on effect should have collapsed Aruba's economy as
well. But the Cuntrera-Caruanas were there and they were in the drug
business, and they helped to turn the corner store into a mall.

Among the local families who grew rich and powerful over the years
are the Mansurs. Arguably the most prominent family on the island, they
are said to be the largest suppliers of Marlboros in the entire Caribbean.
They also own hotels, the local newspaper, commercial real estate, a casino,
stores, a huge import-export holding in the free-trade zone, a shipping
company, retail stores and Interbank. Some of them have been publicly
accused in the United States of being drug-money launderers. Interbank,
for example, backed several Cuntrera-Caruana projects on the island. There
is no doubt that the Cuntrera-Caruanas turned Aruba into the playground
of Caracas and helped to create an infrastructure of offshore secret banking, casinos, a flourishing tourist industry and a prime money-laundering
sink. When the Cuntrera-Caruanas arrived, the Mansurs owned just about
everything. By the time the Cuntrera-Caruanas left, the Mansurs owned
just about everything that the Italians didn't. In between, the Cuntrera-
Caruanas owned enough and controlled enough of Aruba—with or without the Mansurs' acquiescence, and including the politicians—to turn the
island into the world's first Mafia state.

One of the first investments that Paolo and Giuseppe Cuntrera made on
the island, in 1987, was a nightclub called Visage. To do that, they needed a
license from the government. The only significance of the date is that it was
four years after an international warrant had been issued on Paolo and two
years after another family member, Gerlando, had been arrested for heroin
trafficking in Montreal. In both instances, their names and photos had
appeared in the Venezuelan press.

Despite their insistence otherwise, it is categorically impossible that
Aruban officials did not know with whom they were dealing.

If ever two men were destined to form a winning tag team in the battle
against transnational organized crime, it is Alessandro Pansa and Ben Soave.

They're around the same age. Both were born in Italy, except that

Pansa's family stayed while Soave's family migrated to Thunder Bay, Ontario, when he was ten. Both joined the police as young men. Both moved up through the ranks by being intelligent, hardworking and very good at what they do.

By the mid-1990s, Pansa was busting organized crime groups, running the Second Bureau in Rome. Soave was busting organized crime groups as head of the Combined Forces Special Enforcement Unit—a joint task force of RCMP, Ontario Province Police, York and Peel regional police forces, Revenue Canada and the Canadian Immigration Service—from a large, secure office outside Toronto.

Both have the same easy charm.

Both have the same look in their eye, one that warns these are not men to be messed with.

Pansa's background is financial crime and the Mafia.

Soave's background is undercover work—he was so good at it that the RCMP eventually made him coordinator of all undercover operations—and for fifteen years he was the force liaison officer at embassies around the world. Including Rome.

Birds of a feather, Pansa and Soave are old buddies.

Which makes it all the more fitting that these two should bring down the Cuntrera-Caruanas.

The seeds were planted back in the late 1960s, long before they knew each other. Buried deep in reports that came into various agencies during the French Connection days were the names Liborio Cuntrera, Giovanni Caruana and Nick Rizzuto. But at the time, no one realized the significance.

Most of the clan was living in Canada, sheltered there by the Cotroni family. After Paul Violi was killed and Nick Rizzuto had taken over the organization, any Cuntrera-Caruana connection to heroin in Marseilles was either forgotten or put on the back burner while the police went after bigger fish, and then it was forgotten.

Ironically, the dismantling of the Pizza Connection left the Cuntrera-Caruanas with a corner on the North American heroin market. But the family's relationship with the Pizza Connection Sicilians only came to light when Alessandro Pansa accidentally stumbled across something odd.

In the early days of his career, one of his targets was Giuseppe Bono, a man the Italian police suspected of being a main link between the Sicilians and the Bonannos. It was 1982. Pansa had been listening to endless hours of wiretaps when he heard one that didn't sound like the others. This was a condolence call in which Bono was telling a woman how sorry he was to hear about the death of her husband.

A transcript of the conversation probably wouldn't have meant much, even to Pansa, but listening to it was different. Bono was never very talkative, at the best of times. Now he was blabbering on. He'd always struck Pansa as being arrogant. Now, Bono was suddenly a very humble man. And Pansa wanted to know why.

Bono's call traced to a large villa at the beach just outside Rome. It belonged to Pasquale Cuntrera. It was his brother Liborio who'd passed away in London. With a nagging investigator's curiosity, Pansa needed to find out more about these people. Little did he know that that one phone call would be the start of a ten-year preoccupation.

Based on what he found out about their drug trafficking, the Italians issued warrants in 1983 against the three main brothers—Pasquale, Paolo and Gaspare Cuntrera—and Alfonso Caruana. Two years later, now involved in getting evidence out of the Mafia turncoat Tommy Buscetta, Pansa was able to put together enough evidence for a second warrant to be issued against them. They were tried in absentia and convicted.

At the same time, in Canada, Gerlando Caruana—Alfonso's older brother—was arrested for conspiring to import heroin and sentenced to twenty years. He served eight. When two family members were arrested in Germany in 1989, a third warrant was brought against the three brothers and their cousin Alfonso by Giovanni Falcone.

Alfonso had arrived in Montreal in 1968 at the age of twenty-two. He claimed to be an electrician. Family folklore has it that when he got off the boat, he had nothing more than the clothes on his back and $100 in his pocket. Family folklore neglects to mention that in 1968, ten members of the clan had been convicted of drug trafficking in England and Canada, that they had laundered more than $30 million that year through banks in Montreal and that, each week, they had so many hockey bags stuffed with cash, they needed a pickup truck to deliver them all to the banks.

Family folklore also has difficulty explaining how, a decade later, the same guy with the hundred bucks in his pocket was stopped by Swiss police at Zurich airport carrying $600,000 in his attaché case.

Like all members of the family—like many executives in large corporations—he moved around a lot. Alfonso lived for a time in Lugano, one of the world's major money-laundering centers, then in London. Police now say that from Lugano he oversaw the family's financial interests, and from London he controlled the Thailand side of the drug-trafficking empire.

Just before British police could arrest him, he returned to Canada and opened a pizzeria and, oddly, for a man with as much money as he clearly had, worked behind the counter. Unable to indict him in Canada for suspected crimes in Europe, the Caribbean and Asia, the RCMP "Caponed" him—they called in the tax inspectors. Revenue Canada had already questioned him in 1985 about C$21 million that had gone through his bank account in 1981. He told the court then that he didn't know exactly how that happened, but maybe it happened because he'd allowed other people to deposit money into his account. They decided he lived too well for a fellow making pizzas, and seized C$827,962 from his account. In 1995, Revenue Canada decided they wanted his hide—all C$28.5 million worth—which he claimed he never had, didn't owe and, anyway, couldn't pay. He declared bankruptcy.

Not long afterward, he disappeared.

Speculation in the Canadian press was that he was beachcombing in Aruba. There was also, at one point, a rumor he'd been spotted in Brazil. Giuseppe Cuntrera—who was both his uncle and his father-in-law—was living in Brazil, shipping cocaine to Italy from there, and was known to own real estate in both Rio and San Paolo. So that sounded like as good a place as any. Some people around the RCMP who'd been keeping track of Nick Rizzuto's son Vito saw him traveling to Cuba and suggested that Alfonso might be there as well.

The Italians appeared just as anxious to find him—after all, he owed them twenty-one years' jail time—with one report mentioning the bizarre fact that, having lost contact with Alfonso so long ago, they didn't even have a photograph of him to say what he looked like.

As it turned out, the Italians knew exactly what he looked like, and the RCMP knew exactly where he was. Ben Soave not only had photographs, he had Alfonso's phones tapped.

If there ever was a Cuntrera-Caruana corporate headquarters, it had to be in Caracas. From huge, heavily guarded estates, the three Cuntrera brothers oversaw the entire family empire. The Italians had formally asked for their extradition three times since the first warrant that Pansa had helped to instigate. And each time Venezuela had refused, on the grounds that the law simply didn't provide for it. Then Giovanni Falcone made a personal plea. He met with Venezuela's minister of justice, who was on a visit to Italy, and tried to explain what monsters these men were. Chances are this fourth request would also have been rejected. The Venezuelans comfortably hid behind the fact that there was no extradition treaty between Venezuela and Canada or Italy. Nor was there one between Venezuela and the United States.

Three days later, Falcone was murdered.

Then Borsellino was murdered.

And like the 1963 bombs that had killed those seven policemen and driven the family from Sicily, twenty-nine years later the murder of two prosecutors in Sicily would do the same for the brothers in Caracas.

The government of Aruba had already tried to sever its relationship with the family—maybe the Mansurs wanted their island back or maybe the politicians just found religion—and now the Venezuelans decided to call time. It took a bunch of months to arrange, but in September 1992 they bundled Pasquale, Paolo and Gaspare onto a flight for Rome.

Pansa later told an interviewer that he was at the airport to arrest them and that they actually looked like Hollywood versions of godfathers with dyed-black, slicked-back hair, gold watches and white shoes. The three were tried on charges of drag trafficking and "Mafia Association." The 1982 Rognoni–LaTorre law, which makes it a crime to belong to the Mafia, changed the way the Italian police could battle the mob and has been the single most effective weapon in dismantling so many clans in recent years. The trial, which brought guilty verdicts, sent Pasquale to jail for twenty years and Gaspare and Paolo for thirteen years each.

Now the Italians turned back to Alfonso. They'd charged him as well in this case, issued an extradition request to the Canadians and, for the second time in his life, tried him in absentia. The extradition request was not granted and Alfonso was found not guilty.

Word came to Soave that the Italians were going to ask for his extradition on the 1985 conviction. And they well might have, had Soave and Pansa not had other ideas. The request was postponed. Had it been granted, the Canadians would have been obliged to hand over Alfonso. He was in their backyard, alive and well in suburban Toronto. He'd given up pizzas for a car wash, and was working with his nephew in Woodbridge, Ontario. He was making $500 a week. At least that's what he was admitting to.

The Canadians located him in April 1995. While investigating Toronto mobster Enio Mora, they spotted someone in Mora's company they didn't recognize. It was Alfonso.

Soave spent a year plotting Operation Omertá, to finish the job that Pansa had started all those years ago. Over the course of the next two years, his group followed money and drugs through Canada and the United States, through the Caribbean and into Europe. They charted money going into Switzerland and drugs coming out of Turkey. They identified heroin refineries in Thailand, and other family players living in Canada. Throughout it, Soave fought his way through all the complexities of collaboration with law enforcement in different countries.

"One of the biggest problems in law enforcement today," he notes, "is trying to coordinate agencies around the world for a common purpose. Even within one country you can have national agencies bickering among themselves, turf wars, petty jealousies. Now expand that to several. You also run up against a lack of funding. All too often, the financial crunch prohibits long-term investigations. Then there are different jurisdictions, legal and procedural differences and cultural differences."

In this case, it meant he needed to bring onboard the FBI, DEA, U.S. Customs, the Texas Department of Public Safety, the Italian police and the Mexican police. While he was trying to juggle all of their agendas, his men were running nearly one hundred different wiretaps. In fact, they so successfully bugged the gang and had such accurate intelligence information about drugs coming into Canada—by spring 1998 they were picking off large shipments with great precision—that some of the family sussed it out. They were certain the cops were about to pounce and started talking about leaving the country.

Even though it had taken more than thirty years to wear out their welcome in Canada, Venezuela and most of Europe, there were still plenty of places they could go. There was always Brazil. They could always buy their way back into Aruba.

"The Cuntrera-Caruana organization has moved from jurisdiction to jurisdiction," Soave goes on, "specifically to hamper the efforts of law enforcement. Strategically speaking, how more effective can any organization be? They understand the problems we face in trying to apprehend them. They know about our lack of coordinating capabilities, about the lack of political will to provide the funding we need to take them on. They understand how all our problems play right into their hands. And so they thrive."

This time they didn't move fast enough. The man in charge of transport for the family, fifty-year-old Nunzio Larosa, who worked for Gerlando Caruana in Montreal, had gotten sloppy. They'd been following him for eight months, watching him bring drugs from Texas into Canada.

The border crossing the gang used was at Sault Sainte Marie, on the Michigan-Ontario border, where Lake Huron flows into the North Channel to meet Lake Superior. It was always easy there. Most people just got waved through. When spot checks were made, officers asked a few routine questions, but kept traffic moving. That's why Larosa didn't worry that the secret compartment underneath the Ford pickup wasn't ready. Instead, $6 million worth of cocaine was picked up in Texas, stuffed into black garbage bags and shoved behind the driver's seat.

The first shot in the final battle came in May 1998, when Texas troopers grabbed the truck.

The reaction his men heard on the wiretaps came as something of a surprise to Soave. "It didn't even faze them. They just went ahead with plans for another $6 million shipment the following month."

There were more interruptions, and more disruptions to the family's business, and then on July 15, 1998, at just after 7 A.M., Soave took them down. Within fifteen minutes, the fifty-two-year-old Alfonso Caruana was in handcuffs.

"If organized crime was the game of hockey," Soave said that morning, in one of those great-sound-bite quotes that has been broadcast and printed countless times since, "then Alfonso Caruana would be Wayne Gretzky."

Around the same time the RCMP got Caruana, Mexican police in Cancún were capturing Oreste Pagano, the Camorra member who served as the Cuntrera-Caruanas' ambassador to the Colombians. He was the middleman who assured the family of a constant supply of cocaine. They got Alfonso's brothers, too. Pasquale and Gerlando Caruana were arrested in coordinated raids in Toronto and Montreal.

It took two hundred police officers to get five people in Toronto, five in Montreal, two in Mexico and two in the States. In follow-up raids, they collected drugs, jewelry and money. Safe-deposit boxes were located. Bank accounts too. And in one house they found more than thirty kilos of cash.

With Alfonse in custody, the Italians have refiled for extradition and are appealing his earlier acquittal. Whenever the Canadians get done with him, they have plans for at least twenty-one years. The family had been dealt a crushing blow. But anyone who's dealt with transnational organized crime for as long as Ben Soave knows hurt doesn't mean obliterated. He says that younger members are already stepping up to fill the void.

"The game may already be lost," he says, "but that's no reason to give up. Today's organized crime is global. Today's gangs are into everything. They move around the world and take advantage of laws which permit them to stay or reside or operate in other countries. They're like water, they flow to the point of least resistance. The world is no longer confined by borders. We'd been investigating the Cuntrera-Caruana for years. Other international agencies have investigated the group. What took us so long to do something about them was not the lack of will. It was the difficulties of international cooperation and the lack of money."

He had to scrounge around for years for both.

Operation Omertà was budgeted at C$2 million. When his team ran out of money, Soave had to go, cap in hand, to the Criminal Intelligence Service of Ontario to finance the rest of it.

"On a one-to-one basis, cooperation with other law enforcement organizations in the U.S., in Britain, in fact throughout most of Europe, is excellent. Any two organizations will work together. But when you're talking transnational organized crime, you're talking about a lead agency trying to coordinate twenty international agencies with legal, jurisdictional and procedural differences. You have real obstacles. That's where it becomes almost impossible. Just look at the problems we face when borders are imposed. But they're only imposed on us. The criminals don't have borders. They don't have to worry about jurisdiction."

The good guys have borders and no money, the bad guys have no borders and piles of money. The good guys get bogged down in jurisdiction, the bad guys do joint ventures.

He shrugs. "It's not a fair fight."

And transnational criminal organizations know it.

"Just think of them like dandelions," Soave says. "It starts with one weed in the middle of your garden. You rip it out by the stem and the next day there are two more. So now you rip those two out and then there are four of them. You keep ripping them out and they keep coming back, until your lawn is filled with them. So you get someone to dig up your lawn and take them out by the roots, but by then they've started showing up on your neighbor's lawn. He rips them by the stems, until they cover his lawn. Then he gets someone to dig up the roots, except by then they're all over the neighborhood, and they've come back to your lawn too. That's transnational organized crime."

12

BANK IT AGAIN, SAM

Casablanca was a ninth-inning, seventh game of the World Series, grand-slam home run.

—ALLAN DOODY, U.S. Customs

IN 1989, POLICE IN CALIFORNIA STUMBLED ACROSS twenty-one metric tons of cocaine warehoused in Sylmar, California, a sleepy town at the north end of the San Fernando Valley. Along with the drugs, they seized $12 million in cash, accounting ledgers that outlined the movements of some fifty-five tons over the previous three months—more than $1 billion worth—and documentation suggesting that this group had previously tractor-trailered into California as much as two hundred tons.

In size alone, the Sylmar bust was a whopping success. But the most shocking thing about the haul, what really opened eyes, was that it established the magnitude of the joint venture the Colombians had now realized with the Mexican cartels. Juan Ramon Matta Ballesteros's friendship with Alberto Sicilia Falcon and the Guadalajara cartel, and Juan Carlos "Chupeta" Ramirez Abadia's franchising to the Juarez cartel, had spearheaded a full-blown Mexican invasion of America's southern border.

After Sylmar, law enforcement never again routinely spoke about seizures in grams or pounds. The jargon became tons and multitons.

Today, the war along that two-thousand-mile stretch is being fought across it, under it, over it and through it. American law enforcement has become so overwhelmed by the quantities of drugs being smuggled into the country from Mexico, and the sheer size of the logistical problems that must be surmounted to patrol the border, that short of some impenetrable fence that would totally shut down trade between the two countries, the odds monumentally favor the traffickers.

The border stop at Brownsville, Texas, is a huge, open-sided covered shed where tens of thousands of Mexicans arrive daily on foot, tens of thousands of cars pull in to be given a quick look-over and thousands of trucks arrive to be subjected to random searches. And while U.S. Customs and the U.S. Immigration and Naturalization Service do what they can, the small percentage of people or cars or trucks that are closely looked at reveals an even smaller percentage of the drugs coming across the border.

Farther west, toward McAllen, there's a brand-new bridge that crosses the border—with a plaque in the middle indicating Mexico is on that side of the line that runs across the center of the bridge, and the United States is on this side—and every thirty seconds or so a huge cylinder truck, like the kind you see with the word *MILK* painted on the side, comes roaring by carrying something from Mexico to the United States. The border guards stop as many as they can, and try to establish if there is a second, smaller cylinder hidden inside, but that isn't easy, and while they're looking at one, fifty more come into the country.

That's just two roads over the border, fifty miles apart.

The Rio Grande River, which often looks less like a river than it does a wide stream, stretches thirteen hundred miles from Brownsville to El Paso; from there to the Pacific Ocean, the border becomes a flat, arid stretch of land, some of which is fenced, most of which isn't. But then, neither the river nor the land, even where it is fenced, constitutes any real obstacle for large-scale organized smugglers who, regardless of whether their crop is drugs or aliens heading north or drug cash heading back south, operate with near impunity on the Mexican side and near invisibility in the teeming confusion on the American side.

It becomes a percentage game for the bad guys and the good guys. Send a hundred shipments across the border and write off the one or two that will be stopped as the price of doing business. Stop a hundred trucks or cars or people and hope that you can find one or two shipments, knowing that stopping this is impossible, but disrupting a little of it is a reasonable ambition. And even then the traffickers find ways to better their percentages,

flying drugs over the border in 72's which they have gutted and outfitted
to transport multiton loads, or sailing them around it in massive fishing
fleets. They also sometimes dig under it. In 1990 the Americans uncovered
a tunnel operating from Mexico into Arizona. Three years later, they found
a nearly completed tunnel running from Tijuana Airport up to, and almost
inside, an unfinished warehouse on the California side. One DEA estimate
puts the amount of Colombian cocaine coming across the border each day
at up to seven tons.

The amount of Colombian cocaine stockpiled in Mexico, just waiting
to be shipped to the United States—one hundred tons' worth—is enough
to provide one line of coke to every man, woman and child on earth.

Mexico's cartels were born in the famine of the Depression, when families,
one on each side of the border, realized they could make a living moving
people and contraband back and forth. By the 1970s, marijuana had
become their major cash crop. Ever adaptable, enormously resilient and
with stubborn persistence, ten years later all they did was add a little
cocaine to the load, and whatever they got from the Colombians for the
service represented pure profit because they were going that way anyway.

Playing the mule made them rich. But it didn't give them real power.
To manage that, they took a percentage of the coke to market as their own.
Then, because business is business and loyalty has never been a strong suit
among drug traffickers, they went in search of ways to cut the Colombians
out of the picture. They started dealing directly with the Bolivians and
Peruvians for their supplies, which was fine until the Colombians protected
themselves by moving some of shipments through Puerto Rico—they
caught American law enforcement looking the other way—then exerted
enough muscle on the Bolivians and Peruvians to whittle the Mexicans
back down to size.

The group Matta Ballesteros aligned himself with was then called the
Guadalajara cartel. Put together by Miguel Angel Felix Gallardo, Ernesto
Fonseca Carrillo and Rafael Caro Quintero, they were on the ground floor
of Mexican drug trafficking, controlled the high-level end and were, clearly,
on to a very good thing. At least they were until 1985, when they got totally
stupid and murdered DEA agent Enrique Camarena Salazar.

It was an emphatic beginning of their own demise.

Under American pressure, the Mexicans cracked down. Even Matta Ballesteros, then living in Colombia, couldn't escape America's wrath. Tossed into the pot as one of the murderers, he hightailed it to Honduras, where Mexican nationals could not be extradited. Instead, the Americans kidnapped him. They carried him out of the country, bound and gagged, put him on trial, found him guilty and stowed him away for the rest of his life in a federal penitentiary.

The alliance subsequently splintered into two factions. One became the Sinaloa cartel, led by some former Guadalajara lieutenants who set up a joint venture with the Cali cartel and dug tunnels under the border to move their product. They also pioneered more circuitous routes from Mexico into the U.S., as discovered in 1993 when six tons of Cali/Sinaloa cocaine was seized in El Salvador. But the leaders were arrested that same year, and although the cartel still functions, it is no longer significant. It was the second faction emerging out of the Guadalajara group that did become a major force.

The Tijuana cartel was established by the Arellano-Felix brothers— nephews of one of the Guadalajara group's founders—whose claim to fame is the 1993 murder of Cardinal Juan Jose Posadas Ocampo. From their Baja California base, they maintain a violently guarded monopoly on smuggling across the border into California. To further secure their power base, they had the business sense in 1998 to join forces with central Mexico's dominant Sonora cartel. In partnership with the ruling Caro Quintero family—like the Tijuana group, the Sonora cartel was formed with remnants of the old Guadalajara crowd—they dubbed themselves "The Federation." Not only have they continued to smuggle Colombian cocaine into the U.S., but they've expanded their own interests in cultivation, processing, smuggling and distribution of both heroin and marijuana.

For years, the most dangerous of all was the Gulf cartel, run by an ego-maniac named Juan Garcia Abrego who saw himself as heir apparent to Pablo Escobar. Born in Texas and based mainly in Matamoros, just across the Rio Grande from Brownsville, he supposedly got into the trafficking business as a child, floating bundles of marijuana across the river.

Like Escobar, he too courted the media to turn himself into a modern Robin Hood. Tales of his virility were legend—it's said that he fathered several children by many different women—and was apparently so superstitious that he had witch doctors on permanent call to protect him. Yet it was Abrego who completed the metamorphosis of the Colombians, turning them

into a full-blown international franchiser and himself into their primary fran-
chisee. He left the other cartels in the dust when he told the Orejuelas that
he would guarantee delivery of their product anywhere in the United States
for 50 percent of the load. It was a sure bet for the Orejuelas and a major
break for Abrego. Before long, he was handling one third of all the cocaine
used in the United States and was said to be worth, personally, $15 billion.

Mimicking Escobar, he murdered dozens of people on both sides of
the border, including his six closest rivals, which in 1984 helped make him
Mexico's principal cocaine trafficker. Yet he surpassed even his hero when
the FBI honored him as the very first international drug trafficker to make
it onto their Ten Most Wanted list. Arrested in 1996, he was sent to Texas
for trial—the Mexicans agreed with the Americans that because he was
born in Texas he couldn't be protected by Mexico's nonextradition-of-
nationals law—found guilty and sent to prison for life. The Gulf cartel still
operates, but less boisterously than it did under Abrego, much of its business taken away by the just-as-bizarre onetime head of the Juarez cartel.

Set up by Amado Carrillo Fuentes with the help of a former Mexican
federal police commander, the group opted to control the middle of the
border. Within months of Abrego's capture, which served to open the market, Fuentes was smuggling four times as much cocaine as all the other cartels combined, running a global enterprise that is said to have grossed $200
million a week. He maintained a fleet of huge aircraft, including Boeing
727s, to bring drugs from Colombia to Mexico, then passed the drugs off
to youth gangs who would smuggle them into the States. But Abrego's
capture also shifted Fuentes into the bull's-eye as America's primary target.
So, for the sake of old age, he decided he needed to become invisible.
Which he nearly did in mid-1997 by hiring a team of plastic surgeons.

On the morning of July 4, 1997, the thirty-nine-year-old Amado
Carrillo Fuentes lay down on the operating table and expected, later that
same day, to wake up as a younger-looking, vigorous gentleman named
Antonio Flores Montes. Instead, eight hours later, doctors found somebody
expired in his Mexico City hospital bed, the victim of an apparent post-
operative heart attack brought on by eight grueling hours of plastic surgery
to his face and liposuction to his belly.

Immediately, the body was flown north in a chartered plane to
Culiacan for burial. Almost as quickly, rumors spread that Montes was
Fuentes and that Fuentes was dead. Now the world divided into two

groups: it is Fuentes and he died; it isn't Fuentes and he faked it. The DEA matched Fuentes's fingerprints with those of the corpse, and the Mexican government performed DNA tests on the body. Then, and only then, would either comfortably conclude that Fuentes was dead.

Three months after the death, Fuentes's surgeon was reported missing. Jaime Godoy Singh and two doctor friends disappeared. They were found several weeks later stuffed into oil drums that had been partially filled with cement and left on a main highway seventy miles southeast of Mexico City. All three had been handcuffed and blindfolded, strangled and, for good measure, shot in the neck. Their fingernails had been pulled out and their bodies showed signs of burns.

That immediately reignited both camps: the DEA is right, it was Fuentes and his guys who killed the doctors as revenge; the Mexican government's DNA tests are a cover-up, it wasn't Fuentes and they killed the doctors to keep them quiet.

What no one knew at the time—at least no one in Mexico—was that a bunch of guys sitting in a secret office in Los Angeles were almost as shocked and saddened by the death as any close friend of Sr. Fuentes and/or Sr. Montes.

In Mexico, hand in hand with drug trafficking and money laundering, corruption is a fact of daily life. But at no time in recent history has corruption been more evident than during the six-year reign of Carlos Salinas de Gortari.

Salinas was elected president of Mexico in 1988, amid outcries that the vote had been rigged, rumors began circulating almost immediately that the Institutional Revolutionary Party (PRI) in general—which had autocratically ruled Mexico since 1929—and this president in particular were utterly corrupt. But there was little to substantiate those rumors until 1992, when the president's cousin and an employee of the president's father were arrested and convicted of drug trafficking in the U.S. The word was that both had been working for Juan Garcia Abrego.

It was hardly coincidence, then, that Salinas now limited the number and scope of American narcotics agents who were authorized to work on Mexican soil.

The depth of Salinas's venality manifested itself around the same time in the form of a very private, top-secret dinner party at a mansion in

Mexico City's "millionaires' row" Polanco district. The president was the guest of honor. Thirty of the wealthiest men in the country were brought together to demonstrate their support for the PRI and the 1994 presidential campaign. Put more bluntly, this was payback time for the massive depravity which had allowed some of these men to grow megarich under a party that had turned drug trafficking and money laundering into a vital ingredient of the nation's GDP. To no one's genuine surprise, before the night was over, the thirty men said thank you by pledging an average of $25 million each.

For Carlos Salinas, it has been said, this was the birth of his family's dynasty.

Unfortunately for him, though, not everyone in the family was quite as adroit. And brother Raul proved especially clumsy. With illicit drugs quickly becoming the most dynamic sector of a feeble Mexican economy—with the peso crash of 1994, drugs would surpass oil as the prime source of much-needed hard currency—Raul recognized that the leaders of the main cartels were about to become the country's de facto power brokers. So, acting in consort with his brother or with the blessings of the PRI elders or both, he did what any worried but loyal member of a ruling family would do. He invited the drug barons to the banquet.

Within months of that $750 million dinner, newspapers in Mexico were already printing stories about a meeting that had taken place at the Salinas ranch, with Raul present, where envelopes with cash in them were handed over by known drug traffickers.

In hindsight, it shouldn't have been a surprise. From the day Carlos opted to run for president, *Newsweek* magazine had been claiming that the Salinas family was underworld-connected, especially Raul, who was linked to Abrego. Knowing now that Abrego was paying as much as $50 million a month for his own protection, it's easy to understand how, when a police task force sought military help to arrest Abrego, the request was refused by the chief of staff of the president's office, who just happened to be in charge of the national drug and intelligence agencies.

Enter here Deputy Attorney General Mario Ruiz Massieu and his top aide, Jorge Stergios.

In December 1993, Stergios transported bales of cash to the Texas Commerce Bank in Houston. Two dozen cash deposits were made in all by Stergios over the next year, ranging from $120,000 to nearly $480,000, with instructions to the bank not to invest any of it, but rather to leave the full amount in a checking account. During that time, Raul Salinas not only loaned a relative $29 million but also fixed the bid for him to purchase a formerly state-owned television station.

With the 1994 elections about to take place, the PRI candidate, Luis Donaldo Colosio—who'd been chosen to succeed Salinas—was assassinated. This brought the PRI's second choice, Ernesto Zedillo Ponce de Leon, to office, and, along with him, elevation to majority leader of Ruiz Massieu's brother, Jose Francisco. That's when Jose Francisco was assassinated. The very next day, a PRI congressman who would eventually become a suspect in the Ruiz Massieu murder disappeared and was presumed dead. Two months later, Mario Ruiz Massieu mysteriously resigned from the investigation of his brother's assassination.

Raul Salinas was arrested in late February 1995—and four years later convicted—for his involvement in the murder of Jose Francisco Ruiz Massieu, who happened to have been married to his sister Adriana Salinas. Rumors also surfaced that either Carlos Salinas or persons close to his former administration were somehow connected with the Colosio murder.

The same week that Raul was arrested, Mario Ruiz Massieu was questioned by police about his possible role in his own brother's assassination and a potential cover-up to protect Raul. Immediately after being released, Ruiz Massieu flew to Houston. He was arrested the next day at Newark Airport, in New Jersey, about to board a flight for Spain, carrying $40,000 in cash.

Some three thousand miles away, around the same time that Ruiz Massieu was being arrested, Ernest Zedillo was meeting secretly with Carlos Salinas in Mexico City. When that meeting ended, all allegations that the Salinas administration had somehow been involved in the Colosio murder were officially rescinded. The following day, the U.S. government seized $9 million, supposedly belonging to Ruiz Massieu, from the Texas Commerce Bank. Within hours, Carlos Salinas left Mexico.

For the next six months, the so-called Salinas Affair continued to make front-page news around the world, at times pushing other stories to the inside pages. Among them: the arrest of nearly three dozen Mexican Federal Judicial Police officers who'd been part of a $40-million-a-month racket to protect drug traffickers and the seizure of a plane that had been flown from Colombia with seventeen tons of drugs, all of which had been off-loaded by Mexican state and federal police, resulting in the arrest of another twenty officers.

Like any good soap opera, this story took all sorts of twists and turns, but few as odd as the November 15, 1995, arrest in Switzerland of Raul's wife. Paulina Castanon de Salinas had reportedly tried to withdraw $84 million from a safe-deposit box at a private bank which had been opened in the name of Juan Guillermo Gomez Gutierrez, a presumed alias used by her husband. When asked why she would take so much, why she didn't simply take a little at a time, her answer is said to have been, "I was taking a little at a time."

As if this weren't surreal enough, in October 1998, Swiss prosecutors—who'd gone on to discover accounts in six cantons that they believed to have been owned by Raul using false names—dropped their money-laundering charges against Raul for technical reasons. Proceedings were also dismissed against Paulina, although the ever-canny Swiss insisted that $114.4 million in Raul's alleged accounts were indeed drug proceeds and seized it. Another $20 million was subsequently found in London.

In the meantime, Carlos Salinas took up residence in Ireland.

In January 1996, Juan Garcia Abrego was arrested and subsequently deported to the United States. The inevitable void created by his sudden departure from the scene created a battle for succession. After much bloodletting, the thirty-seven-year-old Oscar Malherbe had successfully fought off both his own associates and members of the Juarez cartel who'd tried to take over. Like Abrego, Malherbe would also soon become a pawn in his government's game plan.

Throughout that year, just enough Mexican police and judicial authorities were arrested to make it seem as if the government were taking action. A body was found buried on Raul Salinas's ranch and a story found its way into the newspapers that it had been put there to frame Raul. It was only after a gunman was accused of actually pulling the trigger in the Jose Francisco Ruiz Massieu assassination, and the body on the Salinas ranch turned out to be the missing PRI congressman, that Raul was charged with killing the congressman, whom he'd allegedly paid to handle the contract on Jose Francisco. Abrego received eleven life sentences, Carlos Salinas was questioned yet again about the Colosio murder, Mexico City's chief prosecutor was fired for incompetently handling the Raul Salinas case and Mexico's attorney general was fired, supposedly on similar grounds.

While prosecutors were now asking Carlos Salinas about the murder of Ruiz Massieu, the Mexican army was raiding a wedding, intending to arrest the bride's brother, Amado Carrillo Fuentes. They arrived to find that the party was being guarded by federal police and that the drug baron was nowhere to be found.

Despite as much as seven tons of illegal drugs—particularly cocaine, heroin, marijuana and methamphetamines—now being smuggled daily across the U.S.-Mexican border, Washington continued praising Mexico's spirit of cooperation. Meanwhile, on the front line, U.S. agents were talking of nothing but mutual suspicion, distrust and resentment.

Summing up U.S.-Mexican relations at this point was the photograph of American Drug Czar General Barry McCaffrey alongside General Jesus Gutierrez Rebollo, head of the National Institute to Combat Drugs, Mexico's equivalent of the Drug Enforcement Administration. McCaffrey called Gutierrez "a guy of absolute unquestioned integrity."

Three weeks later, Gutierrez was in jail, accused of being a mole for the Juarez cartel. The agency Gutierrez once headed has since been disbanded for having been corrupt beyond mending; the general was convicted of working for Amado Carrillo Fuentes and was sentenced to thirteen years. An embarrassed McCaffrey was forced to admit, "Our intelligence was wrong."

This on the heels of his March 1996 remark that Attorney General Antonio Lozano Gracia was "a man of tremendous courage and integrity." Nine months later, Lozano was fired for his incompetence and mishandling of the investigation into the Salinas family's affairs. And documents now surfaced from prosecutors in Houston that suggested Raul Salinas, his father and his late brother-in-law Jose Francisco Ruiz Massieu were partners in drug trafficking.

Needless to say, in 1997, when it came time for President Clinton to judge Mexico's efforts in the war on drugs, there was much to criticize. However, the day before Clinton was scheduled to make his decision—a decision that would have serious economic consequences for Mexico should it be a negative one—the Mexicans just happened to stumble across and arrest Oscar Malherbe de Leon. Then, literally hours after Clinton agreed to Mexican certification, Humberto Garcia Abrego—who'd been brother Juan's chief money launderer at the Gulf cartel—decided he didn't like prison life and simply walked out. This despite the fact that his jail cell had apparently consisted of six rooms with telephones and fax machines so that he could keep in touch with his business interests.

With Raul Salinas in jail, his brother Carlos out of the way in Ireland, their family in tatters, Ruiz Massieu and others either awaiting trials or already convicted—and Citibank helping police with inquiries into how they came to funnel more than $100 million into Swiss and other foreign accounts for Raul—the White House was forced to concede in a report to Congress, "Corruption is rife within the ranks of Mexico's police and members of the security forces."

As if that weren't damning enough, a former Gulf cartel trafficker, Juan Antonio Ortiz, testified in one of several cases against Mario Ruiz Massieu: "Everybody could be bribed. From what I know, everybody was being paid all the way to the top."

On August 26, 1999, a federal grand jury sitting in Houston indicted Mario Ruiz Massieu on twenty-five counts of money laundering and conspiracy. Repeated pleas for his extradition to Mexico were rejected by the U.S. government, officially because he was awaiting trial in the United States, unofficially—and more importantly—because no one in the Justice Department trusted the Mexicans to put him on trial, convict him and send him to prison. Some twenty days after the indictment came down in Texas, Ruiz Massieu's drug-overdosed body was found next to a suicide note. In it he wrote, "President Ernesto Zedillo never forgave me for denouncing the leaders of the PRI . . . he took revenge for that." Ruiz Massieu also accused Zedillo of being aware of the plot to murder Jose Francisco Ruiz Massieu. "He had a lot to do with it."

The depth of corruption that is modern Mexico and the endemic avarice that typifies Mexican politics manifests itself in traffickers like Fuentes and the death and destruction they wreak. As Special Agent Phil Jordan, former head of the DEA's Intelligence Center in El Paso, once summed it up, "If Saddam Hussein had done what Amado Carrillo Fuentes has done with the complicity of the government's corruption, we would have declared war."

In fact, we sort of did.

Late in the autumn of 1995, U.S. Customs agents out of Los Angeles began a modest undercover operation with the help of a "CI." That's cop lingo for "confidential informant," a bad guy whom the good guys have convinced to work for them, usually in exchange for various "considerations": a reduced sentence if everything goes well; no sentence if all goes better; a free ride in the Witness Protection Program if things don't work out exactly as planned; flowers at a funeral if the bad guys the CI is double-crossing find out about it before the guys can get his butt out of town.

In this case, the CI—who called himself Javier Ramirez—was hoping for a get-out-of-jail-free card, because, before he switched sides, he'd been running the Emerald Empire Corporation, a one-stop shop for drug dealers with dirty money to launder.

Operating out of a storefront warehouse in Santa Fe Springs, California—a rough-and-ready town east of where the Santa Anna Freeway meets the San Gabriel River Freeway—Ramirez agreed to bring in Customs agents as his partners. He then connected them to high-level money launderers for the Cali cartel and before long, the undercover agents were collecting drug money off the streets of half a dozen U.S. cities.

Through contacts developed with the Colombians, the opportunity soon arose to open an offshoot operation—more cash pickups, but this time for Mexican traffickers—which brought the undercover team inside the financial infrastructure of the Juarez cartel.

In turn, these two operations led to yet another opportunity.

The Feds were picking up huge amounts, ranging from $500,000 to $2 million a time, all of which needed to get into the banking system. The idea was to wire it out of the United States to the Cayman Islands, Venezuela and Mexico, then bring it back to the U.S. as bank drafts or cashier's checks made payable to third parties. But because there was so much money involved, in order to manage it, Emerald Empire put out a call for help. One of the people who seemed interested in Ramirez's plight was Juan Carlos Alcala Navarro—a.k.a. Dr. Navarro—the main fixer for the Juarez group. He agreed that, for a fee of up to 4 percent on each transaction, he would hook up Emerald Empire with some Mexican bankers. He would then pay them an under-the-table commission of 1 percent for whatever amounts they could wash through their bank.

So now, on behalf of Emerald Empire—and with undercover agents watching his every move—Navarro provided a collection of tame bankers who opened accounts under fictitious names in California, Mexico and the Caymans. Before long, there would be more than two dozen of them, representing twelve of Mexico's nineteen largest banks, including Bancomer, Banco Serfin and Confia.

Getting inside the banking system was a major coup, because by the mid-1990s Mexico had become the single most important money-laundering center in the Western Hemisphere.

As the three investigations meshed together, they became known as Operation Casablanca. Overall responsibility for it lay on the shoulders of Bill Gately—then the assistant special agent in charge of the Financial Investigation Division for Customs in L.A.—a superb financial investigator who'd tangled with the cocaine cartels throughout his career. But this was unlike any undercover operation he'd ever worked before. Then again, it was unlike any undercover operation anyone had ever worked before. It was bigger, more complex and more wide-ranging, and offered unbelievably huge prizes if they could pull it off.

Dr. Navarro was one of Gately's prime targets. A notch higher on the list was Jose Alvarez Tostado, a.k.a. "Compadre," the man who apparently oversaw the Juarez cartel's U.S. interests. And just above him, number one on the list, was Tostado's boss, Amado Carrillo Fuentes. It meant that for the first time in any drug-money investigation, three of the most powerful traffickers/money launderers in the world were within reach.

To get them, their flunkies in Mexico and the States, and to round up the bankers too, Gately needed to call on assistance from offices and agencies all over the country. But constructing such a monster operation was a nightmare. Bureaucracies are, by nature, staffed with chiefs who often forget that the tribe needs Indians too. Gately needed constant input from hundreds of people and all sorts of other agencies, many of whom brought with them their own agendas. There were also more than enough petty jealousies to go around. Doubters and begrudgers came out of the woodwork. Later, of course, those same people would line up to take credit. But, in the beginning, they got in the way as Gately fought for approval all the way up the chain of command through U.S. Customs to the Treasury and Justice Departments.

As the operation expanded—which it did with increasing speed, taking on a momentum of its own—Gately established a command post in a secret location away from the Los Angeles Customs offices. More and more agents were moved into the safe house to back up the agents in the field. By mid-1996, such huge amounts of cash were being picked up on the streets of Los Angeles, Chicago, Miami, Houston and New York—much of it owed to the Colombians by the Mexicans for drug consignments—that now a team of forensic accountants had to be given security clearance and moved into the safe house to keep track of it all.

At the same time, administrative support back at headquarters also became more complicated. Time-sensitive material poured in, much of it the kind that needed to be handled no later than yesterday. Agents would find out on a Tuesday afternoon that they needed to fly somewhere to meet a bad guy on Wednesday morning, which didn't give anyone in Washington a lot of time to obtain appropriate approvals.

Before long, the U.S. Customs Service would have two hundred people working on Casablanca.

Underlying all of this was inherent danger. Lives were on the line. Gately and his team needed continually to reassess their strategy, to develop new lines of intelligence, to update the needs of Casablanca, to decide who could do what to whom, to look at what had already transpired and to commit the operation to what would follow. Understandably, at the forefront of their minds was that the price of even a minor failure was unacceptable.

Keeping security tight meant that everything had to be highly compartmentalized. Gately and a few others in Los Angeles knew the big picture. So did a chosen few senior managers at headquarters. But the other people involved—and this was especially important as more and more outside contributing agencies were brought in—were told only what they needed to know in order to accomplish their part. State and local agencies had roles to play, particularly in gathering intelligence. However, with Customs agents risking their own lives undercover, no one was willing to trust anyone else—not even other U.S. law enforcement officers—any more than they absolutely had to.

Making coordination especially troublesome, those outside agencies did need to be told who and what to stay away from. The last thing anyone in Los Angeles or Washington wanted was for some overambitious patrolman to stumble across a money pickup, try to be a hero by busting it up and expose the entire operation. In turn, motivation—getting people to do what was required of them when they had no idea why they were doing it—was that much more laborious. And even with this top-secret, need-to-know restriction set in stone, there was always the sobering reality that, as the operation wore on, the odds continued to increase that something would leak somewhere, that eventually, something would go wrong.

There were contingency plans should the CI get burned, contingency plans if something happened during a pickup, and contingency plans to arrest as many people and to seize as many bank accounts as they could if they had to fold up on a moment's notice. But drawing up contingency plans was one thing. Living with the reality of impending accidents was another. And none of them were emotionally prepared when that accident occurred.

On August 6, 1997, a money pickup was going down at a McDonald's in New York City when one of the bad guys tried to double-cross one of Gately's undercover guys. Emergency backup was in place, as it must be on any undercover transaction—these things are always planned on a worst-case-scenario basis—but warfare in the streets occurs suddenly and violently, and when the bad guy tried it on, all hell broke loose.

One of the undercover agents went down.

Return fire killed the shooter.

But just like that, Operation Casablanca was hurtled onto another plane.

Tony Mangione, who worked on the support team at Customs headquarters in Washington, happened to be in New York when the shooting occurred. "I heard about it the next morning. It's a pretty sickening feeling. At that point, I didn't care much about the operation. I don't think anybody did. The important thing was the agent who got shot and the officer who shot the bad guy. It was only after we found out that our guys would be okay that anyone began thinking of what to do next, of how to salvage the operation."

Gately immediately flew to New York to visit his wounded undercover agent in the hospital and to help the agent who'd killed the shooter get through his trauma as well. Only then did he begin to deal with damage control, focusing on how to save Casablanca.

With the help of the CI, the team in Los Angeles concocted a cover story. Based on partial truths, it went like this: The bad guys who tried to rip us off were rogues, they weren't the people who were supposed to drop off the money, it was an isolated incident, the police just happened to stumble across it and intervened because that's what cops do, the good guys escaped, law enforcement is no wiser about what's going on, it was one of those bad-luck things that sometimes happens, no one expects it to happen again, so the shooting shouldn't change anything.

No one had to remind the undercover teams that if it could happen once, it could happen again. And from that day on, every pickup was an a especially tense time. In the back of everyone's mind was the gnawing question, are they giving us a contract for the pickup because they know we're cops or will they buy our cover story; is this the end of it or are they starting to have doubts; is everything still on or are we being set up?

The Colombians, too, had their doubts. And their discomfort only served to heighten the tension. It was nearly a month later before the Colombians seemed comfortable enough with the cover story that they appeared to put the shooting behind them.

"That was, undoubtedly, the closest we came to being compromised," notes Allan Doody, at the time a senior manager for Customs Criminal Enforcement in Washington. "The shooting in New York was horrible. But because everything was so compartmentalized, I don't think it could have compromised the entire operation. Still, we were very lucky to get through it the way we did. We were able to make up a story that was plausible and they eventually bought it."

He contends that it was clearly in the bad guys' interests to buy in to the cover story. "They needed our service and were willing to accept that there'd been an interruption. Both the Mexicans and the Colombians needed us to continue as the middlemen. Before long, we began to get introductions to Venezuelan business people and bankers who were in the money-laundering end of the drug business. We also met relatives of some of the Mexican cartel folk who were living in Italy, and they introduced us to Italian nationals involved with distributing cocaine in Europe and subsequently laundering money."

The Italian connection began with Emerald Empire being asked if they could arrange pickups outside the U.S. Naturally, the answer came back, yes. But in order to get this phase of it off the ground, a lot of people in Los Angeles, Washington and Rome had to move quickly. What's more, they had to bring in the Italian authorities.

Relationships between U.S. law enforcement and foreign law enforcement tends to hang on what FBI director Louis Freeh describes as "cop-to-cop bridges," those one-to-one relationships where confidence and trust is built up steadily over the years, personalized and carefully maintained. Freeh had forged his own connection with Giovanni Falcone, setting the example; it's no surprise that Italy is today one country where those bridges work best. So the Italians were approached, they understood the problem and, most of all, they trusted their American counterparts enough to sign up.

Now, on the invitation of Emerald Empire's Italian representative—Special Agent Matt Etre, working out of the Customs attaché's office at the U.S. Embassy in Rome—Colombians flew to Italy for a meeting. Etre and his partners—Italian undercover agents—were able to satisfy the Colombians that they were who they claimed to be and the deal was done.

"We worked the Milan area," explains Etre. "We provided the front, which was an investment company, and the Italians managed the money pickups. What I found so amazing was that once the traffickers decided we were all right, no further bona fides were necessary. It was hi, you must be Tony, here's the money. They'd hand half a million dollars in cash to someone they'd never met before and just like that, turn around and walk away."

The six pickups in Italy totaled just under $5 million.

Through information acquired during that phase, U.S. Customs and the Italian National Police were able to identify an important Italian-Colombian alliance, with Colombians stationed in Italy to oversee it. That led to five arrests, including the capture of Alberto Minnelli, a trafficker linked to the Canadian side of the Caruana-Cuntrera crime family.

It also almost opened up yet another front. The Colombians were putting out contracts for pickups, willing to pay commissions ranging from 6 to 20 percent, depending on the currencies involved and the difficulty in handling the money. But as commissions increased, so did competition to service them. Other criminal organizations were always waiting in the shadows to move in on the Emerald Empire business. And it took nothing more than the slightest hesitation by Emerald Empire to hand the contract to a competitor. Which is what happened when the Colombians asked if Emerald Empire could work pickups for them in Great Britain. But unlike the Italians, the Brits took too long to grant permission to authorize American undercover work on sovereign soil, and the contract went elsewhere.

By this time, however, Emerald Empire was hooked into the Cali-Juarez alliance so deeply that the opportunity presented itself for another offshoot. Gately and his men saw an opportunity—and seized it—to take down the Juarez cartel's substantial command and control center in Chicago.

"We'd actually known about Chicago for quite some time," says Doody, "but didn't understand just how much money and how much drugs they had there. We decided to target them and try to disrupt what they were doing there. A lot of their key people got arrested. We seized two to three million dollars at a time, along with large quantities of cocaine. We were in a position of trust, so while we were busting them in Chicago, they were confiding in us in California that something was going wrong in Chicago, that they were in disarray there. They never suspected us."

Terry Neeley had been working as the assistant Customs attaché at the U.S. Embassy in Ottawa, Canada, when he first heard about Operation Casablanca. But he only got involved with it when he was transferred back to Washington in the summer of 1996 and assigned to Allan Doody's group as national program manager for undercover money-laundering operations, of which Casablanca was merely one. He remained in that support role for a year until Gately, an old pal, called on Neeley to risk his life.

For more than a decade and possibly two, Chicago had been the narco-turf of the Herreras from Durango, Mexico. Not a cartel in the Juarez or Gulf sense, it was more a conglomerate of six blood-linked families—something akin to the Camorra branch of the Mafia in Italy—who quietly and effectively had gone about their business building a network of more than one thousand dealers for their Colombian cocaine and "Mexican mud" brown heroin. To service their key markets in New York, Boston, Philadelphia, Dallas, Louisville and Oklahoma City, they took a lesson from the airlines and set up Chicago as their main hub.

Back home, they have traditionally controlled much of the state and local government, doing their Robin Hood act, replacing some municipal services by building sewer systems, hospitals and public housing, and supporting any number of poor farming families by subsidizing legal crops with opium.

After the fall of the Medellín cartel and the imprisonment of the Orejuela brothers, the Herreras seemed to back off from cocaine, content to run what was effectively their heroin monopoly. It was one reason why other cartels tended to stay away from the Herreras—they weren't really in competition. However, the family did develop some sort of relationship with Amado Carrillo Fuentes. And when the Juarez cartel began looking for its own axis in the United States, the Herreras seemed willing to let them superimpose a cocaine structure over their own heroin hub.

Gately had originally seen the Chicago pickups as a chance to develop intelligence against the cartel. Now he concocted a plan to deploy a task force that would report directly back to him as a part of Operation Casablanca.

Neeley recalls that he was invited to head that task force on a Monday. The very next day, Gately arrived from Los Angeles to brief the assistant commissioner for Customs in charge of enforcement, Bonni Tischler, and to list the task force's real-time needs. They decided they would need up to forty people, all hand-picked, their own intelligence section and some help from other agencies, such as the DEA, state and local police. They also needed somewhere to work, somewhere to live, funding and all sorts of equipment. Neeley arrived in Chicago on Wednesday.

"There's an unbelievable adrenaline rush, a real high, when you go out into the field to conduct some very significant enforcement activity. At the same time there's the stress of going away and knowing you're going to be gone for an extended period of time. You worry about who's going to take care of your dogs and who's going to collect your mail and who's going to take the newspaper off the front porch. I sorted all that out, as best I could. Then, as soon as I arrived, I got into a car and started driving around looking for a place to operate from. Bill joined me on Thursday. On Friday, he and I spent the day purchasing some of the equipment we needed. Saturday and Sunday we were still looking for a location and I think we found that by Sunday. We moved in on Monday as agents started coming in from all over the country. We went over information that we'd obtained from previous activities in Chicago, made a determination on where we needed to exercise our authority immediately, briefed the troops and were in business that same afternoon."

They worked out of a suburban motel, using the cover story that they were employees of a company trying to build up sales in the import/export field. Two rooms were turned into a command center and extra phone lines were installed. Other rooms were set aside to house the troops. Gately returned to Los Angeles. But Neeley was on the phone to him at least a dozen times a day.

"Right from the start the pressure was unbelievable. There was no such thing as a day off. Some of the guys would take a few hours to do their laundry or see a movie. But my front-line supervisors and I were always working, always talking strategy, always planning what we were going to do next."

With the motto "We Rock Your World," the task force hit pay dirt with the very first house they raided. In the garage they found a *colleta—*

a secret compartment, professionally built, in which drug traffickers hide cash and contraband. The whole floor had been tiled, but some of the tiles had been grouted above a very big trapdoor. Below that was a room, large enough to drop down into, where they discovered half a dozen guns, some money counters, some cellular phones, and a kilo-press, which is a homemade press to make up kilo packages of cocaine. But this *colleta* had flooded and was filled with four inches of water, so there was no money.

In the second house they raided, there were two *colletas*, both under construction. One was in the garage—again tiled and grouted shut—the other in a laundry room where they'd also tiled the floor. That led them to a third house where the *colleta* was in the basement.

Between the second and third houses, they seized $3.7 million in cash.

Ever aware of the dangers that came along with an operation like this, Neeley and the others continued to identify targets, raid them and use each strike to identify more targets.

"It's like a house of cards that starts falling. During those first few weeks, we pulled off maybe twenty raids. We didn't sleep. We couldn't sleep. We developed intelligence around the clock until we were just too tired to stay up any longer. We then got a few hours' nap and went right back to it. It was our intent to take back the city from the cartels, and the only way to do that was through very, very aggressive investigations and by hitting them nonstop. This was not a nine-to-five job."

Nor was it a job where, for even a second, anyone could afford a lapse of concentration. "The shooting in New York hung over us. We were constantly worried about safety. And we were constantly revising contingency plans should something go wrong. We had our cover teams in place. We knew where the hospitals were. We had our code words established. We had good communications. But Chicago was a Juarez stronghold. We were in their neighborhood, at their homes, where they'd established themselves, inside their *colletas*, inside their command and control centers. Because we were in their face, constantly, there was always a very real chance of someone getting hurt. Regardless of whether your gun is drawn or not, you never know who or what is behind a door."

On more than one occasion, information came back to Neeley at his motel-room command post that the cartels believed they were being followed. On more than one occasion, they needed to drop back fast to regroup and analyze the situation. On more than one occasion, they had to rely on the skills of other agencies and a lot of luck that everything would work out whenever they had to surrender immediate control.

Roberto Orozco Fernandez, a thirty-six-year-old suspected laundry-man and assassin for the Juarez cartel, believed he'd succumbed to bad luck the night a Cook County Sheriff's officer on patrol in the Chicago sub-urbs spotted his Jeep Cherokee making an illegal lane change. The officer pulled him over and, in the course of writing a ticket, discovered two suit-cases containing $1.6 million. Later, an additional $50,000 would be found at Fernandez's house. But the lane-change ticket was only for his sake. He'd been a task-force target, tailed by undercover agents who, according to plan and at just the right moment, brought in the sheriff's deputy.

From what Gately's undercover agents were hearing in other cities, the Juarez cartel was, for the first time, feeling real pressure in Chicago. They didn't understand what was going on. And their initial reaction was to look for someone low-level, on the bottom, who might be leaking information. They even dispatched Dr. Navarro to Chicago. His solution for minimiz-ing the big hits they were taking was to rely more heavily on Emerald Empire to get money out as quickly as possible. He never suspected high-level involvement.

By this time, though, Dr. Navarro's fate was being seriously discussed. That's when Fuentes died. Some of Gately's people, who'd painted Fuentes's face squarely over the bull's-eye, took the loss personally. Not that they were sad for him. They were sad for themselves. They'd come within weeks of getting to him, and now, in a grotesque way, he'd had the last laugh.

"We were so very close to Amado Fuentes," Neeley goes on. "We were in bed with him. We were there. If he hadn't died, we would have put the handcuffs on him. When he died, there was a power struggle. We had to identify who was now controlling the cartel, and we settled on Tostado."

Serious talk about taking the operation down began during the sum-mer of 1997. It arose because some people way up the chain of command were getting cold feet. For many reasons, the decision was made to keep going. And in retrospect, that was the right decision, because they were still developing fresh leads and accumulating better evidence.

Allan Doody admits that he was sitting on the fence about when to call it quits. "I kind of half did want to take it down, and half didn't. The argument to keep working it was that we hadn't yet implicated as many people as we could. We were going off in new directions. I think it could have continued for a very long time."

The argument for stopping it was more political. Pressure was mounting from the top down to bring this to a conclusion. One fear was that Casablanca, in laundering so much money, had become part of the problem. The State Department, Treasury and Justice had their own agendas, one of them being the judgment of Mexico's efforts in the war on drugs which was coming up again in spring 1998. A few very senior people felt it would be better to have Casablanca out of the way before the president made his decision. But it was something a lot more sinister that plagued Gately's team. His agents in the field were starting to bump into other investigations run by other agencies, and none of them meshed with Casablanca's timetable.

Allan Doody again: "There are a lot of agencies out there working their own cases, like the DEA, the FBI, the IRS, plus state and local police. It's not uncommon when you run any major operation that you bump into a piece of a case where someone else might have a wiretap or a search warrant. The problem arises that when you've given them a piece of information they can use, because of the way our legal system works, that information might wind up on an affidavit they then file for a search warrant. Eventually someone gets arrested and the information on the affidavit gets released. Now, in and of itself, that one piece of information may not hurt you. But when you start to add up all those little pieces over the course of time, especially when you have people undercover, you can easily find yourself in a very dangerous situation. Lives are at risk. So you add all of these things up and make a decision."

It wasn't until Thanksgiving 1997 that everyone agreed, at least in principle, that it was time to focus on the end game. That took four months of planning. Gately came up with a time frame for the takedown—he wanted to run it in March—and then he and the senior managers in Washington decided on an actual date. They chose May.

A strategy briefing was called in the final week of April 1998, attended by a small coterie of Customs supervisors and senior managers, plus a few people from Justice, Treasury, the DEA and various U.S. Attorneys' offices—about twenty total—at Nellis Air Force Base near Las Vegas. It was a convenient location for everyone to get to, it would not attract attention and it was close enough to the takedown site that they could scout it. Also, because the base was secure, their meeting would be secure. As it was, just in case, they met in a secure conference room with armed guards outside.

Gately briefed everyone about the case, and told them how he was planning to take it down. He went through it hour by hour. Some bankers would arrive in San Diego. He mentioned who they were and told the group how many people he'd need there. Others would be flown to a casino in Nevada—by coincidence, it was called the Casablanca—and he outlined how many people he'd need there.

Plotting all this took two full days. They started at eight in the morning and were still in the conference room by six at night. They repeated the schedule the next day. When it was over, a few of them drove out to the casino, which was in Mesquitte. It had been chosen because it was isolated in the desert—a good ninety-minute drive from Las Vegas—and with a private airstrip.

No one at the casino knew what was about to happen. The actual arrest plans, and all the legal coordination that needed to go along with them, were made in L.A. The idea was to bring one group to San Diego—because many of those people were fearful of venturing any farther inside United States territory—and invite the others to a jolly Saturday-night celebration in Nevada.

The money going through the system was slowed down so that Customs could grab as much of it as they could before it slipped out of their control. Excuses were easy. They had worked with the traffickers and the bankers for nearly three years. They'd earned a level of confidence. So no one suspected anything when minor errors cropped up—a clerk forgot to sign something, there were typing errors on a form, one of the banks put the money in the wrong account. Pretexts were easy. With one week to go before the takedown, Emerald Empire had almost entirely turned off the money tap.

Those targets who showed up in San Diego believed they were going to win some contracts. They didn't know the city was chosen for its proximity to the U.S. border, making it seem safer for some of them than any location farther inside U.S. territory. The ones invited to Nevada believed they were going to celebrate past successes and discuss the laundering of megabucks in the future. They didn't know the casino had been chosen for its isolation. Neither group knew about the other, because Gately had deliberately set it up that way.

The San Diego takedowns were designed to happen at four different sites and at four different times. The nightmare of putting that together was to make sure they had enough time between takedowns so that the CI could get from one meeting to the next, and also to make sure that if someone was arrested downtown, the next group of bankers wouldn't be sitting in the hotel next door.

In Las Vegas, the bankers had a jovial dinner, talked about all the money they were going to make and were soon being ushered into limos for a trip to "more entertainment." Public descriptions of the event mentioned a night's gambling in Las Vegas. Privately, some of the bankers somehow got the impression that they were off for an evening at a house of prostitution.

Like lemmings, three or four bankers at a time piled into each limo. Departing the casino at well-timed, staggered intervals, they were driven by chauffeurs who happened to be armed undercover agents. The planned route took them into the desert, along a dark, isolated road, where Nevada Highway Patrol pulled them over on the pretext of speeding. The takedown team then showed up to formally announce, you're under arrest. Being in the middle of nowhere, there was noplace anyone could run, noplace anyone could hide.

As soon as one limo was out of the way, word was sent back to the casino to dispatch the next one. Needless to say, every one of them was more than just surprised. Especially Navarro. When the Highway Patrol stopped his limo, the driver announced, "I'm afraid I might have been speeding." But the moment that Navarro spotted a second car arriving at the scene, he knew there was something wrong. He reportedly mumbled, "This isn't just about speeding."

Additional arrests were made across the country, in Aruba and in Italy throughout the weekend. Then, on Monday morning, teams of agents and assistant U.S. attorneys fanned out across the country to seize bank accounts.

When the dust of that weekend settled down, 160 people from six countries were in jail. Criminal indictments had been levied against Bancomer, Serfin and Confia. And Customs agents had seized in excess of $150 million in assets from the Cali and Juarez cartels.

The one who got away was Jose Alvarez Tostado. But only just. Although Gately didn't put handcuffs on him, he seriously disrupted life as Tostado once knew it. Corruption often being the price of freedom in Mexico, the only way he's going to be able to move around is by paying megabribes. Thanks to Casablanca, he may not have that luxury anymore.

News that three major banks had been busted, plus bankers, lawyers and cartel members arrested, sent the Mexican stock and bond markets into a nosedive. Bank stocks plunged 8 percent. Reacting immediately, the Mexican government tried to put a brave face on what was, undeniably, a major embarrassment. Finance Minister Jose Angel Gurria claimed, "This does not mean that the Mexican banking system itself is under scrutiny, only that some employees unfortunately committed illegal acts and were found out."

During the first couple of days after Casablanca, the Mexicans even seemed willing to help. They rounded up half a dozen fugitives, among them Enrique Mendez Urena, whom the Mexican police arrested based on the U.S. indictment. A Juarez cartel investment adviser who'd worked at the Union Capital Bank in Guadalajara, Urena had made very clear statements—which the Americans had on tape—that he was laundering money for the Juarez cartel in his role as a financial adviser to the men at the top of the cartel, and that he also handled money for people within the Mexican government. He was obviously a man who knew a great deal. Which is why it didn't come as a major shock to anyone in the United States that suddenly he was dead.

Two conflicting stories were put forth by the Mexicans. One was that the cartel had captured him and was torturing him as a traitor and that the police had tried to rescue him. This version had Urena dying from cartel-inflicted injuries on the way to a hospital. The second story was that when the police arrived at his home in a luxury neighborhood in Guadalajara, he wasn't there. Instead, neighbors were complaining about a man running over rooftops. The police said they chased the man, who turned out to be Urena trying to escape, that they eventually convinced him to climb down and that he was arrested. But, they added, at some point in his attempted escape, he'd fallen, was injured and had lost consciousness during questioning.

While neighbors did not witness a fall, the fact that he lost con sciousness at some point—and that might very well have been during questioning—sounds reasonable, because somewhere between home and the hospital, he suffered severe head wounds.

He died from those head wounds just after dawn on Tuesday, May 26. For whatever reason, the Mexican authorities did not release his name for more than forty-eight hours. And then, they categorically denied any culpability in the death.

No one in Los Angeles or Washington knows for certain what happened. Nor is anyone ever likely to find out. It could have been an accident. It more likely was murder. After all, if what he told the undercover agents was true, and there is evidence that it was, then there were plenty of people in a position of authority in Mexico who would have a motive. But the news of Urena's death quickly turned into yesterday's news. Almost as soon as it was announced, the Mexicans began venting their anger, accusing the Americans of having violated their sovereignty. The political landscape shifted significantly. The politicians moved in. And cooperation ceased.

The Mexicans now wasted no time in complaining that the undercover operation had severely damaged the trust and cooperation that they'd previously shared with the Americans. Attorney General Jorge Madrazo said that Mexico would fully investigate Operation Casablanca and that he could not rule out formal requests for the extradition of U.S. agents who had illegally operated on Mexican soil.

"I don't know what they [the Americans] will think," Madrazo warned, "but the obligation of the Federal Public Ministry is to carry out this investigation." He continued, "The lack of communication has severely strained cooperation between the two countries. In our joint efforts, we demand respect and reciprocity."

Clearly, the Mexicans had every reason to be embarrassed about having been caught like this, although no one seemed embarrassed enough to explain how or why Mexico's three largest banks had come to launder $157 million worth of drug money. Instead they manifested their embarrassment by attacking the attacker, claiming to be furious that American agents had been operating inside their country for three years without anyone in the government knowing about it. What they didn't want to hear was that had the Mexicans been told, the odds were almost astronomical that someone somewhere in the government would have spilled the beans to the bad guys.

President Zedillo criticized the American tactics. So did the Mexican foreign minister. So did all the opposition leaders. In fact, their rallying calls to Mexican pride—which, without question, had been critically wounded—made this the rarest of political events in that country. It brought together all factions spanning all sides of the political spectrum. Natural enemies joined hands. And for the first time, perhaps ever, the country spoke with one political voice.

Secretary of State Madeleine Albright warned Mexico that prosecution and requests for extradition of U.S. drug agents would be counterproductive. Congress took a more blunt approach, perplexed that Mexico could raise objections of sovereignty while America hunted down narco-traffickers. "Any attempt by Mexico to extradite U.S. law enforcement agents," promised the then–House Banking Committee chairman, James Leach, "would risk irreparable damage to relations between our two countries."

"Sovereignty," added Senator Charles Grassley, "is not meant to be a shield for criminality."

With emotions running raw and tempers flaring, the White House stepped into the fray and opted for mea culpa diplomacy.

The agents who'd worked the case were shocked.

The White House apologized to the Mexicans.

Doing the president's bidding, Attorney General Janet Reno—albeit with carefully chosen words—insisted that Casablanca was neither an indictment of Mexico nor of its banking system. It was, she said, "just an indictment of some corrupt banking employees and three banks."

For some of those undercover agents who'd risked their lives, and some of their managers who'd helped pull off the most massive international drug-money-laundering sting ever, apologies were not merely inappropriate and unacceptable, they were the most heinous of all insults.

13

END RUNS

They're here, they're there, they're everywhere.
When the first rocket ship lands on Mars,
the spacemen will be greeted by Nigerians.

—POLICE INTELLIGENCE OFFICER

IN THE MID-1990S THERE WAS AN INTERNATIONAL heroin conference held in Washington, D.C., cosponsored by Interpol and the DEA, attended by representatives from about sixty countries.

It was the first major conference on heroin in twenty-five or thirty years. Among the delegations attending was one from Nigeria.

And from the very first day, the Nigerian delegates were on everyone's target list. They were verbally beaten up at every turn. Everybody at the conference took shots at them, deriding the country's abominable reputation for heroin trafficking and multiple varieties of fraud.

Throughout the conference, however, the woman who headed the delegation stayed silent, always maintaining her dignity. Finally, on the last day, she politely asked for the floor.

She told the delegates, there has been much talk here over the past several days about Nigerians being involved in smuggling, about being involved in advanced-fee schemes, about Nigerians with false documents, about Nigerians going all over the world to commit all sorts of frauds.

She said, "What I need to explain to this group is, this is what we do in Nigeria."

The gentleman who responded to the official request for his help confessed afterward that he should have known better.

Everyone says that afterward.

It looked like an important business letter from an important company. But it was addressed by hand. It was too good to be true, the gentleman later confessed.

And yet he fell for it.

"Dear Sir: This letter comes to you on the advice of a mutual friend, who thought you might be able to help me. I am acting as an agent for Shell BP . . ."

At least it sort of sounds like a real company.

". . . because a particular problem has arisen with blocked funds. A large sum due the company is being held in a Swiss account and, as the result of a legal complication, the money cannot be released directly to the company. We are anxiously looking forward to securing a foreign partner who can offer us the benefit of having some money remitted into any company's or personal buoyant account. This money runs in millions of U.S. dollars."

The problem duly explained, the proposition seemed straightforward. If the gentleman would allow that money to pass through his bank account, he would be paid handsomely for the service.

"The third party will wire the money due, $20 million, into your account without you assuming any liability. All you have to do is wait for the money to clear, then forward $14 million to us. You are welcome to the $6 million difference as your share. You are not being asked to do anything illegal, just to step into the middle of a legitimate commercial transaction. I would be pleased to meet with you, to show you references and to discuss all of the background paperwork."

The only problem was that the money needed to be paid by a fast-approaching deadline.

"However, to save valuable time, may I suggest you furnish to me your banking details, plus your personal authorization for the transfer, written on your own letterhead so that we may proceed."

The gentleman was much too savvy to send anyone authorization to access his bank account, so he phoned the man who'd written the letter, some sort of Nigerian prince—they're usually royalty or lawyers or government officials or ministers in a church—and asked for more details. His Highness was more than happy to oblige and even arranged a meeting. The gentleman flew all the way to Germany, where the prince was waiting for him with an entourage and plenty of supporting documents.

But now, the prince regretted to explain, there was an additional problem. Unfortunately, in order to make the transfer, the bank was demanding that a fee be paid. Shell BP couldn't pay it because the money was tied up. However, the prince would be willing to deduct the difference once the money came into the gentleman's account, and sweeten the pot for his trouble by adding a few dollars to his share.

The gentleman wanted to know how much the fee would be. The prince said 1 percent. And just how much, the gentleman wanted to know, would His Highness be willing to add to his share to sweeten the pot? The prince wondered if $500,000 would be all right.

When the gentleman seemed to hesitate, the prince suggested that perhaps they should put the half-million pot sweetener in writing. Which is what they did. The prince, acting for Shell BP, signed a contract guaranteeing that the $200,000 bank fee should be deducted from the $14 million the gentleman was agreeing to forward to the company once the $20 million cleared his account. And that he had the right to withhold an another $500,000 as an additional fee.

The gentleman kept telling himself he'd just done a deal of a lifetime. And in one sense, he was right. When the money never arrived, the prince and his entourage asked the gentleman to meet them immediately, again in Germany. In fact, the prince greeted him with the news that the money had been paid but not through the bank. It had been paid in cash and the gentleman was, of course, more than welcome to his share as agreed.

The gentleman asked when he could have it.

The prince told him, right away.

Except there was a new problem. Because of currency controls and a strict tax regime in Nigeria, the money had to be smuggled out. The prince even took the gentleman to see it. Piles of it. $20 million in $100 bills, packed in several huge cases.

Except it was all black.

The prince explained that in order to get it out of the country, they had to coat it with a special chemical. That way Nigerian Customs couldn't seize it. Watch, he said, taking one of the bills and rubbing it with a liquid.

Sure enough, out of the black a $100 bill appeared.

The gentleman was skeptical. The prince allowed him to pick up another piece of black paper and clean it. And again, right there in front of him, a second $100 bill appeared. The problem was, the prince admitted, they were out of the special chemical. But because they'd already caused him so much inconvenience, when he was merely trying to do them a favor, instead of returning $13.3 million, they would be satisfied if he only returned $13 million.

So, just like that, he made an extra three hundred grand.

But to get it, he had to stake them to the money to buy the special chemical. That set him back $75,000. And he's still waiting for His Highness to return from his chemical shopping trip.

A typical advance-fee fraud, it is referred to today as "a 419 scam," named after Nigerian Decree 419, which made it illegal in 1980. It is also, today, one of Nigeria's major exports.

A country that represents one fifth of Africa's population, Nigeria is the most urbanized nation on the continent, and among the most politically powerful. But it is not, nor has it ever been, what might be termed a "natural" country. It is, rather, a confederation of tribal states. Boundaries were imposed by the British, who granted independence in 1960, because those boundaries suited the colonial masters. Within six years the country slipped into post-colonial chaos as the first military coup took place. Since then, ethnic-based wars and coup d'états have been common. There are something like two hundred different tribes in Nigeria and at least as many different dialects are spoken there.

Around 30 percent of the population is Hausa-Fulani. They live in the northern half of the country and are largely Muslim. The Yoruba make up a little more than 20 percent and populate the southwest corner, which includes Lagos. The Ibo are about one sixth of the population and are found mainly in the southeast.

There was an old saying when the British ruled the country that the Hausa were the military, the Ibo were the civil servants and the Yoruba were the entrepreneurs. Opportunistic in the extreme, Nigerians as a group are historically recognized as the best traders in Africa, and were already doing business with the Arabs before the days of the slave trade. But if they are nothing else, Nigerians as a group, are without any doubt, Africa's most talented, freewheeling con men. Their global reputation is based largely, but not exclusively, on 419 frauds.

While the letter the gentleman received is typical, there are dozens of variations. Besides money due that is blocked, there are pleas for help with overinvoiced contracts, currency-conversion problems and the sale of a commodity at below-market prices. Letters may come from an individual claiming to be the benefactor of a will. Some come from what appears to be a church organization, and those are usually aimed at churches and religious groups. Other letters involve the sale or purchase of real estate. In one case, Nigerian fraudsters offered to buy a huge property in Ireland, securing the sale with a pile of black money. The seller of the house was coerced into advancing the fraudsters $950,000 for the chemical to wash the money.

One very odd thing in that case was the presence of another foreigner. There was so much "black money," the seller was told, that certain security arrangements needed to be made. The other foreigner was there to provide muscle. He happened to be Russian. It was the first time any police investigating 419 frauds had ever seen Nigerians teaming up with Russians.

It has not, however, been the last. An FBI investigation in the New York-New Jersey area unraveled a Nigerian gang working a scam in partnership with a Russian organized crime group. But then, besides being con men, Nigerian criminals are perhaps the most relaxed of all the organized crime groups when it comes to forming strategic alliances with other criminals.

Their 419 letters always come out of Lagos. They're thrown into post office sacks and loaded onto flights bound for international postal hubs in London, Frankfurt or New York. There the letters are sorted by the British, German or U.S. post office, which then forwards them on. Or not, as the case may be. Post offices have gotten so good at spotting these letters that they now routinely take them out of the system. In average years, U.S. postal inspectors annually grab 3.2 million.

Although the U.S. Postal Service is, by law, obliged to deliver all letters legally posted, they have the Brits to thank for the loophole that allows them to remove 419 letters before delivery. No one had noticed, until the British National Criminal Intelligence Service pointed it out, that the stamps were counterfeit, lithographic reproductions. The U.S. Secret Service then came into the picture, because they deal with counterfeit instruments of every kind, and under their authorization, postal inspectors now pull those letters out of the system.

But still they keep coming. The Hong Kong postal service, for example, announced not long ago that 95 percent of all the mail from Nigeria is 419 letters. Even with everyone wise to the counterfeit stamps, the Nigerians flood post offices on the principle that a percentage will always get through. It is believed that 1 percent of the people who receive the letters respond, and that the average loss per response is $200,000. Just taking the four million letters the U.K. and U.S. postal services stop each year, that would otherwise represent losses of $80 million. As it is, worldwide, Nigerian 419 scams are believed to be worth nearly $1 billion.

With so much at stake, Nigerian criminals are understandably conscientious when it comes to setting up a scam. Before working in a country, they seed it, bringing people in to live there and to set up their infrastructure. They need addresses for the letters and bank accounts for the money. During the Atlanta Summer Olympic Games, no one could figure out why hotels seemed to be emptied out of all their telephone directories, business directories and Yellow Pages. It turns out that some athletes on the Nigerian national team and loads of fans were paid to bring them home. Within three months of the games, Atlanta was hammered with 419 letters.

The Germans have a massive problem with Nigerian crime. So do the Scandinavians. So do the Dutch. The British keep telling the French they have a problem, but the French won't accept it. Half a million Nigerians live in the U.K.—at least those are the ones that the Immigration office knows about. There could be as many as half a million more they don't know about, not just illegals, but overstayers and people on false passports. There are Nigerians working scams throughout Asia, and on average, in some countries like Korea, one case of Nigerian fraud is reported to the authorities every day. Over the past few years, Nigerians have also begun to establish themselves in Russia. How long that lasts is a matter for conjecture. It's unlikely that groups such as Solntsevskaya are going to be especially receptive to foreigners working their turf. But, given the Nigerian proclivity for doing joint ventures if in the next few years the streets of Moscow aren't filled with dead Nigerian con men, then a deal has been done somewhere.

If not totally ruthless, they are undeniably heartless. One couple who'd been running a company that had done business in Nigeria for years received a 419 letter from a man appealing to their friendship in asking for help to get money out of the country. The couple fell for it and lost their business.

Obviously, these criminal enterprises play off greed. But their understanding of human nature runs deep. In many cases, when a victim realizes he's been hooked, he goes through a distinct personality change. He still somehow believes there might be a light at the end of the tunnel. In one case, an American turned up for a meeting in Britain with $500,000 in cash. The police intercepted him on his way and told him what was about to happen. The man refused to believe it. His half million is gone.

A popular ploy is to let victims think that they'll get their money back by recruiting others into a separate conspiracy. In another case, one victim tried to recoup his losses by luring twenty others into the scam. The group's total losses added up to $7.2 million.

The kind of money that the scam generates was summed up recently by a Nigerian who, over a nine-month period, deposited $46 million in checks plus $9 million in cash in a British bank. He told his bankers that the money was coming in from outside the U.K., although the source of the funds was not disclosed. On one occasion, he handed over forty supermarket shopping bags and announced to the teller, "There's about $4 million in there. You count it. If it's not, tell me."

In addition to banks, they use Western Union to move a lot of their money. Intriguingly, they also have Lebanese banking connections. It seems that in the Muslim north of Nigeria, there is an old, established Lebanese community. For some reason, Nigerian criminal enterprises have come to rely on these Lebanese to move money through their laundering system.

Every six months or so, the Central Bank of Nigeria advertises in world newspapers to warn people away from 419 fraud. The bank takes out full-page ads, but if they have any effect, it is hard to spot. It leads one to wonder why the Nigerians themselves can't do something about it.

The answer is, obviously, they need the money.

Besides the 419 statute, there are other laws that could be used. There are money-laundering regulations on the books, and there is Decree 33. Banks and financial institutions are required to report transactions in excess of 500,000 Naira ($6,500) and presumably some of them do. The Nigerian authorities have even conducted money-laundering investigations which have resulted in property being seized. The Nigerians simply don't trouble themselves by securing convictions. That way, seized property can be returned. What's more, Decree 33 makes it a criminal offense in Nigeria for any Nigerian to commit a criminal offense abroad. Double jeopardy in its purest form, it states that any citizen who is arrested, convicted and sentenced to a jail term in another country will, when deported back to Nigeria, be imprisoned for an additional five years.

It's on the books. The government points to it every time anyone in the West chides them. They just don't bother enforcing it. Nor do they bother fulfilling their obligations to UN conventions, or to cooperate in any meaningful way in the fight against transnational organized crime.

It is therefore down to Western law enforcement to act. But that's easier said than done. The Nigerians are well organized and nothing flaps them. They generally shy away from violence, although there has been violence reported in New York. They use various passports and work in little cells. It is believed that there is a Mr. Big somewhere at the top. But he's likely to be in Nigeria, and that means he's protected.

They are intelligent and understand jurisdictional problems. They try to arrange meetings with victims outside their own country. They prefer to lure Americans to Europe, because borders complicate the investigative process and seriously muddle the judicial process. Britain is one of their favorite places because the judicial system there is tipped in their favor. If they are arrested in Britain, and several victims are located—which they invariably are—the police are then faced with a massive logistical problem. In America, the police can say to the court, there are another twenty-three victims, your honor, and the judge can take that into account in sentencing. But in Great Britain the police have to travel to wherever those twenty-three victims are and take statements from them, and then prove in court that the person they're talking about is the same one they've got in custody. That usually means flying twenty-three people over to Britain to go through a lineup and identify the fraudster. Otherwise the court won't accept that it is the same person. This is costly and difficult to arrange, and the Nigerian criminals know that.

Since 1992, the U.S. Secret Service has been collecting intelligence on these scams. Not just the 419 letters, but all sorts of counterfeit identification documents—pay stubs, employee ID cards, benefit slips, income tax returns, passports—which the Nigerians use to obtain post office boxes. With those, they redirect mail so that they can steal credit cards, redirect bank statements so they can empty accounts, form companies, bilk insurance companies and apply for mortgages and even student loans. They also have a fondness for counterfeit birth certificates from the Virgin Islands. They use them inside the United States to obtain Social Security cards and driver's licenses, with which they can open bank accounts. In response, the Secret Service has databased hundreds of thousands of 419 letters and documents, interviewed tens of thousands of people, and continues to log three to five hundred documents received every day from victims and intended victims. Link analysis on a document can usually pinpoint which group sent the letter or forged the document and, at times, even point to the location of the group's leaders in Nigeria.

The Secret Service is also feeding counterfeit credit card information into that database. The Nigerians start with blanks, stamp them themselves, and use them throughout North America until the cards get stopped. Then they get on a plane and fly to Europe because they know they've got another twenty-four hours to spend on the cards before they get stopped worldwide. West African counterfeit credit cards are becoming so prevalent that police say it is not uncommon to go on busts and find twenty to thirty credit card blanks. They have even intercepted birthday cards sent from one Nigerian to another, with a counterfeit credit card stuck inside as a gift.

The U.S. embassy staff in Lagos admit they are, literally, "inundated" with 419 cases and receive requests daily for help from defrauded Americans. Despite embassy warnings not to come to Lagos—echoed by all of the Western embassies there—some victims insist on showing up. And that's where things can go tragically wrong. Hostages have been taken and held for ransom. Over the past few years, there have also been at least fifteen deaths recorded in Nigeria of foreign victims hoping to recoup their losses.

"Violence attracts attention," notes the FBI's Tom Kneir. "So, if you think about it, violence is pretty stupid. The Nigerian problem in the U.K. is like locusts. They just eat away. We're talking about billions of pounds. It's the same in this country. Now ask yourself, why are they so successful? The answer is, because they go about their business without pissing off anybody. They do frauds, they don't do violence. They come in, do their deals and get out. Most of us go on a two-week trip with multiple pairs of socks and underwear. These guys go on a two-week trip with multiple sets of identification. But that's changing, because they also do heroin. And it's because of the heroin that they're showing up on the radar screens."

Inconceivable abuses, carried out in the name of apartheid, created an extensive breeding ground for crime in South Africa. Among scores of illegitimate acts under the old regime, police used drug syndicates and dealers to get to political opponents. The vestiges of that are manifest today in the nearly eight hundred crime syndicates that are acknowledged to be operating there. Most are street gangs. But some are organized along traditional lines and some have established direct partnerships with major transnational criminal organizations, serving as local franchisees for them.

Of course the major gangs are there as well. Chinese Triads, Russian Maffiya, traditional Italian Mafia, the Colombian cartels and Nigerian criminal enterprises have had the experience and the wherewithal to make their mark. They have updated and modernized the old smuggling networks for drugs, arms, diamonds and stolen cars—Bulgarian gangs move cars out of South Africa and into Eastern Europe, often in conjunction with Russian organized gangs—and have used the nation's financial infrastructure to launder their money. Especially attractive are South Africa's highly developed diamond and gold markets.

Granted, the new government inherited much of this, but since 1994 it has failed miserably to come to grips with the problem. Besides the fact that legislation is insufficient to mount an effective fight against local crime—and absolutely incapable of doing anything about transnational crime—police are underfunded, undermanned, undertrained, outgunned and overworked. Of those eight hundred acknowledged gangs, it is believed that fewer than two hundred are currently being investigated or otherwise actively pursued by the police.

Compounding the problem, the country is surrounded by neighbors whose interests are in direct contradiction to South Africa's. Drug smuggling and weapons trafficking bring them much-needed hard cash, all at South Africa's expense. They moved en masse the moment South Africa's international isolation ended in 1994, taking advantage of South Africa's modern transportation, communication and financial sectors.

The worst offender was Nigeria. In Johannesburg, Nigerian criminal enterprises dominate the cocaine market, frequently in partnership with criminals from other West African states, especially Ghana. Exact figures are not available, but it is estimated that perhaps as many as one hundred thousand illegal immigrants from Nigeria and Ghana live in that city, many of them working in some facet of the illicit drug trade.

The receiving end of a Brazil–to–South Africa air bridge, Johannesburg was a magnate for drug traffickers. As police and Customs at Johannesburg

International Airport began to have some success in stopping drugs from entering the country there, the traffickers—in this case, Nigerian—simply diverted to Cape Town, or brought drugs in overland from Mozambique, Zambia, Zimbabwe, and Namibia. They also began to use courier services, which transship through Britain and Germany. Customs inspectors in both those countries have increasingly stopped shipments of cocaine sourced in South America and addressed to traffickers in Angola, Botswana, Swaziland, Lesotho, Mozambique and Zimbabwe for eventual smuggling into South Africa.

One area where the Nigerians have not succeeded is synthetic drugs, because most of them are aimed at white South Africa and the market is dominated by Dutch and British expatriates. In 1997, South African police busted a drug laboratory and arrested the scientist who'd once been in charge of the nation's chemical and bacteriological warfare program. The lab had been established under the old regime, supposedly to study the use of narcotics as weapon for neutralizing an enemy, and was producing both Mandrax, a strong tranquilizer, and Ecstasy. Both drugs have saturated schools all the way down to junior high. But whether it be cocaine, marijuana, heroin or synthetics, the violence that shadows these markets is inescapable. Pretoria and Durban have both been ravaged by drug-related criminality, while Cape Town has become the Wild West.

In a part of the world that could have as many as one hundred thousand gang members, the most visible and most violent of Cape Town's groups has been the Hard Livings, formed in 1971 by the Staggie identical twins. Rashaad was the brains behind the gang and Rashied was the enforcer, a psychopath who enjoyed his nickname, "Mad Dog." They flourished under the previous government, using much of their wealth and power to expand into Cape Town's prostitution business.

Responding to such lawlessness, and the new government's inability to control such gangs, an equally visible and equally violent vigilante group formed in the Cape Flats, east of Cape Town. Largely Muslim and known as People Against Gangsterism and Drugs (PAGAD), in 1996 they shot, killed and then burned Rashaad Staggie. They also, eventually, shot and seriously wounded Rashied.

Until PAGAD pretty much neutralized the gang's leadership, one of the Hard Livings' rumored alliances was with the Pizza Connection's laundryman.

Vito Roberto Palazzolo was a man who'd escaped American justice. A jeweler by profession, he was in those days running Consult Fin SA, a private bank in Lugano, Switzerland. Both the Americans and Italians asked for his extradition. Instead, the Swiss charged him with money-laundering offenses and, rather than face life in jail in Italy, Palazzolo chose to make his stand in the more lenient Swiss court. He got three years. As a nonviolent offender, about halfway into his sentence in 1988, he was given Christmas leave. Having decided he'd had enough, he skipped. His destination of choice was South Africa, where legend has it that he arrived carrying 16 million Rand ($2.7 million) in cash and even more in diamonds. Within weeks he bought a vineyard and settled into his new life on a fabulous ranch in Fransehoek.

The Swiss found him there when his face appeared in the crowd of a televised report of a National Party fund-raising event, and requested his deportation. Despite his ties to the National Party, the South Africans sent him back to Switzerland, where he served out the remainder of his term, plus an additional two years. Finally released, he returned to South Africa.

Now declared an undesirable by Pretoria, Palazzolo was refused residence. He sidestepped officialdom by obtaining citizenship in the Ciskei homeland, using the name he had in an Austrian passport, Roberto von Palace Kolbatschenko. Someone in the Ciskei agreed to appoint him "ambassador plenipotentiary" to South Africa, which would have allowed him to live in Cape Town with diplomatic status, except Pretoria saw through that and refused his dubious credentials. In 1995, however, the homelands were abolished and his Ciskei citizenship automatically became South African citizenship.

The following year, Andre Lincoln, a colleague of Deputy President Thabo Mbeki, presented evidence to him that the police organized crime unit in the Western Cape was run by a chap with criminal connections to the former government and therefore could not be trusted. He also informed Mbeki that Palazzolo was now living in Cape Town.

Mbeki's solution was to establish the Cape-based special undercover Presidential Investigations Task Unit. He decreed it would bypass all the usual law enforcement chain of command and report directly to him. And he named Lincoln as the Unit's head. With Mbeki's authority, Lincoln went off on a bizarre voyage of inquiry. He contacted the Italians, who told him that Palazzolo was, perhaps, the most important Mafia financier since Roberto Calvi and Michele Sindona, late of the Banco Ambrossiano affair. They claimed that, immediately following Calvi and Sindona, the Cupola had made a decision in Sicily that, rather than control bankers, it was wiser to own banks. As a result, a number of banks were acquired by the Sicilians, one of which was in Zimbabwe. Palazzolo, they said, had been a key part of this transaction and the Italians wanted him back.

Shortly afterward, Lincoln flew to Rome to meet with the Italians—he introduced himself as General Lincoln—received further information about Palazzolo and, in return, invited them to come to South Africa to arrest a whole bunch of suspected Italian mobsters who were living there. Decidedly interested, a few weeks later, a team of Italian policemen arrived in Johannesburg. But all that happened was that they sat around for two weeks. When no arrests were imminent, they went home.

During the time Lincoln was supposedly investigating Palazzolo, he put in a funding request to travel to Angola. It was granted, and he went—with Palazzolo.

A secret South African report had named Palazzolo as the mastermind behind a Western Cape Mafia-style organized crime group and had linked him to the Hard Livings. It also named a South African underboss as a former police intelligence officer and noted that his crew was made up of fugitives from Morocco, Russia, Germany and France. Much of the information on him is widely believed to have come from the Italians, who'd been investigating him for several years. Yet despite his direct association with the Pizza Connection case, Palazzolo has always denied any Mafia links. According to the Italians, Palazzolo is the Mafia's chief laundryman in southern Africa. According to the FBI, which was issued a warrant against him in the U.S., he is one of the top seven members of the Sicilian Mafia.

The Italians have failed at least twice to extradite him. On both occasions, Pretoria turned down the request on grounds of double jeopardy. First Italy wanted to try him for his role in the Pizza Connection case, but South Africa's Department of Justice believed Palazzolo's Swiss jail time had erased that charge. When Italy switched gears, using the Mafia-association law as the basis for extradition, South Africa answered that it could only extradite someone for crimes recognized in South Africa, and that Mafia association is not one of them.

With no alternatives, the Italians decided to try him in absentia. Almost without warning, Lincoln shut down his probe and announced that he was clearing Palazzolo of any wrongdoing. As head of the unit, he wrote on official stationery to Palazzolo's attorney, "None of these activities is the subject of any complaint of irregularity whatsoever. No past or current investigation carried out by myself or my office can implicate your client in the extortion of Italian businessmen in South Africa."

This despite being on Interpol's wanted list.

Since that letter, Andre Lincoln has been arrested for fraud and theft.

In the meantime, Palazzolo continues to be referred to as the God-father of South Africa, and the Italian Justice Ministry lists him as one of their "100 Most Wanted." There are stories that he has given sanctuary to several wanted men and that he oversees the activities of several émigré Italians who have established money-laundering and drug connections in South Africa. His business interests range from ostrich farming, mineral water and toxic-waste disposal to weapons trafficking and drug smuggling. He is known to own a game farm in Namibia and to have a stake in the Angolan diamond industry.

South African police confirm that investigations are continuing and that the most recent Italian extradition request is, in fact, being considered. Unofficially, they admit that two of the things they're looking at are the alleged Palazzolo–Hard Livings link and the Hard Livings–Nigerian cocaine link. Establishing both allegations would connect Palazzolo and the Mafia with Nigerian criminal enterprises. Managing that might be the first step toward reclaiming a country in the midst of being choked to death by criminal organizations.

After all, if the single most important asset of any democracy is its justice system, then it is reasonable to argue that a government unable to convince its citizens that justice will prevail undermines its own legitimacy.

Despite all the international optimism and goodwill that walked alongside Nelson Mandela as he left prison and made his way to political power, the failure of the African National Congress to come to grips with the difference between opposition and power has brought about the bank-ruptcy of law and order throughout much of the country.

It is only one short step from the prosperous future that should be South Africa's to the corruption and anarchy one sees in, say, Colombia.

And while the Nigerians are not alone in raping South Africa, they certainly have much to answer for.

In the very early 1980s, some Nigerian naval officers were sent to a train-ing course in India. They saw how easy it was there to obtain Southeast

Asian heroin and decided that if they could buy some, get it into Europe
or the United States—which they thought they could do by traveling in
uniform—they could earn a fortune. That was Nigeria's leap into drug
trafficking.

Shortly thereafter, the Nigerian economy collapsed. Poverty and political corruption led to substantial migration. Unfortunately, migration coin-
cided with the upsurge in international drug trafficking, which meant
Nigerians found themselves living in centers where drugs suddenly
became available. More and more Nigerians were not only willing to carry
drugs for traffickers—because they needed the money—but were anxious
to do so. At the same time, more and more Nigerian criminals realized that
drugs were their path to riches.

The alarm went out to Customs officers around the world to be
extra-vigilant with anyone carrying a green Nigerian passport. Nigerian
criminals went in search of new passports.

The end of apartheid couldn't have come at a better time. The new
government opened up the country, and Nigerians fraudulently proved
they were South African. It wasn't difficult to manage, with their superior
counterfeiting skills. And anyway, as so much of South Africa is without a
register of births, marriages or deaths, the country has for years run on
completely bogus documentation.

Four million Nigerians now live in South Africa. The retail value
of drugs reportedly flowing through the country represents just over half of
South Africa's GDP. Some 60 to 65 percent of those drugs are then exported
to Europe and the United States by Nigerian criminal enterprises.

A vital ingredient in their South Africa success is the direct air link to
Brazil. It perfectly suited the Nigerians' ambitions because there are five hundred thousand Nigerians living in Sao Paolo. It also suited the Colombians'
ambitions. They'd spotted the possibilities of South Africa and were anxious
to open the market. All the Nigerians had to do was flash their money. The
Colombians now based agents in Lagos and the two groups were in business.

The circuit remains the obvious one. Drugs are trucked down from
Colombia to Brazil, then flown across to South Africa. Some of those drugs
are sold there, the rest are moved north into Europe. Or they're transshipped via West Africa or through Europe—there is heavy traffic in and
out of Italy, giving rise to the suspicion that traditional Italian groups have
joined hands with the Nigerians—and back to North America.

Savvy traders that they are, the Nigerians did not want to be in a position of dependency on the Colombians, so they moved their own buyers into Thailand to supplement their income with an assured supply of Golden Triangle heroin. By 1996, Nigerian trafficking had reached the highest levels of international concern.

A conference of the most senior law enforcement officers in the G-8 put together a subcommittee on Nigerian criminal enterprises. It served to highlight the increasing demand for a coordinated response. Based on that, British Customs and Excise formed a seventeen-man operational response group, with its own integrated intelligence unit.

Called the West African Organized Crime Unit, it is run by a British Customs officer named Tim Manhire. "We've come to think of Nigerians as the world's middlemen. They don't usually source drugs and they don't generally sell them in the marketplace. But they do everything and anything in between."

Their method of choice, he says, is "little and often."

When Customs officers intercept two kilos of heroin, the bust doesn't make headlines. It is still, however, worth a lot of money. The way the Nigerians stay off radar scopes is by sending two kilos today and two more kilos tomorrow. It quickly adds up to a great deal of money.

"It's very easy to underestimate a problem when each seizure you get is very small. We took out ten couriers from one organization going to the States with a kilo or less. But the Nigerians didn't start out working like this, which shows how dangerous they really are. They learned from their mistakes; they've always been willing to make changes along the way. As we've got better at finding them, they've evolved, and have found better ways to get around us."

Initially, Nigerians smuggled large amounts in containers, much as the Colombians still do. As seizures mounted, they saw that they weren't fooling anyone, so they switched to strapping drugs on couriers. At first they used Nigerian women, often prostitutes. That didn't work for very long, so they shifted to "stuffers and swallowers." They paid couriers to hide drugs in body cavities or to swallow condoms stuffed with drugs. The dangers of that became obvious as condoms broke and couriers died. Before long they were also getting caught, as various Customs agencies developed methods to spot them. U.S. Customs uses X rays. U.K. Customs came up with a urine test. It reached the point where anyone carrying a Nigerian passport might as well have had "smuggler" stamped on his forehead. So they side-stepped again, recruiting white European and North American couriers. They reduced the amounts each courier had and increased the number of couriers. It was now a percentage game. One courier with ten kilos might get stopped. Ten couriers with one kilo each means nine might get through. Put ten couriers on ten flights, and they've suddenly got a ninety-kilo bundle for sale.

They pay couriers as little as possible—sometimes $2,000 per kilo—which is not a lot of money considering the value of the drugs and the punishment for getting caught. But they prey on people with no money. They've also been known to pay couriers with a counterfeit U.S. passport so that once they get into the States, they can stay.

Nigerian criminal enterprises have teams of recruiters who employ people as talent spotters. In one recent case, the caretaker of an apartment block recruited two Dominican girls. One was flown to Bangkok to pick up heroin for New York. The other was flown to Rio to fetch coke destined for London. The caretaker was handed $1,000 for his help.

Recruiters cover every category from college kids backpacking around Europe to middle-aged couples traveling with their children. In a well-publicized case, they recruited American sailors based in Italy to smuggle drugs for them, a fallback to their earlier beliefs that men and woman in uniform are not frequently searched by Customs. They've even gone so far as to enlist athletes in wheelchairs on their way to the States for the Special Olympics.

Hedging their bets, they then complicate routings. Couriers no longer travel directly from drug hot spots to drug markets. The first destination is almost never the country where the drugs will be sold, which means they're also relying on the paucity of international law enforcement cooperation. They bring heroin from Bangkok into Africa—currently staging in Ethiopia, Kenya, Ghana and South Africa, in addition to Nigeria—then send the drugs to North America via Amsterdam, Zurich, London and Frankfurt. When a courier arrives from Africa into London's Gatwick Airport, for instance, someone is waiting there with another ticket from London Heathrow to New York, making it look to authorities at JFK as if this person is just arriving from Britain. Or they bring heroin from Bangkok into Zurich and hand it off to another courier who brings it by train into Britain, where a third courier takes it to the States.

They use a route for a while, then change it to keep the cops from detecting patterns. A typically convoluted route was uncovered during a major West African organized crime bust in Chicago called Operation Global Sea. A single courier flew from Chicago to New York, then on to Amsterdam, then Bangkok, where he picked up his heroin. From there he went to Malaysia, where he was handed a new passport and his old one was mailed back to him in the States. With passport and heroin in hand, he returned to Amsterdam, picked up a flight to Guatemala, went from there to Mexico City and then to McAllen, Texas, where he caught a domestic airplane ride home to Chicago.

That a courier took this routing is one thing. That someone actually thought of it shows how far these gangs are willing to go to meet their needs.

Their latest gimmick is the post office. Packages stuffed with drugs are mailed anonymously, addressed to fictitious names at mail drops. The cost is considerably less than airline tickets, accommodations and fees for smugglers, and because delivery dates can be reasonably well predicted, any delay is a signal that law enforcement has taken an interest in the package and it can then be abandoned. Here too, it's the little and often syndrome. Because of the volume of mail that modern post offices have to handle each day, only a very, very small percentage of the Nigerian shipments could ever be stopped.

Their ingenuity is endless, made all the more difficult to impede by their extraordinary ability to communicate. Police agencies all over North America and Europe report that when they make an arrest they find common telephone numbers and addresses in everybody's address book. In one New York case, the name of a housing project near Kennedy Airport had been misspelled in the suspect's address book. Three months later, the same address appeared in another suspect's book—with no connection at all between the cases—misspelled the same exact way. And that same misspelled address continues to pop up.

The gangs are loosely structured and constantly changing. Nigerians who work outside the country can be the boss for one job and a hired hand for another. When $100,000 was needed to finance a recent drug run, the Nigerian in charge contacted four of his friends and they each put in $20,000 in exchange for 20 percent of the profits. The next job the same fellow did was financed by a different group of friends.

As classic free-market entrepreneurs, they're willing to deal with any other organization as long as there is something in it for them. Over the years, they've developed strong alliances—not just with the cocaine cartels in South America, but separately with Dominican street gangs in New York and New Jersey, and Jamaican street gangs in London. And those alliances have created their coke-heroin-swap business.

Although prices vary greatly, depending on market forces, a kilo of heroin in Bangkok will cost a Nigerian trader around $8,000. Bringing that into the U.K. will get him a return of around $50,000. But the U.K. market is for "brown heroin"—sometimes called "mud"—which comes from Turkey. The market for Thai "white heroin" is North America and the price there is three to four times as much. So the Nigerians don't bother with the British market, they get their heroin into North America and now have product worth, say, $150,000.

Another anomaly of the market is that cocaine in North America is half the price that it is in Britain. So the Nigerians hand off their heroin to the Dominicans and sometimes even to the Colombians themselves— whoever needs heroin and has coke to trade for it—and then bring the cocaine back to Britain, which they wholesale to the Jamaican "Yardie" gangs who sell it on the streets of London.

Their $150,000 now gets turned into $300,000.

It's a good deal for everybody, including the Yardies. Until the Nigerians came along, Jamaican gangs were sourcing their own cocaine through the Caribbean. The Nigerians offered them a lower price with no smuggling risks.

"Some Nigerian somewhere had to go to some Jamaican somewhere and cut a deal," a senior British Customs officer notes. "We've never come across any other organized crime group willing to work with as many different groups as the Nigerians. But when you factor in the Jamaicans, it is not without some risk to them. The Jamaicans tend to stick to their own community and are not particularly structured, but they are notoriously violent. Nigerians are notoriously nonviolent. Although in the States we're told they're starting to arm themselves. And that may be what happens in Britain as a result of their alliance with the Jamaicans. Yardies will rip off anyone. They'll take gear and never come up with the money."

All of this now comes full circle, starting with a serious company in a serious industry that takes seriously its own security.

There are electronic security checks to get into the building and electronic checkpoints throughout the building which allow only people who need to go to different floors to do so. Anyone who has not been given the proper clearances is stopped. The chairman himself worked it all out. As far as he's concerned, it's foolproof.

What he never thought about, however, were the ladies with the mop.

Every night, crews of cleaners come into the building. The company hired them through an agency. And all of them can go to every floor. Some of those women are West African. And it only takes one to help herself to a few sheets of company stationery sitting in a desk drawer. From that comes forged letters of recommendation—such as to an embassy for travel visas or to a bank for a loan—and identity fraud, in which a Nigerian con man becomes an employee of the company with all sorts of privileges, including the right to empty out corporate bank accounts. Or they use the letterhead to contact banks, alter addresses on accounts, wait a month, order a statement to see how much is in the account, then order a new checkbook and empty it.

It's not much more than a short step, once someone is inside a building, to penetrate the computer system. Nigerian criminal enterprises have regularly tapped into all sorts of official information—reports from banks and credit bureaus, files from Social Security offices, birth certificates, tax records and voter registrations—allowing them to literally steal an identity and use it to commit a myriad of frauds. Those frauds, along with 419 scams, are the cash cows that supply the down payment for drug trafficking.

The money comes around, full circle.

The chairman worked out his corporate security all by himself.

14

CHASING GHOSTS

*It's like chasing ghosts. Once you think you've identified it,
it disappears, changes its form.*

—Jim Fisher, Criminal Intelligence Service, Canada

It took a strategic alliance of the RCMP,
the Toronto Police and the U.S. Secret Service in 1998 to bust a major
international counterfeit and credit card ring, which turned out to be
something none of them had ever seen before—a strategic alliance
between a Chinese gang, the Italians and the Russians.

One officer called it, "A whole new ballgame."

An Italian organized crime gang had come up with a good method for
counterfeiting Canadian money. That alone might have been enough to make
the case unusual, because the currency of choice had always been U.S. dollars. Counterfeiting Canadian $50 and $100 bills was a relatively new phenomenon. But it was the gang's use of technology that set them one step
above the rest. The banknotes were fed into scanners, the images loaded into
computers and perfect copies reproduced on ink-jet printers. Experienced
officers commented that the reproductions were among the most sophisticated they'd ever seen. The quality was also reflected in the price—30 cents
on the dollar—which is a huge premium to pay for counterfeit money.

Along with the phony banknotes, the gang was also making counterfeit credit cards. They used thermal silk-screen printers to produce and
stamp the cards with the logos of half a dozen major banks. The numbers
assigned to the cards were purchased from a Russian gang who ran gas
stations from which they were doing gas-tax fraud. The Russians were

double-swiping high-value cards—platinum and gold—handed over by unsuspecting clients to pay for gasoline. The money and the credit cards were being marketed around North America by the Chinese gang.

Taking out all three groups was the object of a ten-month operation that had an undercover agent dealing directly with one of the Chinese gang members. But just as the police were about to pounce, things went awry. The undercover officer had negotiated a deal to buy C$3 million worth of counterfeit money. Two days before that was to go down, one of the surveillance units got burned. Someone spotted them. By total coincidence, someone also broke into a car used by another surveillance team that was unrelated to the unit that got spotted. The team's target sheets were stolen.

The officers had no way of knowing whether the break-in had been the work of to a common thief or whether those target sheets were the reason for it and wound up in the hands of the gang. But it was a definite security breach that prompted an immediate rethink. As a result, instead of taking the gang down when they'd originally planned, the officers extended the operation for two months. The criminals also reacted to the surveillance burn. Fearing that an undercover sting might relieve them of their entire cache, they now refused to sell anything more than C$500,000 to any single customer. As it happened, the agent's cover hadn't been blown, but there was no way the gang would go for the original C$3 million.

When the operation finally culminated with simultaneous raids on eighteen locations—including multiple manufacturing sites around Montreal—they only got the credit card end of it. The main players in the counterfeit-money ring got away. The cops also failed to seize the computer, the printer and the scanner, which means the gang is still capable of producing more $10 and $50 bills. Although the police were able to recover $2 million in counterfeit bills—said to be the largest seizure of cash in Canadian history—the police believe that another million is still out there. And if it isn't yet in circulation, there's some Chinese operator somewhere in North America who's sitting on a lot of pieces of paper that are destined to show up eventually.

The term that's most often used is "Asian organized crime," and, as far as catch-all phrases go, it pretty well labels criminal groups with links to Hong Kong, Macao, mainland China, Japan, Korea, Singapore, Malaysia and Southeast Asia.

But it doesn't describe the problem any more than the word *car* tells you what a Cadillac is.

Nor do all the soundbites that show up on the evening news when law enforcement officers talk about "a giant spider spreading its web across the world" and "the invisible empire" and organizations that are "more flexible than the Mafia and more savvy than Colombia's drug cartels."

The problem is that there are various types of Asian organized crime groups, with major structural and philosophical differences, but most of all, cultural differences.

Start with the Japanese Yakuza.

Most experts agree it is are Japan's biggest corporation, turning over $75–85 billion a year, which is more than four times the combined revenues of Sony and Toyota. What's more, nearly one third of its worldwide income is derived from legitimate business.

Descendants of a band of samurai who turned criminals in 1612, known as "the crazy ones," not until 150 years later did the group become an amalgamation of four groups—traditional gamblers, street peddlers, members of the political right and hoodlums—and assume some form that is recognizable today. The name comes from a card game in which the worst hand is eight (the Japanese word is *Ya*), nine (*Ku*) and three (*Za*), although the police in Japan insist on calling them Boryokudan— "Violent Ones"—which is not a name the Yakuza themselves like.

Organized into families—with a father overseeing his children and the children always showing respect to the father—they are also said to be the largest organized criminal group in the world, boasting around eighty thousand members. The relationship the Yakuza have with traditional Japanese society is best illustrated by a story from 1960. Prime Minister Nobusuke Kishi had invited President Eisenhower to make a farewell visit to Japan before leaving the White House. It was a gesture to assure to ratification of a mutual security pact. But because the treaty was so openly opposed by the left wing of Japanese politics, Kishi worried that demonstrators might try to disrupt Eisenhower's visit. He happened to mention that to one of his party's major backers, a Yakuza "godfather," who simply took it upon himself to organize an army of his followers to head off any demonstrations. As it turned out, the visit was canceled. But the relationship between the Yakuza and the political life of Japan remains strong.

The Yakuza have also been used by Western corporations as lobbyists. Some years ago, the group worked itself into a deal as Lockheed's silent partner in securing sales to the Japanese airline industry. At other times, they are blatant corporate extortionists, insisting on payments to stay away from a company. Every few years, for instance, the Yakuza approach publicly held corporations, threatening that, unless the company comes up with protection money, they'll disrupt the shareholders' next annual general meeting. One year, the harassment was so blatant and widespread that two thousand Japanese corporations conspired to hold their AGMs on the same day, for no other reason than to nullify the Yakuza's threats.

As early as the 1970s, with the help of Malaysian Chinese gangs, they opened stock brokerages in Malaysia and Singapore, and quickly expanded into Hong Kong, Australia, New Zealand, Indonesia and the Philippines. When a Yakuza stock market ring was shut down by the authorities in Malaysia, without charges ever being lodged against anyone, the gang showed up intact in London. Some people are convinced that they are also operating on Wall Street. They certainly play the markets, trying to manipulate prices however they can. That's known. But doing it on Wall Street, right under the nose of the Security and Exchange Commission, demonstrates a whole lot of self-assurance.

One of their favorite scams these days is buying and selling the same Tokyo real estate several times to themselves. They artificially run up prices, apply for loans against the buildings, and never pay back the loans. Actually, their loan scams show the gigantic scope of their criminal prowess. In 1991, the presidents of Japan's two largest stockbrokers— Nomura Securities and Nikko Securities—resigned in disgrace when they learned that each had lent 2 billion yen—then around 12 million dollars— to a large Yakuza group. It then emerged that another seventeen financial houses had also lent the group around 2 billion yen each. In 1994, when a bank manager in Nagoya tried to force a Yakuza group to repay its loans, it sent a loud and clear message to other bank managers by murdering him.

When bad debt provoked the financial crises that rocked Japan in the late 1990s, conservative estimates put down 30 percent of those bad debts to the Yakuza.

Policing them is particularly difficult in a country where banking secrecy is absolute. Japanese law enforcement doesn't readily share financial intelligence about them for fear of violating the draconian banking laws and being sued by the Yakuza. The group runs prostitution, drug-dealing, blackmailing and gambling operations. But it does not usually get involved with theft or robbery, which the members consider to be shameful. They murder people—even though that is strictly prohibited by their code—and deal drugs.

Unlike other groups around the world, they seem to have cornered the "ice" market in Hawaii—crystal methamphetamine is a staple of drug users in the islands—where they have distinct cultural advantages. At least fifty major properties in Hawaii are said to be owned by Japanese criminals.

Their major strategic alliance is with the Colombians for the importation of cocaine. They sanction Nigerian criminal enterprises by taxing them for the privilege of operating on Japanese soil. And they have connected with Russian organized crime groups in Eastern Siberia, where they deal together in weapons, metals and prostitution.

Faced with a recent law that makes it possible to seize monies earned in Japan by criminal organizations, and staring at the same economic downturns as the rest of Japanese industry, the group has actively sought overseas investments. So, they're moved into the U.S., Australia, the Philippines and Southeast Asia. There are Yakuza connections with the LCN in gambling on the East Coast of the United States, and interests in oil leases, nightclubs and travel agencies on the West Coast.

Perhaps the most unique thing about them is that they have a very public face. Some of them have seen too many American gangster movies and dress like Hollywood bad guys. Their uniform is dark suits, sunglasses and even crew cuts. They actively mix in nationalist Japanese politics— several twentieth-century Japanese leaders have had ties to the group—and affiliated gangs have been known to publish newsletters, and members sometimes even print their Yakuza association on business cards.

When the Kobe earthquake happened in the mid-1990s, the first group to come on the scene offering help and assistance wasn't the government, it was Yamaguchi-gumi, the largest Yakuza organization in the world, based in Kobe with twenty-six thousand members in more than 944 affiliated gangs. There are many people in Japan who look on them not as a criminal group, but rather, simply as an alternative business.

Next come the Vietnamese gangs.

First it was France's misadventure in Southeast Asia. Then it was America's catastrophic misadventure in Southeast Asia. And when Saigon finally fell, waves of Vietnamese were forced to look beyond their own land for sanctuary. There was a large exodus in 1975 which saw Vietnamese communities spring up on the West Coast of North America, from San Diego to Vancouver, and in Europe, too, notably France.

Five years later, a second, more powerful wave of Vietnamese left home, accounting for nearly 40 percent of today's total Vietnamese population in North America—the largest concentration of them settling in California, Washington and Texas. Hidden inside this second wave, as it spread through the Pacific, North America and Europe, were small groups of criminals and profiteers, who quickly began taking advantage of their own people in these emerging ethnic communities. Typically, extortion and robbery were their entry-level crimes.

With family and village alliances such an important part of their culture, and half a century of military intervention being such an important part of their history, gangs formed along family and village lines, with organized military structures. In several cases, gang leaders were ex-military leaders.

The younger Vietnamese gang members naturally migrated to the bright lights of Chinatowns. Many of them were ethnic Chinese from Vietnam. Those who weren't tended to be too young to harbor their parents' prejudice toward the Chinese. In other instances, they were from villages in the north where, even though Vietnam and China were at war, there was still a lot of trade going on. The presence of soldiers created black markets all along the border region, and the Vietnamese black marketeers traded with the Chinese black marketeers, and they both traded with soldiers on both sides, too.

What now developed out of the contacts these young gang members were making was a symbiotic relationship. The Chinese were the importers. The Vietnamese became their distributors and their muscle. That is now changing as the dynamics of the Vietnamese groups change. They're becoming more sophisticated and beginning to exert themselves on an equal level with the Chinese groups. They're moving up. They're accumulating capital. They're getting the experience. And they're making connections.

Not long ago, a Vietnamese gang spotted a real opportunity—computer chips—and alighted on California's Silicon Valley exactly like a plague of locusts. They forced their way into factories and warehouses at gunpoint and stole millions of dollars' worth of chips and motherboards, which were soon flooding discount electronics markets across the country. It took a joint task force of police from California, Oregon and Washington to break up the gang of some fifty people. Working with them were other Asian gang members, pointing up yet again the Vietnamese tendency to cooperate with anyone who can help get a job done. In this case, it was a $75-million-a-year job.

Where drug dealing is concerned, the Vietnamese come to the game with a real advantage in that they have access to the source. The size of Vietnam's opium crop has doubled in recent years. It's allowed certain gangs to become independent and control a poppy-to-powder business without a Chinese connection. Today, the FBI categorizes Vietnamese organized crime among the most serious threats to national security.

As these gangs have expanded their spheres of influence, violence has expanded accordingly. To date, the violence that typifies Vietnamese organized crime has largely been confined to the Vietnamese community. Where many other gangs would wait for people to leave their house before robbing them, the Vietnamese often do home invasions while the family is there. Understanding that many Asians don't trust banks and keep their money and jewelry at home, they believe they need to terrorize their victims in order to get to the money.

Worryingly, many law enforcement experts feel that it's only a matter of time before this sort of violence spreads outside their own community. If and when it does, it will seriously raise the stakes, because in the violent world of Asian organized crime, Vietnamese violence is notorious. So much so that other gangs also famous for violence sit up and take notice.

Even the Hells Angels motorcycle gang has made accommodations with Vietnamese gangs to head off confrontation. British Columbia is the home turf of the richest Hells Angels club in the world. An organized criminal gang known for manipulating shares on the stock market, running all sorts of lottery scams, prostitutes and drugs, they are anything but a bunch of hairy guys who steal Harleys and drink beer for free because they can intimidate the bartender. A few years ago, one of the chapter presidents in B.C. went missing and the story was quickly passed around that the last place he was seen was entering a house of a Vietnamese drug dealer. The Vietnamese denied having anything to do with his disappearance. It was later learned that he'd owed $400,000 to some California bikers and they'd simply grown tired of waiting for him to pay up.

But his disappearance spurred a meeting between a Chinese gang member and the Hells Angels. The Chinese fellow was trying to work his way into the middle of an alliance. He assured the Hells Angels that he could control the local Vietnamese groups, warning that as long as they authorized him to go ahead and make a deal, there would be peace. If not, there would be war.

When the bikers didn't seem particularly intimidated by the prospect of a gang war, he reminded them that with the Vietnamese, war is eternal. He told the bikers, there are perhaps fifty of you in this whole province, there are perhaps fifty of them in that apartment building down the block. If you start to kill them, then you must accept that, for the rest of your life, you will be at war with them.

The Hells Angels have since come to a "coexistence" accommodation with the Vietnamese.

The Dai Huen Jai are also known as the Big Circle Boys.

In the 1960s, in the China of the Cultural Revolution, the Red Guard was purged by Mao and many of its members were thrown into prisons. As it happened, the prisons were laid out in a circle around Canton City. The ones who survived starvation and torture eventually joined up again on the outside and organized themselves into small working cells. They named their criminal organization after those prisons.

Their military background formed the basis of their discipline. Their criminal instincts drove them. Their long-standing familiarity with violence accounted now for their easy use of it.

One of the characteristics of the Dai Huen Jai—and in many ways this is typical of most Chinese criminal groups—is that they are not organized along any lines that could even remotely be called traditional. There is no one person sitting at the top. There is no Commission. Today's Big Circle Boys have few or no ties with the Red Guard founders. Those men are all in their forties and fifties. Most gang members are half that. So the term *Dai Huen Jai* is used to describe ethnic gangs from southern China. Still, unlike many other Chinese criminal groups, Big Circle Boys do not have initiations and do not swear oaths.

There is a *dy-lo*, or elder brother, and there are *cy-lo*, or younger brothers. There is no set size to a cell. They will fluctuate from half a dozen to whatever is needed. If the *dy-lo* is running a gambling operation, he will need loan sharks, collectors, prostitutes, dealers and security people to guard the place. If he's importing drugs, he needs fewer people. As requirements change, *cy-lo* move on. There is no required lifelong loyalty as there is in the Mafia. Some *cy-lo* stay with the *dy-lo* for their whole career. Others move all the time, depending on who's making the most money.

Therein lies the group's motivation. Money is power. There's no mystique about who the gods have blessed and all the other legends that go along with Triad societies. The Dai Huen Jai are about making money. They market heroin and do massive credit card frauds, and everything is done with a corporate strategy. They don't think of themselves as organized criminals, they think of themselves as organized businessmen.

Accordingly, they will cooperate with any other group to make money. It doesn't matter to them whether they're Vietnamese, Laotian, Fukienese, Taiwanese, Hell's Angels or even the LCN—with whom they have invested in shipments, done importations together and cooperated with distribution projects—it's the deal that matters, not the dealers.

A special mentality, it was well summed up in a letter written by a Dai Huen Jai to his girlfriend from jail. He told her, "I got to know a lot of Dai Huen Jai guys here. They are mostly 28 to 32 years. Their golden years are over. Once in middle age, with half your life over, nothing much to do except to be a criminal. It's difficult to find a job. Why work till 50 or 60 years. They want to earn lots of money then quit. Operate business. Then safely spend the other half of life."

Key to their business, the Dai Huen Jai believe—as do the other Chinese gangs, for that matter—is *guanxi*. It means "connections." The power of the cell is the cell leader's networking. The Dai Huen Jai is like a fraternal organization, where one member can always find a clubhouse in another town. If a Dai Huen Jai cell leader in New York needs heroin, he may pick up the phone and call someone he knows in Toronto, who will call someone he knows in Vancouver, who will call someone he knows in San Francisco, who will call someone he knows in Hong Kong, and once the connection is made, the heroin will wind its way back to New York.

Cell leaders are always networking, calling in favors from other members who pass the request down the line until someone can fill it, regardless of how far down the line it has to go. Which was why, when a cell leader in

New Zealand needed some muscle, the Dai Huen Jai crew that showed up to help him came from England. It has only been since sometime in the 1980s that the group has gone international. They established themselves first in Holland, as a beachhead for the rest of Europe, and have since taken over the Dutch heroin market. From there they moved on to Britain. Their first appearance in North America was in Vancouver. Once they'd established their credentials in that city, they emigrated east across Canada and south into the States, down the West Coast all the way to Los Angeles. Because the Boys of the Circle can go wherever they like, using their reputation as their calling card—they will be accepted into another group, hidden from the police and permitted to do business there—as they've spread out, so have their businesses.

One characteristic of Asian gangs is that they don't restrict themselves to any one area of crime. They're pure opportunists. While wiretaps on, say, an LCN family might reveal that they're into heroin, wiretaps on Asian organized groups pick up talk of gambling, extortion, loan sharking, prostitution, gun running and drug dealing all at the same time. Theirs is a "whatever makes a buck" mentality. Sometimes, though, the signals received by the people listening to those wiretaps can be deceiving.

As part of a heroin investigation, police in Toronto were monitoring the telephones of a Dai Huen Jai group when the leader placed several calls to a Dai Huen Jai group in Montreal. The police didn't know about this second group and were pleased that such a lead had been opened. The two *dy-lo* agreed to a meeting, but kept referring to how they would look for the best dim sum. It was obviously a code of some sort, the police decided, and after rushing off on all sorts of tangents, they decided that *dim sum* stood for heroin. Knowing about the meeting meant they could cover it, which they did. It was in a restaurant. But *dim sum* turned out to mean dim sum. And all the *dy-lo* did was eat lunch.

The most famous of the ethnic Chinese gangs fall under the umbrella of the Triad. The name, coined by the British in Hong Kong, refers to the triangular shape of the Chinese character for "secret society." The three points represent the relationship between heaven, earth and man. Dating back to the seventeenth century, the Triad were resistance groups determined to overthrow the non-Chinese Manchu Qing Dynasty. Today, the

Triad is not a gang but rather a society of member gangs. They are the league, if you will, in which teams play.

Those member gangs are organized in hierarchical structures, although there are no membership cards, commands do not always come from the top down, nor do members send percentages of their profits up the ladder. There are, however, initiation ceremonies and oaths that are enforced through retribution and death. But those are to the Triad. Loyalty is to the secret society. Membership at the gang level is fluid and easily transferred. In fact, members of one group often become members of other groups, including non-Triad gangs such as Dai Huen Jai.

What the Triad does is provide bona fides for access to all the gangs and all the gang members, like a brotherhood where the secret handshake means you've been vetted. Members of one gang can trust members of another and ask for favors. More often than not, those favors are assistance with some criminal scheme.

"The best description I ever heard," explains Jim Fisher, Asian-crime coordinator for the Criminal Intelligence Service of Canada, "came from a fellow in Hong Kong who told me, Triad is the water that allows the fish to survive. His advice was, always focus on the fish."

There could be as many as fifty groups united under the Triad umbrella. Not all are operating. Some are subgroups of a main group and most main groups have many subgroups. The major ones are: 14K, based in Hong Kong with branches in Holland, the U.K., New York, California, Chicago, Boston, Houston, Taiwan, Vancouver, Toronto, Australia and New Zealand; the Wo group, consisting of several elaborately intertwined subgroups, who are fast becoming the most powerful gang in San Francisco; United Bamboo, who are out of Taiwan and based in California, Honolulu, Phoenix, Houston, Miami and Chicago; and San Yee On, the largest single group in the Triad, with branches throughout North America, Asia and Australia, whose membership has been estimated as high as sixty thousand.

While gangs within the Triad compete at the local level, they cooperate with one another internationally. But no matter where they are, they always do so within the context of their own culture. It severely handicaps law enforcement not raised in that culture. Assessments of the threat are all too often based on an inaccurate understanding of the people involved. Their culture is reflected, for instance, in their approach to violence. And all too often, talk of their business skills and prowess hides the fact that they are eminently violent.

Unlike certain groups who will not hesitate to kill a law enforcement officer—the Russians are a good example—Asian gangs in general and Chinese gangs in particular understand that killing a cop is a very dumb thing to do. Instead, they're extremely patient—the culture lends itself to that—and therefore more insidious. They go after the one area where the officer will have real trouble defending himself: his reputation. They make allegations about his honesty that tie him up for years in investigations. However, when it comes to dealing with their own, they are extremely brutal. Instead of putting a single shot to a rival's head, they will punish him by killing his oldest son. And therein lies a defining difference between what the public thinks of as organized crime—Russian and Italian—and Asian groups.

Case in point: a North American gang member named How was trafficking heroin for a man in China. A fifty-kilo shipment was late in arriving. How complained to his boss that he was being severely pressured by his own investors. The boss didn't seem to respond. How told the man that he was losing face with his own investors and that they would evoke revenge. And still the man did not respond. How threatened that if the heroin didn't get to him soon, something might happen to the man's family.

The drugs never arrived.

How invited the boss's mistress out to lunch. She arrived with her two children—both fathered by the man in China—including their five-month-old son. He told the woman that he'd been drinking and asked her to drive. He suggested a restaurant, let her four-year-old daughter sit in the front seat, and climbed into the backseat, where her son was strapped into a car seat, facing backward.

On the way, How kept repeating what a lovely baby she had. And as he did, he took revenge on the man in China by wrapping the strings of the baby's bonnet around his throat and strangling the child.

Alien smuggling is an increasingly attractive alternative to drug trafficking. It offers multibillion-dollar profits without the same severe penalties for getting caught. By the end of the 1990s, it was believed that the international traffic in human beings was a $7 billion industry. It is expected to double by 2005, and perhaps even double again by 2010. The International

Organization for Migration reports that four million people are trafficked around the world each year. The Immigration and Naturalization Service estimates that 90 percent of all illegal aliens are being transported by professional smugglers and transnational criminal organizations.

There is a regular influx of illegal immigrants from China into European Union states, especially those with an indigenous Chinese population, such as Britain. The United States is, however, the first choice of most Asian illegal immigrants, with Canada second. Traffic worldwide has become so huge that the INS believes there are, literally, as many as a million illegal aliens warehoused around the world at any given time, waiting to make the next stage of their journey. There are possibly as many as three hundred thousand just in Moscow, staged there by Chinese organized crime groups with the full compliance of Russian organized crime groups. The Chinese gangs pay "rent" to the Russians for the right to use the staging post. At the same time, Russian gangs cater to the huge market demand in fake passports and visas and other counterfeit travel documents stemming from Afghanistan, Turkey, Iran, Iraq and China. Russian and old Soviet passports sell for around $500, and with visas stamped in them to Sweden, Denmark or Belgium, upwards of $800. American and Canadian visas are said to cost in the $5,000-to-$7,000 range. A visa to Britain can be had for $3,000 to $5,000. It is believed that several hundred thousand people leave Russia every year for the West with counterfeit passports and visas and other forged travel documents.

Up to twenty thousand illegal immigrants are estimated to be warehoused in Prague, thirty thousand in Austria, and possibly as many as one hundred thousand in France. It is known that several Asian organized crime gangs coordinate their operations by stationing members in California, Guatemala, Belize and Surinam.

That's the latest smuggling hot spot. The tiny country on the northeastern corner of South America was originally a Dutch colony. Today, fifty thousand ethnic Chinese live in Surinam, making up 10 percent of the population and offering an easy staging point for illegal immigrants. It is the second poorest country in the Western hemisphere—first prize goes to Haiti—which made it ripe for organized crime gangs to buy their way in, creating a logistics hub for the traffickers. Cocaine passes through from Colombia to Holland, illegal immigrants pass through from China to North America.

The travel routes are usually anything but straightforward. From Fujian Province, there is one well-worn route to Bangkok, then to the subcontinent—either New Delhi or Karachi—and from there to Nairobi, Lagos or Johannesburg. Now the route splits. One heads for Britain via North Africa and Spain. Another crosses the Atlantic to Buenos Aires or Rio de Janeiro, then comes north either to Mexico for the border crossing into Texas, Arizona and California, or to one of the islands, such as Cuba, which is then an easy hop to Florida or Puerto Rico, and from there to New York. Other routes pass through Russia. From there, one goes through Poland to Germany. Another goes through the Baltic states to Scandinavia. The destination with these might be Britain, or it might be the Caribbean for the onward journey into the U.S.

A Chinese gang is based in Sao Paolo, to facilitate the movement of illegal aliens who come across on the southern route. Those who have been staged in West Africa have been aided by Nigerian criminal enterprises, also based in Sao Paolo. There are reportedly fifty United Bamboo members based in Guatemala City who provide a similar service for illegal aliens moved through there and then into Mexico. There are instances of Vietnamese gangs working alongside the Chinese groups, ferrying illegal aliens in fishing vessels across the Pacific, where they are dangerously off-loaded at sea onto smaller boats for the trip to Mexico and north into the States. There have also been occasions when travel has been comfortable and routes direct.

In one recent case, eighty illegal aliens from China—each paying $45,000 for their passage—posed as rich businessmen on a junket to Canada. The criminal gang leader had duped a businessman in Toronto into setting up a tour for these "investors." Paid $2,500 per visitor, the Canadian businessman arranged flights, visas and a weeklong program to show the Chinese what Canada and Toronto had to offer. But shortly after the group arrived, its members disappeared. Only two were found by the RCMP and returned to China. The others made their way into the United States through Akwesasne, with the help of certain St. Regis Mohawk and the Toronto-based members of the Chinese gang.

But for most people trying to escape from their own world, the trip from Fujian to North America can take up to two years, during which time they are subjected to appalling treatment, squalid living conditions, unsafe travel conditions—often herded like cattle onto unseaworthy ships—and in the case of women, constant and serious sexual abuse.

The severity of their traveling conditions was brought to light in the early morning hours of June 6, 1993, when a decrepit old 150-foot rusted-hull freighter called the *Golden Venture* ran aground off the Rockaways, near Fort Tilden, on Long Island. There were 286 illegal Chinese immigrants onboard. Many of them jumped twenty-five feet into the water and tried to swim ashore. Ten died.

Their voyage had begun in Fujian nearly a year before, after each agreed to pay $30,000 to the traffickers. They were taken on a ten-day journey to Bangkok, mostly on foot, where they were forced to wait three months for a freighter called *Nadj II*. They were crammed on that ship for a month until it broke down off Kenya. It was six months before the *Golden Venture* arrived. When it did, they were stuffed into the hull, held there without adequate food, sanitary conditions or even ventilation for the Atlantic crossing, which saw most of them seriously ill most of them time.

The trafficker's original plan was to rendezvous off the New England coast with a smaller vessel operated by Vietnamese organized criminals who'd subcontracted with the Chinese gang to off-load the illegal immigrants at sea, warehouse them in the Boston area, then drive them to what would be virtual servitude in New York. They'd all agreed to work off the monies they still owed, which in every case was a considerable sum. The fate awaiting them was slave labor in a sweatshop or forced prostitution.

That the *Golden Venture* never made the rendezvous with the Vietnamese gang might have been the most fortunate thing that ever happened to the 276 people who lived through the trip. The crew, under orders of one of the traffickers, who'd taken control of the vessel from the captain during a high-seas mutiny, sailed directly for New York instead.

Of the survivors, almost all were subsequently deported. Only forty-two were granted asylum, although additional cases are pending. The crew and the traffickers were arrested and sent to jail. Ironically, almost five years to the day after the *Golden Venture* ran aground, another boatload of Chinese illegal aliens—each of whom had paid $40,000 for the trip—ran aground on the other side of New York harbor, along the New Jersey coast. One illegal alien caught in that incident had already been arrested and deported as a result of the *Golden Venture* disaster.

Generally speaking, gangs in China use two methods to ship people to North America. They come by air to Vancouver—that costs around $45,000—and, interestingly enough, those flights are often arranged through travel agencies in China actually owned by Triad society gangs. Or they come by sea, a treacherous voyage across the Pacific of forty days to four months, which costs about $35,000. In neither case are any guarantees given, and many of these illegal aliens are soon caught and returned to China.

Sea journeys are especially difficult. Smuggling ships, most of them decrepit freighters or fishing vessels flying Taiwanese or Vietnamese flags, have been bringing four to six hundred illegal aliens from China to the West Coast of North America every month throughout the 1990s. While many of them embark from Fujian, smugglers are now opening new "gateways," recruiting from the next province up the coast, Zhejiang. Food and water are scarce. Sanitary conditions are primitive. The passengers are frequently never allowed to leave the ship's hold.

It was the same philosophical level of unthinkable defilement that the British police encountered in June 1998 while investigating what, at first, looked to them like illegal alien smuggling. They called their investigation Operation Kronos. A Triad gang was bringing Chinese nationals from Fujian into Britain. The routing took them across various staging points in Thailand and Burma, into the Czech Republic, then to Holland and into the U.K. At each staging point, the gang phoned back to China demanding of the aliens' families that another payment be made. But once the gang smuggled the people into Britain, the case took a brutal turn. The illegal aliens were now held for ransom.

Six hostages in one house were told that if their families didn't pay, they would be killed. And the method the gang intended to use was horrible. The six would draw lots, and the one with the short straw would be allowed to live as long as he murdered the other five. The gang explained that by letting the sixth man live, he could never testify against them because by doing so he would have to confess to five murders. If the chosen hostage refused to kill the others, his hand would be cut off. And just to make certain the gang could do that effectively, they tied tourniquets around their victims' arms for a couple of days so that when a hand was cut off, the person wouldn't bleed to death. Tourniquets were still in place when the police arrived to save the hostages.

That the gang in Operation Kronos chose to transit through the Czech Republic is hardly a surprise, because Prague is the European base for several organized Asian groups. It is also proof positive that, despite history, the groups can come together.

If the past were the only criteria, it would be fair to say that no two Asian gangs would ever work together, that joint ventures and strategic alliances naturally go against the grain. For centuries, there's been no love lost between the Chinese and the Japanese, or between the Chinese and the Vietnamese. But then, anyone who thinks history matters to criminals has never been to Prague.

Vietnamese immigrants first arrived in 1975 when Czechoslovakia agreed to take one hundred thousand "volunteer laborers" as part payment for Czech assistance during the war with the United States. The first group was solid, hardworking youths. But by the time Hanoi got to the second and third installments, they'd run out of solid, hardworking youths and used the program to get rid of juvenile delinquents. By this point, too, the Czechs had grown weary of this workforce and started withholding monies due them. The promise was that the Vietnamese would get the rest of their pay once they returned home.

Needing to supplement their incomes, the Vietnamese youth responded by orchestrating smuggling networks that brought Asian goods into Eastern Europe. By 1990, with the Iron Curtain down, many of those young men had firmly implanted themselves. When they should have gone home, they married locals or otherwise stayed on as illegal aliens. Smuggling networks matured, they had free access to the West, and the gangs running those networks matured too. They branched out to form international alliances with other Vietnamese gangs—such as the Flying Dragons, which is made up of ethnic Chinese born in Vietnam and aligned to a similar gang in New York—or with established Chinese Triad gangs in Germany.

From smuggling Asian goods they graduated to smuggling cigarettes, and from there to smuggling drugs. Today, Vietnamese gangs in the Czech Republic control the marijuana and hashish markets, supplied by Arab and Balkan state distributors, and are the main client of Kosovar traffickers. They also deal in small amounts of heroin, supplied by two Triad groups—Red Sun and 14K—who likewise see Prague as a revolving door into Western Europe. Triad money is being laundered in Prague through local real estate deals and restaurants.

It is a certainty that any alien smuggling ring staging in the Czech Republic does so with the knowledge of the Triads already there, and might even have used the Vietnamese for protection.

There is a similar situation with Asian presence in Italy. Alien smuggling rings are based in Rome, Turin and Florence. The gangs also traffic drugs, run extortion rackets and oversee some prostitution. Needless to say, respect is always paid to their traditional Italian criminal hosts.

In Spain, the Triad gangs supplant tradition with creativity. The host government has always been concerned about allowing the resident Chinese population to expand. Staging illegal aliens there would thus be too noticeable. So the gangs keep the local Asian population level, topping it up with enough illegal aliens on their way to somewhere else by reusing the identification papers of local residents who pass away.

"To understand Asian crime," explains Jim Fisher, "it is essential to understand the culture. That's the basis of how they operate. That's the basis of how they choose a restaurant. That's the basis of how they make a connection for kidnapping. It's ingrained in everything they do, and if you can understand their cultural connections, you're halfway there."

Unfortunately, he adds, at least for law enforcement, the other half is getting somebody to talk about it in court, finding a victim who isn't too terrified to testify. And that turns out to be as difficult as understanding the culture.

There'd been a street war in Vancouver between Gum Wa, known as the Golden Boys, and the Lotus Family, two fairly historical groups from the late 1960s or early 1970s. Their combat peaked when a boy was beaten to death with a steel bar on the main street of Chinatown at four o'clock in the afternoon. At that hour of the day, and on that one block, there were probably eight hundred to one thousand people, most of whom saw what happened. But when the police asked for cooperation, nobody would say anything. Nobody would come forward. Within seven months, the two group leaders were working together robbing jewelry stores under the control of a Dai Huen Jai group. In fact, the two were arrested together in the same house. The police later learned that someone from the Dai Huen Jai group said to them, There is enough money to be made here, we don't need to fight, when you fight, the police gain more information which makes it difficult for all of us. So they simply stopped fighting and started making money together.

15

MILLENNIUM BUGS

Transnational organized crime will proliferate in the next century because crime groups are among the major beneficiaries of globalization.

—Professor Louise Shelley

It has taken mankind until the earliest hours of the twenty-first century, until the dawn of the third millenium, to arrive at a point where, finally, it is possible to stuff 1 million dollars into an attaché case.

We have the European Union in Brussels to thank for this.

For the first two thousand years since Christ, the only time anyone has been able to manage such a feat was in spy movies when some James Bond or other held up an attaché case and bragged that he had the readies right there. The problem has always been that a million in cash represents far too much bulk for one attaché case. Five would be more suitable. No longer. The bureaucrats in Brussels have come up with the brilliant idea of issuing 500-Euro notes. Roughly the equivalent of $485, it reduces the bulk of a million substantially enough to fit inside an attaché case. Which is precisely what any reasonable cash-rich transnational criminal would welcome. Especially drug traffickers, who will have considerably less trouble transporting their money around the world.

At the same time, this turns out to be a two-birds-with-one-stone situation, because the Euro resolves a second niggling problem for transnational criminals.It automatically separates their money from the origin of the crime, an essential by-product of the money-laundering process.

Take as an example heroin sold in France. Before the appearance of the Euro, traffickers were paid in francs. No matter where they went in the world with their cash—whether they prewashed it in Switzerland, or carted it off to St. Maarten and dumped it in a bank there—the francs were a dead giveaway, pointing straight back to France. So the first thing the traffickers had to worry about was getting rid of their francs. Say they prewashed into German marks, then moved into dollars. Once they'd accomplished that, they could begin to feed their cash into the banking system. Now, as blips on computer screens, the money moved around the world without anyone able to associate the money with drugs sold in France. What the Eurocrats have done is saved the traffickers that step. Drugs sold in Spain will be paid for in Euros and drugs sold in Denmark will be paid for in Euros, and when the day comes that Britain surrenders the pound, drugs sold in Britain will be paid for in Euros. Traffickers will no longer have to worry that an attaché case or two of 500-Euro notes will lead the cops to the crime scene.

On top of that, because it is obvious by volume alone that Euros will eventually earn a place in the world's markets that could someday even challenge the dollar for global supremacy, there will be little need for traffickers to move from Euros into the traditional currency of choice, U.S. dollars. They will be able to stay in Euros, which shortcuts the laundering process again. Better still, now that Europe's borders are gone, Euros earned through crime can be transported anywhere inside the EU without anyone ever asking to look inside that attaché case.

It will take no more than one crooked banker somewhere inside the European Union—or one small bank owned by a criminal—to null-and-void every single money-laundering regulation in every single member state.

If a transnational organized crime group were to be given a magic wand and granted just one wish, it would be a borderless Europe with a single currency that issued 500-Euro notes.

The new century will, thanks entirely to globalization, see smaller gangs join the major league of the big transnational organized groups who, themselves, will form and reform alliances to create a super-league.

Prime candidates for promotion are the Hells Angels. The most famous motorcycle club in the world was born in San Bernardino, California, in

1948 when a bunch of World War II veterans decided they wanted to ride big bikes together. In those days they were just a bunch of big, hairy guys with tattoos. Nine years later, a Hells Angel named Sonny Barger opened the Oakland branch of the club and quickly turned it into the "mother chapter," and out of that came a criminal organization.

He nurtured their rebel image with sound PR techniques, trade-marked their logo and their name, incorporated much of their business interests, kicked out dissenting members, brought in drug dealing as a means of paying their legal bills—and eventually of becoming very, very rich—orchestrated takeovers of smaller groups and nudged the Hells Angels onto the international stage by opening chapters abroad.

It wasn't until nearly thirty years after Barger first came onto the scene that the Feds were able to prosecute the Hells Angels big-time. They'd gone up against the gang throughout the 1960s and 1970s, prosecuting members for firearms offenses, bringing them up on murder charges—a murder case against Barger was eventually dismissed—and even going after clubs as businesses under the Racketeer Influenced Criminal Organizations (RICO) Act. But in the late 1980s they took aim at the Oakland chapter and came out with dozens of convictions. Next, they targeted several chapters on the East Coast which they were able to shut down. They also started forfeiture proceedings against various chapters, seizing property— including real estate—by claiming it had been used for drug dealing.

Of course, Hells Angels are not the only biker-criminals. Counted among their nearest rivals are the Outlaws, in Florida, the Midwest, Canada, and Australia; the Bandidos, in Texas, Washington State, the Deep South, Australia and Marseilles, France; and the Pagans, who operate along the U.S. East Coast. But Hells Angels have the best PR machine—their "toys for tots" program has been skillfully designed to make them look as if they care about society—and are, without any doubt, the most violent. They are also the richest, and the only outlaw motorcycle gang with the firepower to rival the LCN or the Russians.

The structure of this transnational criminal organization is a model of Harvard Business School efficiency. Decentralized, each club is given auton-omy to operate within the overall corporate philosophy. The United States is divided into sectors, with regional officers coordinating activities and settling disputes, while the international chapters—found throughout Europe; in Canada, Australia and New Zealand; and in some South American coun-

tries—operate as separate entities. Although there is no international governing body, all the clubs are linked with a communications network that is
technically superior to anything found in all but the richest police forces.
Each chapter also has a designated intelligence officer whose job is to gather
information about rival gang members and also police officers who might
pose a threat to the gang. Membership is strictly controlled, initiation sometimes entails killing a rival gang member, and dues are paid. All chapters are
violent, but some are more violent than others, and a French Canadian chapter in Quebec is legendary as being the most violent of all. One of its most
celebrated members, Yves "Apache" Trudeau, admitted to killing forty-three
people between 1970 and 1985. It was in 1985 that one chapter in Quebec
decided to wipe out another by killing everyone in the gang. Three bikers
were eventually convicted of six murders.

Because drug money is divided up among the members and not kept
by the club, many Hells Angels today only bother with ponytails and
leather gear for ceremonial purposes. They drive Mercedeses, live in big
houses, sail yachts and wear expensive suits with white shirts and ties.

It was methamphetamine that made them rich. A white powder version of speed, the original connection was through Mexico. They gangs did
a distribution deal with the cartels there, which gave them exclusive rights
to North America. But that deal soon lapsed. The Mexicans got greedy,
decided they didn't really need the Hells Angels because they could distribute meth themselves or, as a last resort, cut a more favorable deal with
the drug-anxious Vietnamese gangs, and keep a bigger percentage. Around
the same time, the Hells Angels started figuring they didn't need the
Mexicans and the worries about smuggling drugs across the southern border with Mexico, because they could cook the drugs themselves and get a
lot less hassle moving them back and forth across the completely porous
northern border with Canada. One infamous Hells Angels meth trafficker,
Kenneth Jay Owen, was arrested in 1987 with $1 million in cash hidden
around his house. He was moving $230 million worth of meth, and after
being sentenced to forty-one years, was fined $2.1 million and had an
additional $2.4 million in property seized.

The gang has since expanded to hydroponic marijuana, a market they
thoroughly own, growing in Canada and distributing throughout North
America. The RCMP reports that there are huge tracts of land in Alberta,
Saskatchewan and Manitoba where they have constructed elephantine

underground hothouses. It has been such a success that almost all the international clubs are studying the possibilities of exporting those hydroponic methods.

Hells Angels all over the world operate exactly along the same lines as their American brothers. But independent of any other groups, British chapters forged their own alliances with the Colombian cartels, held bank accounts in Switzerland and had investments in property throughout Europe.

The brains behind their Colombian connection is said to have been William "English Bill" Anderson, a man with eight convictions for possessing weapons, and who escaped from Sudbury prison while serving a five-year sentence for stabbing someone. To emphasize, again, that these are not just scruffy guys in leather jackets, two of Anderson's associates were Canadian Hells Angels whom British police arrested in their suite at the London Hilton on Park Lane. The gang bought a fleet of merchant ships to smuggle cocaine into the U.K. On one that was eventually seized, Customs officers found three tons of drugs. The off-loading method the gang used was to sink drugs nine thousand feet to the ocean floor and patiently wait until law enforcement was nowhere to be seen before retrieving them with a mini-submarine.

Another group of Hells Angels bought a tanker to run drugs around the world, using watertight containers fixed with electronically activated buoys which they sank. When a local gang wanted to retrieve the drugs, the buoys would be activated and the containers would rise to the surface.

The new century will also be one of old crimes brought up to date.

Start with counterfeiting. Not of negotiable instruments, such as money—there will always be that—but counterfeit software, luxury designer goods, pharmaceuticals and airplane parts. The world market for phony goods is huge, the chances of getting caught are minimal and even if counterfeiters do get caught, convictions and sentences are considerably less than for drug trafficking. What's more, much of the business requires little more than printing cardboard boxes.

Filling a plastic vial with some concocted chemical and putting it inside a box that has all the right markings and all the right colors and all the right minuscule disclaimers along the edge, then shipping it in volume to South America as Viagra—or, even more reprehensibly, as counterfeit baby formula—is worth tens of millions of dollars to Italian and Russian organized crime groups. Printing other perfect-copy cardboard boxes and stuffing them with reconstructed automobile brake pads or oil filters is a $12-billion-a-year business.

Even worse is parts taken off airplanes declared surplus by the Russian Air Force and sold in counterfeit boxes throughout the world to distributors of genuine airplane parts. The potential hazard to the public is staggering. This counterfeit airplane part industry is still in its infancy and, for obvious reasons—not least of which is national panic—government bodies like the Federal Aviation Agency play down the problem. They remind anyone inquiring about this subject that there are all sorts of controls in place among the world's major airlines to limit the horrendous possibility of a wing falling off in midair. But not every airline is a major one. It would only take one company cutting costs on something like a combustion liner—which is a critical component of a jet engine—to create a monumental disaster.

Counterfeit luxury designer goods used to be the exclusive domain of the Mafia. They had factories all over Italy producing knockoffs of every conceivable item labeled Gucci, St. Laurent, Hermes, Vuitton, Chanel, Armani, Dior, Rolex, Piaget, Breitling, Cartier et al. From perfume to clothes to handbags, watches and jewelry, they were into everything.

Successive crackdowns, first by the Italian police because this stuff caused a nuisance, then at the insistence of the French government because millions were being lost by French companies, prompted the Italian counterfeiters to find a better way. They started selling the goods and the labels separately. Street markets all over Europe had what appeared to be knockoff Chanel handbags, Ray-Ban sunglasses or Hermès ties, but because it didn't say Chanel or Ray-Ban or Hermès anywhere on it, the police couldn't do much about it. After the sale, someone would slip the buyer a counterfeit label that said Chanel or Ray-Ban or Hermès.

That worked for quite a while, until the Asian gangs got involved. Organized Chinese gangs manufactured the goods and organized Vietnamese gangs worked the street markets, and together, they pretty much took over the market. They expanded it as well. They didn't just concentrate on high-end European designer goods, they went into Nike, Reebok, Adidas, Lacoste, Hilfiger, Tiffany, Levi's, Swatch and others.

Watches have always been a popular item with these gangs, even more so than they were with the Mafia, because they can be made so competitively in the Orient. A cheap quartz imitation of a designer watch can be manufactured for $3–4 in Hong Kong. The logo, made separately, costs under a dollar. Shipping adds another dollar, tops, bringing the maximum investment to $5. The watch then carries a $75–100 price tag on a street corner and goes for a knock-down, well-haggled price of around $35.

It is such a big-profit, little-risk business that the former head of the Vietnamese street gang Born to Kill testified that he personally was earning $13 million a year just on Rolex and Cartier counterfeits.

With that kind of money in the pot, these gangs approached the business like a business, manufacturing throughout the Pacific basin where so many of these ripped-off designers also manufacture and using smuggling routes established for drugs to move the goods. They then realized that as long as they were counterfeiting the goods, they might as well counterfeit bills of lading, so they set up shell companies that looked like wholesalers—especially gray-market and surplus wholesalers, because they would have access to product outside normal designer marketers—and started bringing goods into the country, even paying duties on them. That has the added benefit of being a way to launder drug money.

Various watchdogs around the world tend to agree that counterfeit goods cost legitimate businesses around $200 billion in revenue each year. If the gangs are working on an average price ratio of say, 30 cents on the dollar, that makes their counterfeiting industry worth at least $60 billion, and probably more. After all, these gangs don't pay tax on that either.

Add into this counterfeit videos and CDs—usually called piracy instead of counterfeiting—and the size of the market becomes clearer. A raid some years ago at a video store in the Detroit area resulted in the seizure of twenty thousand counterfeit cassettes. Expand that across North America and into Europe and the numbers become gigantic.

Music and video counterfeiting goes on all over Eastern Europe—it's a money spinner for organized gangs there, especially Russian—and throughout the Middle East, notably Kuwait and Israel. But it is in the software industry that the numbers are mind-bogglingly big. Not everybody wants or is even willing to pay $35 for a phony Rolex. Not everybody wants a $2 copy of *Casablanca* that risks running out of tape before Sam can tell Ilsa how they'll always have Paris. But as software prices climb and official technical help lines keep you waiting for half an hour, or charge you for advice that used to be free, the idea of paying $30 for a $250 program has its obvious attractions. They even counterfeit the manual.

The industry complains that it loses around $12–13 billion a year through counterfeiting, which is nearly as much as Microsoft's 1998 sales figure. U.S. Customs has gotten good at spotting these fakes—with the help of Microsoft, who makes teams available to police agencies around the world—but the border controls in Asia aren't as good, and counterfeit software there is used in staggering numbers. In Malaysia, for example, 99 percent of all the software in the country is counterfeit. Only one out of every hundred CD-ROMs in the entire country is real. In Russia the figure is 97 percent counterfeit. In China it's 95 percent. In Thailand, where many of the counterfeit CD-ROMs are copied, the figure is 93 percent. In Singapore, 73 percent. In Hong Kong, 72 percent. Managing this end of the industry is only slightly more complicated than printing cardboard boxes. Here, the gangs need to copy CD-ROMs. But once they've managed that—often using the same industry-standard copiers that the major software houses use for their legitimate product—all that's left are the holograms. And they can be done by the same gangs who do them for counterfeit credit cards.

Seizures throughout the U.S. are measured in truckfuls. One shipment stopped by Customs in San Francisco contained twenty-nine thousand counterfeit Microsoft holograms. That was less than a month after they raided a factory in California and seized another batch of forty-seven thousand. In yet another recent raid, seizures included 387,000 counterfeit CDs, forty-eight huge rolls of shrink wrap and more than $1 million worth of CD-replicating machinery. Paperwork was also found that showed that the head of this particular Asian organized crime gang was waiting on an order of an additional $1 million worth of machinery.

Compounding the problem, the nature of transnational organized crime being what it is, there is a frequent overlap of businesses. Increasingly, illegal aliens smuggled into the United States by Chinese gangs are being forced to pay off their debt by working in sweatshops for associated gangs producing pirated software and music CDs. Weapons smuggling is another offshoot. A raid on one gang member in California running a counterfeit-software business manned by illegal aliens produced $2 million worth of phony Microsoft products, a large cache of loaded weapons, two pounds of dynamite and five pounds of C-4 plastic explosives.

But then the inclusion of weapons is hardly surprising when you understand that the global crime cycle that incorporates software piracy often begins with drugs. Asian gangs import heroin into the U.S., wholesale it to Asian and non-Asian street gangs, and use that money to finance the hardware, software and packaging tools needed for their counterfeit businesses. Pirated CD-ROMs and manuals are sold through established distribution networks—which can include unsuspecting swap meets—or internationally on the Net. Profits are then washed through real estate. California is generally considered to be ground zero for these Asian gangs, although their real estate holdings suggest they do not limit themselves to the West Coast.

In early 1999, the FBI made what is said to be their largest-ever counterfeit-software bust. They raided a site in California and confiscated stacks of CD-ROMs with Microsoft logos—destined for the Microsoft Office 97 and Windows 98 markets—as well as a $1.5-million commercial CD duplicator. The cache in this record bust was valued at $30 million. Given the nature of the counterfeit software business—the amounts of money involved and the ease of manufacturing and distribution—the betting line is that the record may not stand for long.

There will always be smuggling, but in the new century there are some high-profit products that will challenge drugs as the contraband of choice.

By international agreement, the 1987 "Montreal Protocol on Substances That Deplete the Ozone Layer" set a timetable for phasing out and ultimately banning the use of chloroflourocarbons (CFCs). They're chemicals that were commonly used as refrigerants in home fridges, commercial refrigeration units and car air conditioners. They're usually called Freon. With other, less harmful substances readily available, 130 nations agreed that getting rid of CFCs was the right thing to do. Except not everybody who agreed to do it did it. Today the hole in the ozone layer is much larger than it was then—it's now bigger than all of Europe—and Freon is up there on the list of highly profitable illicit materials, alongside drugs. In some cases, there is reason to believe that it is trafficked by people with interests in both.

The main culprit is Russia. Although the Soviet Union originally signed, Russia has since opted out of the Montreal Protocol on the grounds of being "a developing country." Russia is a major producer of CFC, and production at seven formerly state-owned factories is now at levels far exceeding demand. Russian organized crime groups control CFC exports through some of those factories.

A European chemical publication estimated that they have been flooding Europe with one thousand tons of CFCs every month. A standard forty-foot container holds around one thousand thirty-pound cylinders of Freon, which is fifteen tons. At around half a million dollars per container—and sixty-five to seventy per month—the Maffiya's European turnover is around $35 million.

Their North American market is half again as important, with an estimated eighteen thousand tons being shipped annually. That's the biggest market for Freon, where an estimated eighty million pre-1994 cars are on the road, and expected to still be on the road in some numbers until 2006. Anyone with an air conditioner in a car built before 1994 needs Freon. It is these air conditioners that feed the smugglers.

The chemical also has industrial and commercial uses—for example, cooling supermarket display cases and also, interestingly enough, cleaning computer chips. A single sixteen-ounce can of CFCs, the kind that used to be sold at auto-supply shops for people to pour into their car air-conditioning systems, can destroy seventy thousand pounds of the ozone layer. It is also said that smugglers, over a three-year period in the middle of the 1990s, brought sixty million pounds of CFCs into the U.S.

In many cases, traffickers take advantage of a loophole in the law which permits some movement of recycled CFCs. They simply label their shipments "recycled materials." It works, because telling the difference between that and the nonrecycled variety is very difficult. And anyway, once it slips past Customs and is mixed with the available supply, it's impossible to prove it is nonrecycled Freon.

Even if it gets stopped by Customs, it's not much easier. The fastest way for inspectors to find out is to check the pressure in the containers. Freon's pressure is less than legal refrigerants. Knowing that, traffickers add inert nitrogen to Freon to raise it to admissible levels. Customs has had to resort to special devices that can identify gasses through wavelengths of infrared light, a lengthy procedure, meaning that only spot checks are possible, one estimate is that 15 to 20 percent of all the CFCs currently in use around the world are contraband.

Knowing that U.S. Customs was on the lookout for CFCs coming in from China, Russia and India, some smugglers started transshipping through Mexico and Canada. Others found supplies in Britain and Australia and moved those into the United States. And just like drugs, when Customs cracked down on CFCs coming into the Port of Miami, the traffickers shifted to the southern border and brought them across from Mexico.

Tijuana, a town where you can buy just about anything—shops and storefronts sell sex, drugs, counterfeit software, pirated CDs, pirated videos and kiddy porn—there are now signs hanging out in front of stores saying, "We Have Freon." A $200 canister there is worth four times as much to a wholesaler in California and ten times as much when parceled out to the retail market.

At times, it looks as if all eighty million of those pre-1994 cars in the U.S. are trying at the same time to get through the border crossing at Tijuana. The world's busiest border crossing—probably the noisiest too—averages thirty-seven thousand cars a day. Customs inspectors do what they can, but it isn't much, because Tijuana is a major drug entry point. Looking for drugs takes up most of their resources. They still get an average of one Freon smuggler per day. And those aren't traffickers bringing a single cylinder across, they are people smuggling two hundred thirty-pound cylinders per trip.

At commercial points of entry, the seizures are bigger. And there, the Russians are not the only traffickers in the business. A woman in Fort Lauderdale, Florida, got caught smuggling three thousand tons of Indian-manufactured CFCs into the U.S. with a street value of $52 million. She wound up with fifty-seven months in prison. Another shipment of eighty-four hundred tons was seized en route from India to Mexico when smugglers attempted to divert it to the U.K. In Philadelphia, one firm was charged with conspiring to smuggle more than fifty-two thousand cylinders of CFCs into the country, which would have made them a $10 million profit. Another smuggler was arrested for shipping forty-six tons from Britain and Australia into the U.S. A company in Maine got caught importing 246 tons from Canada. The U.S. Justice Department even extradited a Freon offender from Costa Rica on charges of conspiring to import three hundred tons of Freon. Following the methods of drug traffickers, he was accused of using shell companies to cover the smuggling, then laundering the profits into offshore accounts. He eventually pleaded guilty.

In Europe, a small German company had imported eighty containers—

with twelve tons of CFCs in each—from China, bringing it into Rotterdam with false paperwork. Once inside the European Union, the accompanying documents were changed to read "recycled CFCs."

In Hong Kong, dozens of companies have been charged with illegally importing CFCs from China—where production is still taking place—for use there and for markets in Australia and the West Coast of North America. CFCs bought in China, for instance, sell for $1 a pound. They can be resold in North America for $15–25 a pound.

For several years after signing on to the Montreal Protocol, one of the worst offenders was Britain. Even though they were clearly illegal, CFCs were still being imported into the U.K as late as 1995. That year, nearly four thousand tons came into the U.K. According to the United Nations, in the eight years that followed the Montreal Protocol, after everyone had agreed to phase out CFCs, production increased nearly 90 percent. Exports increased seventeenfold. India flooded the Middle East with CFCs. The Chinese flooded Asia with CFCs. Despite the supply curve heading sharply upward, the price curve did too. Prices in some countries trebled. In the U.S. and Canada, they increased as much as tenfold. It was after Britain finally complied with the 1987 agreement, nearly ten years later, that the Russians moved in big-time to fill the gap.

In Brownsville, Texas, Ernesto and Antonio Medina ran an export business called Medina Forwarding Corp. They'd contracted to ship twelve hundred thirty-pound cylinders of CFCs from Russia through their warehouse to Mexico. A perfectly legal transaction, as Mexico also enjoys Third World exemptions from the Montreal Protocol. The goods arrived on schedule at the Port of Houston and were trucked in bond down to Brownsville. Six weeks later, the cylinders were driven out of the warehouse en route to Mexico. U.S. Customs inspectors at the Brownsville-Motomoros Bridge did a routine check of the tractor-trailer and the accompanying paperwork. The listed value of the shipment, $10,000, didn't seem right. So now they did a more thorough search of the tractor-trailer. They found an $8,000 invoice from an Ohio company for empty cylinders. That turned their attention to the cylinders being exported. And they were still empty. The Medinas were arrested, and eventually pleaded guilty. But not before their connection was traced. The CFCs had been dispatched from Brownsville to two men in New York who moved them into the retail market. Those two were connected back in Russia.

Production in the Third World won't be stopped—at least officially—until 2010. As that deadline draws closer, supplies will be dwindling. A pack-rat stockpiling mentality will, by then, have driven demand and prices—and profits for transnational organized crime groups—right through the very ozone layer the Montreal Protocol was designed to protect.

Another high-ticket item for smugglers will always be people. As U.S. and Canadian authorities have cracked down, illegal-alien traffickers have diverted south, to Mexico, where organized criminals act as brokers—the remnants of the Amado Carrillo Fuentes drug cartel is said to be one of the main gangs involved—receiving the aliens and moving them north into the U.S. An astonishing 1.75 million people are apprehended every year just along the U.S.-Mexican border. No one knows exactly how many get through.

Other active human-smuggling networks are found in countries with certain ethnic populations—Korean, Thai, Indian, Pakistani and Bangladeshi—and, increasingly, in Europe where people from the former Yugoslavia have settled.

Kosovar and Albanian gangsters exploited the Balkan refugee crisis, as did the Italian Camorra. Gang members patrolled the refugee camps, looking for anyone willing to buy their way out of there and into Western Europe, especially Britain. Because there is no inherent difference between smuggling people and smuggling drugs, the gangs take people across the established drug routes. And for the Albanians and Kosovars, they are well established. Interpol reports that one out of every eight drug traffickers arrested in Europe is either Kosovar or Albanian. The price for the one-way, no-guarantees trip from the Balkans to Britain has been reported to be $5,000. It is considerably less than Chinese illegals have to pay. The best deal for them appears to be a $16,500 one-way trip to the UK which includes a Russian-made counterfeit passport and, Interpol believes, access to a lawyer in Britain if the authorities get involved.

Aliens have been found hidden in trucks, in buses, under trucks, under buses, inside freight and in luggage compartments of trains. According to those authorities, seven hundred to eight hundred million illegals are caught annually trying to come into Britain, although the figure is rising sharply every year. At the beginning of the 1990s, it was only one tenth as many. How many get through is another matter. Those women who don't get caught often wind up forced into prostitution to pay back their smuggling fees. This is in addition to the women and children who are trafficked around the world specifically to supply the sex trade.

Well-organized traffickers using established sophisticated international networks, often with the compliance of corrupt government officials in those countries supplying women, bring women into industrialized countries—especially the European Union—from the former Soviet Union and Eastern European bloc, and from Ghana, Nigeria, Morocco, Brazil, Colombia, the Dominican Republic, the Philippines and Thailand. Exact figures are impossible to come by, but the International Organization for Migration believes that more than five hundred thousand women are illegally trafficked each year—that figure could double by 2010—while the International Campaign to End Child Prostitution in Asian Tourism says that criminal organizations operating in Russia, Ukraine and Belarus are behind much of the trafficking.

A Brazilian man was sent to prison in 1998 for his role in smuggling women into Britain over an eight-year period beginning ten years previously. Over that same period, for his services, he reportedly earned $9.5 million.

In 1998, Operation Seek and Keep broke up an alien smuggling cartel—said to be the largest ever in U.S. history—responsible for bringing nearly twelve thousand people, mostly subcontinentals, through Russia, Cuba and the Bahamas. They were delivered into the United States at the behest of subcontinental businessmen already established in the country who were looking for sweatshop labor.

The complexity of the case—led by the INS, with the help of law enforcement in Canada, Ecuador, the Dominican Republic, the Bahamas and India—was underlined by the fact that during the yearlong investigation, law enforcement agencies monitored more than thirty-five thousand telephone calls. Among those identified as ringleaders were two men carrying British passports with addresses in London. Nitin Shettie used the alias Nick Diaz. He was arrested in the Bahamas. Navtej Pall Singh Sandhu was arrested in Puerto Rico. They stand accused of bringing some twelve thousand people into North America over a three-year period to supply low-cost businesses with cheap labor. The price for the journey was $20,000 to $28,000, making this venture worth $240 million. In a few reported cases, payments were demanded at different points along the smuggling route. If the aliens couldn't pay the fee, the owners of the businesses being supplied were required to put up the money. They then held the illegal aliens in servitude until they paid back the fees, with all the usual interest charges added on. The gang's money was laundered in Canada and the United Arab Emirates before being wired on to India.

Another circuit, used by another group, has subcontinentals being moved through Russia to Nicaragua, then through Guatemala and Mexico. The illegal aliens are then escorted to the Rio Grande, where they are given inner tubes to float across the river.

As long as cash is king, money laundering will be a major preoccupation for transnational organized crime gangs, who will, more and more, form joint ventures to make their cash disappear. But it won't go on for very much longer, because technology is offering up solutions.

The magnetic strip on the back of every credit card tells a computer somewhere that this is your card, that you control a certain amount of money and that, as long as the PIN used with this card is correct, a transaction can be completed. The magstripe can be read by ATM machines in Oslo and Singapore and Ecuador, allowing you to have access to your money globally. But buying something with a credit card or getting a cash advance through an ATM machine involves a third party—a store, a bank, a credit-servicing agency—and therefore leaves a trail of the transaction. Which is why bad guys don't use credit cards. They don't want any record of an account relationship.

The future is theirs. Over the next few years, credit cards will be implanted with microchips that will, effectively, turn the card into a bank. It is already commonplace in its crudest form—phone cards. Completely anonymous, whoever owns the microchip controls the money implanted in it.

Now consider the next two stages. Because the microchip is the money, the difference between $5 and $50,000 is simply a matter of programming. Phone cards' microchips are digital one-way streets, but the difference between a card that is withdrawal only and one that permits deposits too is also simply a matter of programming.

Banking corporations all over the world are rushing to develop and market this particular new product, knowing that demand for it will be substantial. It is no longer a question of if it happens, but rather an undeniable fact that it will happen soon, and when it does, the world as we know it will change yet again. For all intents and purposes, we will have our bank in our pocket. The card with the two-way-street microchip will come along with what's called a "wallet"—something about the size of a pocket calculator—into which two cards will fit. The wallet will read the value implanted on both microchips and transfer some of it between cards. Money will move from microchip to microchip with the simple validation of a PIN. There will be no account because there's no need to have an account. The value goes from one chip to another chip. And it won't even have to be done face-to-face. It will be done long-distance for the price of a local phone call, thanks to the Internet. By slipping the microchip into a special reader attached to a computer with a modem, value can be transferred from the chip you've been carrying in your pocket to a chip in Cali, Colombia or the Cayman Islands. There won't be an account relationship because the value is going directly from one chip to another without the intermediary bank involved.

We will buy our newspapers this way, be paid our salary this way, buy our drugs this way. It is a legitimate product with unlimited advantages. An obvious one is that cash and checks—both of which are expensive methods for making payments—will become things of the past. That will save many businesses enormous amounts of money. It will also save governments great sums because they will no longer have to mint currency, store it or pay it out.

The United States government, for example, sends out one million checks per week, to cover everything from salaries, social security and retirement to welfare and Medicare payments. To cut down on those costs, a law has been proposed that all payments be made electronically, that money be transferred directly into bank accounts. It would be fast, there would be no risk of loss in the mail, it would be convenient for everyone— no one would have to go somewhere to get their government check cashed—and it would be cost-efficient. The only problem is, 15 percent of the American people don't have bank accounts. Obviously, the government can't make someone have a bank account if they don't want one. Smart cards with two-way microchips solve that dilemma.

As long as people trust the value implanted on their microchip, the system will work. And there is no reason why we won't come to trust microchips as money. After all, we've learned to trust pieces of paper as money. There was a time when you could take a dollar bill to the government and they would give you several pieces of silver for it. But quarters aren't silver anymore. The piece of paper is backed by nothing more than the government's word.

Microchips will be equal acts of faith. It's called trusted value. What's more, they will be multicurrencied. You may have £1,000 on your chip and need to spend $500. The card will automatically handle the currency conversion. Until now, cash has been one of the major hurdles that transnational criminal organizations have had to deal with. That problem is now being solved. Suddenly a million will fit into your back pocket. So will ten million.

The future is theirs.

In the meantime, credit card fraud and cybercrime form a new and very dangerous category called identification theft. At the end of the 1980s, sophisticated credit card frauds were negligible because the technology wasn't there to support them. By the end of the 1990s, as gross bank-card volume hits $10 trillion, cumulative credit card fraud losses are fast approaching $15 billion.

It is a major growth industry. Credit card fraud investigators singled out six specific problem areas in the world. They are California—where nearly one fifth of all U.S. credit card fraud losses occur—Florida, Texas, New York, Asia and Great Britain. Regardless of what the credit card companies do to stop it—whatever security measures they put in place—it's almost as if the transnational criminal organizations behind these frauds are one step ahead.

Magstripes were supposed to solve the problem because they contained sophisticated algorithms that were "impossible" to break. So the bad guys learned to copy magstripes and break algorithms. Then someone decided holograms were the answer. So the bad guys learned to make holograms. There has been talk of voice prints and photos, but that won't solve much because the bad guys can easily put their own voice prints and photos on the cards, and set up the magstripes to match. PINs haven't been a cure-all either. The Dai Huen Jai were among the first to crack PINs, by installing video cameras near ATM machines so they could watch people punching in their codes.

Some credit card companies are betting that smart cards will be the future, offering them the protection they need. Some law enforcement officers who deal daily with professional credit card fraud are betting that smart-card chips won't last two months before they're compromised.

In those rare instances when an international effort has been mounted, there have been successes. One recent case began with the arrest of some Malaysians in Britain using counterfeit credit cards to buy diamonds and gold. When that was followed by arrests of more Malaysians using comparable cards in Denmark, Sweden and South Africa, the authorities in Kuala Lampur were notified. They then spent a year to hunt down and break up the ring behind the cards.

Similar successes are few and far between. And the Russians have been unstoppable. They discovered credit cards, created nonexistent shops, used those businesses to charge large sums to stolen cards, took the money and left the banks in the middle wondering how both the customer and the store disappeared.

More sinister is the idea that credit cards are just one facet of identity theft. Access to someone's individuality—which in the age of computers is often represented by a PIN, date of birth and mother's maiden name—is access to that person's bank balance. It is also access to a wide range of credit, cash, goods and services.

In 1997 the FBI arrested Carlos Salgado in San Francisco. He was attempting to sell a CD-ROM that he'd made which contained information about one hundred thousand people. The information had been obtained from credit card accounts held by a company doing business on the Internet. He bought the data from them. Considering the damage that could have been inflicted with this information, his asking price seemed cheap at a mere $2.60 per account.

The Internet is, arguably, the most powerful force on the planet since Christ. The possibilities offered by the Net for both good and evil are unlimited. The extent of criminality already present is staggering and the future is beyond comprehension. In 1994, twenty-year-old Vladimir Leonidovich Levin pleaded guilty to having gained access to a computer system inside Citibank's Cash Management System in New York and to having transferred $3.7 million into accounts that he and his partners controlled in Finland, the Netherlands, Germany, Israel and the United States. He managed it all while sitting in front of a laptop in an office in St. Petersburg, Russia.

Since cyberbanking opened a hornet's nest of potential financial fraud, the FBI has had its hands full. They monitored Levin's intrusion into Citibank, not knowing who or where he was, from July 1994 until October of that year. They recorded forty transactions as he wired money from Argentina and Indonesia to San Francisco, Finland, Russia,

Switzerland, Germany and Israel. In the end, they arrested six foreign nationals and recouped all but $400,000.

Levin himself was arrested at Heathrow Airport in February 1995 by Scotland Yard and extradited to the U.S in September 1997. He pleaded guilty the following January and was sentenced to three years and a fine covering the losses that Citibank hadn't been able to recoup. He is now out. Until his deportation, he'd never set foot in New York. And therein lies the very nature of cybercrime.

Anybody can be anywhere because cyberspace is nowhere. It's almost as if it were another dimension. And, as such, it is almost always beyond the reach of law enforcement. Like so many of the hackers who have come before him, Levin was an amateur working a makeshift scheme, leaving a money trail to be followed. It will not be the same when transnational organized crime groups use their economic power to buy the kinds of skills and set up the kinds of scams that don't leave a money trail.

Not long ago, the Boeing Corporation in Seattle had to change the PINs used by employees to access certain retirement accounts because someone, somewhere, cracked the code. The *Times* of London reported that a number of banks in the city have paid fees to hackers who successfully invaded their computer systems. While the banking industry denies any pay-offs, police officers insist that at least some of the reported stories are true.

Stories abound pointing up the vulnerability of organizations who believed they were secure. And hackers even hold publicly advertised conventions in Las Vegas. In 1996, one group did it to the New York City Police Department. They infiltrated a telephone switchboard so that people dialing a precinct would hear this message: "You have reached the New York City police department. For any real emergencies, dial 9-1-1. Anyone else— we're a little busy right now eating some doughnuts and having coffee."

The Center for Strategic and International Studies claims that cyber-theft from banks averages $250,000, while bank stickups only average around $6,000. Nearly 80 percent of the stocking-mask variety get caught. Fewer than 1 percent of the computerized bank robbers are ever found.

Another huge area of concern is cargo theft. Said to be a $10 billion business, it is managed by organized thieves somewhere in the world who have gained access to freight-forwarding companies and airlines, to seek out shipments of goods and digitally reroute them to their own warehouses. It is fast, efficient, highly profitable and by the time someone realizes the goods are missing, they have disappeared into some untraceable black market. Even if the goods are somehow found, the cyberthieves are usually thousands of miles away. They never come in contact with the goods.

In a very real sense, the Net is being turned into the digital, or "smart," equivalent of what might be called dumb frauds, such as telephone canvassing and various sweepstakes gimmicks. For instance, a company that went on the Net under the Web site name Netware International is said, by the FBI, to have been nothing but a pyramid selling scheme. Their Web site suggested they were forming a private bank with deposits insured by the National Union Fire Insurance Company of Pittsburgh. They then claimed that the bank would declare profits of around 25 percent a year, and that those monies would be divided up among those members—apparently they had already solicited funds from twenty-five hundred people—who sold at least two more memberships. National Union Fire Insurance Company immediately and vehemently denied any affiliation with Netware. The FBI has since seized $1 million from Netware.

Clearly the old rules no longer apply. Cybercrimes affect a wide variety of industries, businesses and citizens. The 1999 Melissa virus illustrates how vulnerable computers have become. Cybertheft of trade secrets illustrates one way in which such vulnerability can cost industry, businesses and citizens billions of dollars.

The Web is a sewer of fraud, scams and piracy. It is unpoliced, and, what's more, unpoliceable. There are good arguments that freedom of speech and freedom of the press demands it stay unpoliced; that it represents the ultimate inalienable right of citizens to speak freely, think freely and congregate freely, even if some of those citizens are speaking, thinking and congregating for criminal reasons. But that does not mean industry, businesses and citizens should not be protected. It simply suggests that such protection should serve industry, businesses and citizens, not governments with their own agendas.

In a white paper titled "Criminal Threats to Business on the Internet," published by Global Technology Research Inc. of Portland, Oregon, the author, Kent Anderson, outlines seven levels of Internet intruders:

Low Level, being stereotypical hackers such as the ones who accessed a computer system in the Czech Republic and walked away with $1.9 million. For-Profit Fraudsters, who are often the digital equivalent of the old tele-

phone canvassers, sweepstakes fraudsters and the people behind the
Freedom Star National Bank of Arizona, who went on the Net, offering high interest rates to depositors, and only got stopped when the
Office of Controller of Currency in Washington happened to notice
that no one had ever granted this bank a charter.

Organized Criminals, such as the gang who successfully penetrated the
security systems of the Bank of Russia in Moscow and walked away
with $4.7 million.

Political, Religious and Anarchists' Fringe Groups, such as the German
Chaos Computer Club, who tried to extort the French telecommu-
nications companies in protest against nuclear testing in the Pacific.

Industrial Espionage and Sabotage—according to an FBI study of five
hundred companies, nearly two thirds of them had suffered computer security breaches during the twelve-month period studied.

International Espionage and Information Warfare, which is the ability to
intercept phone calls, fax transmissions and e-mail, a feat well within
the grasp of an experienced crypto technician—and experienced
crypto technicians are for hire to transnational criminal organizations
around the world.

Terrorists, being an obvious threat to national stability, especially in a scenario where they team up with a transnational organized crime group
first to empty the coffers a national health care or social security network, then to digitally dismantle it.

All of that will, however, pale by comparison in the new millenium.

The main targets will be global banks and those multinational corporations using "electronic data interchange." That's where companies farm
out many of their billing, invoicing and other data services to specialist
companies overseas.

It is only a matter of time before a transnational organized crime
group sets up such a company, runs it successfully for several years to gain a
reputation and trust, then empties out its clients' bank accounts, wreaking
unimaginable devastation on multinational business and possibly even crip-
pling certain sectors of the Western economy. When it happens, with the
bad guys being light-years ahead of the good guys, there may not be a law
enforcement agency anywhere on the planet who will know where to look.

EPILOGUE

CRIME IS NOT A LOCAL ISSUE.

And politicians who seek votes on their track record of having reduced crime are at best disingenuous, at worst dishonest.

It goes without saying that by putting more cops on the beat, fewer little old ladies will be hit over the head for their handbags and fewer cars will be stolen from shopping-mall parking lots. Making the streets safer and our homes more secure is a substantial issue and, understandably, wins votes. But to insist that, as muggings and car theft statistics fall, crime is on the run is simply untrue. Crime—when discussed as a business and measured in terms of that business's turnover—has been increasing exponentially for years.

The business of crime is soaring.

Drug trafficking, for example, now accounts for 2 percent of the world's economy.

What's more, our criminal-justice system—which had always been intended to handle local crime—is archaic, incapable by design of dealing with global matters and, anyway, on the verge of collapse. Petty cases clog the courts. Complex frauds bemuse juries who vote to acquit because it's easier than trying to understand. Loopholes are often illogical and large enough to drive a Mack truck through. Prosecutors have neither the time nor the budget to take on an otherwise important case if it doesn't have a better than a 50-50 chance of ending in a conviction.

Compounding matters, transnational organized criminals hide behind governments they've infiltrated or otherwise subverted; buy lawyers with the skills, know-how and funds to impede the system; buy bankers, accountants and company-formation agents who are in no way held responsible for the obstructions they purposely create; have obliterated international borders that keep law enforcement at bay as a rule rather than the exception; and can count on the assistance of political special interest groups who will, dependably, spend whatever it takes to protect their own balance sheets. For instance, in 1999, a proposed law that would have required U.S. banks to be much more vigilant about money laundering was soundly defeated by a lobby financed by the U.S. banking industry.

The inability of modern society to deal with global crime has reached such overwhelming proportions that it is destined to be a defining issue for the twenty-first century, much the way the Cold War was for the twentieth and colonialism was for the nineteenth.

"No area of international affairs will remain untouched," warns Louise Shelley, director of American University's Center for Transnational Organized Crime and Corruption in Washington. "Political and economic systems and the social fabric of many countries will deteriorate under the increasing financial power of international organized crime groups."

She feels that national security is threatened by continuing trade in nuclear materials; that large-scale arms smuggling is fueling regional conflicts; that the human costs of international drug trafficking and illegal-alien smuggling are observable in both source and destination countries; and that the massive profits of these transnational organized crime groups, laundered in international financial markets, are undermining the security of the world financial system.

Money-laundering expert Jack Blum concurs, convinced that to fight transnational crime we need transnational solutions. "The idea that jurisdiction is a function of geography does not work in the electronic age. Electrons in cyberspace do not read maps. Few if any international frauds (logistically) take place solely within the borders of a single country. We will have to change the way nations deal with each other in matters of exchanging evidence, allowing police to work across borders, and even the way the international community deals with the question of sovereignty."

The key word being *sovereignty*.

After all, what chance is there of anything happening if it means turning over protected rights to some international authority? Justice throughout the English speaking world is a direct descendant of colonial Britain. The French and Belgians have built their system on the Napoleonic Code. The two vary greatly. It is common practice in the United States and Canada, for example, for law enforcement to mount sting operations. As long as they function within set guidelines, the results are admissible in court. The Napoleonic Code specifically prohibits acts of *les agents provocateurs*. German law has come from still other roots. Until recently, wiretaps were totally illegal in Germany. They are now legal, but only under certain, very restricted conditions.

The United States Constitution guarantees, as an inalienable right, Fifth Amendment protection. No defendant can be forced to testify against himself. But the right of the accused to remain silent is not the same under British law. So where do the twain meet? If some super-jurisprudence is drawn up, will it include Fifth Amendment rights? There is no way Americans would subscribe if it doesn't. What then of undercover operations in France and wiretaps in Germany? How ready would those two systems be to accommodate them?

When the European Union established Europol, a police structure specifically designed to investigate drug trafficking and terrorism within the EU, a furious debate raged over what powers Europol would have. In the end, the politicians in Brussels did what politicians everywhere always do whenever faced with difficult questions. They fudged an answer that protects their own interests rather than solving the problem. Europol's powers were so whittled down—in the name of national sovereignty—that it functions today as little more than a repository of whatever information the member states are willing to share. They do not have what might be necessary, which is an operational role. They are not a Europe-wide police force with powers of arrest. They are another level of bureaucracy. The politicians merely built a superstructure on top of the already top-heavy pink elephant that is called international law enforcement cooperation.

And even if, somehow in the next ten years, Europol were to become an operational force, say a European version of the FBI—which will never happen until fifteen member states agree to give up some sovereignty—what then of those nations in Europe who are not part of the European

Union? Switzerland, one of Europe's biggest transit centers for drugs and one of the world's most important money-laundering centers, is outside Europol. And because the U.S. so regularly figures into these matters— being the world's largest market for illicit drugs and the prime target of the transnational criminal organizations—one might expect that there should be full cooperation with American law enforcement. But why should Europol succeed where Interpol has failed?

For public consumption, everybody agrees that these sorts of organizations are important. Privately, American law enforcement agencies are eminently distrustful. There is already enough worry about sharing information among themselves. All too often, trying to get U.S. agencies to share intelligence is like pulling teeth. Mention Interpol and they're outright allergic.

At Interpol Headquarters in Lyon, France, they insist that they only keep post-arrest information. That they don't maintain an intelligence database which might otherwise be accessed by any law enforcement agency anywhere in the world. That while they do handle intelligence material, they always return it to the agency it's come from. That any agency can classify anything they send to Interpol as they see fit, and specify which desks can and cannot see it. In return, when they're on the record—in other words, when they need to be diplomatic—American law enforcement officers claim that Interpol serves a much-needed purpose, that they have full confidence in the organization and that they cooperate at every turn. When they're being frank—and not credited as a source— they admit that's a load of bureaucratic crap.

The working relationship between American and British law enforcement is a perfect illustration of why everybody really needs to start again at the beginning, as to why new rules might be the only answer. Besides being a drug market, the U.K. is also a major transshipment point. Couriers come through on their way to and from the States. Arresting a courier at Heathrow with a few kilos of cocaine is a short-term measure that keeps some drugs off the streets. But getting a courier doesn't put even a minor dent into the much larger, global scope of drug trafficking. To manage that, law enforcement needs to get to the people who control the business. In order to manage that, a cop somewhere has to get the courier to cooperate, which can only be done if he or she can also secure all the authorizations required, locally and internationally, to effectuate what is called a controlled delivery. That means allowing the courier to proceed with the drug run, albeit with undercover supervision. As it happens, controlled deliveries are managed all the time between the U.S. and the U.K. They're a very important law enforcement tool. But if a cop in Birmingham, England, makes a request for assistance that has to go up his force's chain of command, then to the Home Office, then to the Foreign Officer, then across the Atlantic to the State Department, then to the Justice Department, then to the FBI, then to some state authority and then down the chain of command of the police in Birmingham, Alabama, just to get a cop there to look after the courier, it's not going to happen. The cop in Birmingham, England, has to be able to phone someone in Birmingham, Alabama, which gets straight back to Louis Freeh's concept of bridges—street-level planks of wood that ordinary cops can use to step over the puddle. Some sort of system that would deputize authority to act in a case.

Invariably, however, sovereignty gets in the way. Where politicians have their say, jurisdiction will always matter. This acts to the detriment of law enforcement offices around the world, which must be able to form joint ventures and strategic alliances with one another—easily, fluidly and without bureaucrats or politicians in the middle to screw it up—exactly the same way transnational criminal gangs form their mergers.

Given that radical problems merit radical solutions, there are many people now proposing that the intelligence services be given a role in law enforcement, because they are, by nature, extra-jurisdictional. In Britain, both MI-5 and MI-6 have been recruited into the war on organized crime. Funds have been committed and personnel assigned. The only thing missing are answers to questions such as, will intelligence officers with material information in a case be called to testify? If not, what then of the defendant's right to face his accusers? Would evidence presented in such a trial be sufficient to demand someone's extradition from a country that doesn't recognize the use of intelligence-agency eavesdropping or the untested documentation of a James Bond? Putting aside the fact that, over the years, most intelligent services have shown very poor judgment—witness the CIA's record on Vietnam, Iran-Contra, the bombing of the Chinese embassy in Belgrade and their total failure to predict the disintegration of the Soviet Union—there are just too many serious legal hurdles that would have to be jumped in order for the spy services to become effective law enforcement agencies.

By definition, crime is a violation of some law. By definition, law enforcement is about mechanisms, organizations and policies charged with bringing about compliance with the existing laws. Implied is that law enforcement will always operate within the rule of law. But the intelligence agencies are not mandated to operate within the rule of law. Their job is to do whatever they have to—with very few limitations—in order to accomplish their mission. Although political assassination was ruled out by U.S. law after the death of President Salvador Allende in Chile, other nations do not limit the scope of their intelligence services the same way. Would that mean a Pablo Escobar who stayed beyond jurisdictional reach could be assassinated? It seems fair to wonder, for instance, where at CIA headquarters they keep their copy of the Constitution. Is it on the same shelf as their operating manuals? Almost certainly not.

Matty Maher, a former director of international operations for the DEA, has studied this particular point in minute detail. "The intelligence services are the first to tell you, we don't operate inside the country, we operate outside. So then explain to me, how can you declare transnational crime, or drug trafficking, as threats to national security and then say that the intelligence community will only operate outside the three-mile limit on these issues? Because if you're operating outside the three-mile limit and you develop intelligence or evidence about criminal activities that are also threats to national security, then what exactly have you gathered? Is it top-secret national-security information, or is it evidence of a crime that needs to be shared in a law enforcement context and used in criminal proceedings? It's that dichotomy which causes the problem."

He says that the term *threat to national security* is like the term *pregnant*. You are or you aren't. It is or it isn't.

"Is transnational crime up there with Korean missiles and nuclear generators? Is drug trafficking up there with warheads in Ukraine? If it's not, then why are we calling it this? Because once you call it a threat to national security, you have put this thing in a whole new package and the rules should change substantially."

Regardless of the product—weapons, drugs, counterfeit credit cards—the suppliers are outside the country. But the distribution organizations, the profit-making mechanisms, the money-laundering machines are inside the country. The two ends meet in the middle and form a conspiracy. It can be vertical, horizontal, hubbed wheel, whatever, but it's a conspiracy under the definition of conspiracy—two or more people having a common goal of committing a criminal offense.

Maher can't imagine how the intelligence services and law enforcement can come together in such a situation. "You've got the intelligence community on the supply end. At the same time, it's going to be very hard to segregate any information you get on the distribution end or the money-laundering end because it's all one conspiracy. Under a principle of law, all of the co-conspirators are joined. They don't have to know one another. At least in U.S. law, all there has to be is a common understanding and two or more people agreeing on it. So you've got your CIA working outside the country. Inside the country you've got your Secret Service, FBI, Customs, DEA, ATF and everybody else working on the domestic end of this. But it's still all one conspiracy. Does the CIA neutralize their end of this? And then, do the domestic enforcement agencies arrest and prosecute the domestic end of this? If you compartmentalize it, how do you compartmentalize the evidence to prosecute it? What about the judicial process? What about discovery, witnesses, sources and the methods that need to be examined to see if they comply with the law? They're never going to do that."

It's tough enough just trying to get forces inside the country to work together. One of the lessons that law enforcement in the United States learned from the cocaine wars of the 1970s and 1980s was that turf battles between agencies were counterproductive. That when the FBI insisted, this is ours, and locked horns with the DEA and Customs, the energy they expended only served to facilitate the bad guys. So cooperation became the operative word in the 1990s.

Except that not everyone heard it. When you ask other law enforcement agencies about the FBI, they seem unanimous in the opinion that if the FBI doesn't own the bat, the ball, the gloves and the umpires, the FBI doesn't play. The DEA have always shared a culture and kinship with the CIA—in fact, the DEA was born out of the Agency's rib—and they understand the foreign-intelligence mission. But the DEA also plays an important role domestically. That sometimes means stepping on toes at U.S. Customs. The borders are, by law, secured by Customs, but they lay claim to an anti-money-laundering mission as well, which sometimes means stepping on toes of the CID branch at the Internal Revenue Service. Because the two are both Treasury agencies, sibling rivalry is compounded.

The point is that all the best speeches urging cooperation are doomed to fail because egos get involved. So do budgets. It is a fact of life when governments dole out stipends, that whoever has caught the biggest fish will get the biggest dinner.

Internationally, some nations do what they can within the confines of sovereignty. There are Canadian, British, French and German law enforcement investigators stationed in Miami. These are not people doing liaison duty—there are already plenty of those in Washington—these are foreign law enforcement officers working operationally inside the United States. That suggests there are American investigators operationally active inside Canada, Britain, France and Germany.

Jack Blum goes further, believing that nations can harmonize legal systems and can also reach common definitions of crime. Additionally, he would like to see a common international understanding that no nation-state may use its sovereignty to harbor criminals. "We urgently need a global convention on the gathering of evidence in criminal cases. Police must have an easy, uncomplicated way to get the evidence they need admissible from foreign jurisdictions without extensive red tape."

Getting such agreements signed and ratified is not beyond the scope of possibility. Once upon a time, though, the United Nations proposed that money laundering be made an internationally extraditable offense. Some eighty nations agreed to ratify a pact. Granted, that's less than half the UN membership. But even that many would have been great. Five years later, only four had bothered to actually sign it.

Addressing the UN on transnational crime in 1998, President Clinton argued that we must create a world in which criminals must have no place to run, no place to hide. The member states readily agreed. And yet, nearly a quarter of those same member states continue to provide secret banking, much of it aimed specifically at aiding and abetting the concealment of dirty money. Even more of those same member states continue to offer shell companies that can be bought for minimal fees in jurisdictions halfway around the globe, whose specific purpose is to obscure a money trail that might otherwise aid law enforcement in connecting criminals to their ill-gotten gains.

Sure, there is wide agreement in the international community that nations must get together to combat transnational organized crime, that individual efforts are no longer sufficient when faced with this global threat, and that by denying criminals their profits, transnational crime can be reduced. But such rhetoric is little more than the equivalent of approving of motherhood, apple pie and the flag.

Transnational criminal organizations are businesses that rely on cash flow and reinvestment in order to grow. Denying them either—or better still, denying them both—could bankrupt them. That means going after the people who handle their money. But the people who handle their money are often the same people behind those who make our laws. Significantly, not one single nation on the face of the planet has ever even proposed legislation that requires lawyers, bankers, accountants and company-formation agents—who, knowingly or unknowingly, service transnational criminal organizations by laundering their money—to verify, under threat of criminal penalty, the beneficial owner of the money they are handling before they handle it.

If lawyers, bankers, accountants and company-formation agents could be taken out of the equation, if companies and secret bank accounts based in tax havens were denied the right to function in the rest of the world— if the Caymans and the Antiguas and the Arubas and the Colombias and the Nigerias and the Switzerlands and the Liechtensteins and even the Niues of this planet were outright ostracized for their role in transnational criminality—that's when something might begin to change.

ACKNOWLEDGMENTS
AND SOURCES

I OWE AN IMMENSE DEBT OF GRATITUDE TO THE MANY men and women of law enforcement who spoke to me on the record, and to those who for various reasons could only speak to me off the record. In the United States, among those I can name, including retired agents, my thanks to Billy Ahern, Peter Grinenko and Ron Rose of the New York Police Department; Hardrick Crawford Jr., Tom Fuentes, Tom Kneir, Robert Levinson and Jim Moody of the FBI; Allan Doody, Terry Neeley, Fred McGreevy, Tony Mangione, Mark Robinson, Jerry Sullivan, Roger Urbanski and Dick Weart at U.S. Customs; and Brent Eaton, Tom Clifford, John Costanzo, Brian Crowell and Matty Maher of the Drug Enforcement Administration.

In Washington, I am grateful to John McDowell of the Department of State's Bureau for International Narcotics and Law Enforcement Affairs; Tanya Meekins of the Environmental Protection Agency; John Sopko at the Department of Commerce; Frank Cilluffo at the Center for Strategic and International Studies; George Malbois at the Embassy of Switzerland; attorney Jack Blum; Rogene Waite at the DEA; Michael Bopp and Mary Roberts at the Senate's Permanent Subcommittee on Investigations; Professor Louise Shelley at American University; Joyce McDonald at FINCEN; George Abbott at the International Anti-Counterfeiting Coalition; and General Heze Leder at the Embassy of Israel.

Thanks as well to John Moscow, asssistant district attorney for the city of New York; Lee Seglum and the New Jersey State Commission of Investigations; Pam Brown at the DEA in Miami; Tom Cash at the Kroll Agency in Miami; and Alexis Johnson in Arizona.

In Britain, my thanks to law enforcement officers, including Chris Pope at the Dyfed Powys Constabulary; Dave Cooper, Simon Goddard, John Leek and Jim Morrison at the National Criminal Intelligence Service; Paul Cook, Ranald Macdonald and Tim Manhire at HM Customs and Excise; Lindsay Anderson and Graham Saltmarsh at the National Crime Squad; Allan Jones at the Merseyside Constabulary; and Bob Denmark at Royal Lancashire Constabulary. Also, my thanks to Norbert Garrett and Andre Pienaar at the Kroll Agency and Rowan Bosworth-Davies.

There are a number of officers at the Metropolitan Police in London to whom I would like to say thank you. Their cooperation was outstanding. But I won't mention their names for fear of reprisals from a shameful, petty and, I would claim, dangerous cult of secrecy that pervades the force through the disgraceful Palace Guard mentality of the Press and Public Relations Office.

My thanks goes to many people throughout the rest of Europe, especially Alessandro Pansa at the Servicio Centrale Operativo of the Italian National Police and his staff of Marcella Montaina, Aquilino Dortona, Andrea Il Grande, Massimo Mazzarella, Vittorio Rizzi and Amalia Bonagura. Also in Italy, many thanks to U.S. Customs Special Agents Armando Ramirez and Matt Etre, stationed at the American Embassy in Rome. In Holland, among others, my thanks to Hank Zwam. In Austria, I am grateful to three officers from the Vienna Police: Chief of Police Peter Stiedl, Chief of Detectives Dr. Walter Schubert, and Chief of the Major Crime Bureau Max Edelbacher; Michael Sika, director general of the Ministry of Interior; Jean Francois Thony, director of the Money Laundering Program, Office of the Control of Drugs and the Prevention of Crime, United Nations; Bernard LeRoy, senior legal advisor to the United Nations; David Kyd of the International Atomic Energy Agency; and various officers at EDOK.

My appreciation goes as well to Rick McDonnell of the Financial Action Task Force Asia/Pacific and others in Australia; Bernard Delias and others in France; Don Shruhan, Stuart McDonald and others in Singapore; plus several people who assured me they were not officially permitted to talk, and yet did, at the Hong Kong Organized Crime and Triad Bureau and the Australian Federal Police.

In Canada, I am grateful to Pietro Poletti and Brian Scharf at the Criminal Intelligence Service of Canada; Bruce Tuck and Rob MacCallum of the Toronto Metropolitan Police; Ben Soave and Reg King of the RCMP.

I am equally grateful to many journalists, including friends at the *New York Times, Newsday, Wall Street Journal, Washington Post, Miami Herald, Los Angeles Times, International Herald Tribune, London Times, Telegraph, Guardian* and *Independent*.

My appreciation also goes to Alan Williams for his legal advice.

Finally, a special note of thanks to John Forbes and John Hurley in Washington, Bill Malarney in Atlanta, Jim Fisher in Ottawa and Yvon Gagnon in Montreal. Of course, as well, to everyone at The Overlook Press—especially Peter Mayer, Tracy Carns and Aimee Bianca; to Nick Webb in London, to my agent Mildred Marmur and, *comme d'habitude*, to La Benayoun.

A WORD ON ETHNICITY:

In referring to certain types of organized crime groups, I have used a kind of shorthand. I know very well that Italian is not synonymous with the Mafia, that Asian is not synonymous with Triad, that Nigerian is not synonymous with criminal enterprises that originate in Nigeria. And I never meant to imply otherwise. I know very well that the overwhelming majority of immigrants in Brighton Beach in Brooklyn are hardworking, family-loving people simply trying to get ahead in the New World, and that they abhor the criminality that stems from such a tiny sector of their community. To speak then of Italian organized crime or Asian organized crime or Russian organized crime—even when some of the latter is, more correctly, Chechen or Ukrainian, et al—is nothing more than a convenience. To anyone who might still be offended and finds my shorthand politically incorrect, I sincerely apologize.

A WORD ON SOURCES:

The problem with printed sources is that mistakes get repeated. It is often the case that one sloppy inclusion, early on, can take on the air of truth as that inclusion is re-cited, with each new version of the story merely referencing the previous one. Unless an author checks back to the original source, the risk is great that such misinformation will, eventually, simply be accepted as fact. I have, therefore, always considered printed sources with the greatest of jaundiced views. I look on them as no better than secondary or, in most cases, tertiary sources and have tried to limit their use here to that. Where previously printed sources do serve as a great help is as a road map to primary sources. In cases where people have been quoted, wherever possible, I have endeavored to find that person. In instances where circumstances have been described and primary sources are no longer available, I have endeavored to find at least two versions of the story that have come from separate and distinct sources, to check the accuracy of those circumstances. And, except where propriety dictates otherwise, sources are quoted.

BOOKS

ABADINSKY, HOWARD, *Organized Crime*. Nelson Hall, Chicago, 1990.

————, *The Mafia in America: An Oral History*. Praeger, New York, 1987.

ALBANESE, JAY, *Organized Crime in America*. Anderson Publishing, Cincinnati, 1996.

ANASTASIA, GEORGE, *The Goodfella Tapes*. Avon Books, New York, 1998.

APPLETON, PETER, and DOUG CLARK, *Billion $$$ High: The Drug Invasion of Canada*. McGraw-Hill Ryerson, Montreal, 1990.

BALSAMO, WILLIAM, and GEORGE CARPOZI. *Crime Incorporated, or Under the Clock: The Inside Story of the Mafia's First Hundred Years*. New Horizon Press, New Jersey, 1991.

BAUM, DAN, *Smoke and Mirrors: The War on Drugs and the Politics of Failure*. Little, Brown, Boston, 1996.

BEARE, MARGARET E., *Criminal Conspiracies: Organized Crime in Canada*. Nelson, Scarborough, Canada, 1996.

BLACK, DAVID, *Triad Takeover: A Terrifying Account of the Spread of Triad Crime in the West*. Sidgwick and Jackson, London, 1991.

BLUM, HOWARD, *Gangland: How the FBI Broke the Mob*. Simon & Schuster, New York, 1993.

BLUMENTHAL, RALPH, *Last Days of the Sicilians: At War with the Mafia—The FBI Assault on the Pizza Connection*. Times Books, New York, 1988.

BONANNO, JOSEPH, and SERGIO LALLI, *A Man of Honor*. Simon & Schuster, New York, 1983.

BONAVOLONTA, JULES, and BRIAN DUFFY, *The Good Guys*. Pocket Books, New York, 1996.

BOOTH, MARTIN, *The Triads: The Growing Global Threat from the Chinese Criminal Societies*. St. Martin's Press, New York, 1991.

BRASHLER, WILLIAM, *The Don: The Life and Death of Sam Giancana*. Harper and Row, New York, 1977.

BRESLER, FENTON S., *The Trail of the Triads: An Investigation into International Crime*. Weidenfeld and Nicolson, London, 1980.

CARRIGAN, D. OWEN, *Crime and Punishment in Canada: A History*. McLelland and Stewart, Toronto, 1991.

CHIN, KO-LIN, *Chinatown Gangs*. Oxford University Press, New York, 1996.

COOK, FRED, *Mafia*. Fawcett, New York, 1973.

CUMMINGS, JOHN, and ERNEST VOLKMAN, *Mobster: The Astonishing Rise and Fall of John Gotti and His Gang*. Warner Books, London, 1996.

DAVIS, JOHN H., *Mafia Dynasty: The Rise and Fall of the Gambino Crime Family*. Harper Collins, New York, 1993.

DU, PHUC LONG, and LAURA RICARD, *The Dream Shattered: Vietnamese Gangs in America*. Northeastern University Press, Boston, 1996.

DUBRO, JAMES, *Dragons of Crime: Inside the Asian Underworld*. Octopus, Toronto, 1992.

ENGLISH, T. J., *Born to Kill: America's Most Notorious Vietnamese Gang, and the Changing Face of Organized Crime*. William Morrow, New York, 1995.

FIORENTINI, G., and S. PELTZMAN, *The Economics of Organized Crime*. Cambridge University Press, Cambridge, 1995.

FOGEL, JEAN-FRANÇOIS, *Le Testament de Pablo Escobar*. Grasset, Paris, 1994.

FOX, STEPHEN R., *Blood and Power: Organized Crime in Twentieth Century America*. William Morrow, New York, 1989.

FRANZESE, MICHAEL, and DARY MATERA, *Quitting the Mob: How the Yuppie Don Left the Mafia and Lived to Tell His Story*. Harper Collins, New York, 1992.

FRIMAN, H. RICHARD, *Narco Diplomacy: Exporting the U.S. War on Drugs*. Cornell University Press, Ithaca, 1996.

GAGE, NICHOLAS, *Mafia, USA*. Playboy Press, Chicago, 1972.

GAMBETTA, DIEGO, *The Sicilian Mafia: The Business of Private Protection*. Harvard University Press, Cambridge, 1993.

GATELY, WILLIAM, and YVETTE FERNANDEZ, *Dead Ringer: An Insider's Account of the Mob's Colombian Connection*. Donald I. Fine, New York, 1994.

GENTRY, CURT, *J. Edgar Hoover: The Man and the Secrets*. New American Library, New York, 1992.

GIANCANA, SAM, and CHUCK GIANCANA, *Double Cross*. Warner Books, New York, 1992.

GOLDFARD, RONALD L. *Perfect Villains, Imperfect Heroes: Robert F. Kennedy's War Against Organized Crime*. Random House, New York, 1995.

GOODE, JAMES, *Wiretap: Listening in on America's Mafia*. Simon & Schuster, New York, 1988.

GOSCH, M. A, *Last Testament of Lucky Luciano*. Little, Brown, Boston, 1975.

GOTTI, JOHN, and SALVATORE GRAVANO, *The Gotti Tapes: Including the Testimony of Salvatore "Sammy the Bull" Gravano*. Times Books, New York, 1992.

GUGLIOTTA, GUY, and JEFF LEEN, *Kings of Cocaine: Inside the Medellín Cartel—an Astonishing True Story of Murder, Money, and International Corruption*. Simon & Schuster, New York, 1989.

GUNST, LAURIE, *Born Fi' Dead: A Journey Through the Jamaican Posse Underworld*. Henry Holt, New York, 1995.

HANDELMAN, STEPHEN, *Comrade Criminal*. Yale University Press, New Haven, 1995.

JACOBS, JAMES B., *Busting the Mob*. New York University Press, New York, 1994.

KAPLAN, DAVID, and ALEC DUBRO, *Yakuza*. Addison-Wesley, Massachusetts, 1986.

KEFAUVER, ESTES, and UNITED STATES SENATE, *Crime in America: Special Committee to Investigate Organized Crime in Interstate Commerce*. Doubleday, Garden City, New York, 1951.

KELLY ROBERT J., *Handbook of Organized Crime in the United States*. Greenwood Press, Westport, 1994.

KENNEY, DENNIS JAY, and JAMES FINCKENAUER, *Organized Crime in America*. Wadsworth Publishing, California, 1995.

KERRY, JOHN, *A New Kind of War: National Security and the Globalization of Crime*. Simon & Schuster, New York, 1997.

KESSLER, RONALD, *The FBI*. Pocket Books, New York, 1993.

KIRBY, CECIL, and THOMAS C. RENNER, *Mafia Assassin*. Methuen, Toronto, 1986.

KIRKPATRICK, SIDNEY, and PETER ABRAHAMS, *Turning the Tide: One Man Against the Medellín Cartel*. Dutton, New York, 1991.

KLEINKNECHT, WILLIAM, *The New Ethnic Mobs: The Changing Face of Organized Crime in America*. Free Press, New York, 1996.

LACEY, ROBERT, *Little Man: Meyer Lansky and the Gangster Life*. Little Brown, Boston, 1991.

LALLEMAN, ALAIN, *L'Organizatsiya: La Mafia Russe à L'Assaut Du Monde*. Calmann-Lévy, Paris, 1996.

LAMOTHE, LEE, and ANTONIA, NICASO, *Global Mafia: The New World Order of Organized Crime*. MacMillan Canada, Toronto, 1994.

LAVIGNE, YVES, *Hells Angels: Into the Abyss*. HarperCollins, Toronto, 1996.

———, *Good Guy, Bad Guy: Drugs and the Changing Face of Organized Crime*. Random House Canada, Toronto, 1991.

LYMAN, MICHAEL D., and GARY W. POTTER, *Organized Crime*. Prentice Hall, New Jersey, 1997.

LYMAN, MICHAEL, *Gangland: Drug Trafficking by Organized Criminals*. Charles Thomas, Illinois, 1989.

MAAS, PETER, *The Valachi Papers*. Putnam, New York, 1968.

MACDONALD, SCOTT, *Dancing on a Volcano: The Latin American Drug Trade*. Praeger, New York, 1988.

MARTIN, JOHN M., and ANNE T. ROMANO, *Multinational Crime: Terrorism, Espionage, Drug and Arms Trafficking*. Sage, California, 1992.

MERMELSTEIN, MAX, *The Man Who Made It Snow*. Simon & Schuster, New York, 1990.

MUSTAIN, GENE, and JERRY CAPECI, *Mob Star: The Story of John Gotti, the Most Powerful Man in America*. Penguin, New York, 1989.

NADELMANN, ETHAN, *Cops Across Borders: The Internationalization of U.S. Criminal Law Enforcement*. Pennsylvania State University Press, University Park, Pennsylvania, 1993.

NASH, JAY ROBERT, *World Encylclopedia of Organized Crime*. Da Capo Press, New York, 1993.

NAYLOR, R. T., *Hot Money and the Politics of Debt*. Black Rose Books, Montreal, 1994.

NICASO, ANTONIO, and LEE LAMOTHE, *Global Mafia: The New World Order of Organized Crime*. Macmillan Canada, Toronto, 1995.

O'BRIEN, JOSPEH, and ANDRIS KURINS, *Boss of Bosses*. Simon & Schuster, New York, 1991.

O'KANE, JAMES M., *The Crooked Ladder: Gangsters, Ethnicity, and the American Dream*. Transaction Books, New Jersey, 1992.

O'NEILL, GERARD, and DICK LEHR, *The Underboss: The Rise and Fall of a Mafia Family*. St. Martin's Press, New York, 1989.

PADILLA, FELIX M., *The Gang As an American Enterprise*. Rutgers University Press, New Jersey, 1992.

PETERSON, VIRGIL W. *The Mob*. Green Hill Publishers, Illinois, 1983.

PETRAKIS, GREGORY J., *The New Face of Organized Crime*. Kendall/Hunt Publishing, Iowa, 1992.

PILEGGI, NICHOLAS, *Wise Guy: Life in a Mafia Family*. Pocket Books, New York, 1985.

PISTONE, JOSEPH D., and RICHARD WOODLEY, *Donnie Brasco: My Undercover Life in the Mafia*. New American Library, New York, 1988.

POPPA, TERRENCE E., *Druglord: The Life and Death of a Mexican Kingpin*. Pharos Books, New York, 1990.

POSNER, GERALD L., *Warlords of Crime: Chinese Secret Societies, the New Mafia*. McGraw-Hill, New York, 1988.

POSSAMI, MARIO, *Money on the Run*. Viking Canada, Toronto, 1992.

RAUFER, XAVIER, *Les Superpuissances du Crime*. Plon, Paris, 1993.

ROBINSON, JEFFREY, *The Laundrymen* (revised and updated edition). Simon & Schuster, London, 1998.

RYAN, PATRICK J., and GEORGE E. RUSH, *Understanding Organized Crime*. Sage, California, 1997.

SEYMOUR, CHRISTOPHER, *Yakuza Diary: Doing Time in the Japanese Underworld*. Atlantic Monthly Press, New York, 1996.

SHANA, ALEXANDER, *The Pizza Connection: Lawyers, Money, Drugs and the Mafia*. Weidenfeld, New York, 1988.

STERLING, CLAIRE, *Thieves' World: The Threat of the New Global Network of Organized Crime*. Simon & Schuster, New York, 1994.

———, *Octopus: The Long Reach of the International Sicilian Mafia*. Norton, New York, 1990.

STRONG, SIMON, *Whitewash: Pablo Escobar and the Cocaine Wars*. Macmillan, London, 1995.

THEOHARIS, ATHAN, and JOHN STEWARD COX, *The Boss*. Temple University Press, Philadelphia, 1988.

TYLER, GUS, *Organized Crime in America*. University of Michigan Press, Ann Arbor, 1962.

VAKSBERG, ARKADY, *The Soviet Mafia*. Weidenfeld, London, 1991.

NEWSPAPERS AND WIRE SERVICES

ASSOCIATED PRESS
October 10, 1999: *Swiss Officials Add New Case to Russian Investigation*
November 29, 1998: Koppel, Naomi, *Swiss Trial Highlights Russian Mob Influx*
December 20, 1994: *Seized Uranium—Weapons Grade*
December 19, 1994: *Czech Police Seize Uranium*
November 23, 1994: *Soviet Nuclear Complex at Risk*
June 7, 1994: *Yeltsin—Russia a Superpower of Crime*

BOSTON GLOBE:
June 29, 1994: Neuffer, Elizabeth, *FBI Director Presses World Effort on Crime*
January 23, 1994: Constable, Pamela, *US-Colombian Drug War Shifts Its Focus to Cali*

CHICAGO TRIBUNE
November 24, 1996: Witt, Howard, *Gangsters Squeezing Russia*
Ju++ly 21, 1996: Hundley, Tom, *Red Hot Deals Draw Russians to Poland*
May 14, 1993: Hanley, Charles J., *Drug Bust May Signal Colombia-Russia link*

CHRISTIAN SCIENCE MONITOR
May 15, 1998: Kiefer, Francine, *Waging War on Global Crime*
October 8, 1997: Prusher, Ilene R., *Worldwide Webs—Mafia's Reach Grows*

September 17, 1997: *Mexico's Growing Drug Cartels Seep Across American Border*
January 11, 1995: Tanner, Adam, and others, *Russian Mafia Expands into New Areas,
Using the US to Launder Dirty Money*
July 5, 1994: Sloane, Wendy, *FBI's Moscow Mission: The Mob, Nuclear Theft*
June 29, 1994: *Russian Mob Holds Summit in Austria*
May 4, 1994: Burke, Justin, *Russian Mafia Thrives in Berlin*

DALLAS MORNING NEWS
September 10, 1995: Katz, Gregory, *Russian Mafia Sets Off Growing Wave of
Crime—Fall of Communism Opened Gates to Europe, Corruption*
September 10, 1995: Katz, Gregory, *Russia's Underworld Finds Fertile Ground in
America—Profits, Legal System Are Irresistible Lure*
December 17, 1992: Rodrigue, George, *Smugglers of Nuclear Materials Proliferating—
Officials Fear Dealers Will Get More Sophisticated*

DETROIT NEWS
April 9, 1998: Girard, Fred, *Fetisov Denies Links to Mob*

FINANCIAL POST
January 9, 1999: Rubin, Sandra, *RCMP Investigated YBM in Early 1995, Informant
Says Mounties Warned Him of "Something Foul" in Company*

FORT LAUDERDALE SUN-SENTINEL
March 6, 1993: Caribbean News Agency, *Sicilian Mafia Attempts to Buy Caribbean
Island*

GUARDIAN
January 4, 1997: Thomas, Richard, John Hooper and David Hearst, *The Godfather,
Part IV*

INDEPENDENT
June 17, 1997: Cockburn, Patrick, *Ministers Quizzed on Links to Russian Mafia*
December 9, 1993: Doyle, Leonard, *Russian Mafias Carve Up Drugs Trade—The
Bosnian War Has Forced Crime Clans to Find New Balkan Routes for Smuggling
Heroin into Europe*

INTERNATIONAL HERALD TRIBUNE
April 15, 1994: Erlanger, Steven, *In Moscow, the High Life Flowers at Gangland
Funeral*

JERUSALEM POST
March 27, 1998: Derfner, Larry, *The Lerner Legend*
September 19, 1997: Ben-David, Calev, *Crime Time*
June 26, 1997: Harris, David, *Police: Israel Is a Global Money-Laundering Center*
May 23, 1997: Rabinovich, Abraham, *A Man of Means*
March 8, 1996: Hutman, Bill, *Police Concerned Russian "Mafia" Infiltrating Government*
January 4, 1996: Dan, Uri, and Dennis Eisenberg, *The Real Mafia*
July 8, 1995: Rodan, Steve, *In Harm's Way*
June 29, 1995: Hutman, Bill, *Hefetz Warns of Infiltration by Russian Mafia*
June 2, 1995: Marcus, Raine, *New Police Unit to Lead War on Int'l Crime*
April 23, 1991: Rotem, Michael, *Soviets Want Oleh Arrested by Swiss*

LOS ANGELES TIMES
December 12, 1998: *Swiss Court Clears Russian Businessman Linked to Gangs*
December 11, 1998: Alonso-Zaldivar, Ricardo, *Immigrant Ring at US-Canada Border Cracked*
September 23, 1998: Paddock, Richard C., *A New Breed of Gangster is Globalizing Russian Crime*
November 17, 1997: Darling, Juanita, *Colombian Cartels Find New Drug Paths to US Narcotics—In Effort to Cut Out Mexican Traffickers, South Americans Have Forged Ties with Smugglers in Caribbean And Guatemala, Sources Say. Russian Mafia Is Reportedly a Partner In Europe*
January 10, 1997: Gerstenzang, James, and Robert L. Jackson, *US Authorities Try to Put Freon Black Market on Ice—Probe: Fifteen People Are Charged with Smuggling Illegal Air-Conditioning Chemical Linked to Depletion of Ozone Layer*
October 9, 1994: Hood, Marlowe, *The Taiwan Connection*
July 17, 1994: Cole, Richard, *Asian Gangs Could Be the Future of US Organized Crime, Experts Warn Law Enforcement*

MONTREAL GAZETTE
September 20, 1998: Schwarcz, Joe, *The Rise and Fall of a Gas: Freon Saved One Generation from Food Poisoning, but Left Gaping Holes in the Ozone Layer*
June 27, 1998: Marotte, Bertrand, *Another Blow for Troubled YBM: Auditor Resigns, Refuses To Certify '97 Statements Because of Possible "Error or Fraud"*
May 28, 1998: Van Hasselt, Caroline, *TSE Suspends Trading in YBM: Police Probe of Bicycle Firm Hurts Exchange's Reputation*
May 22, 1998: Marotte, Bertrand, *TSE's Listing of YBM Draws Barbs*
October 16, 1994: Marsden, William, and Geoff Baker, *RCMP Traces Cash in Huge Money-Laundering Case*

September 1, 1994: Baker, Geoff, *Many Fish Caught in Mounties' Net; but Biggest Got Away, They Say*

MOSCOW TIMES
October 23, 1994: Gubarev, Vladimir, *The Car Theft Industry*

NEWSDAY
October 7, 1999: Robin, Joshua, *A $7B Laundry in Forest Hills?*
August 24, 1996: Fallon, Scott, *Suspected Mobster Extradited—Italy Hands Over Russian Accused In B'klyn Killings*
March 10, 1995: Gelman, Mitch, *Glittering Palace of Smoke, Mirrors*
March 10, 1995: DeStefano, Anthony M., *Russian Thugs Defy US—Screen Weakness in Refugee System*
March 9, 1995: Buettner, Russ, *Marble Foyer and a Bullet-Proof John*
March 9, 1995: Kocieniewski, David, *Russian Godfather Collar—Italy Cops Grab Him For Us*
March 1, 1995: Gelman, Mitch, *Brooklyn Mystery Led to Russia, Italy*
July 28, 1993: Gambardello, Joseph, and Peg Tyre, *Russian Mob Boss Survives Hit*

NEW YORK DAILY NEWS
April 22, 1997: Mustain, Gene, and Jerry Capeci, *2 Dance Bullet Ballet*
April 21, 1997: Mustain, Gene, and Jerry Capeci, *Infamous from Moscow to NY*
April 20, 1997: Mustain, Gene, and Jerry Capeci with Julia Gorin, *Mob Russian in for Crime Time*
March 10, 1996: Gordy, Molly, *A Russian Goodfella? He'd Ice Agents*

NEW YORK TIMES
October 13, 1999: Bohlen, Celestine, and Neela Banerjee, *Little Known Power Broker Emerges in Kremlin Scandals*
October 13, 1999: O'Brien, Timothy, *Bank of New York Executive Resigns*
October 11, 1999: Bohlen, Celestine, *Energy Companies Are Tools in Russian Power Struggle*
October 7, 1999: Wines, Michael, *Yeltsin Son-in-Law Tied to Oil Giants*
October 6, 1999: O'Brien, Timothy, and Raymond Bonner, *Jury Charges 3, One a Bank Aide, in Russian Case*
September 30, 1999: Gordon, Michael, *Russia Starts Inquiry at Moscow Bank into Money Laundering*
September 29, 1999: O'Brien, Timothy, and Lowell Bergman, *Law-Enforcement Rivalry in US Slowed Inquiry on Russian Funds*
September 23, 1999: Schmitt, Eric, *Bank's Head Admits "Lapse" in Money Laundering Case*

September 21, 1999: Bonner, Raymond, *Bank Affair and a Yeltsin Son-in-Law*
September 11, 1999: Bonner, Raymond, *Reputed Russian Mobster Denies Tie to Laundering and Takes Umbrage*
September 9, 1999: Tagliabue, John, and Celestine Bohlen, *Accusations of Bribery in the Kremlin Mount Up*
December 20, 1998: Olson, Elizabeth, *Ex-Soviets Are Focus of Inquiry by the Swiss*
July 22, 1998: Landler, Mark, *Macao Journal—A Reputed Mr. Big Upholds Colony's Reputation*
January 10, 1997: Cushman Jr., John H., *US Prosecutors in 6 Cities File Charges of Smuggling Refrigeration Gas*
December 8, 1996: Myers, Steven Lee, *Fighting International Crime*
July 9, 1996: Richardson, Lynda, *Russian Émigré Convicted of Extortion*
May 3, 1996: Wren, Christopher, *Mexican Role in Cocaine Is Exposed in US Seizure*
April 28, 1995: Dunn, Ashley, *Golden Venture Passengers Opting for China*
November 2, 1994: Erlanger, Steven, *Scandals Put Russian Defense Chief on the Defensive*
August 23, 1994: Raab, Selwyn, *Influx of Russian Gangsters Troubles FBI in Brooklyn*
April 1, 1994: Fyodorov, Boris, *Moscow Without Mirrors*
August 29, 1993: Faison, Seth, *Gang Leader Is Arrested in Hong Kong*
April 9, 1993: Kristof, Nicholas D., *China Police Have Gang Link in Hong Kong*
June 21, 1992: Cowell, Alan, *Inquiry into Sicilian Slaying Looks for Mafia Link to Colombia Drug Cartel*

OBSERVER NEWS, LONDON
December 15, 1996: Sweeny, John, and others, *Global Gangsters—Russian Maffiya Invades Britain*

OTTAWA CITIZEN
July 9, 1998: McDermott, Jeremy, *Colombian Drug Cartels Hook Up With Russian Mob*
June 29, 1998: McIntosh, Andrew, *Mafia Boss Bribed His Way Back to Canada—RCMP: Internal Mountie Report Says Mob Paid $800,000 to Free Ailing Kingpin*
June 15, 1998: McIntosh, Andrew, *RCMP Sting Broke US Laws: Mounties Changed US Criminals' Cash for Months Without US Authorization*
June 15, 1998: McIntosh, Andrew, *National Bank Executives Worried About Role in Sting*
June 14, 1998: McIntosh, Andrew, *Mounties Didn't Have Government's OK for Covert Drug Sting: RCMP Laundered Cash for Five Months Before Getting Cabinet Approval*

June 13, 1998: McIntosh, Andrew, *RCMP Feared Mob's Mole Might Foil Probe*
June 12, 1998: McIntosh, Andrew, *Agents "Reinvested" Profit in Drug-Money Business: Cash-Strapped RCMP Also Put $400,000 into Failed Dutch Sting*
June 11, 1998: McIntosh, Andrew, *How the RCMP Helped "Push" $2 Billion Worth of Cocaine: For Four Years, the Mounties Laundered Drug Money for the Mob, for Bikers, for the Colombian Drug Cartels, and for Transient Dealers on Montreal's Streets. Few of the Deals Were Ever Investigated*
May 22, 1998: Marotte, Bertrand, *YBM Stock Listing Shames TSE*
May 20, 1998: Marotte, Bertrand, *CEO Attempts to Restore YBM's Flagging Credibility*
March 5, 1993: Clough, Patricia, *Mafia Family Reported Buying Own Caribbean Island*

PHILADELPHIA INQUIRER
January 15, 1999: McCrary, Lacy, *Stock Sensation's Trappings of Success Shape up as Sham*
February 20, 1994: Hanley, Charles J., *As Russian Crime Grows, So Do the US-Russian Police Links*
January 30, 1994: Seplow, Stephen, *In the New Russia, Blood Trails Billions*

REUTERS
August 24, 1999: *Swiss Banks Dispute Money-Laundering Reports*
January 28, 1999: Edmonds, Sarah, *Canadian Regulators Assailed for Laxity on Suspect Firm*
December 10, 1998: Vicini, James, *US Says Chinese Smuggling Ring Used Tribal Land*
December 9, 1998: Anderson, Scott, *Canada, US Break Up China Immigrant Smuggling Ring*
August 23, 1996: Szekely, Peter, *Italy Extradites Alleged Russian Crime Boss to US*
November 24, 1994: *138 Countries Seek to Combat Global Crime*
April 15, 1993: Roche, Andrew, *Hong Kong's Triads Find Odd Bedfellows in Beijing*

ROCKY MOUNTAIN NEWS
March 28, 1995: Jensen, Holger, *Russia Must Break Crime's Stranglehold*

SAN DIEGO UNION-TRIBUNE
October 4, 1992: Lavelle, Philip J., *Sting Put Cocaine's Global Web into Focus*
September 29, 1992: Lavelle, Philip J., *Drug Sting Here Is Massive, International Ruse Nets 260 Suspects*

SAN FRANCISCO CHRONICLE
December 1, 1997: Wallace, Bill, *Chinese Crime Ring Muscles In—Violent Gang Moving into State from Canada*

March 19, 1995: Wallace, Bill, *The Next Red Menace—Organized Crime Syndicates from the Former Soviet Union Have Arrived in Cali*
January 22, 1995: Geiger, Eric, *Austria Feels Chill of Booming Russian Mafia*
December 30, 1993: Burdman, Pamela, *Human Smuggling Ships Linked to One Huge Ring—Bases in California, Guatemala*

SCOTLAND ON SUNDAY
November 26, 1995: Ronay, Gabriel, *Western Businesses Bought As Front for Russian Mafia*

SOUTH CHINA MORNING POST
July 13, 1998: Fraser, Niall, *Infighting Breaks Out for Control of Macau Syndicate*
March 27, 1994: *Spain—Chinese Illegal Immigrants on the Increase*
April 25, 1993: Dobson, Chris, *Police Report—China Initiated Triad Contacts*
April 12, 1993: Torode, Greg, *Triad-PSB Links Threatening Crime Fighting*
April 11, 1993: Dobson, Chris, *PRC Minister Reportedly Met Triad Members*
December 8, 1991: Marsh, Jon, and Chris Dobson, *USA—Government Sets Up Taskforce to Stop Triads*

ST. PETERSBURG TIMES
February 19, 1999: Testerman, Jeff, *Prosecutors—Crime Ring Eyed Casinos. Edward Halloran Is Accused of Bilking Investors by Claiming He Was Connected with the Seminole Casinos*

SUNDAY TELEGRAPH, LONDON
November 20, 1994: Davies, Hugh, *Russian Mobs Have American Dream in Sight*

TORONTO STAR
December 12, 1998: MacCharles, Tonda, *Huge Smuggling Ring Not Unique*
May 30, 1998: Daw, James, *Never Put Your All in One Stock—It's Still Buyer Beware on the TSE, YBM Proves Spot on TSE 300 No Guarantee*
May 22, 1998: *Canada–US Hold Summit on Crime*
February 2, 1999: Van Rijn, Nicolaas, and Dale Brazao, *The Long, Rugged Road to Gold Mountain*

TORONTO SUN
July 18, 1998: Lamberti, Rob, and Scot Magnish, *Cops Seize High-Priced Assets—30 Kilos of Money Snapped Up After Arrest of Reputed Mafia Boss, Associates*
July 16, 1998: Lamberti, Rob, and Scot Magnish, *Cops Topple Mob's Drug Empire—Police, Crime Tentacles Circle the Globe*

July 16, 1998: Lamberti, Rob, and Scot Magnish, *Drug Empire Crushed "Wayne Gretzky" of Underworld, 11 Others Arrested*

UNITED PRESS INTERNATIONAL
December 12, 1998: *Alleged Mafioso Returns to Moscow*
December 10, 1998: *Alien Smuggling Ring Broken*
March 15, 1994: Hail, John, *New York–Based Gang Smuggling Thousands of Chinese to US*
September 1, 1993: Richardson, Paul, *Bail Rejected for Reputed Gang Kingpin in Human Smuggling Case*

WALL STREET JOURNAL
October 6, 1999: Davis, Ann, *First Indications Are Handed Up in Laundering Inquiry*
October 1, 1999: Higgins, Andrew, *Russia Investigating Laundering*
October 1, 1999: Cullison, Alan, *IMF Tells Russia to Sell Offshore Banks*
September 29, 1999: Higgins, Andrew, *Russia's Prosecutor Launches Criminal Case Against Bank*
December 5, 1994: *Global Gangs*
March 22, 1990: Penn, Stanley, *Asian Connection–Chinese Gangsters Fill a Narcotics Gap Left by US Drive on Mafia*
September 15, 1987: Morgenthaler, Eric, *Smuggling Aliens–A Shadowy Operation Shows How Hard It Is to Keep Out Illegals*
February 6, 1987: Pasztor, Andy, and Rose Gutfeld, *Fuel Fraud–Gasoline Tax Evasion Ignites a Crackdown by US and the States; FBI Cites Organized Crime; Treasury May Be Losing As Much As $800 Million*

WASHINGTON POST
October 29, 1999: Hilzenrath, David, *Island Banks a Haven for Russian Criminals*
October 21, 1999: O'Harrow, Robert Jr., *3 Firms Linked to Russia Probe*
October 7, 1999: O'Harrow, Robert Jr., *Bank Probe Seeks Help Abroad*
September 10, 1999: O'Harrow, Robert Jr., *In Queens, Office Intrigue*
June 24, 1999: Hoffman, David, *Russian Oil Battle Goes to Offshore Courts*
April 18, 1999: Hoffman, David, *Out of Step with Russia? Outsiders Battle over Stake in Oil Giant*
February 17, 1998: Kovaleski, Serge F., and Douglas Farah, *Organized Crime Exercises Clout in Island Nations*
March 30, 1997: Farah, Douglas, and Molly Moore, *Mexican Drug Traffickers Eclipse Colombian Cartels*
October 7, 1996: Farah, Douglas, *Russian Crime Finds Haven in Caribbean*
August 18, 1996: Constable, Pamela, *From Russia with Chutzpah*

August 12, 1996: Anderson, John W., and Molly Moore, *Mexican Cartels Diversify*
September 17, 1995: Reding, Andrew, *The Fall and Rise of the Drug Cartels*
August 2, 1994: Drozdiak, William, *European Unity for Organized Crime*
May 26, 1994: Smith, Jeffrey, *Freeh Warns of a New Russian Threat*
April 2, 1994: Coll, Steve, *Russian Crime Syndicates Moving West*
December 28, 1993: Weymouth, Lally, *Organized Crime—The New Russian Menace*
October 5, 1992: Drozdiak, William, *World Crime Groups Expand Cooperation, Spheres of Influence*
October 21, 1989: Parmelee, Jennifer, *Cocaine Trail Forks, Leads into Europe; Colombian Cartels, Mafia in Italy Working Together*

WASHINGTON TIMES
December 30, 1998: Alden, Edward, *Canadian Star YBM Turns Out to Be Sham*
October 26, 1998: Gertz, Bill, *Mafia Runs Half of Banks in Russia*
September 28, 1998: De Borchgrave, Arnaud, *Subsidizing the Kleptocracy*
December 13, 1997: Seper, Jerry, *Russian Mob Figure Met with Clinton*
December 12, 1997: Seper, Jerry, *Man Tied to Russian Mob Met with Clinton, Gore*
September 20, 1996: Hacket, James, *Missile Disaster Wake-Up Call*
November 3, 1995: De Borchgrave, Arnaud, *Clinton Targets Global Organized Crime As Security Threat*
December 17, 1994: Hedges, Michael, *DEA-IRS "Bank" Hits Cocaine Cartel in Pocketbook*
December 5, 1994: Gertz, Bill, *Most of Russia's Biggest Banks Linked to Mob, CIA Report Says*
October 19, 1994: Copeland, Peter, *Traffickers Planning a Deal, Ex-Agent Says*

MAGAZINES

AMERICAN CRIMINAL LAW REVIEW
Winter 1995: *Money Laundering*

AMERICAN SPECTATOR
January 1996: Bernstein, Jonas, *A Fistful of Rubles*
December 1991: Adams, James Ring, *Medellín's New Generation*
September 1988: Adams, James Ring, *Losing the Drug War: Drugs, Banks, and Florida Politics*

ANTHROPOLOGICAL QUARTERLY
April 1996: McDonogh, Gary, *The Sicilian Mafia*

ARMS CONTROL TODAY
March 14, 1996: Holdren, John P., *Reducing the Threat of Nuclear Theft in the Former Soviet Union*
October 1995: Potter, William, *Before the Deluge? Assessing the Threat of Nuclear Leakage from the Post-Soviet States*
Decemner 1994: Mueller, Harald, *Fissile Material Smuggling: German Politics, Hype and Reality*
January 1993: Potter, William, *Nuclear Exports from the Former Soviet Union*

ASIAN AFFAIRS
September 1, 1995: Bolz, Jennifer, *Chinese Organized Crime and Illegal Alien Trafficking: Humans As a Commodity*

ATLANTIC MONTHLY
June 1994: Hersh, Seymour, *The Wild East*

AUSTRALIAN AND NEW ZEALAND JOURNAL OF SOCIOLOGY
November 1987: Trahair, Richard, *Organized Crime: A Global Perspective*

BANKING WORLD
February 1984: Lonsborough, Richard, *Dirty Money in the Caribbean*

BRITISH JOURNAL OF CRIMINOLOGY
Spring 1992: Ruggiero, Vincenzo, *Crime Inc.: The Story of Organized Crime*

BROOKINGS REVIEW
Winter 1995: Leitzel, Jim, and others, *Mafiosi and Matrioshki: Organized Crime and Russian Reform*
Winter 1993: Flynn, Stephen, *World Wide Drug Scourge: The Expanding Trade in Illicit Drugs*

BUSINESS AND FINANCE
October 6, 1994: Dunne, Mark, *Cleaning Dirty Money*
December 9, 1993: Fitzgerald, Kyran, *Laundering the Loot*

BUSINESS TODAY
April 1994: Sakurada, Keiji, *Yakuza Storming the Corporate Ship*

BUSINESS WEEK
June 8, 1998: Weber, Joseph, *Red Flags? What Red Flags?*

January 29, 1996: Bremner, Brian, *How the Mob Burned the Banks: The Yakuza Is at the Center of the $350 Billion Bad Loan Scandal*

April 6, 1992: Reichlin, Igor, *Germany's Brash New Import: Dirty Money—Its Banks Can Legally Launder Cash and Do So, by the Suitcase*

CANADIAN BANKER

September/October 1994: Ballard, Michael, *Money Laundering and the Canadian Banks: An Industry Position*

CANADIAN LAWYER

January 1997: Lundy Derek, *It's a Law Firm, Not a Laundry*

CANADIAN POLICE NEWS

Summer 1989: Desjardins, Fred, *The Mob in Canada*

Winter 1987: *Bikers: A New Kind of Organized Crime*

COMPARATIVE ECONOMIC STUDIES

Winter 1995: Minniti, Maria. *Membership Has Its Privileges: Old and New Mafia Organizations*

CONSERVATIVE REVIEW

September 1996: Douglass, Joseph Jr., *Narcotics Trafficking, Organized Crime, and Terrorism*

May 1995: Douglass, Joseph Jr., *Organized Crime in Russia: Who's Taking Whom to the Cleaners?*

CONTEMPORARY CRISES

March 23, 1990: Gaylord, Mark, *The Chinese Laundry: International Drug Trafficking and Hong Kong's Banking Industry*

CRIME AND DELINQUENCY

July 1993: Kersten, Joachim, *Street Youths, Bosozoku, and Yakuza-Subculture Formation and Societal Reactions in Japan*

CRIME, LAW AND SOCIAL CHANGE

Fall 1995: Paoli, Letizia, *The Banco Ambrosiano Case*

Summer 1995: Myers, Willard H. III, *The Emerging Threat of Transnational Organized Crime from the East*

Spring 1994: Friman, H. Richard, *International Pressure and Domestic Bargains: Regulating Money Laundering in Japan*

Spring 1994:Van Duyne, Petrus, Alan and Block, *Organized Cross-Atlantic Crime*
Summer 1993: Kelly, Robert, and others, *The Dragon Breathes Fire*
Summer 1993: Passas, Nikos, and David Nelken, *The Thin Line Between Legitimate and Criminal Enterprises*
Winter 1993: Maguire, Keith, *Fraud, Extortion and Racketeering: The Black Economy in Northern Ireland*
Winter 1992: Jenkins, Philip, *Narcotics Trafficking and the American Mafia: The Myth of Internal Prohibition*
Fall 1992: Brodeur, Jean-Paul, *Undercover Policing in Canada: Wanting What Is Wrong*
Spring 1992: Lee, Rensselaer W. III, *Dynamics of the Soviet Illicit Drug Market*

CRIMINAL ORGANIZATIONS
Spring 1997: Builta, Jeff, *Mexico Faces Corruption, Crime, Drug Trafficking and Political Intrigue*

CURRENT DIGEST OF THE POST-SOVIET PRESS
December 1995: Levchuk, Sergei, *Ukrainian Mafia Has Found Its Niche Doing Shady Business in Europe*
October 1995: Kryshtanovskaya, Olga, *Russia's Mafia Landscape*

CURRENT HISTORY
May 1995: Lee, Rensselaer, *Global Reach: The Threat of International Drug Trafficking*

DEFENSE NATIONALE
December 1992: Sola, Richard, *L'Internationalisation de la Mafia Chinoise*

ECONOMIST
February 12, 1994: *The Covert Arms Trade*

EQUITY
June 1992: Dubro, James, *The Big Circle Boys*

EUROMONEY
February 1996: Celarier, Michelle, *Stealing the Family Silver: From Mafia Ties and Drug Trafficking to Bribery and Insider Dealing, Allegations of Corruption Have Tainted Numerous Privatizations Around the World*

EUROPEAN JOURNAL OF INTERNATIONAL AFFAIRS
Summer 1990: Naylor, Thomas, *Criminal Empires*

EUROPEAN SOCIOLOGICAL REVIEW
December 1985: Gambetta, Diego, *The Entrepreneurial Mafia*

EUROPE-ASIA STUDIES
July 1996: Kryshtanovskaya, O., and S. White, *From Soviet Nomenklatura to Russian Elite*

L'EXPRESS
December 8, 1994: Raufer, Xavier, and Philippe Coste, *Les Multinationales du Crime*
October 1994: Raufer, Xavier, *Du Rififi dans les Triades*
March 1993: Lecomte, Bernard, *L'Empire du Milieu*

FAR EASTERN ECONOMIC REVIEW
November 23, 1995: Chen, Shu Ching Jean, *Pungent Prices: Taiwan's Triads Have Taken Over the Garlic Trade*
November 23, 1995: Thayer, Nate, *Cambodia: Asia's New Narco State?*
February 2, 1995: Aniskiewicz, Rick, *Taiwan: Organized Crime Pushes into Politics; Pingtung Just Like Sicily*
February 9, 1995: Smith, Charles, *Out of Gangland: A Glut of Illegal Guns Worries the Authorities*
January 20, 1994: Lintner, Bertil, *Khun Sa: Asia's Drug King on the Run*
August 5, 1993: Baum, Julian, *Human Wave: Rise in Illegal Immigrants from China Alarms Taipei*
April 8, 1993: Mooney, Paul, and Melana Zyla, *Braving the Seas and More*

FBI LAW ENFORCEMENT BULLETIN
April 22, 1990: Florez, Carl and Boyce, Bernadette, *Laundering Drug Money*

FINANCIAL POST MAGAGZINE
February 10, 1992: Capeci, Jerry, *Why the Mob Loves Canada*

FINANCIAL WORLD
February 1, 1994: Cordtz, Dan, *Dirty Dollars: Uncle Sam Looks for New Ways to Stymie Crooks and Their Smurfs, Who Launder $300 Billion a Year*

FORBES
December 15, 1989: Stern, Richard, *How the Mafia Manipulates Stocks*

FOREIGN AFFAIRS
March 1994: Handelman, Stephen, *The Russian Maffiya*

FOREIGN POLICY
Spring 1993: Lee, Rensselaer W. III, and Scott B. MacDonald, *Drugs in the East*

FORTUNE
November 30, 1992: Serwer, Andrew, *Hells Angels' Devilish Business*
June 22, 1987: Rowan, Roy, *How the Mafia Loots JFK Airport*

FUTURES RESEARCH QUARTERLY
Spring 1995: Moore, Richter, *Twenty-First Century Law to Meet the Challenge of Twenty-First Century Organized Crime*

FUTURIST
September 1994: Moore, Richter, *Wiseguys: Smarter Criminals and Smarter Crime in the 21st Century*

GLOBAL FINANCE
October 1996: Leander, Ellen, *Finance's Top Cops*
January 1996: Shibata, Yoko, *Quaking Lenders: How Gangsters Complicate Japan's Banking Crisis*
January 1994: Celarier, Michelle, *Laundering Dirty Money in Russia*

IASOC MAGAZINE
Summer 1997: Williams, Phil, *Drugs & Democracy*

INTERNATIONAL CRIMINAL JUSTICE REVIEW
Summer 1992: Huang, Frank, and Michael Vaughn, *A Descriptive Analysis of Japanese Organized Crime: The Boryokudan from 1945 to 1988*
Summer 1992: Song, J. H. Long, and J. Dombrink, *Asian Emerging Crime Groups: Examining the Definition of Organized Crime*

INTERNATIONAL CURRENCY REVIEW
October 1993: MacDonald, Scott, *Asia Pacific Money Laundering*

INTERNATIONAL JOURNAL OF COMPARATIVE AND APPLIED CRIMINAL JUSTICE
Spring 1991: Martens, Frederick, *Transnational Enterprise Crime and the Elimination of Frontiers*

INTERNATIONAL JOURNAL OF INTELLIGENCE AND COUNTERINTELLIGENCE
Winter 1990: Bacon, John, *The French Connection Revisited*

INTERNATIONAL JOURNAL OF OFFENDER THERAPY
    AND COMPARATIVE CRIMINOLOGY
Spring 1993: Jones, Mark, *Nigerian Crime Networks in the United States*

INTERNATIONAL QUARTERLY
May 1993: Rothacher, Albrecht, *Yakuza, The Socioeconomic Roles of Organized Crime in Japan*

INTERNATIONAL RELATIONS
August 1995: Clutterbuck, Richard, *Peru: Cocaine, Terrorism and Corruption*
May 1990: Jamieson, Alison, *Mafia and Political Power 1943-1989*

INTERNATIONAL SPECTATOR
January 1997: Rutland, Peter, *Business Lobbies in Contemporary Russia*

INTERNATIONAL TAX JOURNAL
Spring 1997: Barrett, Richard W., *Confronting Tax Havens, the Offshore Phenomenon, and Money Laundering*

JANE'S INTELLIGENCE REVIEW
January 1993: Galeotti, Mark, *Red Mafias and National Security*

JEUNE AFRIQUE ECONOMIE
September 2, 1996: Ndir, Mansour, *Blanchiment d'Argent*

JOURNAL OF CONTEMPORARY CRIMINAL JUSTICE
March 1995: Albanese, Jay, Contemporary Issues in Organized Crime
December 1994: Carter, David, *International Organized Crime: Emerging Trends in Entrepreneurial Crime*
September 1993: Ryan, P. J., ed., *Organized Crime II*
March 1992: Vito, Gennaro, ed., *Organized Crime*

JOURNAL OF CRIME AND JUSTICE
Spring 1993: Gay, Bruce, and James W. Marquart, *Jamaican Posses: A New Form of Organized Crime*

JOURNAL OF ECONOMIC ISSUES
June 1, 1998: Tomass, Mark, *Mafianomics: How Did Mob Entrepreneurs Infiltrate and Dominate the Russian Economy?*

JOURNAL OF MODERN ITALIAN STUDIES
Spring 1996: Chubb, Judith, *The Mafia,the Market and the State in Italy and Russia*

JOURNAL OF RESEARCH IN CRIME AND DELINQUENCY
November 1994: Joe, Karen A., *The New Criminal Conspiracy? Asian Gangs and Organized Crime in San Francisco*

JUSTICE REPORT
March 1996: Laplante, Laurent, *Counteracting Criminal Biker Gangs*

MACLEAN'S
December 21, 1998: *Nabbing Smugglers*
October 12, 1998: Noble, Kimberley, *Battling the Mob: An Unlikely Group Tackles a Russian Gangster*
February 17, 1997: Sheridan, Maureen, *A Trade in Criminals: Canada's Policy of Deporting Lawbreakers Helps Fuel Jamaica's Soaring Crime Rate*
April 29, 1996: Kaihla, Paul, *The People Smugglers: Canada Is a Top Destination in the Global Trade in Humans—How Criminals Victimize the Innocent*
July 10, 1995: Kaihla, Paul, *The Cocaine King: How a Poor Colombian Became Canada's Biggest Drug Baron and Got Away*
October 2, 1995: Kaihla, Paul, *Inside an Immigration Scam: More Than 80 Chinese Posed As Investors to Be Smuggled into Canada*
December 6, 1993: Fennell, Tom, *Up in Smoke*
October 7, 1991: Bruning, Fred, *Taking Money from Gangsters: Political Leaders Have Permitted the Mafia to Flourish and Infiltrate Extensively What Is Laughingly Called Legitimate Business*
October 23, 1989: Jensen, Holger, *Hiding the Drug Money: Criminals Are Using Canada to Launder Billions of Dollars in Drug Profits*

MEDICINE, CONFLICT AND SURVIVAL
January 1996: Walker, William, *International Responses to the Threat of Nuclear Smuggling from Russia*

NARCOTICS CONTROL DIGEST
July 22, 1992: *26 Biker Gang Members Indicted on Drug Charges*
October 24, 1990: *Authorities Strike a Blow Against Hells Angels*

THE NATION
December 1994: Kwong, Peter, *China's Human Traffickers: Wave of the Golden Venture*

NATIONAL FORUM
Summer 1992: McKeown, Patrick, *Computer Crimes and Criminals*

NATIONAL SECURITY STUDIES QUARTERLY
Summer 1996: Richard, Daniel, *Overseas Tasking of the CIA for Domestic Law Enforcement*

NEW AFRICAN
June 16, 1995: Rake, Alan, *Drugged to the Eyeballs*

THE NEW REPUBLIC
April 11, 1994: Sterling, Claire, *Redfellas: Inside the Russian Mafia*

NEWSWEEK
October 4, 1999: Several contributors, *Where Did Russia's Money Go?*
March 10, 1997: Brant, Martha, *Most Wanted Kingpin?*

NEW YORK TIMES MAGAZINE
January 24, 1993: Handelman, Stephen, *Why Capitalism and the Maffiya Mean Business*

ORGANIZED CRIME DIGEST
May 11, 1990: *Bandidos Outlaw Biker Gang Survived Nationwide 1985 Crackdown by Feds*

PARADE
February 25, 1996: Maas, Peter, *Who Is the Mob Today?*

POLICE CHIEF
June 1995: Noble, Ronald, *Russian Organized Crime a Worldwide Problem*
June 1994: Chu, Jeannette L., *Alien Smuggling Syndicates Are Increasingly Involved in Other Criminal Activities, Infiltrating Legitimate Businesses and Deriving Millions of Dollars in Illicit Proceeds*
October 1993: Mosquera, Richard, *Asian Organized Crime*
January 1989: Schramm, R. R., *Organized Crime*
January 1988: *Special Issue on Organized Crime*

POLICE STUDIES
Winter 1990: Burke, Tod, and Charles O'Rear, *Home Invaders: Asian Gangs in America*

Winter 1990: Florez, Carl, and Bernadette Boyce, *Columbian Organized Crime*
Autumn 1989: *Corruption As a Fundamental Element of Organised Crime*

RCMP GAZETTE
September 1998: Nyhuus, Kim, *Chasing Ghosts*
September 1998: *Motorcycle Gangs*
September 1987: Hamilton, R. B., *Triad and Crime Gangs of Vietnamese Origin*
October 1980: Martin, W. G., *Motorcycle Gangs*

READER'S DIGEST
November 1997: Wilkens, Russell, *Biker Gangs: Getting Away with Murder*

REVUE DE CANADIEN CRIMINOLOGIE
October 1993: Alain, Marc, *Les Bandes de Motards au Québec*

SATURDAY NIGHT
December 1993: Elliott, Patricia, *A Life in the Drug Trade*

SCIENTIFIC AMERICAN
January 1996: Williams, Phil, and Paul Woessner, *The Real Threat of Nuclear Smuggling: Although Many Widely Publicized Incidents Have Been Staged or Overblown, the Dangers of Even a Single Successful Diversion Are Too Great to Ignore*

SOCIAL AND LEGAL STUDIES
March 1996: Ruggiero, Vincenzo, *War Markets: Corporate and Organized Criminals in Europe*

SOCIETY
March 1995: Godson, Roy, and Olson William, *International Organized Crime*
January 1990: Lee, Rensselaer, *Cocaine Mafia*

THE SPECTATOR
May 27, 1995: Clark, Ross, *Do We Really Want Opium Dens?*

STUDIES IN CONFLICT AND TERRORISM
October 1994: Filippone, Robert, *The Medellín Cartel: Why We Can't Win the Drug War*
January 1992: Jamieson, Alison, *Recent Narcotics and Mafia Research*

TIME

July 14, 1997: Drummond, Tammerlin, *Enter the Redfellas: Are Russian Mobsters Dallying with Drug Lords?*

February 8, 1993: Walsh, James, *Triads Go Global*

November 4, 1991: Richard Behar, *Offer They Can't Refuse: Mob Families in the US Are Considering a Merger*

TRANSNATIONAL ORGANIZED CRIME

Summer 1997: Blickman, Tom, *The Rothschilds of the Mafia on Aruba*

Spring 1995: Lupsha, Peter, *Transnational Narco-Corruption and Narco Investment: A Focus on Mexico*

US NAVAL INSTITUTE PROCEEDINGS

July 1996: Tomney, Christopher, and Joseph DiRenzo, *Countering High Tech Drug Smugglers*

US NEWS AND WORLD REPORT

August 3, 1998: Kaplan, David E., and Christian Caryl, *The Looting of Russia*

April 14, 1997: Witkin, Gordon, *One Way, $28,000: Why Smuggling Aliens into America Is a Boom Business*

September 30, 1996: Kleinknecht, William, *The Hottest Import: Crime*

October 23, 1995: Cooperman, Alan, and Tim Zimmermann, *The Russian Connection*

June 19, 1995: Parshall, Gerald, *The FBI Nabs a Russian Gotti*

March 7, 1994: *The Mobsters Who Now Rule Russia*

June 21, 1993: *The New Slave Trade: A Shocking Story of Human Smuggling; the Growing Backlash Against Immigrants*

October 19, 1992: *Cocaine Kings and Mafia Dons*

January 18, 1988: *Ethnic Gangs and Organized Crime*

February 3, 1986: Powell, Stewart, *Busting the Mob*

WASHINGTON QUARTERLY

Winter 1995: Williams, Phil, *Transnational Criminal Organizations: Strategic Alliances*

Fall 1985: Nadelmann, Ethan, *International Drug Trafficking and US Foreign Policy*

WORLD AND I

December 1997: De Borchgrave, Arnaud, *Organized Crime's Global Shadow*

June 1989: Seper, Jerry, *Dirty Money Finds New Laundries*

WORLD POLICY JOURNAL

Spring 1995: Paternostro, Silvana, *Mexico as A Narco-Democracy*

THE WORLD TODAY
January 1995: Dunn, Guy, *The Russian Mafia*

MONOGRAPHS, PAPERS, DISSERTATIONS, SPEECHES AND REPORTS

ANDERSON, KENT, *Criminal Threats to Business on the Internet: A White Paper*. Global Technology Research, Portland, Oregon, 1997.

BRANDT, DANIEL, *As Criminal Capitalism Replaces Communism-Organized Crime Threatens the New World Order*. NameBase NewsLine, January–March 1995.

CENTER FOR STRATEGIC AND INTERNATIONAL STUDIES, *Wild Atom: Nuclear Terrorism*. Webster, William, project chairman. Washington, D.C., 1998.

————, *Russian Organized Crime*. Webster, William, project chairman. Washington, D.C., 1997.

————, *The Nuclear Black Market*, Webster, William, project chairman. Washington, D.C., 1996

————, *Global Organized Crime: The New Empire of Evil*, Raine, Linnea and Frank Cilluffo, editors. Washington, D.C., 1994.

————, *Report of the Project on the Global Drug Trade in the Post Cold War Era: The Transnational Drug Challenge and the New World Order*. Flynn, Stephen, and Gregory Grant, editors. Washington, D.C., 1993.

COUNCIL OF EUROPE, *Convention on Laundering, Search, Seizure and Confiscation of the Proceeds from Crime and Explanatory Report*; Council of Europe Publishing, Strasbourg, France, 1995.

CRIMINAL INTELLIGENCE SERVICE CANADA, *Annual Report on Organized Crime in Canada*. Ottawa, 1998.

————, *Annual Report on Organized Crime in Canada*. Ottawa, 1997.

————, *East European–Based Organized Crime*. Ottawa. 1997.

————, *Hell's Angels and Other Outlaw Motorcycle Gangs*. Ottawa, 1997.

————, *Aboriginal Organized Crime in Canada and the United States*. Ottawa, 1997.

————, *Italian Organized Crime in Canada*. Ottawa, 1997.

————, *Colombia Drug Cartels in Canada*. Ottawa, 1997.

————, *Asian Organized Crime in Canada*. Ottawa, 1997.

————, *Annual Report on Organized Crime in Canada*. Ottawa, 1996.

————, *Asian Organized Crime Workshop Papers*. Ottawa, 1996.

Canadian Security Intelligence Service, *Smuggling Special Nuclear Materials*. Ottawa, 1995.

FINANCIAL ACTION TASK FORCE, *Report on Money Laundering Typologies*. Paris, 1997.

GRASSLEY, CHARLES, *The Emerging International Mafia;* speech made before the Heritage Foundation, Washington, D.C., February 23, 1996.

OBSERVATOIRE GEOPOLITIQUE DES DROGUES, *Annual Reports;* Paris 1997, 1998.

————, *Atlas Mondial des Drogue;* Presses Universitaires de France, Paris 1997.

PROVINCE OF BRITISH COLUMBIA, Ministry of Attorney General—Interministry Committee on Criminal Gangs and British Columbia, *Action Plan Summary,* Victoria BC 1994, 1995.

ROYAL CANADIAN MOUNTED POLICE, *Aboriginal Organized Crime and Tobacco, Weapons and Gaming.* Ottawa 1992.

STATE OF NEW YORK, ORGANIZED CRIME TASK FORCE, *An Analysis of Russian Emigre Crime in the Tri-State Region.* Albany, NY, 1996.

UNITED NATIONS, *Report on the Conference for the Adoption of a Convention Against Illicit Traffic in Narcotic Drugs and Psychotropic Substances.* New York, 1994.

UNITED STATES DEPARTMENT OF JUSTICE, Bureau of Justice Assistance, *Urban Street Gang Enforcement.* Washington, D.C., 1997.

UNITED STATES DEPARTMENT OF STATE, *International Narcotics Control Strategy Report.* Bureau for International Narcotics and Law Enforcement Affairs, Washington, D.C., 1998.

————, *Report on Ethnic Chinese Organized Crime: Triad Structures and Capabilities.* Washington, D.C., 1994.

UNITED STATES FEDERAL BUREAU OF INVESTIGATION, *Vietnamese Activity in the United States: A National Perspective.* Washington, D.C., 1993.

————, *An Introduction to Organized Crime in the United States.* Washington, D.C., 1993.

————, *An Analysis of the Threat of Japanese Criminal Organizations to the United States and Its Territories.* Washington, D.C., 1992.

————, *Wanted by the FBI the Mob: FBI Organized Crime Report 25 Years After Valachi.* Washington, D.C., 1988.

UNITED STATES HOUSE OF REPRESENTATIVES, Committee on Banking and Financial Services, *Hearing on Russian Money Laundering.* Washington, D.C., September 21–22, 1999.

————, Committee on Banking and Financial Services, *The Money Laundering Deterrence Act of 1998;* and *Money Laundering and Financial Crime Strategy Act of 1997.* Washington, D.C., June 11, 1998.

————, Committee on Banking and Financial Services, *Money Laundering by Drug Trafficking Organizations.* Washington, D.C., February 28, 1996.

————, Committee on Banking and Financial Services, *Organized Crime and Banking.* Washington, D.C., February 28, 1996.

————, Committee on Banking and Financial Services, Subcommittee on General Oversight and Investigations, *Use by the Department of the Treasury of the Geographic Targeting Order as a Method to Combat Money Laundering.* Washington, D.C., March 11, 1997.

————, Committee on Banking and Financial Services, Subcommittee on General Oversight and Investigations, *U.S. Law Enforcement Response to Money Laundering Activities in Mexico.* Washington, D.C., September 5, 1996.

————, Committee on Banking and Financial Services, Subcommittee on General Oversight and Investigations, *Money Laundering Activity Associated with the Mexican Narco Crime Syndicate.* Washington, D.C., September 5, 1996.

————, Committee on Banking and Financial Services, Committee on Government Reform and Oversight: *National Drug Policy-A Review of the Status of the Drug War.* Washington, D.C., March 19, 1996.

————, Subcommittee on General Oversight and Investigations, *The Counterfeiting of U.S. Currency Abroad.* Washington, D.C., February 27, 1996.

————, Committee on Foreign Affairs, Subcommittee on International Security, International Organizations, and Human Rights and the Western Hemisphere, *U.S. Relations with Colombia.* Washington, D.C., August 3, 1994.

————, Committee on Foreign Affairs, Subcommittee on International Security, International Organizations and Human Rights, *The Threat of International Organized Crime.* Washington, D.C., November 4, 1993.

————, Committee on Government Reform and Oversight, *National Drug Policy: A Review of the Status of the Drug War.* Washington, D.C., March 19, 1996.

————, Committee on International Relations, *Threat from International Organized Crime and Terrorism.* Testimony of Louise Shelley, Center for Transnational Organized Crime and Corruption, American University, Washington, D.C., October 1, 1997.

————, Committee on International Relations, *The Threat from Russian Organized Crime.* Washington, D.C., April 30, 1996.

————, Committee on International Relations, *Global Organized Crime.* Washington, D.C., January 31, 1996.

————, Committee on International Relations, Subcommittee on Asia and the Pacific, *Drugs in Asia: The Heroin Connection.* Washington, D.C., June 21, 1995.

————, Committee on International Relations, *International Organized Crime.* Washington, D.C., June 27, 1994.

————, Committee on the Judiciary, Subcommittee on Crime, *The Growing Threat of International Organized Crime.* Washington, D.C., January 25, 1996.

————, Committee on the Judiciary. Subcommittee on Immigration, Refugees and International Law, *Alien Smuggling.* Washington, D.C., June 30, 1993.

————, Permanent Select Committee on Intelligence, *Intelligence Community in the 21st Century.* Washington, D.C., April 9, 1996.

————, Select Committee on Narcotics Abuse and Control, *The Federal Strategy on the Southwest Border.* Washington, D.C., December 10, 1990.

UNITED STATES SENATE, Committee on Appropriations, Subcommittee on Foreign Relations, *International Crime*. Washington, D.C., March 12, 1996.

————, Committee on Armed Services,*Intelligence Briefing on Smuggling of Nuclear Material and the Role of International Crime Organizations*. Washington, D.C., January 31, 1995.

————, Committee on Finance, Subcommittee on International Trade and United States Senate, *Threat to U.S. Trade and Finance from Drug Trafficking and International Organized Crime*. Washington, D.C., July 23 and 30, 1996.

————, Committee on Foreign Relations, Subcommittee on European Affairs, *Loose Nukes, Nuclear Smuggling, and the Fissile Material Problem in Russia and the NIS*. Washington, D.C., August 22–23, 1995.

————, Committee on Foreign Relations, *International Drug Trafficking Organizations in Mexico*. Washington, D.C., August 8, 1995.

————, Committee on Foreign Relations, *Terrorism, Narcotics and International Operations*. Testimony of Willard H. Myers III, director, Center for the Study of Asian Organized Crime, Washington, D.C., April 21, 1994.

————, Committee on Governmental Affairs Permanent Subcommittee on Investigations, *Fraud on the Internet: Scams Affecting Consumers*. Washington, D.C., February 10, 1998.

————, Committee on Governmental Affairs Permanent Subcommittee on Investigations, *Global Proliferation of Weapons of Mass Destruction*. Washington, D.C., October 31, November 1, 1995; March 13, 20 and 22, 1996; March 27, 1997.

————, Committee on Governmental Affairs Permanent Subcommittee on Investigations, *Russian Organized Crime, Security in Cyberspace*. Washington, D.C., May 15 and 22, June 5 and 25, July 16, 1996.

————, Committee on Governmental Affairs, Permanent Subcommittee on Investigations, *Russian Organized Crime in the United States*. Washington, D.C., May 15, 1996.

————, Committee on Governmental Affairs Permanent Subcommittee on Investigations, *Criminal Aliens in the United States*. Washington, D.C., April 7, 1995.

————, Committee on Governmental Affairs, Permanent Subcommittee on Investigations, *International Organized Crime and Its Impact on the United States*. Washington, D.C., May 25, 1994.

————, Committee on Governmental Affairs, Permanent Subcommittee on Investigations, *The New International Criminal and Asian Organized Crime*. Washington, D.C., December 1992.

————, Committee on Governmental Affairs, Permanent Subcommittee on Investigations, *Current Trends in Money Laundering*. Washington, D.C., December 1992.

————, Committee on Governmental Affairs, Permanent Subcommittee on Investigation, *Asian Organized Crime.* Washington, D.C., October 3, 1991; November 5–6, 1991; June 18, 1992; and August 4, 1992.

————, Committee on Governmental Affairs, Permanent Subcommittee on Investigations, *Arms Trafficking, Mercenaries and Drug Cartels.* Washington, D.C., February 27–28, 1991.

————, Committee on Governmental Affairs, Permanent Subcommittee on Investigations, *Nontraditional Organized Crime: Law Enforcement Officials' Perspectives on Five Criminal Groups.* Washington, D.C., 1989.

————, Judiciary Committee, *Gangs: A National Crisis.* Washington, D.C., April 23, 1997.

————, Judiciary Committee and Committee on Indian Affairs, joint hearings, *Criminal Gangs in Indian Country.* Washington, D.C., September 17, 1997.

————, Judiciary Committee, Subcommittee on Technology, Terrorism and Government Information, *The Identity Theft and Assumption Deterrence Act.* Washington, D.C., May 20, 1998.

————, Judiciary Committee, Subcommittee on Technology, Terrorism and Government Information, *Methamphetamine: A Newly Deadly Neighbor.* Washington, D.C., April 6, 1998.

————, Judiciary Committee, Subcommittee on Technology, Terrorism and Government Information, *Internet Crimes Affecting Consumers.* Washington, D.C., March 18, 1997.

VAN DER HEIJDEN, TOON, *Policing in Central and Eastern Europe: Comparing Firsthand Knowledge with Experience from the West.* College of Police and Security Studies, Slovenia, 1996.

WILLIAMS, PHIL, ed., *Russian Organized Crime: The New Threat?* Frank Cass, London, 1997.

WILLIAMS, PHIL, *Hysteria, Complacency and Russian Organized Crime.* Russia and Eurasia Programme Post-Soviet Business Forum Briefing No. 8, the Royal Institute of International Affairs, London, October 1996.

INDEX